COUNTERING AL-QAEDA IN LONDON

ROBERT LAMBERT

COUNTERING AL-QAEDA IN LONDON

Police and Muslims in Partnership

HURST & COMPANY, LONDON

First published in the United Kingdom in 2011 by
C. Hurst & Co. (Publishers) Ltd.,
41 Great Russell Street, London, WC1B 3PL
© Robert Lambert, 2011
All rights reserved.
Printed in India

A Cataloguing-in-Publication data record for this book
is available from the British Library.

ISBN: 978-1-84904-166-9

This book is printed on paper from registered sustainable
and managed sources.

www.hurstpub.co.uk

CONTENTS

CONTENTS

DEDICATION

From July 2008 until his death in February 2011 Adam Lambert played a pivotal role in establishing Strategy to Reach, Empower and Educate Teenagers (STREET) as an effective and legitimate youth outreach project in Brixton. As operations manager it often fell to Adam to demonstrate to outsiders how STREET tackled violent gang crime and violent extremism without undermining the integrity and credibility of its youth workers in their local communities. Therein lay a crucial balance between public safety and community confidence that sits at the heart of this book. At his funeral Abdul Haqq Baker, STREET's founder and director, paid tribute to Adam's unique ability to foster and nurture this two-way trust-building process. When I met Adam for the last time he was working hard to ensure that STREET would continue this pioneering work notwithstanding serious political opposition. This book explains why I hope his efforts were not in vain and why I dedicate it to his precious memory.

I also dedicate the book to the trustees, management, staff and local partners of the Finsbury Park Mosque, who worked bravely and tirelessly to combat the influence of al-Qaeda and restore the mosque to its rightful place at the hub of an engaged multicultural local community in London. That they have done so in the face of concerted political opposition in their own time and almost entirely with their own resources, is to their immense credit and typical of the community they represent.

DISCLAIMER

From 1980 until 2006 I was employed as a Metropolitan Police Special Branch (MPSB) detective countering threats of terrorism and political violence in Britain. Formed in 1883 MPSB was wound up in 2006 and I retired from the police service a year later. This book benefits from my MPSB experience but at no point does it enter into areas of classified operational counter-terrorism activity. No statement or comment is made that is premised on strands of classified intelligence—still less is any confidential counter-terrorism activity disclosed or compromised. Such a blanket restriction does nothing to obscure a clear exposition of the topic of counter-terrorism partnerships between Metropolitan Police officers and representatives of mosques and Muslim organisations during the period January 2002 to October 2007. It follows that references to Abu Qatada, Abu Hamza and Abdullah el Faisal as al-Qaeda apologists or propagandists are not based on any use of classified or other operational intelligence. Instead, all such references are based on publicly available material and the community-based research conducted for this book. By the same token I should stress that the book reflects only my personal perspective and experience and not Metropolitan Police, Association of Chief Police Officers (ACPO) or British government counter-terrorism policy or strategy. Where I challenge British counter-terrorism policy and strategy I do so constructively in the strong belief that the war on terror has undermined British policing and that much hard work is needed to restore its reputation as the best in the world.

ACKNOWLEDGEMENTS

I am indebted to a number of individuals for their advice, encouragement and support in writing this book. They fall into three categories: academics; former police colleagues; and representatives of mosques and Muslim organisations in London. First to thank among the academics—the one and only Bill Tupman. Bill has unique experience of guiding police officers through the hazards of academic research and I tested his skill and patience to the full in undertaking the PhD research that provides much of the material for this book. I have also benefitted from the guidance of Abdul Haqq Baker, another Tupman protégé, who has undertaken parallel PhD research to my own. Other academics who have provided invaluable support include Salwa El-Awa, Jonathan Githens-Mazer, Gwen Griffith-Dickson, Michael Kenney, Richard Jackson, Orla Lynch, Laura McDonald, Jeffrey Murer, Bashir Nafi, Tim Niblock, Tariq Ramadan, Marc Sageman, Marie Breen-Smyth, Basia Spalek, Azzam Tamimi and Max Taylor. However, it is a small number of former police colleagues and partners from London mosques and Muslim organisations who made the book possible and for whose co-operation and support I am most indebted. They will understand if I do not name them all here. In spite of such expert guidance I remain stubbornly attached to error and claim complete responsibility for my own mistakes. Most importantly, I wish to thank my wife Julia who has graciously tolerated my preoccupation with the topic of the book over a long period.

PREFACE

Like the subterranean metros under the streets of New York and Paris, the London Underground tube service connects different parts of the city that vary enormously in terms of wealth, culture, architecture and public safety. For the vast majority of travellers—workers, students and tourists—the tube serves as a link between home, work and places of education and entertainment. The individuals who feature in this book are among a very small minority who use London tube trains for entirely different purposes. Since modern terrorists first bombed late Victorian London, the Underground has served both terrorists and the counter-terrorists employed to detect and deter them equally well. For their part, terrorist strategists, propagandists and operatives have travelled the tube to different London neighbourhoods for their various clandestine purposes which include recruitment, support, reconnaissance, targeting and, of course, the execution of terrorist bombings—the action that defines them, whatever their motives or causes. Counter-terrorism has many sub-specialist roles and no doubt surveillance officers have spent more time than desk-bound analysts travelling the tube so as to discreetly monitor the movements of suspected terrorists. Such is the close proximity of terrorists and counter-terrorists during clandestine phases of terrorism and covert counter-terrorism police work.

Sadly, over a century of effective counter-terrorism surveillance on and off the tube has been overshadowed by the shooting dead of Jean Charles de Menezes by police officers on a stationary northbound train at Stockwell underground station on 22 July 2005. Menezes had no connection with terrorism and was wrongly identified as a suspect wanted in connection with a series of failed bomb attacks on the London Underground and a London bus the previous day. Those failed terrorist attacks took place at Shepherds Bush on the Hammersmith and City Line, Warren Street on the Victoria Line, Oval on the Northern Line and on a number 26 London bus in Shoreditch. They mirrored successful suicide bomb attacks carried out between Liverpool Street and Aldgate, between Edgware Road and Paddington on the Circle Line, between King's Cross and Russell Square stations on the Piccadilly Line and on a number 30 London bus in Tavistock Square on 7 July.

During the hours before Menezes was shot dead surveillance was focused on a block of flats in Tulse Hill where a failed terrorist bomber and Menezes both lived. In my view, failures in the management of communications between surveillance officers and firearms officers who shot Menezes in the mistaken and genuine belief that he was a terrorist suspect should not be allowed to impugn the professionalism and bravery of the junior police officers involved in the incident. Rather, Menezes's tragic death should be seen as an unintended but inevitable consequence of a 'shoot to kill' policy put in place by ACPO officers in the wake of 9/11. Known as Operation Kratos the 'shoot to kill' policy was wholly reasonable and proportionate given that the British government helped create a serious risk of al-Qaeda 'suicide' terrorist attacks on London by embracing the war on terror in general and the war in Iraq in particular. Rather than blaming individual police officers for Menezes's death it would be far more realistic to see the innocent Brazilian electrician as another example of civilian 'collateral damage' arising from an ill-conceived war on terror driven by politicians in Washington DC and Westminster.

To recognise that Menezes's family suffered the same anguish as other families who lost loved ones to terrorist attacks inspired or directed by al-Qaeda just two weeks earlier is to begin a consideration of effective counter-terrorism—of the kind that a long denied public inquiry into 7/7 might have produced. To consider that Menezes experienced terror in the moments before he died is to recognise that al-Qaeda strategists have the ability to prompt counter-measures that serve them better than the democracies they attack. In addition, to adopt the perspective of bereaved families is to embrace the victims of other disasters on the London tube during the last century in which specific causes of negligence, criminal and terrorist intent and warfare dissolve into the shared loss of loved ones.[1] This kind of empathetic effort has its own rewards, but it also serves to undermine both al-Qaeda strategists and the neo-conservative architects of the war on terror who thrive equally well on the unique status they attach to their existential battle. It is also the kind of empathetic effort that underpins much of the partnership work I describe in this book.

When the strategic planners of 7/7 decided to target the London Underground, they were following an established pattern of target selection that marks London out as one of the most routinely bombed European cities since the invention of dynamite. Although the tactic of suicide bombers was new to Britain, the impact on stoic and phlegmatic Londoners was minimal, seasoned as it was with experience, resilience and a collective urban memory. For specialist counter-terrorism police officers belonging to MPSB, a police department that had been specifically concerned with terrorism and political violence in Britain for over a century, that collective urban memory was harnessed alongside professional experience to produce unequalled expertise, experience and local knowledge in counter-terrorism. Significantly, MPSB expertise was already being diluted and dismantled on the day Menezes was killed. It will need another book to do justice to the skill and bravery of MPSB officers between 1883 and 2006 but having had the privilege of working with so many of them I am duty bound to correct the impression created by outsiders that their experience had somehow become outdated with the advent of 'new terrorism' on 9/11. That is a purpose that sits at the heart of this book.

I have used four stations on London Underground's Victoria Line—represented on tube maps in light blue—to help organise this book into four parts: King's Cross, Finsbury Park, Brixton and Victoria: *King's Cross* the station where the 7/7 bombers were last seen together introduces the MPSB experience on which the book is based; *Finsbury Park* just two stops northbound from King's Cross explains how that experience was utilised in tackling the influence of al-Qaeda at and around the Finsbury Park Mosque in St. Thomas' Road; *Brixton* at the southern end of the tube line examines the same phenomenon at and around the Brixton Mosque in Gresham Road; and *Victoria*, close to the heart of government in Westminster, serves to conclude the book by drawing lessons from the experiences described in *King's Cross*, *Finsbury Park* and *Brixton*.

The four stations also serve to chart the development of my own experience in counter-terrorism. From the day I joined MPSB in 1980

daily journeys on the Victoria Line provided time to reflect on my counter-terrorism role while travelling to carry out the tasks my specialism
entailed. In 2002 I had an office in King's Cross from where I would
travel by tube and bus to visit mosques and Muslim organisations
around London. *King's Cross* is therefore the place where my prior
experience in counter-terrorism policing is brought to bear on the terrorist threat to London in the wake of 9/11. *Finsbury Park* and *Brixton*—respectively, northbound and southbound from King's Cross on
the Victoria Line—were two of my first destinations in 2002 and by the
time I retired from the police at the end of 2007 they had become the
venues for two pioneering and controversial counter-terrorism partnership projects. In 2004 I returned to an office at New Scotland Yard
(NSY) just a ten-minute walk from Victoria station so it is appropriate
that I should attempt to draw lessons from my experiences in Finsbury
Park and Brixton in *Victoria* to conclude my journey in this book.

Like any other tube journey my interest below ground is strictly limited and focused instead on what can be gleaned at street level where
people reside, work, socialise and conspire. This is a necessarily tight
geographical focus that will help to illuminate the importance of local
context when thinking about the most effective ways to tackle al-
Qaeda influence in Britain. It does not, however, seek to deflect or
exclude attention to equally important lessons that exist in other parts
of London and around Britain. Still less should I give the impression
that purposeful journeys on the London Underground provide the sole
basis for the reflections on experience that this book consists of. I commenced regular train journeys from Paddington to Exeter St. David's
in September 2005 and from King's Cross to Leuchars in September
2008 and these longer train rides away from London provided the
time to reflect on my changed role from counter-terrorism practitioner
to counter-terrorism academic. Notwithstanding the separate demands
of each discipline I was struck by a basic requirement that each role
has in common: a need to listen closely to voices of experience in local
communities.

ABBREVIATIONS

ACPO	Association of Chief Police Officers
ACSO	Assistant Commissioner Specialist Operations (MPS)
ATB	Anti-Terrorist Branch
BNP	British National Party
CAMPACC	Campaign Against Criminalising Communities
CSTRV	Centre for the Study of Terrorism and Political Violence
CTC	Counter Terrorism Command
DCLG	Department for Communities and Local Government
EMRC	European Muslim Research Centre
FBI	Federal Bureau of Investigation (US)
FCO	Foreign and Commonwealth Office
GMP	Greater Manchester Police
HT	Hizb ut Tahrir (UK)
HMIC	Her Majesty's Inspectorate of Constabularies
IAG	Independent Advisory Group (MPS)
IHRC	Islamic Human Rights Commission
MAB	Muslim Association of Britain
MCB	Muslim Council of Britain
MCU	Muslim Contact Unit
MI5	Security Service
MPS	Metropolitan Police Service
MPSB	Metropolitan Police Special Branch
MSF	Muslim Safety Forum
MWH	Muslim Welfare House
NAMP	National Association of Muslim Police
NBPA	National Black Police Association
NCCL	National Council for Civil Liberties

ABBREVIATIONS

NSY	New Scotland Yard
NYPD	New York Police Department
PSC	Palestine Solidarity Campaign
PIRA	Provisional Irish Republican Army
RUC	Royal Ulster Constabulary
SMC	Sufi Muslim Council
STREET	Strategy to Reach, Empower and Educate Teenagers
STW	Stop the War
SWP	Socialist Workers Party
WTC	World Trade Centre

GLOSSARY

'adat	principle of custom in fiqh
Amir	leader
Dar al-Harb	House or abode of War
Dar al-Kufr	House or abode of Disbelief
Dar al-Islam	House or abode of Islam
dawah	missionary work; call to Islam
deen	religion
dhimmi	non-Muslim living under Islamic rule
faqih	expert in fiqh
fatwa	juridical verdict
fiqh	Islamic jurisprudence
hadith	narrative of the Prophet
hajj	pilgrimage
halal	allowed, permissible
haram	forbidden
hijab	headscarf
hijrah	migration from Mecca to Medina
hudud	punishment
ijma	consensus
ijtihad	process of independent reasoning in fiqh
imam	belief
izzat	family and community honour
jahiliyyah	state of ignorance
jannah	paradise
jihad	sacred struggle
jizyah	head tax on non-Muslims under Islamic rule
Khalifah	Caliphate, Islamic state

'kafir	non believer
kufr	unbelief
madhab	school of fiqh
majlis	council or assembly
mujtahid	scholar of ijtihad
nafs	the self
qisas	lawful retaliation
qiyas	deduction by analogy
riddah	apostasy
Sahabah	Companions of Muhammad
Shahid	martyr
Shari'ah	Islamic law
shura	consultation
Sirah	sacred biography of Muhammad
Sunnah	recommended according to Shari'ah
tabligh	preaching
takfir	excommunication
taqlid	imitation
ulema	religious scholars
ummah	nation, people or community
wajib	duty
zakat	almsgiving

PART ONE

KING'S CROSS

1

LEARNING FROM EXPERIENCE

After he retired from distinguished service in the Metropolitan Police (the Met), Inspector Ernest Lambert, my grandfather, lived for nearly forty years. Although he never received official confirmation, once he became an octogenarian Ernest proudly boasted he had become the Met's longest serving pensioner. Throughout this long 'retirement' his experience of London policing from 1899 to 1924 served to inform his thinking and subsequent work in Britain's capital city. By retiring from the Metropolitan Police at the same rank in 2007 I have therefore only just begun to emulate him. While our police careers in London are separated by over fifty years I can at least claim that we jointly served the Met in three centuries—another unique, unofficial family record in the Met I feel sure. I am also tempted to claim that we policed London when it faced similar threats from terrorist bombers. On the one hand we both had to be vigilant against skilful Irish republican bombers who regarded London as their prime target. On the other hand, and surprisingly unacknowledged in a welter of academic and popular literature on terrorism and counter-terrorism, we were also both occupied with 'new' threats from international terrorists who each regarded London as a prime target as well.

In another unremarked parallel, late nineteenth century London-based anarchist bombers often displayed ineptitude in bomb making that has been mirrored by al-Qaeda bombers in the first decade of the twenty-first century. This lack of technical skill meant that anarchist terrorists risked accidental death when exploding their unstable bombs while al-Qaeda terrorists risked living when their poorly constructed bombs failed to detonate—the same lack of tradecraft reducing the effectiveness of different tactical approaches to their chosen method of political communication. The same deficiency in tradecraft also undermined strikingly similar revolutionary goals notwithstanding competing ideologies and different political contexts.

Something of this shared approach to bombing London as an appropriate tactic with which to advance and promote revolutionary change is captured in an innovative documentary made by Joe Bullman in 2009.[1] His artistic technique of juxtaposing Londoners' experience of terrorism in two eras is illuminating and helps my purpose of breaking down artificial barriers erected to distinguish between 'old' and 'new' terrorism.[2] Like Bullman, I am concerned to examine and compare the impact London-based terrorists and counter-terrorists in different eras have on each other and on the communities where they each seek support and intelligence. For me, this is an extension of what I have always understood to be a professional requirement of learning from experience in counter-terrorism. Having spoken with convicted terrorists who have undertaken their own academic research in prison it is a very similar approach of learning to theirs—combining lived experience with reflection, academic rigour and an appreciation of a requirement to enhance organisational learning for future benefit. At its heart sits a willingness to acknowledge and learn from mistakes.

'Everyone knows society is on the verge of another great revolution', a Muslim 'radical' reads a late Victorian London anarchist tract against a backdrop of 'suspect' Muslim Londoners monitored by surveillance cameras and covert counter-terrorism technology.[3] 'For my part' the Muslim reader continues, 'I'm willing to suffer for my ideas ... they will not crush this movement by repression they will only make it more revolutionary and more dangerous'.[4] This is a realistic and recurring terrorist aspiration that governments in both eras have unwittingly done much to bring about, thereby giving rise to the notion of 'counter-productive counter-terrorism'.[5] Bullman's documentary also reveals an understandable police preference in both eras to respond covertly to clandestine terrorist activity. In both respects, the documentary usefully sets the scene for two lessons I have learned from experience: covert counter-terrorism responses that are not narrowly focused, reasonable and proportionate risk falling into a perennial trap of counter-productivity set by all kinds of terrorists; and counter-terrorism's necessary reliance on covert methods should not preclude complementary responses that are wholly transparent and aim instead to foster

trust and partnership in the same communities where terrorists seek recruits and support.

In both eras these are lessons more readily understood by police officers than politicians in government. Certainly, Ernest and I had to contend with Home Secretaries who would interfere in the day-to-day business of counter-terrorism at the drop of a hat. Whether in late Victorian or post-7/7 London, such interventions might do more for a politician's public profile than the narrow purpose of effective counter-terrorism policing. Equally, in pursuing popular acclaim Home Secretaries in any era might overlook the needs of minority communities where terrorists seek recruits and support. Thus during Ernest's service a high profile 'hands-on' intervention by Winston Churchill at the Sidney Street siege did nothing to reduce the popular stigmatisation of a local East End Jewish community as terrorists and subversives.[6] Similarly, when John Reid spoke to a Muslim audience in Leyton, East London in the aftermath of high-profile local terrorist arrests in 2006 he did nothing to reduce the popular view that politically active or strictly observant Muslims were part and parcel of a home grown or al-Qaeda terrorist threat to Britain.[7]

Ernest had no great expectations of Home Secretaries in regard to policing except that they should not try and do it themselves. Like Sir David McNee, who joined the Met as Commissioner at the same time I joined as a recruit, Ernest believed that policing was independent, somehow above politics. McNee went so far as to express his independence tangibly and symbolically. 'The political neutrality of the police service and the political independence and impartiality of chief police officers' he declared, 'is central to the British policing system'.[8] To the surprise of his new colleagues at NSY he added that this was such an important principle that 'I no longer exercise my right to vote, nor have I since I was appointed a chief officer of police'.[9] I think Ernest, who died in 1963, would have agreed with McNee when he explained that 'police officers must be men and women of the middle, bound only by the rule of law'.[10] Fine sounding words, yet both Ernest and McNee found no conflict of interest when it came to police officers being bound by secret oaths of Masonic fraternity.[11] This masonic blind-spot serves to illustrate how easy it can be for police officers—no less than the politicians and public they serve—to sometimes overlook their own vested interests when proclaiming political neutrality and transparency in the maintenance of law and order.

As a boy I was most impressed by my grandfather's story of policing the first ever FA Cup Final at Wembley Stadium in 1923. His personal eye witness account was made even more vivid by an old newsreel showing a policeman on a white horse called Billy preventing injury and loss of life by patiently easing thousands of fans off the football pitch after the stadium became seriously overfull. I saw that grainy black and white newsreel at the same time that George Dixon, an avuncular 'bobby' on the beat in an iconic television series *Dixon of Dock Green*, introduced me to a vision of community-based policing in Britain.[12] 'Protection of life and property' and 'the preservation of public tranquillity' remained cornerstones of police training when I became a Metropolitan Police recruit in 1977.[13] I was taught that the 'co-operation and approval of the public' was an essential pre-requisite in securing the primary object of police, 'the prevention of crime'.[14] Such was the importance of this primary duty I was required to commit to memory my new role as 'the servant and guardian of the general public' in which I was obliged to 'treat all law-abiding citizens, irrespective of their race, colour, creed or social position, with unfailing patience and courtesy'. If I had not learnt that instruction by heart I would not have begun my police career.[15]

Equally, if I had not learnt to balance the requirements of police training school with the demands of real London policing my police career might have been much shorter. Later on, as a counter-terrorism specialist I would learn of a balance to be struck between the requirement for good intelligence and the need to foster strong community relations. Although often neglected these were competing imperatives that tapped into a rich seam of police experience coalescing around John Alderson.[16] Even though Alderson retired from the police service in 1982, his reputation as a champion of community policing was enhanced over the next two decades through his work with Bill Tupman, director of the ground-breaking Centre for Police and Criminal Justice Studies at the University of Exeter from 1986 until 1995. According to an experienced MPS detective, Tupman was able to encourage his students—generally senior or aspiring police officers—to challenge conventional and conservative police thinking on a number of key topics but most effectively in relation to communities:

Bill was good at getting us to see other points of view—to appreciate that community criticisms of police were sometimes well founded. And whereas John Alderson had been written off by many former colleagues as a well-meaning

left-leaning do-gooder Bill was able to restore [Alderson's] reputation to some extent and get us to examine the difficult issues he had raised.[17]

In 1982 Alderson certainly confounded his conservative police colleagues by giving a frank interview to the far-left journal *Marxism Today*.[18] The interviewer raised the issue of tensions between community policing and intelligence gathering and quoted Tony Bunyan arguing that a community police officer was gathering intelligence 'on the people on their patch' for the benefit of all police departments including Special Branch:[19]

Community policing, despite its high-sounding purpose is a double-edged tool to penetrate the community through other professional agencies and by spying on the community under the guise of offering a protective, friendly approach. Consent is thus to be engineered and, in case this fails, intelligence is gathered to pre-empt dissent.[20]

Significantly, exactly the same allegation was made at the Muslim Safety Forum (MSF) in 2006 by a Muslim community leader,[21] whereas in a thorough-going Home Office review of community policing literature in 2006 the issue of spying was not raised once.[22] In the circumstances Alderson's reply is worth quoting not least because interviewees who worked with him say it is characteristic of his ability to accept criticism while deftly re-framing the issue under scrutiny in favour of his own analysis:

I think what Tony Bunyan describes is a plausible scenario and I wouldn't deny that. Therefore a premium is placed on accountability, on consultation and scrutiny. If one accepts, as I do, that what Tony Bunyan describes is a corruption of community policing, then you've got [to] build in safeguards to prevent that. There has to be a form of social contract, there have to be codes, there have to be bills of rights, there have to be scrutineers—I would accept all that.[23]

Of course, what Alderson declines to say is that the vast majority of his police colleagues would have seen no problem at the time with the notion that a community police officer might be 'spying on the community'—on the basis that the law-abiding majority would have nothing to fear.[24] By the same token—according to this majority police view—communities that provided a home for criminals and political activists warranted close attention. Significantly, notwithstanding a grudging respect for Alderson and a high regard for Tupman, many Association of Chief Police Officers (ACPO) members have not moved far from the naturally conservative position outlined by Assistant

Commissioner David Powis in 1977 in which 'political radicals', 'intellectuals who spout extremist babble' and 'people in possession of "your rights" cards such as those issued by the National Council for Civil Liberties (NCCL)' are deemed to be inherently suspicious and subversive.[25] 'The liberal concerns expressed by Alderson' one interviewee suggests, 'have helped inform debates about policing but invariably police chiefs have opted for a tougher "*Daily Mail*" line when push comes to shove'.[26] In contrast, because I worked with police colleagues outside a cadre of senior police politics I was free to think about the principles of policing without undue pressure to follow an agreed ACPO line. I was also extremely mindful of the fact that many of the young radicals deemed subversive by Assistant Commissioner Powis in 1977 had matured into pillars of the New Labour establishment in government, most notably Jack Straw, Peter Hain, Jack Dromey and John Reid.

Moreover, I had seen many good opportunities for community intelligence being squandered by ACPO officers who failed to grasp the importance of Alderson's commitment to engagement with critical community representatives. That said, David Veness and John Grieve were two notable exceptions who had clearly learned the lessons provided by Alderson. Essentially they had experience to indicate that a commitment to the principles of community policing was more likely to produce good intelligence than its abandonment. It followed that a remedy was needed when members of minority or marginalised communities were found to be prone to poor service from a minority of police officers who failed to uphold the highest standards of British policing.[27]

Similarly, a notion of cultivating community contacts, as opposed to recruiting informants, especially community leaders in touch with their communities, is best informed by a close appreciation of effective community policing. In some respects this departs from a systematic approach to community policing extolled by Sir Ian Blair[28] (Met Commissioner 2005—2008) and ACPO[29] and instead places value on the expert street skills individual community police officers bring to bear on their posts over a long period of time.[30] I first learned this lesson when an established long-term community police officer dispelled a police canteen stereotype when he arrested a man who was wanted for rape. Both in the police canteen and in popular TV dramas like *The Sweeney* and *Life on Mars* natural 'thief takers' like Regan, Carter and Gene Hunt are understood to achieve results by showing scant regard for the sensibilities of minority communities, the restrictions of 'political correctness' or the niceties of due process.[31] In contrast, community police officers are often derided as 'hobby bobbies' or 'uniform carriers' who are as far removed from serious crime as George Dixon.[32] The 'hobby bobby' I had the privilege of working with exposed that stereotype in spectacular fashion—he secured an important rape arrest because he befriended and helped members of a local squatting community by fixing their broken down van—hardly something Regan and Carter or their real life role models ever had time or inclination for.[33] When the community bobby subsequently asked the squatters for help in identifying a man wanted for rape, they provided the information that led to his arrest.

Moreover, apart from achieving results and building trust, this kind of approach also tends to break down barriers and reduce stereotyping on both sides. Unfortunately, trust did not last long in this particular instance because two weeks later the same squatters were injured and their home was ransacked during a search for cannabis by the Special Patrol Group[34]—which highlights two very different approaches to policing. Sometimes, the patient work of trust building by community policing can be undone by unwitting and heavy-handed police action. Then, as now, softer approaches to policing problems—and this includes terrorism as much as any other area of crime—are often misunderstood by a significant minority of police officers as being weak. Similarly for some detectives, community policing continues to be ridiculed as something that is done for the sake of political correctness or for the sake of avoiding situations like the Brixton riots. In an interview with the academic Richard Jackson I describe this viewpoint as short-sighted and often based on a lack of real exposure to the communities where criminals and terrorists operate:

....it is possible to build police careers away from the local communities that are most critical of police, and also the most valuable in terms of community intelligence. This lack of exposure to the real world of inner city London might seem antithetical to policing, but it has been allowed to develop. It has been a particular problem in specialist departments where some officers have worked in relative isolation from the communities that are affected by their work. Needless to say, it is even more of a problem in those arms of counter-terrorism outside of policing that have no engagement with communities at all.[35]

In contrast, experience taught me that community policing had a crucial role to play in helping minority communities tackle terrorism and political violence. Unfortunately, for the main part, ACPO officers tended to treat counter-terrorism as something separate where the rules of good community policing might easily be set aside and counter-manded by operational necessity. Again Alderson, Veness and Grieve come to mind as pioneers in challenging this risk-averse default position. Suffice to say they have had a positive impact on my thinking in writing this book.

Most retired police officers, like my grandfather, are content to limit their reflections on their police careers to sharing a few anecdotes amongst family and friends. Generally, only police chiefs take the time to write about their work in retirement. For instance, two police chiefs I worked for, Sir Ian Blair, Metropolitan Police Commissioner from 2005 to 2008 and his colleague Andy Hayman, Assistant Commissioner responsible for Specialist Operations from 2005 to 2007, have both published books that deal extensively with the counter-terrorism issues that dominated the latter stages of their police careers.[36] Indeed, both books serve to answer criticisms that were levelled at them in the media in a counter-terrorism context. Neither book, however, answers media criticism levelled at my work for them in the same arena. More disturbingly, both books contend that Muslim Londoners have largely failed to make a significant contribution to counter-terrorism policing, an assertion that I am duty bound to challenge. On the contrary, in my experience, Muslim Londoners have made many outstanding contributions to the public safety of the capital both in a counter-terrorism context and more widely. I would therefore be disingenuous if I did not admit at the outset that these accounts by Blair and Hayman spur me to publish my own. For the record, I need only add that I had conducted the research on which my book is based before either of their books were published.

As a rule, only occasional sensationalist books like Harry Keeble's *Terror Cops*[37] break the monopoly ACPO officers have on insider accounts of counter-terrorism policing. Even here, however, there is a case for suggesting that a series of books co-authored by Keeble (of which *Terror Cops* is the latest) if not tacitly endorsed by ACPO officers at least serve to bolster and popularise ACPO counter-terrorism policy, in the way that Andy McNab's bestselling books might be said to glamorise and popularise the role of the SAS and the British military in the war on terror. In any event, the same monopoly usually applies in the media where Blair and Hayman are among a handful of retired

ACPO officers who provide context and authority when policing operations and policing issues are in the news. In much the same vein academics and think-tanks will invariably seek authoritative views on counter-terrorism policing issues from ACPO officers—either currently serving or recently retired. Most notably, Policy Exchange's annual *Colin Cramphorn Memorial Lecture* serves both to promote and influence ACPO counter-terrorism policy, often with particular reference to retired ACPO officers such as Peter Clarke, former head of the Met's Counter-Terrorism Command, who shares the late Colin Cramphorn's perspectives on the topic.[38] It follows that Clarke's talk *Learning from Experience* rests on a different perspective from my own.

I should therefore declare that my book breaks new ground by offering a specialist counter-terrorism perspective that is not informed by ACPO policy and challenges it in places—especially where ACPO policy slavishly endorsed the war on terror. Instead I have written a book based on my own counter-terrorism policing experience in London. While I certainly learned important lessons from ACPO officers over the years if I am honest it is the lessons I learned from fellow constables, sergeants and inspectors that served me best during my police career and that made the biggest contribution to my own learning experience. In particular my account is informed by informal on-the-job learning acquired during a long specialist career in the MPSB. This chapter introduces this perspective and locates it in King's Cross, the part of London where I was based at the beginning of 2002 when I began my final role in MPSB, running the Muslim Contact Unit (MCU) the topic of the book. I then shift my focus from King's Cross to Finsbury Park and Brixton where the experience of Muslim Londoners informs my counter-terrorism work. To conclude my journeys up and down the Victoria Line I travel to Victoria, a place where I often sought to convey the experience and perspectives of Muslim Londoners to ACPO officers, civil servants and politicians.

At any rate this is the way I have organised the book to reflect the geography and chronology of my counter-terrorism police work. At the outset I am conscious of two major deficits. In Finsbury Park and Brixton—both case study sites in my PhD—I do little more than scratch the surface of rich, voluminous primary data I have gathered as both interviewer and participant observer over a long period. Worse still, by omitting close attention to MCU experience in Whitechapel, Walthamstow, Leyton, Ilford, Forest Gate, Parsons Green, Baker Street, Regents

Park, Westbourne Park, Wembley, Edmonton, Finchley, Harrow, Hounslow, Croydon and elsewhere in London I am in danger of skewing attention in favour of partnership successes against al-Qaeda influence. In essence these deficits are both aspects of insider bias that I will endeavour to mitigate in *Victoria* the concluding part of the book. Even if I succeed in that task it will still leave me an opportunity to do full justice to my research data and the wider experience of Muslim Londoners in this important arena in a subsequent account. I am in no doubt that this book serves as an introduction to the issues it raises and not the final word. In offering a personal policing perspective I rest heavily on a PhD research thesis in which I analyse the legitimacy and effectiveness of the MCU's work.[39] Naturally, like this book, the thesis carries the necessary defect of insider bias. To explain how I went about the task of mitigating that deficit I will include an outline of my research methodology in an Appendix.[40] I should add that just as this book is introductory rather than definitive so too is my ongoing research in this arena assisted enormously by collaborations with academic partners.[41]

My experience is also informed and enriched by discussions with victims of terrorist attacks and victims of political violence, especially members of bereaved families with whom I have a strong empathy. In fact there is a levelling equality of suffering in bereavement that is best known to police officers. The job of communicating 'sudden death' messages to parents who are about to begin new lives without the beloved children they have nurtured is especially heart rending and often falls to young officers who have not long left police training school. No training prepares them for the experience of delivering such devastating news. For some police officers, myself included, the experience of drinking tea with newly bereaved parents is a crucial part of spontaneous, unstructured on-the-job training in which we come to appreciate the vital importance of the victim's perspective.

When a more experienced Metropolitan Police officer sat with a mother whose son had been killed near to King's Cross by the 7/7 bombers she was struck by the mother's ability to articulate pride in her son's achievements in his short life just an hour after the devastating news of his death had been broken to her. The police officer in this case was repeating a task colleagues had carried out in 1987 when a negligently discarded match is thought to have caused a fire at King's Cross underground station which killed 31 people, a short distance from where several 7/7 victims died two decades later. Those officers, in turn, were repeating the task of breaking heart rending news to the families of 43 victims of a London Underground accident at Moorgate, just three stops from King's Cross on the Northern Line, in 1975. Such, too, is the equality of suffering between sudden bereavements caused with and without criminal intent—an insight that flows from the policing experience of interviewing bereaved victims who have lost their loved ones in a variety of contexts.

In making this observation about the equality of suffering I do not overlook another lesson of police experience—that all cases and all situations must be assessed on their individual and particular merits. This is especially important so as to avoid copying the media where one case of victim suffering will be highlighted while others will be neglected, whether caused by terrorism, serious crime or negligence. I am also conscious that I am relying on British policing experience that would not resonate in many other countries. For instance in those dictatorships where police play key roles in the disappearance of the regime's political opponents family suffering is taken to an altogether different level where the natural healing process of bereavement cannot even begin. Before 9/11 I never dreamt that my policing role in London might become connected to and contaminated by another kind of policing heritage abroad that promotes practices that cause greater suffering than the bereavements they invariably culminate in. Suffice to say, one of the many unintended negative consequences of the war on terror has been the juxtaposition of international policing methods in which the Peelian notion of 'policing by consent' has often been overshadowed and eclipsed by the practice of state terror, torture and coercion.

Certainly, no British police officer can afford to be complacent after a number of British citizens have been tortured by foreign police colleagues in the name of a global war on terror. Such departure from the rule of law and civilised conduct seemed inconceivable two years after the Moorgate underground tragedy when I delivered my first 'sudden death' message to parents whose son was killed in a road traffic accident in the Finchley Road just fifty yards north of Finchley Road underground station. I subsequently recalled that experience when a young police officer came to deliver a message concerning my daughter's sudden death in 1992. Like many other bereaved parents I have tried since then to put the experience to the best use that I can. In a number of ways, including an attempt to address the grievances that result from unacknowledged and unrecorded civilian bereavements in the war on terror, this book represents part of that process. To be sure, when delivering and receiving sudden death messages police officers, like nurses and doctors, learn to respect and support the dignity and sanctity of this first stage of bereavement. British police officers who have also served abroad in war torn countries such as those in the Balkans region report similarly powerful and painful stories confirming the universality of the suffering of parental bereavement.

The crucial importance of affording equal importance to the suffering of all bereaved families is captured in a moving diptych by war artist Steve Pratt. The two paintings *The Ultimate Sacrifice in the name of God, Queen and Country* (2009) and *Collateral Damage* (2009) evoke an equality of suffering between Afghani Muslim and British Army victims of the present counter-insurgency campaign in Afghanistan.[42] While Pratt's military experience adds weight to his profound artistic vision, the failure of US and British politicians to appreciate the importance of the universality and equality of suffering he captures has been skilfully exploited by al-Qaeda strategists and propagandists, most notably al-Qaeda's iconic leader Osama bin Laden. While nothing a terrorist propagandist says should ever be taken at face value still less should we allow our own politicians to ascribe meanings and motives to terrorists that their words and actions do not allow. Certainly bin Laden is sufficiently clear in this extract as to reduce the need for any gloss:

What happened in September 11 and March 11 is your own merchandise coming back to you. We hereby advise you ... that your definition of us and of our actions as terrorism is nothing but a definition of yourselves by yourselves, since our reaction is of the same kind as your act. ....Our actions are a reaction to yours, which are destruction and killing of our people as is happening in Afghanistan, Iraq and Palestine. By what measure of kindness are your killed considered innocents while ours are considered worthless? By what school [of thought] is your blood considered blood while our blood is water? Therefore, it is [only] just to respond in kind, and the one who started it is more to blame...[43]

Alex Schmid is the first academic to analyse the way terrorist strategists—of all kinds—take advantage of a symbiotic relationship between the terrorist acts they plan and the counter-terrorism measures employed against them. Terrorism, he suggests, is a form of communication that 'cannot be understood only in terms of violence'.[44] Rather, for Schmid, 'it has to be understood primarily in terms of propaganda'[45] so as to penetrate the terrorist's strategic purpose:

Violence and propaganda, however, have much in common. Violence aims at behaviour modification by coercion. Propaganda aims at the same by persuasion. Terrorism can be seen as a combination of the two. Terrorism, by using violence against one victim, seeks to coerce and persuade others. The immediate victim is merely instrumental, the skin on a drum beaten to achieve a calculated impact on a wider audience.[46]

In 2002 I was part of a small group of specialist counter-terrorism police officers, based at a former police station in King's Cross, who embarked on the work that I now seek to document and analyse in this book. Although I was not then familiar with Schmid's work I had learned from practitioner experience that effective counter-terrorism did not alienate the very communities where terrorists sought recruits and support. Having learned from mistakes made in countering Irish republican terrorism it was sufficiently clear to me that the tactic of terrorist bombings should be the target of counter-terrorism policy not the political cause that terrorists seek to exploit. Throughout more than a century of sporadic terrorist bomb attacks in London political activists campaigned lawfully and peacefully in and around King's Cross for the same causes terrorists used to justify their violence. This included regular, lawful meetings in support of Irish republicanism at a pub in the Grays Inn Road just a ten-minute walk from my office in King's Cross Road. Effective counter-terrorism understood the value of distinguishing between the two kinds of behaviour and the need to prosecute one while facilitating the other. This was to anticipate and make use of Schmid's terrorist insight and to recognise the kind of learning that took place in the specialist police department I belonged to until 2006.

Just a hundred yards from the rear of the building where I was based a blue plaque marks the house where Vladimir Lenin continued Karl Marx's revolutionary London-based work. Like the revolutionary Lollards[47] and reformist Chartists[48] who lived in the neighbourhood before them Lenin and Marx exposed the kind of political inequities that can lead to political violence, terrorism and retaliatory state terrorism and suppression by governments. To walk from my office to King's Cross tube station was to witness poverty, alcoholism, drug addiction and social dysfunction alongside thriving business success in a way that once caught Lenin's attention:

[Lenin] was greatly impressed by the variety of London life, by the evidences of great wealth and great poverty side by side. Krupskaya mentions in her book

15

how in face with these contrasts she heard him muttering through his clenched teeth, and in English, 'Two nations', which seems to indicate a lapse from the natural Marxist form of 'Two classes' into a form made familiar by Disraeli.[49]

Indeed Lenin often shared exactly the same purpose in walking northbound along King's Cross Road from Percy Circus as I did: to eat a lunch of fish and chips with comrades. London's traditional working class meal made such a favourable impression on the Russian revolutionary that he took Trotsky and Stalin to eat it with him in a restaurant near King's Cross station.[50] Although Osama bin Laden's physical presence in London is less clear than Lenin's there is no doubt that he too used it as a base for his revolutionary activities. In 1994 the al-Qaeda leader established a media office known as the Advice and Reform Committee in suburban Dollis Hill, served by a quiet station on the Jubilee Line. That office operated freely until 1998 when the individuals running it were arrested under US arrest warrants in connection with the al-Qaeda bombing of US embassies in Nairobi and Dar es Salaam. Interestingly, at key points Osama bin Laden offers a very similar critique of capitalism to Marx and Lenin and provided a clear focal point for my job of assessing al-Qaeda's influence in Britain in the period 2002–2007.

Counter-terrorism, like many other specialisms, relies on expertise, experience and sound local knowledge. Those were the attributes that informed my role as one of a small team of London police officers working in partnership with an equally small number of Muslim Londoners to share expertise, experience and local knowledge in countering and reducing the adverse impact of al-Qaeda terrorist strategists and propagandists in London. Like my grandfather I was dedicated to the task of preserving the capital city's public safety—not just for the benefit of those in power or with influence but for its poorest and most marginalised citizens as well. Part of the expertise my colleagues brought to this new partnership table as specialist counter-terrorism police officers was a strong professional memory of lessons learned from mistakes in the past. Perhaps the lesson that draconian counter-terrorism measures tended to boost terrorist recruitment and support—thereby becoming counter-productive—was the most crucial in the immediate aftermath of 9/11 when we conceived our new role.

For their part Muslim Londoners brought lessons learned from harsh experience that would serve the partnership well when faced with the negative impact of the war on terror. Like other immigrant Londoners a small number of Muslims had settled in the capital having suffered torture and oppression in their countries of origin simply for being politically active. They provided powerful testimony of the inherent dangers of a global war on terror that granted legitimacy to some of the world's most practised state torturers—including those who had tortured individuals now exiled in London and working against al-Qaeda. London has been an established safe haven for political asylum seekers of all kinds for over a century. During my grandfather's police service effective policing served Jewish and Irish immigrants well and avoided conflating them with a handful of terrorists who sought their support. On occasions such as the early media frenzy that surrounded the famous Sidney Street siege in 1911 this might entail working against the grain of political and official police policy. As Stephen Gates observes:

The siege of Sidney Street carries startling resonances even now. It was, arguably, the first breaking-news story: a film shot by newsreel cameramen was shown that evening in a West End theatre. The presence of the 36-year-old [Home Secretary, Winston] Churchill, who can be seen in the film gesticulating towards the police, was an early photo opportunity. Sir Robert Anderson, a former head of the CID at Scotland Yard, denounced 'the mollycoddling attitude towards criminals by the Radical government [sic] and a certain so-called humanitarian section of the general public'.... Two Latvian gunmen killed in the shootout were at first thought to be Jewish anarchists and views on immigration ran through the coverage of the event. The Times described them as 'some of the worst alien anarchists and criminals who seek our too-hospitable shore'.[51]

As in my police service, Ernest dealt with far more suspected terrorist attacks than ones that came to fruition. Moreover, suspected terrorist activity by a small group of London-based Jewish anarchists was used by popularist politicians and commentators to invoke and incite anti-Semitism towards peaceful, hardworking London Jewish immigrants.[52] While all sections of contemporary, diverse Jewish London faced anti-Semitic 'guilt by association' it was minority, anarchist and politically radical Jewish communities in the capital that faced the greatest risk of stigmatisation, disapprobation and suspicion both from other London Jewish communities and in wider London society.[53] Then, as now, the capital's guardians of public tranquillity, the Metropolitan Police Force (only now a *Service*) had the task of protecting all sections of the capital's diverse citizenship from terrorism and the fear terrorists intend it should generate and which politicians invariably amplify.[54] On that basis newly arrived London Jewish immigrant communities had as much right as any other majority or minority section of London society to expect fair and impartial policing.

Such an expectation would have been warranted given the notion of policing by consent first established in the capital by Sir Richard Mayne in 1829.[55] The extent to which this policing model took root in the capital is highlighted in a *Times* editorial in 1908 which noted: 'The policeman in London is not merely guardian of the peace, he is the best friend of a mass of people who have no other counsellor or protector'.[56] It is not hard to imagine how such an avuncular approach to community engagement might appear attractive to new immigrant Jewish Londoners familiar with more oppressive and intrusive policing models in Russia and elsewhere in contemporary Europe. However, then, as now, policing in London became less effective when it owed more to the consent of powerful, majority interests than the consent of stigmatised communities that lacked influence.[57] Moreover, immigrant London Jews who were politically active in pursuit of international socialist causes at the end of the nineteenth century and the beginning of the twentieth century faced far greater risks of stigmatisation than their non-Jewish socialist comrades who were regarded as belonging to indigenous London communities.

This tension between a police objective to serve minority immigrant communities and popularist political leadership permeates British counter-terrorism in all eras. In whatever context, it should be set against the notion of competition for community support between terrorists and counter-terrorists and the ensuing police adage 'communities defeat terrorism' that became popular during my police service. Of course, it is impossible to overstate the pressure of tabloid media opinion on politicians when faced with terrorist outrages—real or imagined. Just as Home Secretary Winston Churchill played up to it in 1911 so too would the more considered Roy Jenkins do likewise in 1974 when introducing draconian new anti-terrorism measures to a febrile House of Commons in the aftermath of a Provisional IRA (PIRA) bomb attack in which 21 civilians were killed and 182 injured. Two improvised explosive devices exploded in two central Birmingham pubs—the *Mulberry Bush* and the *Tavern in the Town*— and a third device, left outside a bank in Hagley Road, failed to detonate. Noting parallels with the atmosphere in the House of Commons after the al-Qaeda tube bombings in July 2005, the *New Statesman* usefully marked the first anniversary of 7/7 by reprinting an article written by Mary Holland after she witnessed the House of Commons debate on the introduction of the Prevention of Terrorism (Temporary Provisions) Act. The following extract from Holland's 1974 article certainly resonated in 2006:

The most depressing aspect of the House of Commons debate on Mr. Jenkins' new laws against terrorism was not the desire of most MPs to be seen as more vociferous in their demands for retribution than all but the most vengeful of their constituents, Holland noted. Nor was it the fact that so few seemed to have given thought to how Mr. Jenkins's measures might work in practice. The character of the debate which should have induced near despair was the passionate desire of a British Parliament to batten down the hatches, to shut out the ugly, dangerous infection which threatens us from the outside. ...If the new laws are seen as labelling all Irish people here as potentially suspect, that is what those people could become.[58]

Most tellingly, Holland captures the wilful failure of the Labour government to acknowledge the legitimacy of the political grievances the PIRA sought to exploit for terrorist recruitment. An omission, I should add, that built on earlier Conservative failings that would prove hugely counter-productive for the reasons Holland anticipated. Fascinating and neglected parallels exist here between an Old Labour knee-jerk government response in 1974 and its New Labour counterpart in 2005. Moreover, just as politically active Jewish and Irish immigrants to Britain have in different eras often faced unfair and counter-productive conflation with a handful of terrorists so too have politically active Muslims suffered unwarranted stigmatisation as terrorists and subversives in the decade since 9/11.[59] That at least is my assessment and it sits at the heart of my account. It is also the assessment that has proved hugely controversial and prompted the criticism I seek to address. To be clear, the Bush-Blair war on terror is founded on a competing assessment of al-Qaeda as part of the wider threat posed by political Islam, often described as Islamism and regularly distinguished from Islam. In London, often considered the home of political Islam, this is a policy that disqualifies some of al-Qaeda's most effective opponents and puts my work at odds with government policy.

My first task is to challenge the twin arguments that al-Qaeda is wholly different from 'old' terrorism and that political Islam represents a subversive threat to Britain (and the US and the rest of Europe), that is similar to, if not worse than, communism. I therefore seek historical parallels and both professional and family experience—as well as my

19

academic research—to assist me. Although it is not certain it seems very likely that my forebears were French Huguenots who arrived in London to escape religious persecution in France. They certainly succeeded in terms of escape and merely had to overcome the kind of hurdles most immigrants face—accusations that 'their presence threatened jobs, standards of housing, public order, morality and hygiene…' and the like.[60] A familiar story of gradual London integration is only interrupted by one notable, negative incident in 1769 when two immigrant weavers—one French, one Irish—employed in the Huguenot weaving industry were arrested and hanged outside the *Salmon and Ball* public house in Bethnal Green. According to the officer who commanded the soldiers who captured and executed them the two men were guilty of conspiring with fellow weavers (or cutters) to protect their jobs in the face of sudden redundancy.[61]

While such savage curtailment of political protest had ended long before my police career began nevertheless many ACPO officers worked enthusiastically with Margaret Thatcher's government to help restore the reputation of the Metropolitan Police as the enemy of the workers during the miners' strike and the News International print dispute during the 1980s.[62] That was certainly the view of a police constable who came from a mining community in Derbyshire who experienced hostility from family and friends because of his role as one of 'Maggie Thatcher's strike breakers'.[63] After police launched a charge on a miner's demonstration in London he was confronted by angry miners' wives who abused him as a sell-out and scornfully remarked 'and you're going to go home to your wife and children…!' He was deeply distressed and subsequently resigned from the police.[64] Suffice to say John Alderson was a lone ACPO figure prepared to challenge Thatcher's exuberant embrace of political policing. By all accounts the Prime Minister was decidedly unimpressed when Alderson was photographed drinking tea and chatting happily with anti-war protesters at a peace camp Home Office officials had rather anticipated riot police would shut down.[65] Alderson was also a clear voice against the use of the military in policing roles. 'The need to act' he said, 'without bias or prejudice to be a servant of the law and of society as a whole is the *sine qua non* of police action', and therefore, 'military involvement in policing operations should be avoided if at all possible…'[66]

Alderson's observation about the crucial separation of police and military in Britain sits at odds with the war on terror:

The distinction between the military and police functions, at least since the formation of the modern police in 1829, has been marked in Great Britain. The distinction is not so clear in France and other countries much influenced by the Napoleonic police systems where the *gendarmerie* are in fact under military command but have a normal policing function as well.[67]

It is only that absence of military thinking that allows British policing to build partnerships with minority and marginalised communities. William Lyons argues that counter-terrorism must learn to police in ways 'that build trusting relationships with those communities least likely to willingly assist the police: those often marginalized communities where criminals and terrorists can more easily live lives insulated from observation'.[68] The point is re-enforced by M. C. de Guzman who argues that a 'community-police relationship that is based on mutual trust is more likely to uncover matters that are helpful in identifying prospective terrorists':

A more formal or authoritarian police-community relationship would distance police from the rest of the community and only reports of actual law breaking are likely to be reported... Enlisting the community in its own defence encourages it to take control of its own destiny.[69]

As witnessed in Sidney Street the military role in policing was still very much in evidence during Ernest Lambert's police service. In addition to major terrorist and criminal operations, the Home Secretary of the day would invariably call for military support whenever political or industrial protest was the issue. While nothing ever occurred in London to match the military slaughter of protesters in Manchester's Peterloo massacre nevertheless early socialist demonstrations still cast workers as subversive threats requiring military options to support an unarmed police force. For example, shortly before Ernest joined the police an orderly socialist demonstration in Trafalgar Square was marshalled jointly and brutally by military and police resulting in the death of three protesters and serious injuries to 200 more.[70] Similarly, when I joined the police the shooting dead of demonstrators by British soldiers in Derry in 1969 was the subject of annual 'Bloody Sunday' marches in London. In both instances British governments showed little interest in the problem such incidents posed for the concept and practice of 'policing by consent'. In the latter case, still less was there much government interest in the extent to which such actions prove counter-productive in terms of boosting terrorist recruitment and undermining community support for counter-terrorism.

At least in the Lambert family, cumulative experience suggests that draconian state measures of all kinds that harm political activists who often share the same political grievances as terrorists fail to achieve their purpose in all but the most despotic states. In 1923 Ernest and fellow police officers were led to believe that their role in combating IRA bombers in London was over—that the IRA was crushed—following the execution of 77 political activists and the imprisonment of 12,000 more in Ireland.[71] Not only was that assessment premature it also serves to highlight the false premise on which the war on terror was launched in 2001. Instead, al-Qaeda, like any terrorist movement, would be more likely to be defeated if the legitimate political grievances it seeks to exploit were addressed and not ignored. Of course, *real politic* demands tough political responses at such times, but it is regrettable that British political leaders have not devised coherent strategies to present soft and effective counter-terrorism strategies to the public and media in ways that would make them legitimate to both majority and minority communities.

To be sure, during my police service, outstanding success has been achieved by British security and police officers in innumerable counter-terrorism cases regardless and in spite of the political rhetoric in Westminster and the extraordinary powers and special legislation that has been sought and won there. Invariably, success in these cases arises from the application of specialist intelligence and investigative skills that focuses narrowly on legitimate terrorist suspects without recourse to exceptional police powers granted by Parliament. In terms of operational counter-terrorism this is no different to success in other areas of detective work tackling serious violent crime where perpetrators of murders and assaults are investigated, tried and convicted at trials where the evidence is tested by a judge and jury. Where miscarriages of justice have arisen—the Birmingham Six and the Guildford Four cases being the most notable—they have been due in part to the political notion that being tough on terrorism licenses derogations from normal police practice. In contrast, the significant body of successful UK terrorist prosecutions where junior security and police officers have behaved professionally and proportionately owes everything to specialist detective and security skills and not extended or exceptional police powers.

If ever derogation from due legal process can be justified then it would have to be when Britain is under attack by foreign military forces.[72] That was certainly the case when my father interrupted his apprenticeship in the London print trade to enlist in the British Army to resist Nazi Germany's military campaign in Europe. While he fought across Europe, his family faced a bombing campaign at home in London that makes both the Irish republican and al-Qaeda bombing campaigns I dealt with pall into insignificance. Nothing in the language or application of the war on terror persuades me that al-Qaeda or the existential Islamist threat it is supposed to represent is in anyway an equal threat deserving of the same kind of responses:

It began with attacks upon outer London. Croydon and Wimbledon were hit and, at the end of August, there was a stray raid upon the Cripplegate area. Then, at five p.m. on 7 September 1940, the German air force came in to attack London. Six hundred bombers, marshalled in great waves, dropped their explosive and high incendiary devices over east London. Beckton, West Ham, Woolwich, Millwall, Limehouse and Rotherhithe went up in flames.[73]

For the main part London underground stations were a safe haven and shelter for wartime Londoners. My grandfather was a volunteer steward and my father spent much of his rare and precious leave time in them. However, strict wartime censorship restricted news reporting of a dreadful incident at Bethnal Green underground station in which 172 people were killed in a crush caused by a panic following the discharge of a prototype anti-aircraft rocket from nearby Victoria Park.[74] One local resident recalls how shock and surprise caused the panic that led to the disaster.[75] Locals responded calmly and orderly to frequent German bombing campaigns but because they had no experience or knowledge of the secret anti-aircraft rocket in their midst they were unprepared for its noise and impact and panicked.[76] There was an unexpected and fatal gap in their local knowledge. Thus a well-intentioned counter-measure against the German bomber planes proved to be counter-productive by virtue of unintended and unforeseen consequences. Public servants charged with the primary responsibility of public safety have a duty to learn from the wider lessons afforded by tragedies of this kind. In contrast, when a Nazi bomb penetrated a shelter at Balham underground station and killed 68 people it was wholly unavoidable.[77] Both incidents serve to contextualise the PIRA's frequent terrorist bomb attacks on London's transport infrastructure and al-Qaeda's bomb attacks on the London Underground on 7 July 2005. Neither terrorist movement has accounted for such a high casualty rate on the tube as the Nazi air force.

A perfunctory official inquiry and a small, belated memorial plaque in the stairwell at Bethnal Green station stand in marked contrast to an expansive and exhaustive 7/7 inquest and a glistening steel memorial for the deceased in Hyde Park pointing skyward in poignant contrast to the mangled, jagged metal of the train carriages devastated underneath London's streets. It is to be hoped that plans for a more fitting tribute to the more numerous Bethnal Green dead will reach its funding target soon.[78] According to eye-witness Alf Roberts, survivors of the Bethnal Green tragedy were advised to keep the circumstances of the incident hidden. Aged thirteen at the time and trapped amongst the dead and dying in the station stairwell Roberts recalls 'a lady air-raid warden put her arms underneath my armpits and literally lifted me out'.[79] She said to Roberts, 'You, go downstairs and say nothing of what's happening here'.[80] He spent the night underground with 1500 others and when he went up to ground level the next morning, still nothing was said. 'The stairs were washed and cleaned, the bodies cleared away', he recalled.[81] It was only 'as incomplete families returned home that the Bethnal Green community discovered what had happened':[82]

There was a little girl who my mother looked after. She didn't turn up, so I went to school without her. When I got to school, there were children missing. In one case, there was seven went to the Tube and only one came up, the whole family was gone.[83]

Recounting his hidden experience over half a century later Roberts cries in distress at the suffering he has kept bottled up throughout his life. In contrast, survivors of 7/7 have been encouraged to articulate their experiences as a means of post-traumatic stress management. None have done so more thoughtfully than John Tulloch who had the misfortune to be close to the bomber Mohammed Siddique Khan when he detonated his rucksack bomb on a Circle Line train at about 8.56 am on the morning of 7 July 2005. Only the luck of having his suitcase in front of his legs saved Tulloch's life. Having met Tulloch and having read his insightful book *One Day in July: Experiencing 7/7* I have been struck by the probability that the death toll would have been far higher if Khan had detonated his bomb before and not after scores of passengers disembarked from the train at Edgware Road station.[84] A small and widely unremarked fact that speaks against Khan's strict adherence to al-Qaeda's purpose of carrying out mass or maximum casualty terrorist attacks.

In addition Tulloch describes the enjoyable, leisurely breakfast with friends that immediately preceded his walk to Euston Square underground station to board the same train as Khan. For many of the survivors and bereaved from 7/7 the memory of breakfasts, coffee and conversations with their loved ones before they left home that morning mark the last moments of their old once familiar lives. Since then they have entered a new and unfamiliar world. Tulloch also recalls the cynical depths New Labour political spin sunk to when recounting how *The Sun* placed a photo of his bandaged face next to the full page headline 'Terror Laws: Tell Tony he's Right'. On the contrary, Tulloch responds, he had no confidence that Tony Blair was right about anything, least of all the war in Iraq, the war on terror more widely or his tough-talking—'the rules of the game have changed' response to 7/7.[85] Mohammad Siddique Khan and fellow bomber Shehzad Tanweer were adamant that the war in Iraq, the war on terror and the UK's uncritical support for Israel's oppression of Palestinians motivated them.[86] Tony Blair consistently denied this and insisted that Khan, Tanweer and their fellow bombers hated the West, not his Washington-driven foreign policy.[87]

Tulloch went to Beeston and Leeds, Khan's and Tanweer's home patch, to seek the views of young Muslims.[88] He discovered what most Muslims knew already—that Khan's and Tanweer's al-Qaeda-produced 'martyrdom videos' sought to exploit widespread anger about precisely these policies. The anger was real—neither al-Qaeda nor the bombers manufactured it. Tulloch could empathise with the grievances Khan and Tanweer exploited but take serious issue with their method of response. To deny or suppress the grievances was, he concluded, to boost support for al-Qaeda. Today al-Qaeda propaganda videos continue to exploit the same widespread anger but with a greater emphasis on the UK war in Afghanistan. The new coalition government shows little sign of changing from Blair's flawed diagnosis. Instead of recognising the legitimacy of opposition to UK foreign policy the government funds and supports the Quilliam Foundation, so-called counter-extremist experts, who seek to de-radicalise 'radical' Muslims instead of empowering them against the ongoing al-Qaeda threat to UK cities. In London some of the most successful opponents of al-Qaeda propaganda have been denounced by Quilliam and shunned by government because of their support for Palestinian resistance against Israel.[89]

Of course victims' responses to events like 7/7 vary but Tulloch is not alone in enquiring empathetically into the perpetrators' motivation. Tulloch exemplifies a victim's desire to get to the root causes of an incident that was intended to take his life. Although much shorter,

Tulloch's journey of discovery is not dissimilar to one made by Jo Berry when she set out to meet the man who planted the bomb that was intended to kill Margaret Thatcher but which killed her father, Sir Anthony Berry, and others instead.[90] Now she presents workshops with her father's murderer—the PIRA's Brighton bomber Pat Magee—in which reconciliation and constructive dialogue is offered as a viable alternative to state and non-state terrorism. In similar ways Berry and Tulloch develop the well-known adage, 'hate the crime, not the criminal'. Tulloch's probing response does not sit well with the 7/7 Inquest that had no remit to investigate the root causes of the terrorist bombing and thereby fell a long way short of the public inquiry many victims have demanded. To that extent carefully limited official responses to the wartime deaths at Bethnal Green tube station and the deaths that occurred on underground trains and one London bus over half a century later may not be so dissimilar as appears at first sight. Whereas Tony Blair was alive to the demands of a counselling age his predecessor Sir Winston Churchill simply ordered silence and a stiff upper lip. In both instances they led governments 'at war' and were anxious to avoid questions that might highlight their own unwitting role in the tragedies. Blair showed no greater willingness to listen to victims' perspectives than Churchill.

Ernest served in the Metropolitan Police during the First World War and had his fair share of 'sudden death' messages to deliver. At 6.52 pm on Friday 19 January 1917 he was on duty in central London when approximately fifty tons of trinitrotoluene (TNT) exploded at a munitions factory in Silvertown, West Ham killing 73 and injuring over 400 workers. This was a massive blast and would have killed hundreds more had it happened just one hour earlier or an hour later, instead of during a changeover between the day and the night shifts. Ernest heard the explosion and saw windows shatter in buildings over six miles away—other witnesses said the explosion could be heard as far away as Sandringham in Norfolk. Other deadly incidents at munitions facilities in First World War Britain included an explosion at Faversham involving 200 tons of TNT which killed 105 in 1916, and another at the National Shell Filling Factory in Chilwell which exploded in 1918, killing 137.[91] These deaths occurred at a time when government felt under no pressure at all to examine and explain how efforts to protect Britain backfired so badly against its own civilian population. Police officers and the bereaved victims they notified in

Bethnal Green and West Ham during two world wars were offered none of the counselling that was made available to their counterparts after 7/7. To that extent these earlier generations of London police officers and bereaved families share unspoken, harrowing experiences with police officers and the families they serve in Iraq and Afghanistan where even greater death tolls of unremarked civilians have occurred as a direct if unintended consequence of the war on terror.

I have long argued for a full public inquiry into 7/7 because it would help to settle the questions at the heart of this book: what motivates al-Qaeda-inspired bombers in Britain and what is the best way to tackle the threat they pose? Such an inquiry would serve the best interests of bereaved families. But if the needs of the bereaved and an ongoing threat from al-Qaeda are not sufficient causes for the coalition government to hold a belated public inquiry into the causes of 7/7 then I should offer one other compelling reason: an increase in violence against Muslims that is directly related to the al-Qaeda terrorist threat. My recent research makes clear that many violent attacks against Muslims and the mosques they pray in are motivated by a false belief that Muslims are terrorists or terrorist sympathisers intent on repeating 7/7.[92] One only has to view a *Guardian* undercover video of English Defence League thugs to see what this looks like in 2010.[93] Muslims are being stigmatised and attacked merely for holding a widespread and legitimate view that UK foreign policy in the Muslim world compounds rather than solves the al-Qaeda terrorist threat to the UK. It is not just British Muslims who question the Blair-Brown-Cameron mantra that the war in Afghanistan helps prevent further 7/7-like attacks in the UK. However, many British Muslims fear speaking out on the issue for fear of being vilified as a subversive fifth column.

7/7 has had a profound impact on all British Muslims. While many who are distinctively religiously observant or publicly politically active have faced the greatest risk of demonisation and attack those who are not have also had to come to terms with a changed landscape. On the fifth anniversary of 7/7 Murtaza Shibli launched a ground-breaking new book *7/7: Muslim Perspectives* in which twenty-five ordinary and diverse British Muslim voices explain the impact of 7/7 on their lives.[94] No one has worked harder to build bridges between Muslims and counter-terrorism policing since 7/7 than Fatima Khan, vice-chair of the Muslim Safety Forum in London, and an important contributor to Shibli's book. Nevertheless, she has seen friends and colleagues vilified as 'radicals' and security threats when in fact they are valuable allies against al-Qaeda terrorism. This is the ongoing legacy of the Bush-Blair analysis of al-Qaeda and the root causes of 9/11 and 7/7. Fascinatingly the coalition government contains ministers who enthusiastically endorse it—most notably Michael Gove and Dame Pauline Neville-Jones—and those who oppose it—most obviously Nick Clegg and Sarah Teather. An authoritative public inquiry would help them resolve their competing perspectives, do a real service for the victims of 7/7, reduce street violence against Muslims and keep London safe in the future. That at least is an example of the learning from experience that characterises the approach I take towards countering the influence of al-Qaeda in London. As I make plain in the next chapter it is precisely the same approach that is assessed by my detractors to be evidence of appeasement of radical and conservative Islam.

2

RESPONDING TO AL-QAEDA

Over the last four decades the British government's responses to terrorist bomb attacks by the PIRA and al-Qaeda have perforce reflected the moral outrage of the public and the media. Although there is an understandable need for political leaders to be seen to be 'tough on terrorism', such reactions have generally resulted in knee-jerk legislative responses that have not achieved a reduction in the terrorist threat. Instead they often unintentionally benefitted the strategists planning the terrorist attacks more than the police and security services seeking to detect and disrupt them. Rarely, have political leaders felt inclined to advise the public or the media that softer, often counter-intuitive responses to terrorist attacks are inherently more likely to achieve success than the draconian measures invariably adopted instead. Whether that failure results from ignorance or political expediency or a combination of the two is a moot point. Both terrorist movements have targeted London and other UK cities in which their own supporters are resident yet have benefitted from poorly-focused, disproportionate policies from British governments.

In particular, Margaret Thatcher and Tony Blair led government responses to terrorist attacks that were insufficiently focused on the terrorist conspiracies themselves and liable thereby to stigmatise surrounding communities that hitherto only shared some of the terrorists' political grievances. In both instances disproportionate government responses were seized upon by terrorist propagandists who sought to bolster their claims that communities adversely affected by draconian counter-terrorism measures should join or support their

29

cause. The fact that Tony Blair was able to adopt a tough posture after 9/11 and 7/7 and repeat mistakes made by Margaret Thatcher speaks volumes for the power of terrorist outrages to impede rational and proportionate responses by politicians who are generally persuaded to appease tabloid anger and outrage instead. I seek to articulate a response to terrorism that resists such political pressure.

I am also motivated to defend a controversial strand of public safety partnership work I helped develop during the latter stages of a lengthy specialist career in counter-terrorism policing in London. Given that the work in question was successful in tackling al-Qaeda's influence in specific local communities in London, it will be helpful at the outset to explain the basis on which the work has been criticised and undermined so as to introduce the nature of my defence. I should also stress that even though the partnership work in question was between specialist police officers and representatives of mosques and Muslim organisations it was not inherently controversial. It became so precisely because it was skilfully undermined by influential voices in think-tanks and the media. Indeed, even if the work had been praised rather than vilified a media profile would still have raised problems for police-community partnerships in which both partners sought to avoid undue media attention so as to achieve the best possible results against al-Qaeda. Certainly, every fibre of my professional experience argued in favour of low-key partnership activity away from the spotlight of the media. That is still my default position. Only the most sustained and wide ranging think-tank and media campaign has encouraged me to offer a public defence.

In defending work I have become committed to I do not seek to denigrate the strongly held views of my media friendly and well-orchestrated critics. I recognise that the counter-terrorism policing work I undertook with London Muslim partners between 2002 and 2007 is anathema to them. Moreover, I concede that I would find the work indefensible myself if the views and behaviour of my former London Muslim partners were as objectionable as my critics claim they are. In addition to attempting to correct or modify an erroneous analysis of individuals and the mosques and Muslim organisations they represent I am also motivated by an ambition to persuade my critics to recognise the paucity of their objections. This might seem like an ambitious objective but it has not been attempted before and clearly every effort should be made to do so given a shared commitment to tackling al-

Qaeda's influence in Britain. Instead, to date, far more has been written by researchers, observers and commentators than by the participants in the partnerships themselves. By capturing the insider perspectives of police and Muslim community partners in London for the first time I hope at least to articulate perspectives that have hitherto been largely hidden.

I do not underestimate my task. My critics include some of the most influential voices in the British media and their transatlantic allies. By way of illustration, and not least because it is credited with masterminding successful Conservative election campaigns for the London mayor in 2008 and in the British general election in 2010, the think-tank Policy Exchange best epitomises the strength and depth of my opponents' power base.[1] Certainly, Dean Godson, research director for foreign policy and security at Policy Exchange and Martin Bright, author of Policy Exchange's influential pamphlet *When Progressives Treat with Reactionaries: The British State's flirtation with radical Islamism* were the first publicly to analyse the work I undertook and with which I have consequently become publicly associated.[2]

Given my long-standing professional antipathy towards media exposure for counter-terrorism work it is worth recalling how my critics first became aware of my work and how they chose to expose it to media attention. Bright, then news editor for the *New Statesman*, literally stumbled across it in the classified government documents Derek Pasquill, then a civil servant at the Foreign and Commonwealth Office (FCO), leaked to him in 2005.[3] In one particular memorandum I am quoted as assessing that Sheikh Yusuf al-Qaradawi played a positive role in countering al-Qaeda influence in Britain.[4] Suffice to say Qaradawi is regarded by my detractors as the most important voice of radical Islam to be countered in the entire world. As Bright was primarily concerned to expose what he deemed to be Islamist appeasement in the FCO, my own role as an alleged appeaser was little more than a footnote for Bright at that stage. Post-7/7, Bright and Pasquill became infused with a sense of urgency in their task of exposing the frailty of the British state towards radical Islam. In an article published by the *New Statesman* when Bright was political editor, Pasquill explains how he was persuaded to forsake the constraints of the Official Secrets Act and become a whistleblower:

By the summer of 2005 I was getting seriously worried. It is impossible to overstate the effect of the London bombings. I was really shaken by the events

of 7 July and they played a huge role in informing my thinking. I took a holi-
day in August and devoted it to reading up on political Islam and, in particular, the ideology of the Muslim Brotherhood, Egypt's main Islamist group. The
dominant view at the FCO was that it was a moderate organisation with which
the UK could do business. My reading suggested otherwise, and I gradually
became convinced of the totalitarian nature of its ideology. I found statements
by its founder, Hassan al-Banna, glorifying death in the service of Islam, particularly disturbing.[5]

There is at least a glimmer of hope in Pasquill's account that I might
be able to persuade him of a gap in his rapidly gleaned knowledge of
radical Islam. Although he does not vouchsafe the titles of the books
he read on the subject of the Muslim Brotherhood it may be safe to
assume that they were of the kind likely to have been recommended by
his new journalist collaborator Martin Bright. Thus books and articles
by Daniel Pipes, Lorenzo Vidino and Michael Whine come to mind.[6]
Pasquill would certainly have found it difficult to access literature that
offered a positive view of the Muslim Brotherhood in 2005 albeit an
article by Robert Leiken and Stephen Brooke published in 2007 offered
a more optimistic perspective.[7] Interestingly, Leiken and Brooke's positive account rests on field research conducted in London and in many
respects my own research for this book develops the same methodology. Certainly, Pasquill's evident concerns about the long deceased
Hassan al-Banna 'glorifying death in the service of Islam' might have
been ameliorated had he taken the opportunity to read less dogmatic
and negative accounts of the Muslim Brotherhood. Leiken himself has
been quick to concede that his own view was greatly improved by
engaging directly with the subjects of his study. That, at any rate, is the
basis for my modest optimism when aiming to add positive firsthand
experience to well-orchestrated and negative accounts of vilified Muslims and Muslim organisations in Britain.

Significantly, when Bright found a publisher for his anti-Islamist
pamphlet in Dean Godson at Policy Exchange it signalled a marriage
of convenience between equally proactive anti-Islamists. Unlike Bright,
however, Godson was fully aware of my counter-terrorism role in London and had already written about my partnership work in *The
Times*.[8] In doing so Godson based a *Times* article on the counter-terrorism partnership I was involved in following a Ministry of Defence
workshop he attended with me at Shrivenham.[9] To the best of my recollection we were not introduced then and we have not met since.

Given Godson's extensive network of police contacts and his interest in my work this lack of face-to-face contact is surprising. Nevertheless, over the last six years he has argued consistently that my partnership work was illegitimate and should not inform the British government's counter-terrorism policy. Initially I felt no compulsion to respond publicly to Godson myself but I was disappointed that neither the Commissioner of the Metropolitan Police nor the Home Secretary chose to defend the work against such allegations.

That official silence is not altogether surprising, however, when considering the public disapprobation that would surely follow any such endorsement of police partnership work with close associates and supporters of al-Qaradawi in London. To be clear, Godson and Bright also represent an alliance between Conservative and Labour supporters that has its roots in support for the war on terror and support for hardline Israeli policies towards Palestine. It follows that their criticism of my counter-terrorism work extends far beyond a consideration of public safety in Britain.

Of course, I do not seek to argue that many of the Muslim Londoners I worked with to counter al-Qaeda influence are not fierce opponents of Israel's policy towards Palestine. On the contrary, it is part of my case that their credible opposition to Israel's Palestinian policy at times played a key role in countering al-Qaeda influence in local communities in Britain. Suffice to say that is the part of my defence that is least likely to cut any ice with my neo-conservative critics. It does, however, serve to underline the extent to which the war on terror was premised on a conflation of different terrorist threats that have only one thing in common—they are each motivated wholly or in part by support for the Palestinian cause. I will describe how democratic protests against the war on terror and against Israel's policy towards Palestine have shown the potential to undermine al-Qaeda's recruitment strategy in Britain. It is a tribute to Godson, Bright and their allies' influence that such potential was never allowed to become embedded in Britain's counter-terrorism policy. Instead the work I sought to promote—never any more than a pilot project—was eventually sidelined. When it was subsequently superseded by a national strategy known as the Prevent programme it had been manipulated by civil servants to become something quite different, at points the polar opposite of the counter-terrorism work I had pioneered with police colleagues and Muslim partners.[10]

It would be misleading to suggest that Godson, Bright and their allies have been solely concerned with my work in counter-terrorism. Far from it, my work merely serves to illustrate what they diagnose as a widespread malaise in the British state—the unwitting appeasement of radical Islam. Godson, in particular, has an abiding interest in counter-terrorism policing and argues that my partnership work was ill-conceived and fatally flawed because it granted legitimacy to subversive and socially divisive Muslims.[11] If instead I had treated these purportedly subversive and socially divisive Muslims as informants to be met, controlled and paid 'in a dark alley' instead of affording them the legitimacy of partnership status Godson would not have criticised the work, indeed he may well have commended it.[12] That is to summarise Godson's case and by contradicting it—to argue instead that the Muslims in question are not subversive or socially divisive—I set the scene for my defence.

In doing so I will also correct a line of defence that has often been made on my behalf. Doubtless, offered with the best of intentions it has been suggested that Lambertism—a term that has been coined to characterise my approach to this strand of community-based counter-terrorism work—is concerned to employ radical Muslims as a bulwark against al-Qaeda.[13] The more charitable analysts of Lambertism suggest that I may have been well intentioned when granting legitimacy to radical Muslims for this purpose and that the partnership work I was involved in served a limited purpose at the time that I did so.[14] In this connection, both my adversaries and my apologists reference partnership work I was involved in at the Finsbury Park Mosque, colourfully described as 'the suicide factory' in a bestselling book.[15] However, as even my keenest allies make clear, a time came when the subversive and socially divisive nature of my Muslim partners in Finsbury Park (and in Brixton and elsewhere in London) should have become clear enough for me to realise that they were inherently ill-suited for partnership status for the reasons Godson makes plain.

To be frank I prefer Godson's trenchant criticism—it is transparent and cogent—even while I reject it. However well intentioned, apologists often seek to interpret my work in a way that is partial and sometimes misleading and I therefore reject their analysis too. To be clear, so far as I am concerned, the Muslim Londoners who I was privileged to partner when I was paid to maintain public safety in London were perfectly suited for the task and remain so today. That was my professional opinion when I retired from the Metropolitan Police at the end of 2007 and the academic research I have undertaken since re-enforces it. My critics argue that the Muslim partners I credit with overcoming and reducing al-Qaeda influence in and around Finsbury Park are as hate filled as the man they ousted from control of the local mosque—Abu Hamza. I present compelling evidence to disprove their claims and I am happy for readers to assess the degrees of my success or failure at the end of the book. In the circumstances it serves my case ill to rely on apologists who excuse my error of judgement on the basis that I partnered non-violent Islamists to tackle violent Islamists—a kind of colonial divide and rule strategy. That is to misconstrue the partnership work I was involved in.

Initially my work just involved me and a close friend and colleague in MPSB. In the immediate aftermath of 9/11 the two of us conceived and implemented the Muslim Contact Unit (MCU). Between us we had sufficient credibility within MPSB to be allowed to pursue our own initiative but insufficient leverage to muster resources which were being ploughed instead into implementing Britain's role in the war on terror. Despite the modesty of our aims it was sufficiently clear to senior police management that our plan did not sit well with the war on terror. At the outset our simple purpose was to discuss the al-Qaeda threat to Britain with representatives of mosques and Muslim organisations in and around London. Had we kept the MCU's remit to that function our critics would not have objected. Instead, as head of the MCU from January 2002 until October 2007 I helped form partnerships that empowered representatives of mosques and Muslim organisations against the influence of al-Qaeda propagandists, strategists and apologists in local communities in London. We each developed our own critical thinking as the initiative unfolded and although we saw eye to eye on most issues I am only speaking for myself in this book. I trust it is now sufficiently clear that it was the identity of my Muslim partners that undermined it in the eyes of Godson and Bright. If instead I had worked in partnership with Muslims who they deemed to be moderate and to be hostile to the Muslim Brotherhood—not connected to it—then they and their allies would not have sought to denigrate the work.

Although he is far less forthcoming than Godson, it seems reasonable to assume that Tony Blair might also have been far more comfortable with the work I undertook while he was British Prime Minister had I chosen different Muslim partners from the outset. Of course, for the greater part of the period we were both concerned with Britain's public safety, Blair also stood accused by Godson and his allies of bestowing ill-considered legitimacy on radical, subversive and hate-filled Muslims. On his own account, it took 7/7 to shake Blair to his senses and to adopt Godson's prescriptions in all but name for a solution. Thus many notable Muslim allies of the Blair government became excommunicated, ex-partners once Ruth Kelly and subsequently Hazel Blears took charge of Blair's new community engagement policy at the newly formed Department of Communities and Local Government from 2006 onwards. Those Muslims who had previously been used to wielding small influence in Westminster's corridors of power were left in no doubt that they now had none. If they wanted it back, Blair made plain, they would need to abandon their links with radical Islam and adopt a wholly conciliatory and accommodating approach to what he suggested were core British values. This is not to suggest that Blair needed 7/7 to awaken him to a reality Godson described before Britain was attacked by al-Qaeda. Instead, I suggest that 7/7 provided Blair with the impetus to put into effect a policy the need of which he had conceived after 9/11.

It is only since reading Tony Blair's *A Journey* that I have come to appreciate the full extent and significance of the gulf that separated the former British Prime Minister's response to 9/11 to my own.[16] I do not mean to suggest that I needed to read his memoir to understand the difference between his role and responsibilities as British Prime Minister as distinct from my own as a London detective working in counter-terrorism. Nor do I seek to obscure the fact that my long-standing reservations about Blair's enthusiastic engagement in the war on terror provided much of the impetus for this book of my own. Rather it was through reading Blair's riveting account that I came more fully to understand the way personal perceptions of our different roles accounted for such contrasting conceptualisations of 9/11 and our opposite ways of responding to it. Not least because it is written in a prose style that skilfully evokes Blair's familiar gifts as a public orator and media communicator, I found the book helped me comprehend the lived reality of Blair's personal involvement in the execution of the war on terror from day one.

In addition, *A Journey* provides rich unwitting testimony in support of two illuminating accounts I have found helpful when writing this book: David Owen on Blair's susceptibility to what he has coined as 'hubris syndrome'[17] and Peter Oborne on Blair's expedient approach to the facts of counter-terrorism investigations in Britain.[18] Owen is especially illuminating on the power of Blair's vanity to guide him unerringly to the forefront of the most comprehensive international interventionist policy of the modern era: the war on terror. Similarly, on a local level, I rely on much of the detail of Oborne's surgical analysis of Blair's 'use and abuse' of a counter-terrorism operation at the Finsbury Park Mosque in 2003 later in this book. For now I venture to suggest that Godson shared some of Owen's and Oborne's insights and skilfully exploited Blair's public aspirations in the war on terror so as to achieve the kind of domestic and foreign British policies that matched the ones being rolled out in the USA by the Bush administration. Needless to say, there was no place for a soft power project that potentially empowered enemies of Israel.

Of course, in contrast to my own narrow focus, Blair's book deals with far more than his response to 9/11. However, he recognises how when travelling on a train from Brighton to London just hours after the terrorist attack in New York he calmly and presciently anticipated that this was a defining moment in his political career and that his response to it would dwarf all his other political decisions.[19] To that extent we share a consuming personal interest in the responses we made to a terrorist attack planned and executed by the terrorist movement al-Qaeda. We also share one conclusion now that we both came to in the immediate aftermath of 9/11: we are dealing with a long-term terrorist threat. It is therefore no coincidence that we both continue to rationalise and justify our opposite analyses of the al-Qaeda threat to Britain. After retiring from public service we might have turned our attention elsewhere but instead we both remain voluntarily wedded to our earlier actions and decisions. Instead, if anything, our opposing prescriptions for countering al-Qaeda are more fiercely debated now than at any point when either of us was in post. While far from explaining the full nature of the debate the fact that Blair is understood to favour Israel and I am understood to favour Palestine will at least help to introduce the polarisation that makes constructive engagement elusive.

Shortly after retirement from government and party politics Blair established the Blair Faith Foundation to help tackle what he describes as radical Islam. Through this charity he is now at the forefront of a campaign to tackle Islamophobia in Britain. His solution is for Muslims to renounce radical Islam so that they will become more congenial to their non-Muslim neighbours and thereby reduce the threat they face of violence, intimidation and abuse. It is not a formula he would ever have contemplated in a parallel anti-racist context. Instead, it flows from his trenchant analysis of the al-Qaeda threat as representing merely the violent end of a continuum of radical Islam that needs to be tackled by moderate Muslims working in partnership with their non-Muslim neighbours.[20] There is no doubt in my mind about the sincerity of Blair's position on this issue. It fills me with genuine regret that my own modest role working in partnership with representatives of Muslim organisations, with a more narrowly defined remit of tackling al-Qaeda propaganda and influence, should be assessed as illegitimate by Blair's most avid supporters. Indeed, *A Journey* has been especially illuminating in helping me reconcile Blair's instinctive populist political opportunism with genuine social convictions inspired by his Roman Catholic faith. At key moments like the immediate aftermath of 9/11 the two elements appear to be mutually re-enforcing and help to account for the rapturous reception he received when launching his book in New York in 2010.[21] Not for a second did it occur to Blair (or the journalists interviewing him) that the rampant Islamophobia that had engulfed New York on the ninth anniversary of 9/11 was a direct consequence of the war on terror's false conflation of al-Qaeda with radical Islam.[22]

Like Blair, I also turned my attention to tackling Islamophobia after retirement.[23] Which is not to suggest that I ignored the problem when I was a serving police officer, but simply to highlight the fact that I was paid to keep Britain safe from terrorist attacks and that required me to focus principally on al-Qaeda during the latter stages of my career in counter-terrorism policing. Unlike Blair it did not occur to me in retirement that Muslims should be expected to relax their attachment to Islam as a political touchstone, as a method of reducing arson attacks on mosques and violent anti-Muslim hate crimes in the street. Instead, I found myself offering contrary advice to British parliamentarians on how best to tackle Islamophobia.[24] Indeed, I went so far as to suggest that Blair's remedy was part and parcel of the same flawed analysis of radical Islam that allowed him to defend the invasion of Iraq to the Chilcot Inquiry.[25] It follows too that just as my critics might forgive my post-9/11 police partnership with radical Islam on the basis that it was well intentioned but ill-considered, so too might I concede that Blair made an honest and naïve mistake when first buying into the war on terror. Both of us might claim pragmatism in support of our opposite approaches. However, in retirement our voluntary attachments to our opposed remedies leaves observers with no option but to conclude that we are both freely and equally committed to the cause of Britain's public safety in ways that are fundamentally opposed.

In any event, not for one day since 9/11 has the British security service assessed that the threat from al-Qaeda has been anything less than serious or significant. Few would challenge the account I give in this book of partnership work between Muslims and police as representing an effective bulwark against al-Qaeda propaganda and influence in specific local communities in London during the period 2002 to 2007. So effective indeed only one objection might conceivably be made to undermine it according to the Blair-Godson standard: that the Muslim partners were as subversive as al-Qaeda and thereby potentially more dangerous because they adopted a conditional non-violent stance towards Britain and the West. Moreover, in Blair's book, this is a kind of subversion that is more profound even than that posed by communism. More profound and more corrosive because radical Islam has, on his account, abused Britain's relaxed multiculturalism and come to threaten the country's very social cohesion in a way that communism had not. In such circumstances I am described as having granted legitimacy to deadly enemies of democracy and to be an appeaser of radical Islam. Crucially, however, had I treated these enemies as criminal informants without granting them legitimacy by insisting on a partnership relationship with them then my post-9/11 police role would have passed Blair's post-7/7 test and Godson's too.

As Blair set off to meet George Bush to discuss the war on terror for the first time I was travelling on the London underground to listen to a recording of a speech by Abu Hamza in which he praised al-Qaeda's attack on the World Trade Center (WTC). It was recorded at the Finsbury Park Mosque in London a venue that had become the hub of Abu Hamza's self-styled 'Supporters of Sharia' operation. At the time neither Blair nor I had any sense that we were embarking on different journeys that would come to represent opposing approaches to countering al-Qaeda. Still less, was either of us aware of the unintended and unforeseen consequences of our actions. For Blair, it would not have been immediately apparent that his brilliantly crafted resolve to stand shoulder to shoulder with George Bush would bind him inexorably to the invasion of Iraq and the normalisation of torture. For me the notion that Lambertism would become a label that describes the appeasement of Muslims known as Islamists and salafis was even more remote. Yet with hindsight both outcomes can be seen to be the direct consequence of our opposite analyses of the threat posed by al-Qaeda in the wake of 9/11. To be more insightful, the only reason 'Lambert-ism' became a term of heartfelt disapprobation was because it signalled a counter-terrorism policy that departed from Blair's central analysis of the al-Qaeda threat. To be clear, 'Lambertism' is not defined by my criticism of the war on terror's counter-productivity which is an argument made well by others but rather by my refusal to accept that Islamists and salafis are ideologically bound to al-Qaeda, inherently antithetical to democracy and social cohesion and ill-suited to be partners of police or government.

In fairness, Blair appears to have been crystal clear in his instinctive conviction that he was about to begin a profound journey as a result of the terrorist attack on the WTC. He had watched it calmly on a television in a hotel room in Brighton before embarking on a train journey through the Sussex and Surrey countryside to London. Whereas for me party political conferences and the Grand Hotel in Brighton forever evoked a terrorist bomb attack that nearly killed his predecessor, Margaret Thatcher, for Blair the venue had no symbolism or significance whatsoever. Instead, as he recalls, Blair was extraordinarily quick to envisage the terrorist attack on the WTC as an unprecedented act of evil Islamic extremism and to discern a high profile political opportunity to partner George Bush, the US president, in response to it.[26] I was much slower to order and formulate my thoughts but from the outset I sought to draw on my long professional experience of counter-terrorism for guidance. Unlike Blair, I was predisposed to put myself in the shoes of the strategists who conceived and executed the most spectacular and audacious terrorist attack of all time. It was a lesson I was taught when I first joined MPSB in 1980. Not a formal classroom lesson but a piece of advice over a cup of tea on the seventeenth floor of NSY: 'you get paid to think like they do'. Like the other counter-terrorism advice I valued it was the distillation of an informal on-the-job training process that stretched back unbroken and unstructured to 1883 when MPSB was formed in response to Irish republican bomb attacks in London.

It would be wrong to suggest that all the advice I was offered as I developed a career in counter-terrorism was as insightful and influential as this particular gem. Certainly, a different calibre of freely available MPSB advice might have served me better had I been more conventionally ambitious. Instead, I was drawn to the company of streetwise detectives who built low-level specialist careers outthinking and outsmarting terrorist opponents. Or more accurately, attempting to do so. I was fortunate to have entered this arena before risk aversion took hold of counter-terrorism management and when detectives might still learn from their mistakes. In this intriguing company I learned to appreciate that terrorists can be distinguished from political activists by reference to their capacity for risk taking.[27] Hence the notion of 'doers' versus 'talkers': terrorists as risk takers and political activists as invariably risk averse. Which is not to say that political activism is risk free—far from it—but rather to emphasise that planting a bomb in a public place generally affords an act of political violence the element of random harm necessary for it to qualify as terrorism and to attract the kind of penalty most political activists seek to avoid at all costs.

By comparing Blair's recollections with those of his closest advisor Alistair Campbell it seems safe to conclude that Bush and Blair did not discuss an aptitude for terrorism when they met to launch the war on terror.[28] Both leaders were, however, fixated with the religious ideology they believed accounted for the savagery of 9/11 and most especially the bomber's recourse to suicide. Both ideology and method combined to convince Blair that his contemporaneous experience of negotiating with the PIRA was in no way relevant. Consequently, it became an article of faith for Blair that al-Qaeda represented a wholly new kind of terrorist threat.

In contrast, as Blair joined Bush to announce their war on terror partnership, I met a Muslim Londoner who shared many of the political grievances al-Qaeda sought to exploit in their bid to use 9/11 as a rallying cry and a recruiting sergeant. We both recalled how we had first met during an Federal Bureau of Investigation (FBI)/MPSB investigation into the first WTC terrorist attack in 1993. Neither of us could conceptualise significant differences between the two attacks on the same building that were merely separated by eight years. Indeed, we speculated on the likelihood that the two terrorist cells may have been motivated in largely the same way. Neither of us anticipated that the war on terror would so thoroughly undermine the outstanding transatlantic counter-terrorism partnership work that resulted in the successful prosecution of the men who plotted and very nearly succeeded in toppling the twin towers of the WTC in 1993. Instead, we shared a naïve belief that London would remain a hub of counter-terrorism excellence: a city where the rule of law and due criminal process were proven to be the best weapons when looking to preserve public safety and undermine the efforts of terrorist strategists, who wanted to provoke draconian measures that would alienate communities and potentially boost recruitment to their ranks.

When terrorist bombers first attacked the WTC I had been able to assist FBI investigators when they came to London to establish background details of Ramzi Yousef, a prime suspect in the case who had previously studied at a university in Britain. Yousef would later be prosecuted and convicted for his part in the terrorist conspiracy in which a massive truck bomb exploded in the underground car park of the WTC killing six people, injuring over a thousand more and narrowly failing to destroy the landmark building—something it was clearly intended to achieve. I kept a close professional eye on the case during the next decade not least because the blind Egyptian scholar Omar Abdel Rahman, otherwise Sheikh Omar, who was convicted for seditious conspiracy in relation to the same bomb attack had a small but significant following in London. Indeed, Sheikh Omar's support in New York and London is one of the key topics I have discussed with representatives of mosques and Muslim organisations in Britain in the research interviews on which this book is based.

To illustrate, Abu Hamza al-Masri (referred to throughout as Abu Hamza), a London resident throughout much of the 1990s, was at the hub of support for Sheikh Omar in Britain. A London mosque representative recalls attending an event in Luton[29] in 1996 when Abu Hamza called on his audience to support Sheikh Omar when he was standing trial in New York:

Abu Hamza made it clear that he knew Sheikh Omar and that they had spent time together during one of the Sheikh's visits to London. Typically, Hamza accused the US of framing Sheikh Omar while at the same praising the attack on the World Trade Center as a brave and just act.[30]

Abu Hamza would return to the significance of the first attack on the WTC when celebrating the second attack on the same target venue on the first anniversary of 9/11.[31] For now it is worth noting that Sheikh Omar's role in respect of the 1993 attack was very similar to the empowering roles played by Abu Hamza, Abu Qatada and Abdullah el Faisal in London throughout the 1990s. Sheikh Omar's statements in court express sentiments that all three London-based propagandists repeated on a regular basis:

This case [...] is nothing but an extension of this fierce, lengthy attack of American war against Islam, and this war, it is not new to us, but it has been taking place since the beginning of the 20th century.[32]

When Sheikh Omar attacks US support for President Mubarak of Egypt he raises issues that Abu Hamza echoed many times in his own talks in the UK:

America loved Mubarak and supported his regime....He cheated and stole, he raped and accepted bribes, and suppressed freedom... America loved Mubarak ...because he killed thousands of Muslims and he jailed many hundreds of thousands of them.... He built other prisons paid for by American dollars, and he terrorised the peaceful and he attacked the homes and the mosques after midnight and took the wives and the mothers as hostages in the police precincts.[33]

As I watched the iconic twin towers collapse to the ground eight years later I recalled how close these earlier terrorist bombers had come to achieving the same goal by more conventional terrorist means. Watching the second terrorist attack on the WTC live on television screens in the public order control room at NSY in London I had no reason to suppose that my government would respond to it in such a wholly different way to the first attack. Over and above my professional duty to assist in such a vital task I felt a strong bond of empathy with New Yorkers who had suffered a terrorist bomb attack of the kind that had become commonplace in my home city. To that extent it was the same reaction I had to the 1993 attack yet on that occasion no war on terror ensued and instead the FBI was allowed to conduct a relatively low-key international criminal investigation without recourse to the wholesale infringement of the civil rights of Muslims in the USA and abroad. Indeed, in response to the first bomb attack on the WTC, the demands of justice and the needs of victims were met in the finest traditions of the US judicial system.

The same scrupulous attention to judicial integrity marked the painstaking investigation into what was, prior to 9/11, the most devastating terrorist attack in the USA. In 1995 the Oklahoma City bomb attack killed 168 people, injured 680 more, destroyed or damaged 324 buildings within a sixteen-block radius, destroyed 86 cars and left a further 258 buildings engulfed in hazardous shards of shattered glass. Once informed speculation that this bomb attack was carried out by Arab Muslims gave way to the evidence that Timothy McVeigh, an extremist nationalist US army veteran, was responsible for it, the ensuing political and media commentary was notable for its restraint and responsibility. While criminal investigative attention properly fell on McVeigh's close associates in the violent extremist nationalist milieu in the USA every effort was made to avoid stigmatising a significant minority of US citizens who shared some of the bomber's political grievances.

In fact, in stark contrast to 9/11, in response to both the 1993 and 1995 terrorist attacks in the USA, rigorous and successful criminal prosecutions were mounted against committed violent extremists without in any way criminalising or alienating the communities from which they came. To that extent the investigations were, for the most part, models of best counter-terrorism practice whereby due attention was paid to maintaining positive relations with those minority or alienated communities where terrorist movements seek recruits and supporters. Notwithstanding notable occasions when it fell short this was also the tried and tested approach to countering terrorism in the UK before 9/11. Thus, when the FBI asked their UK counterparts to investigate the background of Ramzi Yousef, a suspect who would later be convicted and sentenced to imprisonment for the first WTC bomb attack, there were no concurrent briefings to the news media about Yousef's activities in the UK. Instead, UK police officers were able to piece together useful information about the four years Yousef had spent studying electrical engineering at what was then the Swansea Institute of Higher Education without undue media intrusion.

Much has been written during the last decade that either supports or criticises the war on terror, with the major part of a prodigious literature seeking to defend the military-led response to 9/11 on the basis that al-Qaeda represented an existential and irrevocable threat to the West that rendered all prior understanding of counter-terrorism redundant. Consequently academics talk about 'new terrorism' to denote al-Qaeda and most other kinds of terrorism conducted by Muslims and 'old terrorism' to encompass all other terrorism including bomb attacks conducted in the name of Irish and Basque independence. Interestingly, when the term 'old terrorism' was coined insufficient regard was given both to its durability and also to its similarities with 'new terrorism'. The conceptual thinking that underpinned the war on terror was undertaken by politicians who either had a prior plan to launch a battle against political Islam—neo-conservative ideologues like Paul Wolfowitz—and instinctive politicians like Blair and Bush who trusted their ability to tap a popularist and media appetite for vengeance.

To be sure, from the moment the dust settled on the ruins of the WTC, academics and political commentators interpreted the terrorist attack as an act of Islamic or Islamist radicalism or extremism and thereby provided valuable if unwitting support for the neo-conservative architects of the war on terror.[34] Michael Ignatieff expressed a dominant academic view and also the prevailing cross-party political wisdom in Washington and Whitehall:

> The nihilism of their (al Qaeda's) means—the indifference to human costs—takes their actions out of the realm of politics, but even out of the realm of war itself. The apocalyptical nature of their goals makes it absurd to believe they are making demands at all. They are seeking the violent transformation of an irremediably sinful and unjust world.[35]

While Ignatieff expressly cautioned against disregarding the rule of law his analysis was nevertheless useful in creating an exceptional threat where due legal process might not apply.[36] This approach helped create a sense of legitimacy for extra-judicial counter-terrorism measures such as detention at Guantanamo Bay and extraordinary rendition which became features of the war on terror.[37] Richard Ashby Wilson represents a coherent body of human rights scholarship that challenged Ignatieff's influential notion that the war on terror required a new 'ethics of emergency' that licensed the 'suspension of many cherished human rights'.[38] Legitimacy might normally be lost by abandoning human rights but, for Ignatieff (and the war on terror he defended), 'emergency powers and radical counter-measures' were lesser evils 'forced on unwilling democracies by the exigencies of their own survival'.[39] As Wilson notes 'consequentialist reasoning, rather than a concern for intentions or motivations' underpinned this rationalisation for the war on terror.[40]

Moreover, it is clear that Ignatieff's case was premised on a notion of a necessary trade-off between legitimacy and effectiveness: that a cornerstone of liberal democracy might be removed in the interests of national (and international) security. To this end Ignatieff's focus on the irrational and fanatical nature of the threat posed by al-Qaeda was pivotal and distinguished a dominant 'new terrorism' discourse from 'old terrorism'.[41] The logical frailty of this position is articulated by

Isabelle Duyvesteyn who describes the argument that 'religious terrorists have no motivation because the achievement of their goals is impossible' as untenable.[42] In addition, she identifies 'essential continuities with previous expressions of terrorist violence, such as the national and territorial focus of the new terrorists, their political motivations, their use of conventional weaponry, and the symbolic targeting that is still aimed at achieving a surprise effect' that combine to reduce the conceptual gap between old and new terrorism.[43]

The conceptual gap between old and new terrorism is reduced further when considering, as Brynjar Lia does, how the experienced al-Qaeda strategist Abu Mus'ab al-Suri reflects on the politics of 'old' terrorism and the successes and failures of the PIRA's bombing campaign in the UK in particular.[44] Lia illustrates perfectly well the extent to which al-Qaeda strategists share political and tactical goals with terrorist groups that have never been described as posing an 'apocalyptical' threat.[45] In particular by presenting key extracts from al-Suri's *Global Islamic Resistance Call* Lia brings al-Qaeda's engagement with contemporary politics into sharp relief. This highlights the importance that al-Qaeda strategists attach to al-Qaeda's political legitimacy in the Muslim world. For example when al-Suri explains the need to overcome an individual recruit's sense of national identity imposed by 'the borders of Sykes-Picot, drawn in his mind by colonialism'[46] his approach is comparable to that of PIRA and many other 'old' terrorist strategists concerned to overcome nationalist 'colonial' borders in reality but first to erode their legitimacy in the minds of potential recruits and supporters.[47]

David Lehany insists 'the problem is political, not primarily religious, military, or even conventionally ideological'.[48] Al-Qaeda's leaders are, he suggests, 'strategic actors', who 'believe themselves to be embedded in long-term, iterative struggles over outcomes', who have 'chosen their tactics accordingly'.[49] Al-Qaeda terrorism 'is largely about the use of potent symbols to hearten supporters and to intimidate enemies. The tactics do not make sense outside of the symbolic contexts in which they are chosen'.[50] Legitimacy then is key to al-Qaeda's vision of success and counter-terrorism strategies may, as Tupman and O'Reilly suggest, unwittingly boost it when counter-terrorism is being orchestrated for the benefit of a different audience or agenda.[51]

It follows, in this account, that 9/11 was a carefully crafted act of 'old' political terrorism. According to al-Qaeda propagandist Saif al-Adl, 9/11 was intended to provoke the USA to 'lash out militarily against the ummah' in the manner if not the scale of 'the war on terror'.[52] 'The Americans took the bait' he continues, 'and fell into our trap', doubtless using hindsight to describe al-Qaeda's ability to predict the massive scale and range of the response to 9/11.[53] As P. Eric Loew observes, 'a key al-Qaeda objective would have been to provoke US retaliation so that the USA was seen as 'brutally repressive'.[54] Jessica Wolfendale interprets the war on terror as a US government blind-spot that fails to understand the need to undermine al-Qaeda's legitimacy in the audiences where it seeks support. This, she argues, has a negative impact on the effectiveness of counter-terrorism responses.[55] Wolfendale also assesses that the UK government imported the same failure of legitimacy and effectiveness into its strategies in the war on terror.[56] The extent to which my choice of Muslim partners—made in King's Cross—ran counter to the war on terror is the topic of the next chapter.

3

CHOOSING MUSLIM PARTNERS

In whichever way the al-Qaeda threat is conceived, individuals con-victed in the UK of terrorism inspired or directed by al-Qaeda since 9/11 are nevertheless always Muslims and invariably British.[1] Conse-quently policing of, or with, Muslim communities raised policy issues that politicians of both the left and right expected government to deter-mine and police to implement.[2] Elected to government in 1997 on a manifesto that included commitment to the socially excluded[3] the Labour Party was united in its support for Lord Macpherson when in 1999 he upbraided the Metropolitan Police for being institutionally racist.[4] Notwithstanding different agendas, Conservatives and Liberal Democrats were equally concerned that the Metropolitan Police should henceforth implement policies agreed in parliament and not operate in isolation from central or local government.[5] As Robert Reiner notes, failures of police accountability generally and specifically in regard to minority communities dated back to the Scarman report[6] and exposed what he regards as a fundamental problem: 'how to control police actions, especially in the light of their considerable discretion'.[7] Indeed, institutional racism was perceived to be part of a wider failing of insti-tutional police isolation from the political process.[8]

For clarity I will refer to the partnerships between individual MCU officers and representatives of mosques and Muslim organisations in Finsbury Park and Brixton as 'the London partnerships'. Police initia-tives such as the MCU and the London partnerships it gave rise to might appear to commentators on both the left and right to be acting above and beyond a legitimate police mandate.[9] Such concerns would only be amplified when a police unit was perceived to be licensing community interventions that were religious rather than ethnic or secular in complexion.[10] Clearly a balance had to be struck between police independence and political control yet the notion of police neutrality was often difficult to maintain in practice.[11] Just as left-wing concerns about the politicisation of the police reached a high-water mark during the miners' strike in 1984,[12] so too would identical right-wing concerns begin to coalesce around the 'New Labour partnership' of Tony and Ian Blair, prime minister and police commissioner respectively.[13] However, specific concerns that counter-terrorism policing should be independent of the government's key role in the war on terror were also shared in the 'Old Labour' margins.[14] Academic debates about the nature and extent of policing roles in a counter-terrorism context therefore shed light on issues of police legitimacy and effectiveness that lie at the heart of this book.

Following Charles Tilly, I argue that effective counter-terrorism policing and effective al-Qaeda propaganda and recruitment activity are both in the business of building and nurturing trust networks in the same communities.[15] Trust, legitimacy, and reputation are crucial issues for both parties and a gain for one will invariably involve a loss for the other.[16] However, when sections of Muslim communities perceive that policing has been suborned by hostile political imperatives driving a deeply resented war on terror, trust building will become difficult. More importantly, by word of mouth, in ways Tilly suggests are characteristic of trust networks the reputation, legitimacy and effectiveness of police and community partnerships like the London partnerships would be bolstered or weakened within communities and within the wider policing and counter-terrorism fraternity.[17]

In support of the notion, another social movement theorist Sidney Tarrow usefully highlights the critical but often neglected role of trust networks in spreading 'frames and repertoires' which become vital when both terrorists and counter-terrorists are 'operating in clandestine environments and have been forced to rely on informal networks, often facilitated by face-to face contact'.[18] 'These informal networks' he observes, 'allow movement leaders to try to shift the goals and preferences of colleagues and followers, while educating members about tactical possibilities'.[19] Illuminating and insightful, these 'network' perspectives may nevertheless have the unintended consequence of problematising and criminalising Muslim communities where al-Qaeda and counter-terrorism compete for influence. Thus, in an influential research project sponsored by the US Department for Homeland Security, social psychologist Clark McCauley conceives al-Qaeda as 'the apex of a much larger pyramid of sympathisers and supporters'.[20] His willingness to locate 'all who sympathise with terrorist goals' at 'the base of the pyramid' licenses counter-terrorism (and counter-subversion) strategies against large numbers of Muslims whose opposition to US foreign policy in the 'Muslim world' forms the basis of al-Qaeda recruitment strategies and antidotes to it.[21] This tension between terrorist 'sympathiser' and potential counter-terrorism 'partner' runs through the debates about the work of the London partnerships.

In the first modern policing response to an urban terrorist threat MPSB was formed to provide specialist intelligence and investigative capability and a bridge between what would later become known as high and low policing.[22] Over a century later, however, MPSB had been amalgamated with the Anti-Terrorist Branch (launched in 1972 as the investigative arm of MPSB) and subsumed within the Counter-Terrorism Command of the MPS, playing a much reduced, supporting role with the Security Service (MI5) and Home Office assuming greater control of intelligence gathering and strategy.[23] As a result and in the context of the war on terror counter-terrorism policing can be conceived as one strand in a multi-faceted global response.[24] In his review of post-9/11 counter-terrorism policing in the UK Darren Thiel describes three main areas of activity: intelligence collection, analysis and distribution (what he calls 'high policing' following Brodeur[25]); target hardening activity including 'stops, searches and screening practices administered by uniformed police'; and the 'generation of community intelligence and community co-operation through uniformed 'low-policing' consultation with British Muslim community members' including 'a related policy to intensify and develop neighbourhood policing-style practices in areas deemed at risk of producing violent Islamists'.[26] In theory there may be no inherent conflict between each field of activity but as Thiel demonstrates in practice tensions have arisen between the notion of 'high' and 'low' policing; between the notion of community intelligence and community support; and between the notion of 'neighbourhood policing as risk reduction' and as spying on 'suspect' communities.[27] Moreover, a post-7/7 shift in focus towards 'home-grown' terrorism and 'radicalisation' raised a number of issues concerning the legitimacy and effectiveness of counter-terrorism polic-

COUNTERING AL-QAEDA IN LONDON

ing practice, in particular in relation to a tension that was perceived to exist between 'hard' investigative counter-terrorism and 'soft' community policing in support of counter-terrorism.[28]

In fairness, these are issues that a small number of academics had raised in the aftermath of 9/11.[29] Thus, for instance, in arguing that 'strategies against terrorism negate assumptions of community cooperation and trust that are implicit in community policing' Melchor de Guzman highlighted a policing dilemma that the London partnerships sought to overcome.[30] In addition, by arguing that 'the war on terror necessitates broader collaborative policing' than 'parochial' community policing,[31] de Guzman drew attention to a key issue of police legitimacy that impacted upon the London partnerships. Similarly, William Lyons was concerned that the need to build trust with marginalised communities where terrorists sought support was insufficiently understood by the architects and administrators of the war on terror:

Until we learn to police in ways that build trusting relationships with those communities least likely to willingly assist the police—those often marginalized communities where criminals and terrorists can more easily live lives insulated from observation—no amount of additional funding or legal authority, consistent with living in a free society, will increase the capacity of our police forces to gather the crime and terror-related information we desperately need.[32]

Implicit in Lyon's observation is the notion that counter-terrorism policing (whether hard or soft) needs to achieve legitimacy in marginalised, distrustful communities so as to become effective. This interconnectedness between legitimacy and effectiveness had significant ramifications for the London partnerships, not least because it acknowledges another important but sensitive connection—between community policing and community intelligence.[33] It is a link supported by Basia Spalek,[34] Douglas Sharp[35] and a handful of academics outside the counter-terrorism and security arena. Unfortunately Lyon's concerns did not feature in UK government counter-terrorism strategy, which was designed instead to support US military action at every turn.[36] Given the extent to which the UK emerged as a major contributor to al-Qaeda's global campaign it is not fanciful to suggest that the oversight proved costly—most especially for the UK itself. Although by the end of my research study period (October 2007) government policy was far more attuned to winning Muslim community support there was a strong sense that considerable alienation may already have been caused by the government's close association with the worst excesses of the war on terror.[37]

In contrast, most post-9/11 literature on counter-terrorism policing focused on security and intelligence issues such as terrorist networks[38] and the systems and mechanics of intelligence necessary to counter it,[39] rather than the nature of community engagement required to obtain it. As Willem de Lint notes, the 'shadow cast by 9/11' resulted in intelligence becoming a very urgent issue albeit 'the control of actionable governance-relevant knowledge and its dissemination [had] been a long-standing focus of top-level policy development'.[40] He also captures the sense in which so much post-9/11 intelligence policy was fashioned with little thought whatsoever of credible Muslim community leaders as potential partners. Whereas, partnership involves sharing, intelligence gathering was predicated, de Lint suggests, on ownership and exclusivity.[41] In highlighting the primacy given to the demands of an 'intelligence community' de Lint drew attention to a tension between all areas of law enforcement and notions of community policing. As one policing academic observes community policing is an 'oxymoron', for, he argues, 'if the police could serve the *whole* community there would be little point in having the police at all'.[42]

For police to offer and win the trust and partnership of marginalised, minority community groups more used to being treated as suspects was to break the mould and required inspirational and committed leadership of the kind displayed by Deputy Assistant Commissioner John Grieve in the aftermath of the Macpherson report.[43] Under Grieve's leadership a zealous movement within the police service was formed to foster a new diversity paradigm in policing.[44] The defining feature of the new paradigm was a commitment to support black and Asian ethnic minorities, Jewish communities, gay and lesbian communities, and women both in the workplace and in all policing encounters. The 'diversity' movement was marked by an intense commitment to ensure the catastrophic damage caused to the reputation of the MPS by the Stephen Lawrence Inquiry was never repeated.[45] In contrast, Muslim community leaders often interpreted partnership overtures from the MPS as being based on a wholly different premise: as being part of a 'cold war' attempt to monitor 'suspect' communities and curb 'radicalisation'.[46]

Initially, to overcome such reasonable suspicions MCU officers were required to utilise what David Thomas and Kerr Inkson call cultural intelligence[47] so as to empathise and communicate effectively.[48] For Thomas and Inkson cultural intelligence consists of 'being skilled and flexible about understanding a culture, learning more about it from your ongoing interactions with it, and gradually reshaping your thinking to be more sympathetic' to it.[49] This might be counter-intuitive for police as research has shown they have a tendency to control and manage partnerships.[50] Nevertheless, as Tilly and Tarrow remind us, the potential benefits for counter-terrorism policing might be significant.[51] To infiltrate the same trust networks in communities where terrorists seek to win recruits, support and influence would be a major achievement. Not, perhaps, infiltration in the traditional sense but of a kind practised by the London partnerships where credible community voices were empowered against competing al-Qaeda propagandists—pre-figuring work that would later be branded 'counter-radicalisation' or 'de-radicalisation' under the Home Office 'Prevent' counter-terrorism work stream.[52]

Post-9/11 police needed to understand the diversity and complexity of London's Muslim communities. As Humayun Ansari notes British Muslims had grown used to their faith identity being relegated to a private space while their 'Asian' or 'ethnic' identity was actively engaged by government, police and public servants.[53] In consequence a small number of Muslims had grown used to engaging with police prior to 9/11 in precisely those circumstances. Typically, senior MPS officers Tariq Ghaffur and Ali Dizaei only came to describe themselves publicly as Muslims after 9/11, prior to that their faith backgrounds were subordinate to their cultural or 'ethnic' identities and so typically they would be referred to within the police service and in the media as 'senior Asian police officers' prior to 9/11.[54] Tahir Abbas helpfully locates approaches to British Muslim identity before and after 9/11 within a wider discourse on multiculturalism.[55] As a result of a major terrorist incident in the USA, he notes, 'young British Muslims are increasingly found to be in the precarious position of having to choose one set of loyalties in relation to the other (Islamic v British)'.[56] To focus as advocates and detractors of multiculturalism do on issues of 'assimilation' and 'integration' was, Abbas argues, to fail to grasp a complex story of social exclusion.[57] When he observes that 'multiculturalism has strong limitations because it rejects 'cultures' that do not correspond to nation states' he is unwittingly describing the difficulty the MPS faced at a local level in respect of Muslims and its diversity agenda.[58]

In addition, counter-terrorism policing was prevailed upon by influential politicians, lobbyists, public intellectuals and academics against forming close partnerships with 'extremist', 'oppressive', 'homopho-bic', 'anti-Semitic' salafis, Islamists and other Muslim 'fundamen-talists'.[59] One major Rand report, *Civil Democratic Islam: Partners, Resources and Strategies*, written by Cheryl Benard, was especially influential.[60] Lumping salafis and Islamists together as 'radical funda-mentalists' Benard cites their antipathy to modern democracy and 'to Western values in general, and to the United States in particular' as an incontrovertible basis on which to treat them as enemies.[61] Any coun-ter-terrorist policy maker, strategist or practitioner reading the report would be bound to conclude that salafis and Islamists should only be viewed as targets for investigation or source recruitment.[62] Benard cau-tions against accommodating 'traditionalists' (by this she appears to mean any seriously practising Muslims) because to go too far down this road 'can weaken our credibility and moral persuasiveness'.[63] 'Given the fact that core values are under attack', she argues, it is 'important to affirm the values of Western civilization'.[64] Benard's position here is fully representative of US and UK policy in the war on terror and centrally relevant to the London partnerships. By extrapo-lation, the MCU was clearly wrong to have forged close, reciprocal partnerships with 'radical fundamentalists'.[65] In addition, when in a subsequent Rand report[66] Benard explicitly links her approach to George Bush's expansion of the war on terror into a 'struggle against ideological extremists who do not believe in free societies, and who happen to use terror as a weapon',[67] she reveals the extent of the dis-connect between mainstream top-down counter terrorism and a dis-senting bottom-up counter-terrorism project in London.

Instead of entertaining salafis and Islamists as partners, Benard makes a case for cautiously co-opting modernist Muslims (by this she appears to mean individuals on the margins of traditional Islam) so as to 'enhance their vision of Islam over that of the traditionalists by pro-viding them with a broad platform to articulate and disseminate their views'[68] 'They, not the traditionalists' she concludes, 'should be culti-vated and publicly presented as the face of contemporary Islam'.[69] Sub-sequent Rand reports by Kim Cragan, Scott Gerwehr and Angel Rabasa similarly insist on the long-term deficit of empowering Muslim commu-nity counter-terrorism initiatives that are not premised on a clear under-taking to relinquish political and cultural Islamic imperatives.[70]

In consequence the leading terrorism research institute in the West came remarkably close to a position adopted by vocal activists campaigning to denude Islam of any political or cultural identity that conflicts with Western democracy.[71] In an assessment routinely made by politically active Muslim Londoners to MCU officers, Abdus Sattar Ghazali argues that Rand academics are encouraging and promoting 'so-called modernist Muslims to play one section of society against another' so as to 'split the society'.[72] He describes the Rand strategy as 'neo-Orientalism' and dismisses Benard's report as a 'Machiavellian manifesto that seeks to enforce Western hegemony and cultural imperialism through the policy of "divide and rule"'.[73] When he concludes that 'the type of Islam that Benard espouses is a passive and weak Islam that can be easily penetrated and hence reformulated to suit the West's agenda'[74] he is anticipating a role that would be created for Quilliam and other organisations.

Following Lord Macpherson's ruling every London police officer underwent compulsory community awareness training so as to appreciate and empathise with Afro-Caribbean cultural and historical perspectives.[75] ACPO clearly considered it was important for police officers to appreciate how black Londoners had cultural roots that linked them to the slavery and exploitation their forebears had endured under the yoke of the British Empire. At no point did this level of organisational cultural empathy extend to London Muslims and the concerns expressed by Ghazali about an ongoing 'neo-Orientalism' being directed against them. On the contrary, Muslims felt increasingly scrutinised by counter-terrorism policing, and under an obligation to establish their loyalty in a way that did not apply to other communities.[76]

In 2006 in a departure from the Rand formula a US academic think-tank produced a report that highlighted the potential value salafi (but not Islamist) groups might bring to the table in terms of an advantageous counter-terrorism capacity.[77] Such novelty might be welcomed by the London partnerships but it needed to be tempered by the report's overwhelming sense of reluctance to offer any meaningful partnership status to salafi groups (with Islamist groups completely off limits).[78] Instead, practitioners are advised, to brace themselves for the 'distasteful' work of engaging with 'non-violent salafi leaders' so as to 'monitor the activities of the more militant elements of their movement'—hardly the basis on which to build trust and mutual respect.[79]

Who should police partner in counter-terrorism? A debate about Muslim partners turns on notions of legitimacy and effectiveness. If Benard is right then police must partake of a policy that explicitly seeks to 'divide and rule' Muslim communities in the way that any counter-insurgency or counter-subversion strategy sets out to do. If there is merit in Ghazali's analysis, then for police to follow Benard would be to risk losing legitimacy in exactly the kind of communities most effective in helping police to identify and tackle al-Qaeda terrorism. No doubt the dilemma would not exist for police if the al-Qaeda threat did not exist. That acute political, media and academic interest in the debate was prompted by the al-Qaeda threat ensured that policing responses would be influenced by them. When police followed Macpherson and embraced previously 'suspect' ethnic minority groups it was with the full support of all three main political parties and the mainstream media with virtually no dissenting voices.[80] To embrace 'suspect' minority Muslim groups in the same way would be to risk controversy and intense political pressure—which is to locate the London partnerships in a political context that extends beyond Brixton and Finsbury Park where most of the data was collected and demonstrates a connection with policy directed in Washington and Whitehall and debated by the most influential sections of the media, think-tanks and academics.

At various locations in London, perhaps most notably in an abandoned office on the second floor in a former police station in King's Cross Road in 2002 and 2003, a small group of MCU police officers exchanged ideas and experiences that would shape their approach to the London partnerships. With hindsight the fact that there was no available office space for the MCU at NSY in 2002 had a beneficial effect. To be housed instead at an abandoned police station in King's Cross Road meant that the handful of officers joining the unit could formulate and discuss ideas in isolation away from the operational and administrative demands of a headquarters' environment. Although only a thirty-minute journey by foot and tube separated MCU officers from their colleagues at New Scotland Yard it was sufficient distance to grant them a sense of autonomy not least because they spent most of their time at meetings in the community. By capturing the reflections of MCU officers it helps establish the sense they had of their function and especially the legitimacy and effectiveness of the Muslim partnerships they became involved in, especially in Finsbury Park and Brixton.

Contrary to outsider accounts that assume a top-down imperative[81] the MCU was conceived, implemented and managed by two veteran

MPSB officers, myself, a Detective Inspector and a long-time colleague, a Detective Sergeant. Informal discussions between us took place in October and November 2001 and with agreement from senior management we launched the unit in January 2002—three days after the high-profile arrest of Abdul Raheem, otherwise Richard Reid, an al-Qaeda shoe-bomber from Brixton. Our basic idea was that the unit should consult Muslim community leaders to establish what understanding they had of the al-Qaeda terrorist movement and its influence within Muslim communities in London. By doing so we calculated that we would make a contribution to the MPSB function of assessing the extent and nature of the terrorist threat posed to Britain. It was not our intention that the unit should recruit Muslim community leaders as informants (known officially as 'covert human intelligence sources'[82]) but rather to enter into dialogue on a partnership footing—in the way community leaders would be approached for any other policing function.

It was during an informal meeting over a cup of coffee in a café near the entrance to St James's Park underground station in October 2001 that we first discussed the idea of a partnership engagement with Muslim community representatives. The meeting took place in the morning after night time air strikes on Afghanistan launched the war on terror in response to 9/11. By successfully targeting iconic symbols of political and economic power the strategists behind 9/11 demonstrated the key purpose of terrorism: political communication, what the Russian anarchist Peter Kropotkin called *propaganda of the deed* at a meeting in London in 1881,[83] two years before MPSB was launched to safeguard Londoners from terrorist bomb attacks.[84] By simultaneously achieving a massive impact on live television the same strategists took the business of terrorism into a new global media arena for the first time.[85] All around the world people stopped what they were doing to ponder unbelievable images on their television screens. While the majority could not comprehend any rational purpose to what they saw, the terrorist act immediately communicated itself as a reciprocal act of violence amongst a minority already in tune with al-Qaeda's revolutionary ideology.[86]

The empowerment of minorities is always more important to terrorist strategists than the condemnation of their actions by the majority.[87] So too is the prospect that governments might overreact and introduce counter-productive counter-terrorism measures that unintentionally boost support for the terrorists.[88] In response, the war on terror was immediately characterised by a fierce resolve and a 'you're either with us or against us' message from George Bush and Tony Blair to potential allies and enemies around the globe. Over coffee we came to the conclusion that the war on terror was in danger of playing into the hands of al-Qaeda strategists by failing to distinguish between terrorists and the communities where they operated. More specifically we assessed that Muslim Londoners might begin to feel so alienated by the rhetoric of the war on terror that police would lose their critical support in combating al-Qaeda's established influence in the capital.

In 2002 the Metropolitan Police Service (MPS) employed over 31,000 police officers from which approximately 600 had volunteered and been selected to work in MPSB, a department principally concerned with counter-terrorism intelligence. Several MPSB officers had previously worked effectively in partnership with community representatives to better understand terrorist threats and to help community leaders reduce the risk of young people becoming terrorists or terrorist supporters. Rather than recruiting informants they believed it was often advantageous to approach community representatives as potential partners or contacts. Significantly, while the police duty to foster community support to counter terrorism was reasonably well understood in policing circles it was easily misinterpreted in Muslim London communities as being the thin end of a coercive wedge. Similarly, a corresponding Islamic imperative to provide precisely that kind of support to police was less widely understood by police and Londoners generally. At the time the MCU first entered into dialogue with Muslim Londoners, it was not uncommon for London police officers to gain their knowledge of Muslims and Islam from *The Sun* and other tabloid newspapers. Invariably this consisted of negative stereotypes that were often Islamophobic. In the circumstances, it would be reasonable for London police readers of *The Sun* and other tabloids, no less than *Sun* readers generally, to conclude that the negative representations of Muslims they read virtually every day were broadly accurate and justified. In response, Muslim London police officers who joined the MCU played a small but vital role in helping to overcome negative media portrayals and identifying and cultivating a common purpose between their colleagues and their co-religionists.

At the outset MCU officers consulted Muslim community leaders about the al-Qaeda threat to London and the full remit of the London partnerships in terms of empowering community action against all-

Qaeda influence developed later. As the two founding members of the MCU we shared prior experience of working in partnership with community representatives to assess a wide range of international and domestic threats of terrorism and political violence from the early 1980s onwards. The nature of these relationships was crucial: although informants were an important source of terrorist intelligence—just as they were for criminal intelligence—our experience suggested that community leaders and representatives were more likely to co-operate with police if they were treated as partners and not as informants. To be an informant, in our experience, was to risk losing credibility, legitimacy and effectiveness in the communities to which they belonged. In contrast, in our experience, that credibility, legitimacy and effectiveness could be safeguarded if community leaders or representatives engaged with police in a wholly transparent manner.

At its inception in January 2002 the MCU was located within MPSB albeit our office was in King's Cross and in October 2006 the unit was subsumed into the Counter Terrorism Command (CTC), an amalgamation of the Anti-Terrorist Branch and MPSB. Given the key intelligence-gathering role of MPSB in respect of threats of terrorism and political violence to the capital from 1883 to 2006 it is the concomitant consolidation and expansion of Security Service (MI5) primacy in respect of this intelligence gathering function that assumes greater significance than the creation of a new hybrid police department. In fact, ever since the diminution of the subversive Cold War threat MPSB had faced a challenge to the management of its core business from the Security Service.[89] 9/11 and 7/7 served to expedite the takeover process that brought to an end a department with a record of countering terrorism dating back to 1883.[90] Although the major part of that record would hardly be hailed as being synonymous with the principles of community policing[91] it did nevertheless contain strands of community experience that MCU officers sought to utilise and develop. Like our parent department, however, we were destined to be out of step with a new counter-terrorism mandate that was sceptical about bringing past experience to bear on a terrorist threat conceived to be so wholly different in scale and purpose compared to anything that MPSB had dealt with in the past.

The specialist learning that provided the impetus for the MCU had parallels in the learning that was taking place simultaneously throughout the 1990s in a Finsbury Park Islamist community and a Brixton salafi community. Unbeknown to the three parties a combination of all three learning experiences would coalesce after 2002 to form the London partnerships. The first impetus for the London partnerships was therefore the formation of the MCU and the founding officers' analysis of terrorism and counter-terrorism as possessing vital community components. In summary, a distinguishing characteristic emerges of a sense that counter-terrorism policing is in competition with the terrorist movement it is tackling for influence in the same communities—where the latter want recruits and tacit supporters and the former seeks active support to undermine the terrorists.

In effecting major organisational and cultural change in the MPS in the wake of the Stephen Lawrence Inquiry, John Grieve highlighted the importance of listening to challenging community voices and not simply talking to 'nodding dogs'.[92] Essentially Grieve, like Veness, had experience to indicate that a commitment to the principles of community policing was more likely to produce good intelligence than its abandonment. That provided a rationale for us. The first Muslim officer to join the MCU had worked closely with John Grieve and had this extract from a report co-authored by Grieve highlighted on his office desk:

In Britain after Stephen Lawrence, every individual and institution has a responsibility to examine their behaviour, perception and prejudices. The defence of unwitting racism is closed. As a member of my Independent Advisory Group explained: 'Passive non-racism is no longer acceptable'. For the Met this is a time of profound change. We have made terrible mistakes and my determination is that, in working more closely than ever before with the communities we serve, we seek to build a police service ready to face the challenges of the new millennium—a millennium that is hostile to racists.[93]

Regrettably, from an MCU perspective, some of Grieve's and Veness' successors appeared to take the view that the war on terror allowed the MPS to derogate from these new obligations in respect of ethnic minorities who happened to be Muslim—much in the same way that the Bush and Blair governments tolerated human rights violations on the same premise.

I was struck by the fact that the overwhelming majority of mosque managers, mosque trustees, Imams and community groups had virtually no understanding of the al-Qaeda phenomenon.[94] In the wake of 9/11 they were as stunned and as bereft of explanations as other Londoners.[95] When reporting this finding in 2002 MCU officers would remind colleagues that it was consistent with other London communities (Irish, Sikh, Kurdish) where religious leaders tended not to know much about terrorism in their communities and where expertise was found instead in small politically active enclaves.[96]

An organisational failure to appreciate the amount of time and commitment that is required to build trust and confidence appears to be endemic and not confined to police. Given the importance that attaches to time and confidence building in all partnership endeavours it is unsurprising that government and police tendencies to move ministers and officials at regular intervals has militated against their intended purpose.[97] This highlights an issue raised by other researchers who have studied working partnerships—that there can be considerable difficulties arising from, and tensions within, partnership approaches.[98] The fact that MCU officers were aware of the problem highlights an important aspect of reflexivity that includes reflection:

Reflection might be thought of in terms of individuals, collective groups and/ or institutions intentionally and rationally reflecting upon the part that they play in the perpetuation of identified social problems as well as reflecting upon ways in which they can intervene and act so as to minimise harms.[99]

When MCU officers first discussed the al-Qaeda threat separately with Brixton salafis and Finsbury Park Islamists in 2002, it soon became clear that they shared two key reference points: the first WTC attack in 1993; and the roles of Abu Qatada, Abu Hamza, Abdullah el Faisal and other extremist propagandists in London. Whereas the overwhelming majority of Muslim Londoners had little knowledge of the al-Qaeda phenomenon, expertise tended to be confined to small salafi and Islamist enclaves. In addition, in the same way that former FBI undercover officer Mike German identifies strategic and tactical parallels between terrorist movements with widely divergent goals and ideologies[100] so did MCU officers in the aftermath of 9/11. According to one officer al-Qaeda and PIRA propaganda was identical in the way it described British foreign policy as being neo-colonial and imperialistic.[101] Young London Muslims and young London Irish Catholics were both 'encouraged to believe that Britain was responsible for emasculating indigenous religions and cultures in countries they had subsumed into the British Empire'.[102] The only difference being that Britain's own empire had dissolved to be replaced by 'the great Satan' [the US] and 'the special relationship' now made Britain 'the little Satan':[103]

Teachers at a grammar school in North London were shocked when Muslim kids cheered as the planes struck the twin towers. There were similar reports around the country. It was the same in school playgrounds in Kilburn and Holloway when the IRA nearly killed Margaret Thatcher[104] in Brighton.[105]

Osama bin Laden became a hero overnight. The man who gave the Americans a bloody nose.[106]

A group of young Muslims in Finsbury Park put Osama bin Laden ahead of everyone except Thierry Henry in their list of heroes and role models.[107]

Reminded me of the Bobby Sands mural in Belfast.[108]

Bobby Sands and Mohammed Siddique Khan? Same propaganda purpose. Exploiting grievances about British colonial policy. Galvanise recruits.[109]

After discussions like these with MCU colleagues I developed the notion of a significant connection between Mohammed Siddique Khan and Bobby Sands in presentations to counter-terrorism colleagues at NSY in 2006.[110] By focusing on two religiously devout and high-profile terrorist propagandists—Bobby Sands and Mohammad Siddique Khan—it challenged the notion that al-Qaeda was beyond negotiation and wholly different to the PIRA.[111] This was an attempt to break down the disjuncture between 'old' and 'new' terrorism that permeated counter-terrorism strategy in the wake of 9/11.[112] Contemporaneous Irish Catholic community concerns and contemporaneous salafi and Islamist community concerns could be seen to be skilfully exploited on behalf of two distinct terrorist ideologies that were otherwise outside the scope of Catholic, salafi and Islamist understanding.[113] Both terrorists, Khan and Sands, insist they are part of oppressed communities that have to resort to violence to oppose the overwhelming might and treachery of an inherently hostile neo-colonialist power.

While all Irish communities might have suffered to some degree the evidence is clear in demonstrating that one religious group—Irish Catholics—bore the brunt of stereotyping, profiling and stigmatisation.[114] In interview, specialist police officers with firsthand experience of PIRA terrorism concede that one of the major unacknowledged lessons of that long campaign was UK counter-terrorism's failure to adequately distinguish terrorists from members of the Republican or Nationalist Catholic communities where they sought support. Indeed, a key motivational factor for the specialist officers launching the MCU was a recognition of the need to reassure minority Muslim communities that they would not be conflated with al-Qaeda terrorists in the same way Irish Catholics were sometimes conflated with PIRA.[115] No more—according to this hard won experience—was Irish Catholicism a key pointer to PIRA terrorism than salafism or Islamism was to al-Qaeda terrorism. Rather, just as Irish Catholic community sentiments were exploited by PIRA propagandists so too have salafi and Islamist community sentiments been exploited by al-Qaeda propagandists. By focusing on two religiously devout and high-profile terrorist propagandists—Bobby Sands and Mohammad Siddique Khan—it is possible to challenge the received wisdom that al-Qaeda was beyond negotiation. In both cases contemporary Catholic community concerns and contemporary salafi and Islamist community concerns are seen to be skilfully exploited on behalf of two distinct terrorist ideologies that are otherwise outside the scope of Catholic, salafi and Islamist understanding. Both terrorists, Khan and Sands, insist they are part of oppressed communities that have to resort to violence to oppose the overwhelming might and treachery of an inherently hostile neo-colonialist power. In Khan's words, addressed to the British government, 'until you stop the bombing, gassing, imprisonment and torture of my people we will not stop this fight'.[116] In Sands' words: 'I am a casualty of a perennial war that is being fought between the oppressed Irish people and an alien, oppressive, unwanted regime that refuses to withdraw from our land'.[117] Both are self-consciously approaching death as a form of martyrdom so as to elevate themselves to an imagined moral high ground. In Khan's words, 'I and thousands like me have forsaken everything for what we believe'.[118]

In Sands' words:

I am a political prisoner because I believe and stand by the God-given right of the Irish nation to sovereign independence, and the right of any Irishman or woman to assert this right in armed revolution. That is why I am incarcerated, naked and tortured.[119]

Both Khan and Sands highlight the significance of their respective religious allegiances. In Khan's words:

It is very clear, brothers and sisters, that the path of jihad and the desire for martyrdom is embedded in the holy prophet and his beloved companions.[120]

In Sands' words (in the final days of his hunger strike):

I can ignore the presence of food staring me straight in the face all the time. But I have this desire for brown wholemeal bread, butter, Dutch cheese and honey. Ha!! It is not damaging me, because, I think, 'Well, human food can never keep a man alive forever', and I console myself with the fact that I'll get a great feed up above (if I'm worthy). But then I'm struck by this awful thought that they don't eat food up there. But if there's something better than brown wholemeal bread, cheese and honey, etcetera, then it can't be bad.... I am standing on the threshold of another trembling world. May God have mercy on my soul.[121]

Both aspire to lead by example. In Khan's words:

Our words are dead until we give them life with our blood... By preparing ourselves for this kind of work, we are guaranteeing ourselves for paradise and gaining the pleasure of Allah.[122]

In Sands' words:

I have considered all the arguments and tried every means to avoid what has become the unavoidable: it has been forced upon me and my comrades by four-and-a-half years of stark inhumanity.[123]

Both are anxious to attack religious leaders in their own communities who fail to support the terrorist movement. In Khan's words:

'...by turning our back on this work, we are guaranteeing ourselves humiliation and the anger of Allah. Jihad is an obligation on every single one of us, men and women'. Whereas, he says, 'our so-called scholars of today are content with their Toyotas and semi-detached houses' in their desire for integration. They are useless. They should stay at home and leave the job to real men—the true inheritors of the prophet.124

In Sands' words:

I was very annoyed last night when I heard Bishop Daly's statement (condemning the hunger-strike). Again he is applying his double set of moral standards. He seems to forget that the people who murdered those innocent Irishmen on Derry's Bloody Sunday are still as ever among us; and he knows perhaps better than anyone what has and is taking place in H-Block. He understands why men are being tortured here—the reason for criminalisation. What makes it so disgusting, I believe, is that he agrees with that underlying reason. Only once has he spoken out, of the beatings and inhumanity that are commonplace in H-Block.[125]

And both men, Khan and Sands, it follows, are self-evidently addressing themselves to supporters and would-be recruits rather than a wider public. This helps demonstrate the importance for counter-terrorism to distinguish between the terrorists' tactical use of communities' religious and political beliefs and the communities' religious and political beliefs themselves. This approach also encourages an exploration of important instances where counter-terrorism has fallen short of that goal. By doing so tentative guidance can be offered for future counter-terrorism policies that are more attuned to terrorists' and communities' political grievances, thereby more ably distinguishing between the two positions so as to engage more productively with the latter to the detriment of the former.

According to many of my interviewees, it is axiomatic that by the time a young male British Muslim has become an al-Qaeda suicide bomber (or other active terrorist) he has bought into an ideology that distorts strands of Islamic belief as it is understood by the salafi and Islamist communities that practise it. Which is simply to argue that al-Qaeda does not seek to distort strands of Islamic belief as it is understood by Barelvi, sufi and other related quietist Muslim communities in the UK. Al-Qaeda may deride sufism just as the PIRA from time to time derided loyalist Protestantism as an implacable enemy of Irish Catholic communities but al-Qaeda ideology is not premised on a superior sufi account of religious belief and practice. Rather al-Qaeda seeks to disguise its revolutionary political ideology in salafi and Islamist clothing.[126] Therefore, to continue the comparison, just as PIRA never appealed to loyalist Protestant approaches to Christianity in its propaganda neither does al-Qaeda seek to present its message as arising from or bearing upon Barelvi or sufi approaches to Islam. For counter-terrorism it is important to reflect on the extent to which both PIRA and al-Qaeda have sought to align and embed their terrorist ideologies within communities where religious belief and practice is a minority position often opposed by more powerful majority Christian and Muslim communities. It follows that a dominant strand of counter-terrorism has failed to appreciate this reality by seeking to impose outsider solutions to salafi and Islamist community problems. This is shown to be as unrealistic as having expected the Reverend Ian Paisley to persuade young Irish Catholic men away from involvement with PIRA.

Of course, a young British Muslim might traverse the religious and cultural distance from a Barelvi or sufi community's religious understanding and practice to become an al-Qaeda terrorist far more readily than a young male from a British loyalist Protestant community would ever have contemplated joining PIRA. From an al-Qaeda perspective, however, the ground to be covered in recruiting a young British Muslim from salafi and Islamist communities is generally likely to be less than in recruiting a young British Muslim from Barelvi or sufi communities. While there will be important exceptions to this rule an effective al-Qaeda recruiter is shown to have much in common with counterparts in PIRA in terms of their mutual skill at embedding and concealing themselves in supportive communities. Which is why salafis and Islamists are often best at spotting them and generally have the best counter-narratives to al-Qaeda propaganda once it has begun to have a telling influence upon individuals and communities. To conflate salafis and Islamists with the problem is, therefore, to inhibit their willingness to protect their communities against it. Which is not to make the additional error of conflating salafis with Islamists because important differences exist between them.

In drawing attention to links between Sands and Khan I am suggesting a notion of al-Qaeda that was at odds with ACPO, government and the prevailing wisdom of terrorist 'experts'. My willingness to draw comparisons between al-Qaeda and PIRA was out of sync with the underlying ethos of the war on terror. In the event Tony Blair's willingness to dismiss PIRA experience in favour of George Bush's account led British counter-terrorism into a US-dominated domestic policy for the first time.

Unique in Western counter-terrorism policing during the war on terror the MCU was a small scale, bottom-up, community-focused initiative managed and staffed by police officers with either extensive MPSB counter-terrorism experience or extensive knowledge of the London Muslim scene, the latter practising Muslims and experienced police officers.[127] According to a long-serving MPSB senior officer any success the unit achieved was the result of a synthesis of those complementary yet distinctive experiences and skill sets.[128] The same officer expressed the view that the unit's departure from conventional wisdom and ultimately the disapprobation it received from influential commentators arose for the same reason.[129] All of my interview and observation data concurs that it was a combination of two kinds of expert experience that the officers themselves—and police associates and Muslim community representatives who came into contact with them—regarded as giving the unit its distinctive character. Moreover, it was during the course of lengthy informal discussions that MCU officers shared their two areas of expertise with each other.[130] Muslim police officers with no experience of counter-terrorism policing (least of all MPSB work) listening to the experience of new colleagues who had been involved in intelligence gathering against domestic and international terrorist threats for over two decades.[131] MPSB veterans, for their part, listening to the experience of Muslim police officers who knew Muslim London intimately, in a way that was hitherto unknown in counter-terrorism policing.[132] According to an MCU officer who had worked as a surveillance officer against domestic and international terrorist targets in London, conceiving al-Qaeda became a process of shared learning.

Michael Kenney is one of only a small number of academics to have explored the informal learning processes that take place in counter-terrorism policing and to compare them with similar processes within terrorism and organised crime groups.[133] His fieldwork with the MCU in 2007 tends to confirm the importance of tradecraft and informal on-the-job learning on the streets where skills are honed, as opposed to classroom or taught learning which does not always test individual's aptitude to operate in real counter-terrorism scenarios so well.[134] In his detailed comparative study of Colombian drug traffickers and al-Qaeda terrorists Kenney elucidates key similarities in the learning experiences of two very differently motivated groups and usefully separates their taught skills from their learned 'on-the-job' skills.[135] For both groups—one economically driven and the other motivated by political and religious zeal—the pressure of intrusive and coercive policing serves to ensure their skill-sets are honed and sharpened in covert, high-risk environments. Taught 'abstract technical knowledge' such as drug and bomb-making procedures and 'experiential, intuitive knowledge' such as 'ingenuity, elusiveness, cunning and deceit' combine to serve successful counter-terrorists and drug traffickers equally well.[136] Invariably good tradecraft skills are employed by drug traffickers and terrorists to safeguard the products of their taught skills—such as drug shipments and primed and timed bombs—and to counter security and policing tactics that seek to disrupt their activities.[137]

An MCU officer argues that the same street skills separate effective counter-terrorism operatives from those that do not make the grade, especially for those roles that require aptitude for high-risk close engagement with terrorist suspect targets.[138] Interestingly, he adds, just as terrorist recruits who lack street skills may be given a 'safe' job in propaganda dissemination so too will poor counter-terrorism operational trainees return to the safety of desk jobs.[139] Much to his chagrin he noted one such 'failure' had become a notable terrorism expert commentator in the media after 9/11.[140] On the other hand, he argued, the combination of street skills that converged on the MCU gave it a unique insight into the way terrorists directed or inspired by al-Qaeda operated in London.[141] Mutual learning of this kind between the MPSB and Muslim community experience on the MCU grew as the new unit matured. Focusing on this shared learning experience helps explain how responses to al-Qaeda were conceived on the MCU.

Against the grain of the war on terror the MCU made a significant early contribution to counter-terrorism policing by demonstrating that it was reductionist, illogical and counter-productive to conceive of al-Qaeda as an Islamic threat. This achievement was due entirely to the authoritative input of Muslim MCU officers and their friends in the community. For example, to illustrate, it is worth noting that Mehmood Naqshbandi had a considerable influence on this formative thinking about the nature of the al-Qaeda problem.[142] Naqshbandi would go on to become a key advisor for the Home Office in respect of the 'Prevent' agenda and to host the most authoritative guide to Muslim Britain on the internet.[143] However, neither Muslim nor secular members of the MCU would find it so easy to disabuse colleagues of the widely propagated notion that Islamists and salafis were part and parcel of the al-Qaeda problem.[144]

Given their wholly different career paths to the specialist (non-Muslim) counter-terrorism officers working alongside them on the MCU the dynamics of the unit as a partnership in and of itself becomes relevant. This relationship is particularly instructive given the dearth of insider Muslim community experience in counter-terrorism policing more generally.[145] Occasions when Muslim MCU police officers have faced the double jeopardy of suspicion from within their parent organisation and criticism from within their home communities reveal the extent to which mediation between counter-terrorism policing and distrustful sections of the community has been exacerbated during the period under review (2002–2007).[146] In terms of balance, however, many situations have been observed where a Muslim MCU police officer has been instrumental in bridging a treacherous gap in understanding and interpretation to the mutual benefit of both a suspicious parent organisation and a hostile home community.[147] In achieving these unique results Muslim MCU police officers have capitalised on a strength that sits outside their professional and cultural skills—their local reputations as sincere and strictly observant Muslims.[148] This quality takes on added significance when both counter-terrorism policing and diversity policing more generally are shown to have recruited Muslim police officers during the period under review on an entirely contrary basis. As one Muslim officer explains:

Up to 2003 Muslims arriving at Hendon Training School were left in no doubt that they would get on better in their police careers if they adopted a secular lifestyle. Refusal to drink and insistence on observing Islamic codes of decency and a requirement for halal food would be tolerated but not encouraged. The idea that a Muslim police officer might be excused to attend a local mosque for jumma prayer on a Friday was not sanctioned. Generally speaking most Muslims joining the police knew this was likely to be the case and either joined because they were not practicing or because they were willing to compromise. Some of those Muslims who wanted to practice their religion strictly left after a few weeks at Hendon.[149]

Not surprisingly, as part of only a handful of strictly practising Muslims in the Metropolitan Police in 2002 the individuals were cautious when approached by two veteran Special Branch officers about joining a newly formed unit, the MCU. 'There was already a lot of concern in my local community about the extent of anti-Muslim sentiment being voiced as part of the war on terror' explains one, 'all of that vilification of Muslims as being barbaric was very disturbing':[150]

And the idea of joining a unit in Special Branch needed very careful thought. I knew there would be criticism from some sections of the community who would see it as spying. That was a real concern but I was personally satisfied that the MCU was not part of that business. The question for me was whether I could do a useful job for Muslims and Londoners by joining the unit. In the end I was convinced I could help the situation more by joining than by remaining in my current post. I was keen to help young Muslims stay away from terrorism and at the same time separate terrorism from Islam.[151]

Concerned from an early stage to set an objective of reducing the number of London Muslims recruited or inspired to commit terrorist acts in the name of al-Qaeda, the MCU conceived the problem as a battle for hearts and minds within Muslim communities in January 2002—a pioneering approach that only gained wider acceptance five years later.[152] Most significantly the unit identified sections of London Muslim youth as targets for counter-al-Qaeda propaganda strategies, youth communities to be won away from support for terrorist narratives and rehabilitated as valuable citizens.[153] Such a 'soft' approach has been epitomised by patient trust building with Muslim community partners who as outreach workers have been assessed to have the necessary skills to carry out such work on Muslim London streets.[154]

This insider understanding of the notion of partnership is best summarised as having three stages: approach, engagement and consolidation. 'Approach' covers initial meetings between MCU officers and community representatives at which the prospect of partnership is discussed. This also involves an examination of the prior circumstances that give rise to the 'approach' invariably but not always instigated by an MCU officer. Since inception in January 2002 the MCU had an express purpose of forging partnerships with Muslim community groups that had experience and skill in countering the adverse influence of al-Qaeda propaganda and recruitment in sections of London's Muslim youth community. Employing counter-terrorism experience and Muslim community understanding the MCU identified these qualities as existing in parts of Muslim London that al-Qaeda had targeted from 1993 onwards. For their part certain salafi and Islamist community partners provide compelling accounts of their experience of tackling this threat and seeking police support without success between 1993 and 2002. Thus, although 'approach' best characterises an MCU initiative it is also an assessment of prior community efforts to elicit police support for the same purpose. Finally, and crucially, 'approach' also covers those instances where relations between the MCU and given Muslim community groups have not progressed beyond an initial exploratory encounter. By acknowledging the existence of such cases it is possible to see the Brixton salafi and Finsbury Park Islamist case study sites as unique in terms of sustained pro-active partnership endeavour.

By adopting the term 'approach' to describe initial encounters between potential police and community partners it is important to acknowledge that the term has a more common meaning in policing. Here, 'approach' is regularly used to describe the procedures and methodologies surrounding a first meeting between police officers and a potential informant. Indeed, this first stage of 'covert human intelligence source recruitment' is subject to stringent regulatory guidelines[155] that help to distinguish one kind of 'approach' that is essentially coercive from another that is intended to provide a sound basis for a partnership relationship built on trust. Participant observation usefully contrasts the two methodologies, characterising one as an established model where police control and management is vital and the other as a new and tentative model where police are obliged to accept the normal and familiar rules of partnership engagement.

'Engagement' covers the period following an 'approach' when the police and community partners engage together in a joint project. Two examples are examined in considerable depth. Firstly, an engagement between the MCU and Islamist partners to counter the influence of al-Qaeda in sections of a Muslim youth community in the Finsbury Park area of North London between January 2002 and October 2007. Secondly, an engagement between the MCU and salafi partners to counter the influence of al-Qaeda in sections of a Muslim youth community in the Brixton area of South London between January 2002 and October 2007. The two prime case study sites also help distinguish important differences and highlight essential similarities between salafi partners—in Brixton—and Islamist partners—in Finsbury Park. Thus, most notably, while salafi partners place complete reliance on re-educating Muslim youth according to a salafi rendition of essential religious texts the Islamist partners place more emphasis on scholars who are best described as belonging to the Islamic revival and who do not flinch from addressing the same political grievances that al-Qaeda uses to license terrorist attacks like 9/11 and 7/7.

Consequently Muslim youth who were engaged by salafi partners in Brixton were given compelling religious authority for renouncing the relatively shallow claims of al-Qaeda propagandists to be following a correct interpretation of Islam. Such rehabilitation work took place as part and parcel of youth outreach initiatives that include such familiar activities as football matches and group-bonding activities. The same activities also formed part of Islamist approaches to youth engagement in Finsbury Park. In contrast, youth engaged by the Islamists were drawn into political activity such as participation in 'Stop the War' and 'Justice for Palestine' demonstrations and voting for candidates in national and local elections who support the same causes. However, a close examination of the two sites also reveals similarities in respect of a political analysis. The fact that salafi partners adopted strict neutrality should not be confused with an absence of engagement with the political grievances that al-Qaeda seeks to exploit. Even less should it be conflated with outsider challenges to al-Qaeda narratives by groups like the Sufi Muslim Council that are essentially quietist and quiescent. Similarly because Islamist partners expressed strong criticism of US and UK foreign policy in terms that bears comparison to al-Qaeda narratives it becomes vital to distinguish their remedies—and their effectiveness as a counterweight to it. In both instances MCU partners offered discreet facilitation and support so as to allow the outreach work to take place as effectively as possible. A key concern for the MCU became an increasing need to support both salafi and Islamist partners in the face of sustained criticism from powerful critics, of the kind already noted.[156]

'Engagement' also covers instances where MCU and Muslim community groups developed a productive dialogue without developing joint partnership activity of the kind described above. In fact this category forms the majority of encounters the MCU had with Muslim community groups during the period under review—January 2002 to October 2007. Given the large scale of Muslim community activity in London in comparison with the meagre resources of the MCU this apparent failure is hardly surprising. As one MCU officer explains:

For the first two years we never operated with more than four officers and sometimes with only one. After the summer of 2004 we sometimes had as many as eight officers on the unit. But we often failed to recruit officers who wanted to join us who we thought would be good. Staffing the unit has never been seen as a priority by senior management. Other areas of counter-terrorism work warranted one officer on each of London's thirty-two boroughs but we had to concentrate our efforts where we thought they would be most effective.[157]

Consequently, a picture emerges of the MCU giving clear priority to Brixton and Finsbury Park partnership activity for the major part of the period under review (January 2002—October 2007). In addition, however, a paucity of community expertise also featured prominently in Muslim London during the period under review. To be clear, MCU officers gave primacy to proactive partnership engagement at Brixton and Finsbury Park because they were important and because of limited resources. Elsewhere in London positive 'engagement' between the MCU and salafi or Islamist groups did not result in such sustained partnership activity aimed at curbing the adverse influence of al-Qaeda propaganda and recruitment of susceptible youth because of a lack of MCU resources. Instead, clear evidence emerges of a realistic potential for increased activity in this field if increased resources had been made available.[158]

'Consolidation' describes the period when the police and community partners reflected on their joint venture and seek to learn lessons from each other. This is an ongoing process that is best characterised by reference to two examples from both case study sites (Finsbury Park and Brixton). In one instance, in March 2005, members of the MCU met Islamist community partners in Finsbury Park to discuss security responses to attempts by supporters of the terrorist propagandist Abu

Hamza to regain control of the Finsbury Park Mosque. At the conclusion of a productive meeting both sides recognised that they had been able to discuss important and sensitive issues frankly and with confidence as a result of the trust they had built up over a long period prior to the meeting. Without this ability key security information would have been lost. In the other instance, in April 2004, new police and new community members of the London partnership initiative in Brixton were introduced by established police and community partners to their new surroundings and new responsibilities. This was a successful exercise in consolidation and continuity recognising that partnership building relies heavily on personal commitment that can be undermined if new relationships are not nurtured carefully by existing partners. Both examples highlight a recurring theme in the case studies—the critical importance of trust and confidence building.

Both case study sites—Finsbury Park and Brixton—provide rich seams of information about the extent to which al-Qaeda propagandists and strategists are concerned that the London partnership initiative presents a viable challenge to their effectiveness. Essentially al-Qaeda strategists are revealed as taking challenges to their legitimacy seriously when they are mounted by salafis and Islamists. This contrasts with their dismissal of challenges to their narratives that are mounted by outsider communities such as sufi Muslims, lapsed Islamists, Christians and secularists. Surprisingly, the MCU has had to labour such an obvious point to counter-terrorism audiences when defending the legitimacy and effectiveness of its partnership with salafi and Islamist community groups.[159] Thus I explained how during the PIRA terrorist campaign it was perfectly well understood that the Reverend Ian Paisley would have had no positive impact if he had ever sought to persuade fellow Christians in the Irish Nationalist community that PIRA violence was disallowed in the Bible. I provided this example to illustrate the similar absurdity of a conservative US sufi scholar Sheikh Kabbani being promoted as a model and guide for young British Muslims susceptible to al-Qaeda propaganda.[160] Instead, the MCU was at its strongest when advocating the knowledge and skills of its salafi and Islamist partners: street credibility; religious credibility; understanding al-Qaeda ideology; understanding al-Qaeda recruitment methodology; counselling skills; and commitment and bravery. Knowledge and skills, MCU officers argued, that were corroborated by the extent to which al-Qaeda propagandists and supporters took them seriously.

In the eight years between the two terrorist attacks on the WTC, London played host to extremists who applauded the first attack and encouraged attempts to emulate it.[161] Interviewees with MPSB experience in the 1980s and 1990s provide persuasive evidence about the extent to which support from Abu Qatada, Abu Hamza and other London-based extremists for the first attack on the WTC in 1993 prefigured and characterised their active endorsement of the second attack in 2001. Ramzi Yousef, convicted for his part in the bombing, is reported to have mailed letters to various New York newspapers just before the attack, that made three demands: an end to all US aid to Israel; an end to US diplomatic relations with Israel; and a demand for a pledge by the USA to end interference 'with any of the Middle East countries' interior affairs'.[162] The letter stated that the attack on the WTC would be merely the first of such attacks if its demands were not met.[163] Precisely prefiguring al-Qaeda's claims for 9/11 and subsequent attacks Yousef admitted that the 1993 attack on the WTC was an act of terrorism, but that it was justified because 'the terrorism that Israel practices (which America supports) must be faced with a similar one'.[164]

Abu Hamza considered himself to be a follower of Sheikh Omar and a London advocate of an established Egyptian discourse of violent opposition to a corrupt US-backed regime that included Sayyed Qutb and al-Qaeda strategist Ayman al Zawahari.[165] Like Sheikh Omar, Abu Hamza had charismatic qualities that inspired supporters to follow him. It is also germane to recognise the influence that charismatic individuals can achieve through their personal commitment to and availability for a small group of followers and supporters.[166] That is the context in which we travel next to Finsbury Park where Abu Hamza held court for over seven years.

PART TWO

FINSBURY PARK

4

ABU HAMZA IN CONTROL

Just two veteran MPSB officers started work as the MCU in January 2002 and continued to staff the unit for the first three months of its life. Our first meeting on 2 January 2002 was with two active trustees of the Finsbury Park Mosque.[1] While we had given ourselves the ambitious target of visiting every mosque, Islamic institution and Muslim organisation in London we decided this should be our first visit. The adverse impact Abu Hamza and his hard-core supporters were having on the mosque was well known locally and nationally. Our priority was to establish a relationship with the mosque trustees, assess the situation and establish ways in which we might support them.

Our first meeting was facilitated by an outstanding local community police officer who had built up a good rapport with the two trustees and took place in the rear of a halal butcher's and grocery shop in Blackstock Road—owned by one of the trustees—just two hundred yards from the mosque.[2]

The community police officer was herself a key witness to the extent of Abu Hamza's adverse influence over many local young people. Throughout 2001 but especially after 9/11 she had grown used to scores of Abu Hamza's young supporters adopting aggressive behaviour in and around the mosque especially on Friday afternoons after Abu Hamza had delivered a fiery khutbah during the jummah prayer. On occasions she was the target of abusive comments and disrespectful behaviour outside the mosque and in Blackstock Road nearby. Gangs of mainly Algerian youths would often congregate outside cafes and shops in the street and deny free and easy passage to pedestrians including the diminutive but feisty police officer. On one occasion she was warned by a youth that what had happened recently to the WTC would soon be repeated in London. When the police officer challenged the speaker—a youth she recognised as one of Abu Hamza's entourage and a friend of one of his teenage sons—he attributed the assessment to Abu Hamza and warned her that she be careful not to step inside the mosque. She had other experience to suggest that Abu Hamza was concerned that her regular presence outside the mosque on Fridays was inappropriate and that her close relationship with the mosque trustees was evidence of their collaboration with the enemy.

During the course of introductions to the mosque trustees we were keen to emphasise our willingness and determination to help them. That seemed important because the community police officer who knew them well had explained to us that they felt let down and neglected by 'the authorities' in their efforts to tackle Abu Hamza. Part of our initial work was therefore to establish ourselves as specialist detectives with enthusiasm and problem-solving skills rather than officials who might easily hide behind the limitations of their parent organisations. Experience taught us that we would have succeeded in our initial task of approaching in the right way when they felt confident to ring us on our mobile phones out of office hours when they were experiencing a problem that needed our immediate help.

Action speaks louder than words in partnership building. It was clear that the mosque trustees had often listened to bureaucratic and legalistic reasons for inaction rather than active problem-solving approaches when in dialogue with officials over several years in connection with their efforts to manage or remove Abu Hamza from the mosque. They had become disillusioned when officialdom appeared unable to convert empathy into practical support. We sought to explain and demonstrate the value of our specialist role in dealing with terrorism and political violence in London over a long period. In our experience community representatives of all kinds appreciate it when they can talk to experts with a track record of tackling problems of the kind they are facing. To illustrate, at any early meeting with the two mosque trustees I shared my experience of arresting and interviewing Omar Bakri Mohammed in 1991. Bakri, like Abu Hamza, was well known to the mosque trustees and locally as an extremist who was gleefully promoting al-Qaeda in the wake of 9/11. My assessment of Bakri was built on my interview with him in Edmonton Police station

a decade earlier but that close connection served as a valuable introduction to the kind of shared expert knowledge we hoped to build up
with the trustees.

The mosque trustees were therefore able to compare my experience
of Bakri—a close associate of Abu Hamza—with their own. In much
the same way I was able to explain to them that my long-standing
association with leading members of the Muslim community in London went back to 1989. Much of this experience centred around the
London Central Mosque where Abu Hamza had once held a post as a
cleaner. Zaki Badawi, who had been a senior figure at the London Central Mosque in 1989, was one of several prominent figures who could
vouch for my record at the time of the Salman Rushdie affair. More
specifically, I could point to the success of the London Central Mosque
in combating violent extremism and maintaining order in the face of
serious challenges as a role model and source of partnership support
for the mosque trustees who were clearly lacking support from the
wider London Muslim community. In the months ahead my long
standing relationship with Fasli Ali, the security manager at the London Central Mosque, that went back to 1989 would prove invaluable
in trust building in Finsbury Park and elsewhere in London.

The reason our first meeting with the Finsbury Park Mosque trustees
took place in the back of a shop was because Abu Hamza and his supporters were present inside the mosque and the two trustees had grown
used to avoiding confrontation with him. We introduced ourselves and
offered to assist them in their efforts to address the problems posed by
Abu Hamza and his supporters and encouraged them to tell their story.
Unlike many Charity Commission and council officials they were used
to meeting we did not restrict them by fixing a time limit on the meeting or on how long they should speak for. We wanted to hear their
accounts on their own terms. The two trustees expressed frustration
that 'the authorities' had been unable or unwilling to arrest Abu
Hamza for terrorist offences because they were at the end of their
tether trying to cope with the increasingly aggressive behaviour of his
supporters. They also gave a summary of the long and protracted civil
litigation that had been intended to restrict Abu Hamza's influence at
the mosque but which had ultimately proved unsuccessful. The same
lack of success, they explained, surrounded concerted efforts by the
Charity Commission to restrict Abu Hamza's activities at the mosque.
All in all a picture emerged of two dedicated and responsible individ-

uals who were heartbroken at having lost control of their beloved mosque to Abu Hamza and his supporters.

In 1994 the new Finsbury Park Mosque marked the culmination of a vision shared by a small group of Muslims from Gujarat in India, Pakistan and Bangladesh who had settled in the area in the 1970s. Previously using an adjoining house for prayers, finance for the new building came from their own hard-earned savings and also from a significant donation from benefactors in Saudi Arabia—not an unusual event at that time. However, the grand opening of the mosque tended to obscure a high level of infighting amongst trustees and founding members of the mosque community. Again, this was not unusual but it took on added significance when in 1997 trustees employed Abu Hamza in the mistaken belief that he would help reduce friction and improve the service offered by the mosque to a growing Algerian youth audience, especially because he spoke good English and Arabic. Although Hamza had shown due courtesy and charm when being interviewed once he was in post he began to challenge the trustees' authority and to impose his own brand of teaching on the mosque. His charismatic style and willingness to help young Muslims new to London with all their welfare needs soon made him very popular. Indeed as his popularity grew with young Algerians and other young members of the community so the mosque trustees and elders became more disenchanted.

Local police first became aware of the situation in 1998 when trustees complained that Abu Hamza's supporters had manhandled an imam and ejected him from the building. In the same year police started to deal with incidents where suspects for credit card frauds and other crimes were reported to be living in the mosque. Overall, despite the good intentions of the mosque management it soon became apparent that Abu Hamza and his core supporters were beyond their control. One of the two active mosque trustees describes how it felt at the time:

We would have crisis meetings and decide how best to tackle Abu Hamza. But when we met him he would get his supporters to threaten us. We were unable to exert our authority. When we told the Charity Commission they were supportive but the legal remedies they proposed were very drawn out and time consuming.[3]

Protracted civil proceedings aimed at reducing Abu Hamza's influence were unsuccessful and the mosque trustees were obliged to accommodate him. Although the court proceedings proved debilitating for the trustees, for Abu Hamza it was just a minor distraction from his purpose of engaging with youth audiences and teaching them about their duty to fight jihad. Soon an office on the first floor of the building became the hub of a small enterprise known as Supporters of Sharia, a base from which to spread Abu Hamza's message that ran along the lines established by Osama bin Laden and other al-Qaeda propagandists.[4] The two mosque trustees played an active role at the mosque and worked tirelessly to curtail the influence of Abu Hamza and his increasingly belligerent supporters. However when they challenged him about his breach of Charity Commission regulations in allowing young Algerian immigrants to sleep in the basement of the mosque he poured scorn on them and threatened violence. The same two trustees established a good rapport with a community police officer but she was generally only able to offer them encouragement. The main responsibility for dealing with Abu Hamza fell to the trustees and internal divisions proved a handicap. Apart from the two active trustees the others were more typical of British mosque trustees in that they were not local and did not regard their responsibilities as being proactive in any way.[5]

In 2001 police were called to an incident where one of Abu Hamza's supporters had assaulted one of the two active trustees.[6] The victim had already endured bullying at the hands of Abu Hamza's supporters for a protracted period. According to one of the active trustees by 2001 it had become a puzzle to them that Abu Hamza had not been arrested in connection with his high-profile activities in support of terrorism:

Later on when we read in the papers that Abu Hamza had been talking to the Security Service and to the police we were surprised and disappointed. When we wanted support against him we had to struggle on our own.[7]

At the same time Abu Hamza's circle of close supporters were beginning to flex their muscles and threaten anyone who opposed their *emir*. For many of them it was their first experience of responsibility when they performed tasks on behalf of the Supporters of Sharia such as serving in a bookshop on the ground floor of the mosque and recording, copying, cataloguing and distributing talks by Abu Hamza. One of the active mosque trustees explained how their authority was gradually undermined, in doing so he was repeating an account first given to MCU officers in January 2002:

At first I complained to Abu Hamza that one of his young followers had been rude or aggressive towards me. He would listen to us and say he would do something about it. But really didn't do a thing except encourage it. One day one of his bodyguards told me I was a *kafir* dog and said he would kill me.[8]

As well as bullying Abu Hamza also enjoyed the charade of pretending to be a mediator between his enthusiastic young followers and mosque trustees and local elders who he despised as being weak and lacking in commitment to their religion. A local community police officer recalls how skilful Abu Hamza was at manipulating community support in his favour:

We were called to an incident at the mosque where a dispute broke out between youths inside the building and two men outside who said they had property inside to collect. Abu Hamza was the one who emerged as the mediator and leader and calmed things down. He was polite to us and thanked us for attending. He was always ready to crack a joke as well. The trustees were never really in control.[9]

Discussions with the two mosque trustees continued over cups of tea in the cold storage room during February and March in 2002. In-between we spoke to local police officers, Charity Commission officials, local council officials and officials at the nearby Muslim Welfare House (MWH) and Muslim Association of Britain (MAB). A picture began to emerge of the trustees having been outmanoeuvred and bullied by Abu Hamza and his supporters over a long period. The kind of physical opposition that the Brixton Salafis had shown in defeating Abbullah el Faisal (see *Brixton* Part Three) had not been an option for the mosque trustees. When one of them died of a heart attack the following year many of his friends blamed the enormous stress he had been under at the mosque:

Big headache, big worry. All the time. We do our duty all the time. No one really help us. Abu Hamza turn our world upside down. [Deceased trustee] was a good man—always working right way. Too much headache for him.[10]

Much of that stress, friends agreed, was compounded by a sense of deep regret at having voluntarily appointed Abu Hamza to an important post that had enabled him to build his power base and to undermine the trustees' authority. It was also considered to have been exacerbated by the proximity of his shop to the mosque and a consequent vulnerability to threats and abuse from Abu Hamza's supporters.

Although the trustees were somewhat circumspect during their early meetings with us they were reasonably relaxed, having become used to dealing with Islington police officers, officials from the Charity Commission and officials from Islington Council. I was struck early on by the extent to which the trustees had been losing a war of attrition to Abu Hamza and his supporters for a long period and as they became accustomed to failure their expectations of proactive support from police or 'officialdom' had begun to recede. In the circumstances we were careful to strike a balance between their genuine willingness to help and a realistic appraisal of their own capabilities and resources.[11] I noted the extent to which the problems caused by Abu Hamza had come to dominate and cast a shadow over their lives. According to the late trustee's closest ally the greatest stress had been caused by a sense of shame.[12] When friends from Pakistan came to stay at his North London home they saw a photograph of him smiling alongside Prince Charles on the day the mosque was officially opened.[13] That was the proudest day of his life. At the time it was the most ambitious mosque-building project in London. News of its subsequent, unhappy fate as a hub of 'international terrorism' had reached Pakistan and his friends would ask how he had allowed it to fall into the hands of extremists:

It wasn't his fault but he took the blame personally. He felt responsible. Others were far more at fault but it had been his life's work and he took it to heart.[14]

According to one local community interviewee the two active trustees were also victims of in-fighting within the trustee body that was neither uncommon nor necessarily problematic of itself but which proved costly in this case:

Mosque committees are notorious for petty rivalries and Finsbury Park was no different. They could have embraced different sections of the community but they preferred to be insular. There was also the familiar problem that most trustees lived away from the immediate area and viewed the mosque as a business interest rather than an active role. That was why they appointed Hamza in the first place. They thought he could do the work the trustees couldn't. But what was missing was a proper management structure. It was based more on village politics from India and Pakistan and it began to suffer.[15]

There was also the problem that the policing that the trustees had grown up with in Pakistan was often corrupt. The community police officer in Islington had achieved a significant breakthrough in terms of confidence building by establishing a genuinely supportive relationship with the two trustees so they felt they were being served honestly and without obligation. That was the strong foundation we were able to build upon in our own trust-building initiative. Nevertheless, according a colleague of the local community police officer who introduced us to the two mosque trustees there was also a strong sense that collectively the MPS had not been able to support the trustees sufficiently in the face of increased intimidation from Abu Hamza and his supporters:

We grew anxious about the two trustees. You could see how Hamza's thugs had bullied them. Although we could give them some support we could not be there all the time and we could only do so much. And because of all they had been through they were reluctant to press charges and go to court. I was pleased when the MCU started up because it needed a strong focus on the case to help the trustees and many of the ordinary worshippers at the mosque. Up until that point no one was looking at the case from a community perspective.[16]

When asked to expand upon this apparent lack of police attention to the problems posed by Abu Hamza, the same officer explained:

It was a case of falling between two stalls. Islington police like all borough policing was focused on crimes figures—the need to cut street crime, burglaries, and anti-social crime in partnership with the council. Until Barry Norman[17] took charge Finsbury Park Mosque was seen as more of a security issue—something the Security Service, Anti-Terrorist Branch and Special Branch dealt with.[18]

This was precisely the issue we hoped to address. I noted the comments of a local CID officer who was involved in the prosecution of three Abu Hamza supporters for credit card fraud:

By 2002 a number of gangs from Algeria had taken control of the Blackstock Road [a busy thoroughfare 200 yards from the Finsbury Park Mosque] and some of them could be quite menacing. Some attached themselves to Abu Hamza and some were just involved in crime. I would say there was a cross over between them. I dealt with a number of cases of credit card fraud, false identification, etc., and also helping a few immigration raids. There was also a problem of intimidation of pedestrians on Blackstock Road itself.[19]

We began to explore these issues with other trustees, local police, the Charity Commission, local councillors and other community leaders. It soon became clear that the MCU could fill a vacuum that existed by co-coordinating the various and disparate activities of trustees, police, council, Charity Commission and other interested parties. At the same time we sought to build trust with key figures in the local Muslim community. This enabled us to fathom the sometimes complex relationships and histories that had enabled Abu Hamza to divide the trustee body in the past. Some of the most revealing interviews took place with Fadi Itani and Ahmed Sheikh Mohammed at the neighbouring MWH. It transpired that their offers to help their neighbours at the

Finsbury Park Mosque had been rejected because of a fear that they would threaten the control of the trustees. To a certain extent this reflected cultural tensions between the Deobandi-oriented mosque trustees and their Arab neighbours at the MWH.

Not that defections from Abu Hamza to the MWH or the MAB were commonplace before February 2005—merely sufficient to highlight an untapped potential. Instead Abu Hamza built up an impressive grassroots support network that provided services that were geared towards the needs of young Muslims—especially those newly arrived from Algeria. On the one hand word spread rapidly on the street that the moment a young Muslim arrived at Waterloo International and successfully negotiated immigration controls he should make his way to Finsbury Park Mosque, or one of the nearby cafes in Blackstock Road, to obtain immediate welfare support and advice about short-term needs. For many North Africans arriving from or via France Abu Hamza had already become a folk hero. On one account his role at Finsbury Park Mosque was described as setting up a jihadi base in the heart of London.[20]

Abu Hamza also showed great skill in building team spirit between Muslims with very different ethnic backgrounds. Whereas in other parts of Muslim London mosques tended to perpetuate the divisions that existed between different ethnic and cultural identities Finsbury Park Mosque, under Abu Hamza's influence, became one of the few to break down traditional barriers. Unfortunately, he did so for the benefit of al-Qaeda influence and not for the benefit of Londoners' safety and social cohesion. An interviewee recalls how young Muslims from Algeria would begin to build relationships with young Muslims who had family connections in Pakistan and India as well as with convert British Muslims. This integration was not always successful but it is interesting that Abu Hamza was anxious to bring Muslims with different backgrounds and experiences under one umbrella. British converts, generally black, were highly regarded by Abu Hamza because of their local knowledge, language skills and ability to help integrate newly arrived Muslims who might have problems with their immigration status. They were also good for morale, as one interviewee recalls:

Abu Hamza was very fond of [name supplied]. He was good at martial arts and was a good instructor. Before he became Muslim he was a big man in drugs and supposedly guns. He still had friends who were supposed to be big in Jamaican crime stuff. Abu Hamza liked reverts because he could show to young people who were born Muslim that were being shown up by their brothers who had given up all the so called pleasures of the corrupt West. He would also help new Muslims find wives. He paid attention to everything like that. Some people probably joined him just for that.[21]

One of Hamza's regular techniques was to explain the political background concerning the countries where his small circle had family connections. So in the cases of Algeria and Egypt he would explain how corrupt leaderships had abandoned Muslims in preference to enjoying the benefits of good relations with the West. The corrupt leaderships should be attacked and killed because they were no longer Muslim. The West that supported corrupt regimes like Algeria and Egypt should also be attacked—given 'a bloody nose' as he puts it. In this way he was giving his young audiences a history lesson and allowing them to place their own memories and the stories they had heard from parents and friends into a wider context. In doing so he would often mock Hizb ut Tahrir (HT) who shared some of his political analysis yet none of his willingness to solve the problem with political violence. Occasionally one or two young recruits who had previously been to HT meetings would join his circle and he was always keen to demonstrate how lacking that group was in any real connection to a global jihad. By joining his circle, he would make clear, young Muslims were gaining access to a world of real action—real jihad, not 'empty talk' about the Caliphate.

Abu Hamza's own visible injuries, he would indicate, were evidence of his active leadership role—something that placed him at considerable variance with the first UK HT leader Omar Bakri Mohammed who had a contrary street reputation as a physical coward. If you were a fit and able young Muslim, Abu Hamza would urge, you should be ready to train for jihad. This, it should be noted, is a wholly different environment from the one Ed Husain describes where as a HT activist meetings were an end in themselves.[22] Husain, on his own account, sees participation in a 'controversial' march through the East End as the limit of his own risk taking.[23] Whereas, if a young Muslim came to an Abu Hamza circle for over six months Abu Hamza would want to know why he wasn't training for jihad instead.[24] Husain's popular thesis that HT was a conveyor belt for al-Qaeda[25] looked decidedly threadbare at a typical Abu Hamza outdoor training camp where young adherents who were struggling to make the grade were mocked that failure would mean joining HT to give out leaflets instead.[26]

One of Abu Hamza's circle who later joined the MWH explained that while he avoided giving precise details of how he lost his hands Abu Hamza often referred his young audiences to his own frontline presence in Afghanistan between 1991 and 1993.[27] Again Abu Hamza was at pains to let them know about his experiences in Bosnia in 1995. In the latter case he would explain how Muslims were often let down by fellow Muslims who failed to show sufficient resolve. In 1999 Abu Hamza's reputation as a man of action was further enhanced when he was arrested and questioned in connection with a failed terrorist operation in Yemen, in which two of his sons had been imprisoned and allegedly tortured along with others connected to Finsbury Park Mosque. Similarly, in 2000 a few in his close circle became aware that two young recruits Feroz Abbasi and James Ujaama had travelled to training camps in Afghanistan.[28] These are just a handful of examples of how he built up a reputation as a facilitator of 'jihad' amongst his followers. Some of his more public clowning, he would argue, was to deceive the authorities. Be that as it may he made the most of his undoubted communication skills. When Abu Hamza took a young audience under his wing he was able to empower them:

You kill each other so this is your repentance, this is when you spill blood in the cause of Allah. Those who worship Allah fight those who do not worship Allah. This is a practical repentance from you. This is to show that you indeed have repented to Allah. So the original matter when you talk about the *kafir*, the *kafir* blood it is allowed for anybody who listens to the orders of Allah— *go and get him*. And also for his money if it is to be distributed among the Muslim among the believer of Allah so they can use it and they don't have to go and wash dishes and they don't have to go and clean the toilets. No. Muslim shall always be full time Mujahid in the cause of Allah. Muslim shall not be tempted by dunya [earthly concerns].[29]

At moments like this it becomes possible to discern how Abu Hamza was so influential over a sustained period. He had the ability to promote violence as being right behaviour and non-violence as being a compromise. He also sets a high moral tone:

Muslim shall not be watching pornography because he cannot get married. It is haram. Allah said go and take those who are making pornography take them home captive they become sabiyah for you. Allah does not want it. It is haram for you to watch pornography but it is halal and a duty for you to capture those who are making this pornography, have them home as an owner master. If they refuse to become slaves of Allah then they become the slaves of the slaves of Allah.[30]

No other Muslim leaders in London at the time were able to offer young Muslims such a tantalising glimpse of licensed control over women who might otherwise be outside the legitimate reach of young Muslim men.[31] At this point many learned Islamic scholars had dismissed Abu Hamza as a raving fool. Once he became a media hate figure it became commonplace for reputable Muslim scholars and community leaders to ridicule him.[32] In doing so they generally displayed their own ignorance of street culture and, often, how disconnected they had become from the Muslim street. In addition, they failed to appreciate the level of skill Abu Hamza demonstrated in connecting to his audience and harnessing their energy. Abu Hamza was also adept at promoting himself to the detriment of more qualified voices by dismissing them as 'dollar scholars'. Sometimes this effective slur is misunderstood as denoting an official connection to a government but in Hamza's world (and of course in Abu Qatada's and Abdullah el Faisal's worlds) it extends to include condemnation of scholars and community leaders who have 'sold out' even without accepting government 'bribes'.[33] This notion of active versus apathetic Muslim representatives was highly effective when notably adopted by Mohammed Siddique Khan in his martyrdom video where he compares his action with 'useless' community leaders content with their 'semidetached houses and Toyotas'.[34] It follows that only those small sections of the community that are in touch with their own streets may have the necessary tools to combat such powerful rhetoric.

Whereas MCU officers expected to spend months absorbing the Finsbury Park scene on a daily basis before feeling qualified to offer a tentative assessment about it, Evan Kohlmann, manifesting a methodological approach to terrorism studies highlighted by Silke,[35] considered himself eminently qualified to pass definitive judgement after one short meeting with Abu Hamza during a flying visit to London in 2002.[36] I was especially concerned that Kohlmann conflated Islamist antidotes to al-Qaeda, as evidenced by the work of the Finsbury Park Islamists, with the terrorist threat itself. Moreover, it soon became apparent to me that the Finsbury Park Islamists at the MWH and the MAB had the requisite skills and experience to challenge Abu Hamza. What was required was a partnership understanding that would empower and licence them to educate young Muslims further afield. In the meantime I was able to observe their local success in challenging Abu Hamza's version of jihad. This was no small achievement given Abu Hamza's powerful message on the topic:

This is frankly Islam. If you don't understand this about Islam you will be killed while you are staying at home. Because you'll be very busy try to make ibaadah, you'll be very busy try to pray Fajar and you do azkar and you try to teach your son while the non-Muslims, the *kafir* are preparing to kill you. Or at least humiliate you and take your son from you. You teach him at home and they undo this teaching at school and make him turn against you and against Islam. At school you give him advice in his ear they give him full time advice in television in the media and you will see your son becomes your own enemy, and the enemy of Allah. You made him so.[37]

Again a sense of moral panic takes centre stage. Muslims are besieged and must defend their families and their honour from the pervasive threat of a corrupt and comforting *kafir* lifestyle. This sense of moral superiority over Muslims who do not fight jihad is evidenced in many of the martyrdom videos made by British Muslim 'suicide bombers' post-9/11. What Abu Hamza demonstrates is that this is a very effective way to persuade young Muslims to abandon the comfort zone of their daily lives.[38] Abu Hamza's was an especially powerful message for young Muslim men who had started a family of their own. Instead of it seeming incredible that young men like Jermaine Lindsey[39] could embark on a 'suicide mission' and abandon their families it becomes clear that Hamza was instilling in them a contrary sense of duty towards their children:

Muslims if you want really to worship Allah then you must keep an eye on *kafirs*. You can't go to the mosque all the time and spend all the time for your own worship and not planning for your children and not securing that your children can have the same access to that mosque 20 years later. This is how you mislead yourself and mislead your children. This is how your selfishness because you love duniya and you want to go to paradise without thinking how can your children have the same path how can people who are being attacked and humiliated now how can you reduce that suffering from them.[40]

Of course, prior to 9/11 Abu Hamza enjoyed great latitude and the efforts of his neighbours to countermand him had little impact on his day-to-day activities, especially inside the Finsbury Park Mosque.[41] When a new follower approached Abu Hamza for advice after listening to one of his talks inside the mosque in August 2000 he was surprised and delighted to be given an immediate clerical role in his office. Abu Hamza was especially powerful when encouraging his young followers to contemplate the religious rewards that awaited them once they shook off their daily shackles and became jihadis. Just like a military instructor must ensure that his recruits are capable of fighting for their lives so was Hamza absolutely concerned to ensure that his followers would not blanch at the prospect of mortal combat:

Don't you know Allah is happy when a *kafir* is killed. Don't you know that? Don't you know Allah SWT is happy when a Muslim is taken out of his prison by force and you humiliating the *kafirs* who put him in. Don't you know that? Don't you know that Allah SWT is happy when you stop the evil from every society so the people can have good ears and they go have good listen to the reality of Islam. Don't you know that? Don't you know that the Prophet has praised people who will change people in life so they can change them into janaah also in the hereafter.[42]

Contrary to the popular stereotype of al-Qaeda influence inhibiting creativity, Abu Hamza was especially empowering when he explained to a young audience that they were licensed and encouraged to use their senses as good Muslims but especially when preparing to fight the *kafir*:

So Allah SWT he gave us these senses. He told us to use it. So we can increase our benefit on earth and also we can be guided generally to know the main outline between Islam and kufr... It is important we use these senses. Allah SWT says in the Qur'an on many occasions that we have given human being these three things. The hearing, ability of seeing, the ability of understanding and they never and they never used it. Use your senses. This is an important introduction for all of us.[43]

Generally delivered to groups of about twenty supporters Abu Hamza concludes his talk by combining the theme of 'using your senses' with an exaltation of the superior Muslim taking the blood of the inferior *kafir*:

My dear brothers no, the blood of a Muslim, the money of a Muslim, the honour of a Muslim is preserved at all costs ... But the blood of a *kafir*, the money of a *kafir*, the honour of a *kafir*—you can take it. This is the difference between a Muslim and a *kafir*. A *kafir* is not allowed to own anything. Except if he goes to Islam or to have a proper oath from a legitimate Muslim leader. And also to pay a tax for that. The sale for his life like a sheep, unrespected, his money, his life his honour, for anybody who wants to take it.[44]

This talk has been highlighted to illustrate just one part of a propaganda and recruitment process that also included training camps and close one-to-one counselling and welfare support. In essence, no different in principle to what any conventional military training would entail. It is so far removed from the responsible training in Muslim citizenship being undertaken at the same time in the nearby MWH as to make the conflation of the two versions of Islamism wholly misplaced. On the north-west side of the Great North Eastern railway track young Muslims were being offered guidance that would see some of them enter mainstream British politics and on the south-east side of the railway track just 500 yards away young Muslims were being given instruction that would see some of them become al-Qaeda terrorists. That was the clear difference that prompted the MCU to form a partnership with the former with a view to tackling the latter.

In Abu Hamza, the mosque trustees found themselves confronted with a gifted and sometimes reckless operator who was determined to use their mosque for his own activities. Up until his arrest in May 2004 Abu Hamza was a magnet for the tabloid media.[45] He was always available to be interviewed and although his performances made the majority of Muslims angry and embarrassed his own supporters were thrilled to see him speaking defiantly to the British media that they despised.[46] According to research conducted by Elizabeth Poole he became 'the most prominently featured British Muslim in the British press', a regular 'feature of the tabloid front pages' whose 'demonisation parallels that of the media's global Islamic monster, Osama bin Laden'.[47] As she suggests:

This works to make the attributes associated with him easier to digest. Given that these centre around his appearance (freak), expressions of hatred and violence, and radicalism, this has significant implications for the way British Muslims are perceived.[48]

It was this very point that explains some of the mixed feelings many Muslim Londoners had towards Abu Hamza.[49] Even those who abhorred his behaviour felt some sympathy towards him when he was viciously attacked by an obviously Islamophobic gutter press.[50] Massoud Shadjareh, chairman of the Islamic Human Rights Commission (IHRC), made this point forcefully in interview:

The Sun, The Express and The Mail were guilty of Islamophobic attacks on Abu Hamza. Really, they just used Abu Hamza as an excuse to express hatred towards Muslims generally. He came to symbolize all that was supposed to be unacceptable about Islam. The situation became especially bad when his solicitor Mudassa Arani was singled out for attack and harassment. All of this had the consequence of encouraging verbal and physical attacks on Muslims.[51]

On the first anniversary of 9/11 Abu Hamza organised a meeting at the mosque under the banner 'A Towering Day in History'.[52] The trustees were powerless to prevent it going ahead despite their strong opposition to it. Following publicity in the London *Evening Standard* members and associates of the National Front, the British National Party and allied extreme right-wing groups protested outside the mosque while over 300 mainly young Muslims packed into the building to listen to talks from Abu Hamza, Omar Bakri Mohammed and other al-Qaeda propagandists and apologists. Conscious that they would be monitored the speakers were circumspect in what they said, at least by their own standards, but that still meant their comments were highly effective in terms of boosting al-Qaeda propaganda messages. In fact this meeting occurred at a time of brief reconciliation between Abu Hamza and Omar Bakri Mohammed.[53] That accommodation was short-lived—both egos and aims preventing a longer-term partnership.[54] On the night far-right protesters were prevented from coming face-to-face with the extremists inside the mosque by the Metropolitan Police who ensured that public tranquillity was maintained.[55] However, this event marked the beginning of irregular protest activity by right-wing extremists outside the mosque. Protests by groups of around fifty demonstrators became familiar on Fridays when Abu Hamza was leading prayers in the street when the mosque was closed down. One MCU officer who was on duty that evening observed some similarities between both sets of extremists:

Both groups had elements that were familiar with street violence. Both groups contained young men who were nursing political grievances that had been nurtured by exploitative leaders. In many ways they were alike. Abu Hamza stoked anger on one side and individuals like Nick Griffin did the same on the other.[56]

In making this observation the officer was drawing on long experience of monitoring violent political groups in London. By highlighting similarities that exist at the street level between two opposing groups he offers access to crude street politics that is impervious to conventional political interventions. The juxtaposition of al-Qaeda and BNP-inspired street politics also indicates the importance of narratives of political grievance that prompt recruitment and activism in both groups. The same officer explains:

BNP and NF street activists have a clear understanding of what is wrong in the world. The white working class has been shat on. First Jews were to blame. Then it was the blacks and Asians. Now Muslims are to blame as well. Just because their grasp of politics is unsophisticated does not mean it is incoherent. It's a mistake to write them off as thugs just because they can't speak the political language of Westminster. It's the same with Abu Hamza's supporters.

They get motivated by grievances. The relationship between them and the leaders they relate to is crucial.[57]

After a high-profile police raid on the Finsbury Park Mosque in January 2003, the trustees suffered increasingly hostile responses from many competing sections of the local and wider Muslim community.[58] Inevitably by the end of the year frustrations began to boil over concerning the continuing closure of the mosque on the grounds that it needed significant repair work being carried out before it would be deemed fit for use by Islington Council's health and safety department.[59] To a large extent the repair work was occasioned by the misuse and neglect that arose during Abu Hamza's de facto control of the building.[60] Damage caused by the police operation was repaired and paid for by the Metropolitan Police.[61] MCU officers supported the trustees in their efforts to keep the building secure while it was closed. This proved difficult at times, as one officer recalls:

There were one or two break-ins at the mosque. Although it was boarded up it was not 100% secure. Abu Hamza's supporters' regarded it as belonging to them. It was also vulnerable to individuals who just wanted to see what they could steal inside the building.[62]

Moreover, in the three months following the police search of the building the premises were without an electricity supply and basic services because Abu Hamza and his supporters had left the building in a state of disrepair and bills unpaid.[63] MCU officers worked well beyond the familiar boundaries of normal police work by investing their own time in assisting the trustees to gain access to support from electricity and other services.[64] This was a difficult task because the reputation of the mosque made companies wary about conducting business at the venue. Often emergency workers would only come to the building if they received reassurance from MCU officers that they would be at the venue to ensure safety. Companies also sought reassurance that future bills would not go unpaid. Jeremy Corbyn and Barry Norman, MP and local police chief, were also key supporters at this time. It was during these kinds of activities that MCU officers built alliances with Jeremy Corbyn and local council officials. For their part council officials were reassured to see that a police unit was able to balance the needs of local communities and counter-terrorism policing. Corbyn, Norman and MCU officers also displayed a willingness to take risks and get involved in support activity that others might have avoided on the basis that they were not prepared to take action that fell outside the confines of their job descriptions and a growing health and safety culture. A commitment to problem solving became our hallmark.

Throughout 2003 MCU officers brokered meetings with community groups, local authority officials, police and the Charity Commission to support efforts to raise funds to enable the repair work to be carried out so that the mosque could re-open.[65] In London the best support came from the London Central Mosque where the director lent his personal authority to the task.[66] Potential sponsors were reluctant to commit funds to the repair work at the building because they feared that when the mosque re-opened it would return into the hands of Abu Hamza (who was not arrested until August 2004).[67] This concern was compounded by the fact that the trustees struggled to convince potential donors that they had the necessary ability to resist Abu Hamza's attempt to re-assert his control at the mosque once it re-opened. For their part the trustees were desperately hoping that their task would be made easier in the event that Abu Hamza was arrested—an eventuality that could not be anticipated with confidence in 2003. As one trustee recalls:

It was a very difficult period. Abu Hamza was praying in the street outside the mosque every week. Up to a hundred worshippers would listen to his speech before he led the prayers. I received phone calls from friends in Pakistan and the Middle East who saw this on TV and naturally thought Hamza was still in charge.[68]

The same coverage also fed into growing anti-Muslim sentiment in the tabloids and in extremist nationalist politics. In turn this would manifest itself in small demonstrations against Abu Hamza while he was leading Friday prayers in the street. The demonstrators sometimes called themselves the English Defence League—anticipating a more formal use of the name later from 2009 onwards. Police would keep them at a distance from the worshippers while they sang abusive songs and shouted insults across the road at the Muslim worshippers who generally numbered around 100. On one occasion the demonstrators brought pork sausages with them to throw at the Muslims and a copy of the Qur'an to burn. From their comments they appeared to be motivated by the same moral outrage that was regularly expressed by tabloid pundits. As usual police officers prevented the demonstrators from causing violence, albeit on one occasion a demonstrator accidentally set fire to his own clothing when seeking to burn a copy of the Qur'an in the street—just twenty yards from where 100 Muslims were praying in the street. On another occasion demonstrators sang 'Where's your Hamza gone, far, far away' to the tune of 'Chirpy, chirpy, cheep, cheep' to mark Abu Hamza's arrest in 2004 and within earshot of his supporters praying in the street.

This was during the period when the mosque was closed for repair after the police raid and Abu Hamza was leading Friday prayers in the street. During the same period *The Sun* newspaper sent its battle bus and page-three girls to the venue in an attempt to galvanise the kind of confrontation that would make good copy. On more than one occasion the Islington police commander, Barry Norman, warned journalists about their behaviour. Why, *Sun* journalists asked, weren't police arresting the Muslim worshippers rather than allowing them to pray in the street? In fact, police tactics were aimed at differentiating between Hamza and his hard-core supporters on the one hand and ordinary local Muslims who wanted to pray on the other. I was also concerned that young Muslims who were briefly attracted by Hamza's rhetoric and reputation should be encouraged by responsible Muslims to channel their concerns in positive ways rather than be stigmatised as part of the same problem posed by Hamza and his hard-core supporters. This approach was supported by the local police chief Barry Norman and the local MP Jeremy Corbyn but it was not popular with the gutter press.

I also became concerned about the extent to which key parts of the BNP's analysis had become common coinage outside of extremist politics. Seeking to exploit widespread anxiety in white working-class communities in London as well as in towns such as Bradford and Burnley that had witnessed Asian (essentially Muslim) riots in the summer of 2001 the BNP produced an audio tape: 'Islam: An Enemy of Democracy'.[69] Having played a major part in provoking the riots the BNP used the tape to explain to its supporters why they should never expect to see improved relations with their Muslim neighbours. The rioting by young Muslims that they —'the oppressed indigenous white community'—had witnessed and suffered was, according to the BNP, just a symptom of a growing clash of cultures that would inevitably lead to more violence. The tape features the BNP leader Nick Griffin explaining that Islam is wholly incompatible with Western values and that Muslims have no intention to ever adopt an English way of life. On the contrary, Griffin argues, Islam seeks to convert Britain to Muslim values.[70] History, Griffin seeks to evidence, confirms the endemic nature of hostility between the West and the Muslim world. Our fore-bears, he concludes, were unequivocal in their opposition to a danger-ous and opposing culture: our current political masters, in contrast, were hamstrung by their blind commitment to immigration from Mus-lim countries and the concept of a 'multi-cultural society'.[71] This was certainly the sentiment and analysis I heard expressed by demonstra-tors outside the mosque on several occasions during 2003—2004.

When the same line was being peddled in the tabloids or radio phone-in programmes there would be one significant difference. Writ-ers and broadcasters would be careful to find Asian allies so they could avoid the charge of racism or of being fellow travellers with the BNP. Denigrating Muslims was altogether a different proposition and the war on terror gave licence to what might otherwise have been cen-sured. According to a member of the Muslim Safety Forum (MSF), 'Muslims were suddenly in the media spotlight and made to feel they were to blame for 9/11 and even more so for 7/7':

In the broadsheets, critics launched their Islamophobic attacks under the guise of a campaign against multiculturalism. They defended themselves against charges of anti-Muslim sentiment by promoting apolitical Muslims, who could be distinguished from Islamists. A simplified version of this tactic was then used in the tabloids.[72]

On the same evening as the 'Towering Day in History' meeting (11.9.02), in the nearby MWH the Finsbury Park Islamist community held a regular training session for Muslim youth wishing to improve their skills in applying for jobs. Police officers who were patrolling the area because of a concern that far right demonstrators might attack Muslims made regular visits to the MWH to offer reassurance and check that no incidents had been reported. Such liaison also helped build trust between police and an increasingly beleaguered Muslim com-munity. In the first twelve months since 9/11 several Muslim women were known by the MWH to have been assaulted and abused in the street and on buses simply because they were visibly Muslim. Typical assaults involved a Muslim woman having her hijab pulled off and being insulted as a 'f....ing Muslim'. Whatever the exact motivation of each attacker it was an experience that the victims had not suffered before 9/11. In conjunction with police the MWH sought to ensure that these incidents were reported by the victims to the police but that proved difficult and in most cases these incidents went unreported.

MCU officers were also able to explain the importance of reporting these incidents to friends and relatives of the victims. In a handful of cases they were able to facilitate the reporting process where the victims were too upset and too suspicious to come forward. That became part of a process whereby MCU officers could build trust in sections of the community where confidence in the police was at a low ebb. Moreover, while MCU officers had not anticipated this level of engagement with issues of Islamophobia it soon became a regular feature of their day-to-day work. One particular case highlighted the problem caused by growing anti-Muslim sentiment. A quiet and pious Muslim postgraduate student was travelling on the top deck of a London bus on a Friday lunchtime. He was wearing his best traditional Muslim clothes having prepared himself for jummah prayers. A group of youths started abusing and threatening him for being a 'terrorist Muslim'. Typically, no other passengers intervened to help him. The youths started hitting him and followed him off the bus when he tried to escape. On the pavement they struck him with a heavy broom and inflicted grievous bodily harm that left him severely injured, mentally and physically.

Although the victim's family were eventually satisfied with the police prosecution of the attackers they were perturbed when investigators initially questioned them in detail about the victim's religious practice in circumstances that left them in no doubt that he was a 'suspect' as well. I later used this case to highlight to colleagues how the support of Muslim communities might be alienated if they were treated as 'terrorist suspects' without due cause. What surprised me was that colleagues in diversity policing who were so in tune with minorities sometimes failed to acknowledge the extent of the problems being faced by Muslim communities.[73]

By the beginning of 2004 another significant local group, calling itself the North London Central Mosque Working Party (referred to as the working party), began to campaign against the mosque trustees.[74] The working party consisted of a diverse core group of around ten individuals with varying levels of legitimacy as interested parties in the running of the mosque.[75] On the one hand the working party contained members who had been involved in the management of the mosque in its infancy before the new mosque building was opened in 1994.[76] On the other hand it had members who had worked with Abu Hamza in the past.[77] They complained that the mosque trustees were out of touch and were negligent in keeping the mosque closed and campaigned on that basis. They received support from Massoud Shadjareh, the chairman of IHRC, who offered his considerable mediation skills in a search for a solution to re-open the mosque. However, when his role as broker became known to Abu Hamza's supporters they threatened him with violence.[78]

The working party complained to the police borough commander, Barry Norman, that the trustees were acting against the wishes of local Muslims by keeping the mosque closed and put themselves forward as potentially better custodians of the mosque. They made similar approaches to the Charity Commission and the local MP, Jeremy Corbyn. In arguing their case for legitimacy they claimed to have credibility among young supporters of Abu Hamza and to be able to mediate effectively between them and the authorities. MCU officers assessed that the working party lacked the credibility and skills they claimed to possess. In the event both Jeremy Corbyn and Barry Norman proved to be effective authority figures who were willing to invest time meeting with working party members and the mosque trustees in an effort to mediate and find solutions that would allow the mosque to re-open without it falling back into the hands of Abu Hamza and his supporters.[79]

By listening to local Muslims I came to understand that the ongoing closure of the mosque represented a significant Islamic shortcoming once it was repaired and fit for use. Police were coming under increased pressure at this point to reduce the costs associated with policing the Friday prayers that had now been taking place in the street outside the mosque for eighteen months. MCU officers were able to explain how by allowing the prayers to take place in the street police were better able to build and maintain trust with young Muslims who might otherwise become more alienated. We were also instrumental in helping Charity Commission and local authority officials to understand Islamic imperatives and local Muslim politics so as to explain sometimes complex intra-communal rivalries and tensions. Islington police commander Barry Norman later commended MCU efforts during this difficult period.

What became increasingly clear was that the mosque trustees would need significant help and support when they finally decided to re-open the mosque. That decision was made in August 2004 after months of negotiations brokered by MCU officers and supported by Barry Norman and Jeremy Corbyn. Abu Hamza had been arrested and the trustees were consequently more confident they could cope with his supporters in his absence. In addition the trustees had entered into dialogue with members of the working party and although there were hostilities there was an element of co-operation to build upon. In the months leading up to the re-opening of the mosque intensive discussions took place with both community and official stakeholders.[80]

By this time Barry Norman had become a familiar and respected local figure leading a low-key police presence each week outside the mosque during the prayer service in the street. On numerous occasions he defused potentially threatening situations and dealt with all parties firmly and fairly.[81] Norman's success in this regard is documented at length by Dave Bones, an independent filmmaker and blogger who attended and filmed many of the Friday prayer sessions in the street. In fact Bones got to know police and worshippers very well over a long period of time, and his website contains insightful film and comment of the events.[82] Whereas the mainstream media descended on Finsbury Park in the hope of an incident, an outrageous comment from Abu Hamza or any other 'story', Bones was simply fascinated to observe the behaviour of individuals and the interaction between police and members of the community. By way of example, Bones filmed this conversation with Barry Norman during a regular Friday prayer session led by Abu Hamza in the street outside the Finsbury Park Mosque:

Bones: I'm very interested, how long have you been serving as a policeman?
Norman: 25 years.
Bones: 25 years. And what is your rank here?
Norman: I'm Chief Superintendent.
Bones: So you're in charge of what's happening here?
Norman: Well I'm more than that I'm the Borough Police Commander.
Bones: Well I'm just very interested how you feel as a policeman and as a human being about what's happening here and what your role is.
Norman: Well our role is to facilitate people's right to free speech. No part of my role is to have my own opinion about what people are saying. My opinion doesn't count. What I am paid for is to make sure that there's no breach of the peace.
Bones: And have you seen a lot of racial tension in this country, or ... or an increase in racial tension?
Norman: It's very patchy isn't it from time to time of course there is. In a cosmopolitan society like ours of course we get racism,
but these demonstrations here, or these prayer meetings on a Friday have not caused us any problems at all.

Bones: None at all?

Norman: No.

Bones: And there's been no err... When your in the middle of err. The Islamists and the Media, what can you do?

Norman: Not get in the middle of them.

Bones: (laughing) Cos sometimes I've seen policemen err ... try and get in between the media and the err ... Do you think it's a Kangaroo court?

Norman: No I think the media have got their own agenda, and the media aren't necessarily supportive of anybody. They're certainly not always very supportive of the police are they?

Bones: No.

Norman: But providing the media aren't causing any aggravation, they can get on with their job and I'll get on with mine.

Bones: I mean... I've been involved with lots of different protests; I've travelled a lot with people who often have a very, very bad view of the police. Yet I see here, err ... British Police in British society, doing their job in a very, very interesting way, like. You know, it's been fascinating.

Norman: We don't see our job as anything more than keeping the peace. We're not pawns of the state. You know, we don't have a mandate to express our point of view and we don't wish to. All we want to do is keep the community safe.[83]

At the end of this interview Bones makes the following observation:

As I moved away from him he turned round, was joined by his fellow officers and did a fantastic little jig on the spot. If my doc [documentary] is ever made I hope you will get to see it. More police should dance like this. Why just a token gesture once a year at Notting Hill? More policemen dancing that's what I say![84]

Behind the scenes, however, Barry Norman and Jeremy Corbyn were taking part in complex, often fraught negotiations to ensure the safe reopening of the mosque. In 2004 members of the working party brought Abu Abdullah (otherwise Attila Ahmet), Abu Hamza's deputy who assumed leadership of Friday prayers after Abu Hamza's arrest, to a meeting at Islington police station.[85] Much later, in February 2008, in a trial arising out of activities at a 'terrorist training camp' in the New Forest, Abu Abdullah pleaded guilty to three counts of soliciting murder after the prosecution dropped five other counts.[86] Other members of the same group convicted in the same trial had also been supporters of Abu Hamza. At the time he met police, however, Abu Abdullah was a familiar participant in the regular weekly Friday prayer sessions held outside the mosque. Once Abu Hamza was arrested and could be seen to be facing a significant period of imprisonment Abu Abdullah and other core supporters sought to secure their ongoing presence in the mosque once it re-opened. In contrast the multi-agency alliance, led by Jeremy Corbyn and Barry Norman and marshalled by MCU officers, was determined that the mosque management should be sufficiently empowered so as to exclude them. To further complicate matters, one or two members of the working party saw themselves as alternative brokers seeking to negotiate a deal between the mosque trustees and Abu Hamza's supporters. In this respect and especially in relation to the negotiation tactics of Abu Hamza's supporters we had entered into an arena Tilly identifies as 'illicit trust networks operating in uneasy symbiosis with the regime [in this case the police and state agencies], and underground networks practicing evasive conformity or clandestine opposition'.[87] According to an MCU officer this aspect of the negotiations was not wholly unfamiliar territory:

During the terrorist campaign conducted by PIRA there were important individuals working for the IRA in London who passed themselves off as activists of one kind or another, often operating in support of prisoners or with campaigning groups. One of their roles was to gather intelligence about the counter-terrorism activities being mounted against them. Like Abu Hamza they sometimes found it useful to meet police and other officials. One IRA terrorist convicted of bomb attacks in London had spent years posing as a street activist in London. He was a regular visitor to New Scotland Yard where he arranged demonstrations. To an extent like Abu Hamza he valued the opportunities to talent spot and recruit young supporters that his overt role provided him.[88]

After lengthy discussions, deliberations and preparation the day chosen for the mosque re-opening was a Friday in August 2004 and the trustees opened the building an hour before jumma prayers were due to begin.[89] Police attendance was low key and Barry Norman was on duty as usual to provide additional reassurance to the trustees and local worshippers.[90] However, notwithstanding efforts by the trustees and their supporters to ensure that they retained control it only took Abu Hamza's supporters about an hour to wrestle control away from them. Largely through their sheer physical presence Abu Hamza's supporters took control of the first prayer service to take place inside the mosque in over a year. Many of Abu Hamza's supporters were thrilled to be back inside the building they had been excluded from for over a year and which they regarded as rightfully belonging to their imprisoned *emir*. Intimidated, the trustees looked on in frustration. Barry Norman and his team of officers were powerless to do anything other than keep the peace. Although contingency planning had included scenarios in which trustees might request police assistance in removing individual troublemakers such activity required that the trustees retain at least an element of authority.[91] The bulk of police were therefore obliged to stand by outside the building while Barry Norman and one colleague assessed the situation inside. To their frustration all that could be achieved was the evacuation and closure of the building at the conclusion of prayers—no small achievement in the circumstances.[92] Muslim partners inside the mosque witnessed the collapse of the trustees' authority at close quarters and explained that it had one small benefit, one crumb of comfort to be taken from a very demonstrable failure of authority:

The trustees tried as hard as they could to muster sufficient support to ensure that Abu Hamza's supporters did not regain control of the mosque. Some of the individuals who had agreed to attend in support failed to arrive. Only the presence of Barry Norman prevented the trustees from being assaulted. Shaken and disappointed they were at least forced to accept they did not have the resources on their own to combat the threat. I think they had hoped that Abu Hamza's arrest might have reduced his influence, instead his supporters were fired up to reclaim the mosque 'in honour of their *emir*'.[93]

Subsequent negotiations witnessed a new realism about the limited capacity of the existing trustee body to tackle the threat posed by Abu Hamza's supporters.[94] While the working party continued to put themselves forward as the group with the legitimacy and influence to take on the role they were weakened by their close association with some of Abu Hamza's supporters. Instead, the multi-agency team urged the trustees to consider inviting support from their neighbours at the nearby MWH at 233 Seven Sisters Road, on the opposite side of the mainline railway. This entailed re-visiting relations that had been strained for a long time. MCU officers were instrumental in persuading the trustees to recognise that they needed to act generously on behalf of the community. Similarly, Jeremy Corbyn was a major ally because he had built strong links with both groups.[95] Charity Commission officials were key allies too because they were able to vouch for the excellent stewardship of the MWH over a long period of time. Last but not least key officials at Islington Council were also able to highlight the valuable community work that had been undertaken by the MWH over a significant period of time as well.[96]

While tensions between mosque trustees had prevented MCU officers from forging a cohesive partnership relationship with the mosque management as a whole no such impediment hampered the evolution of their partnership relationship with officials at the MWH and the allied MAB which was also housed at 233 Seven Sisters Road.[97] Indeed, when MCU officers visited officials at one organisation it was invariably followed by a visit to officials of the sister organisation upstairs in the same building. MCU officers found both sets of officials to be similar to the Brixton salafis in important respects: unified; credible; and willing to take risks.[98] As such a London partnership blossomed on one side of the Finsbury Park railway bridge but remained restricted on the other. Thus, having first raised the issue of playing a major role in managing the mosque in 2002, the potential solution of involving MWH and MAB officials was revisited in negotiations that resembled shuttle diplomacy between the two sites on either side of the railway bridge.[99] While this was taking place the trustees came under strong pressure to re-open the mosque for a second time in 2004 specifically in time for Ramadan in October 2004.[100]

As a result the trustees were involved in a series of discussions with interested parties and such was the extent of Abu Hamza's supporters' infiltration of the working party that they were able to find out most of what plans were being made, again echoing Tilly's analysis of illicit trust networks and social movements.[101] When the mosque re-opened in time for Ramadan the trustees hoped that Abu Hamza's supporters would respect their authority on this occasion. The multi-agency partnership was prepared to support them but remained cautious about their ability to retain control. To highlight the anger that was building up within the Abu Hamza camp one of his supporters punched a mosque trustee in the face during an altercation in St. Thomas Road outside the mosque.[102] This was the second assault the trustee sustained from Abu Hamza's supporters. Another trustee had been thrown down the stairs at the mosque in 2001.[103] Although the assaults were reported to police the trustees were unwilling to press charges because they were anxious about giving evidence in court.[104] That said, the trustee assaulted in 2004 did give evidence at Wood Green Crown Court in 2006 against Abu Hamza's son who was charged with criminal damage and assault.[105] By that time the threat from Abu Hamza's supporters had diminished.

In the event although the trustees retained outward control of the mosque they gradually lost control to Abu Hamza's supporters again, albeit this time Abu Hamza's supporters were careful to proceed by stealth. By paying lip service to the trustees' authority Abu Hamza's supporters discreetly reasserted themselves inside the building, seeking especially to re-occupy the first floor office at the front of the building that Abu Hamza had previously made his own. By the end of 2004 Abu Hamza's supporters had re-established a foothold inside the mosque and felt sufficiently confident to submit their own plan for management to the Charity Commission. In response MCU officers stepped up their 'shuttle-diplomacy' between the mosque trustees and the MWH and MAB officials in an attempt to produce a new management regime that would have the necessary authority to remove Abu Hamza's supporters from the mosque once and for all.[106] Eventually a deal was agreed that gave controlling power to new trustees with backgrounds at the MWH and MAB alongside two existing trustees who played a key role in the transition and remained important members of the trustee body after the process was completed.[107] In addition two Labour MPs Mohamed Sarwar and Khalid Mahmood who had become trustees worked with their Labour colleague Jeremy Corbyn.[108] However, most of the dialogue involved what might best be described as the core part of the London partnership in Finsbury Park—two MCU officers and three senior figures in MAB. The MAB officials had to sell the proposal to their wider constituency at a shura council meeting and wanted to be sure about the extent and level of police support.[109] Because the MCU had built trust with them over a long period the MAB officials had the confidence to argue in favour of the proposal.[110] Nevertheless, they faced stiff opposition from colleagues who were cautious about taking on such a big and onerous responsibility as the Finsbury Park Mosque.[111] As one key MAB negotiator describes the dilemma:

We had to overcome a natural reluctance [to get] involved in such a controversial project. Inevitably it would cast us in the role of government or police stooges. But we argued that it was important to take action that was in the interests of the community. Abu Hamza had damaged the Muslims' reputation and we wanted to repair it.[112]

Asked to develop this insight in terms of internal group decision making, the interviewee explained more about the factors involved:

Most of us come from Muslim Brotherhood backgrounds. Some from Palestine, some from Egypt, some from Iraq, some from North Africa, Lebanon, Somalia, all over in fact. Most of us have had very bad experience with the police in our home countries. To say we are working this closely with the police is a big issue. Especially when it feels like we are being asked to do the dirty work of removing extremists from the mosque. But we had a strong case and one important factor was that most of our brothers had met the officers on the Muslim Contact Unit and could believe in their sincerity. Even our brothers who lived outside London were convinced on this point especially because of the [unit's] work during the Sheikh's [Yusuf al Qaradawi's] visit the previous year. That made a big impression on everyone. The Sheikh [Qaradawi] liked to tell everyone about his first meeting with the MCU at Heathrow Airport when he was surprised and delighted to see one of the police officers was wearing traditional Islamic clothes...![113]

Notwithstanding its written constitution and administrative protocols there was a strong sense in which the MAB mirrored the MCU in conducting its decision making informally and basing its key judgements on an on-the-job assessment of the individuals it was dealing with. To that extent both parties were following lessons learned from experience and their street skills.[114] That is to say there was little attention to process and system in the way senior police officers and senior civil servants were used to conducting business.[115] Instead, trust building relied on risk-taking by both sides, as the MAB interviewee describes:

We were putting our trust in the MCU to be able to persuade the old trustees that they should share control of the mosque with us. That was not easy because of their sense of ownership. But we had come to see the officers had the skills to do this. And they had brought all the right people together to make a success of it—Barry Norman and his team, Jeremy Corbyn, the Charity Commission and the local council. It became a joint effort and we could see we would not be let down. When the shura was split fifty-fifty on whether to go ahead with the plan to take ownership of the mosque the reputation of the MCU officers helped win it.[116]

In addition MCU officers and Islington Police officers made the point that trust and mutual respect although a crucial pre-requisite is not sufficient when dangerous and demanding work has to be carried out in partnership.[117] In these circumstances it is essential that both parties have made positive and accurate assessments about the capacity of their opposite numbers to deliver, largely in the manner Tilly suggests is at the heart of successful trust networks.[118] An MPSB officer who worked closely with the MCU puts the issue into context:

I met one of the MCU officers who was heavily involved in the case at a compulsory staff training day on health and safety. In the intervals he briefed me on the negotiations two days before Abu Hamza's supporters were ejected from the mosque by MAB. I remember asking him if he was worried about someone in MAB leaking the plan to Hamza's supporters so they could be forewarned to prevent access to the building. He said that was the least of his worries! It was everyone else apart from MAB he said he had to worry about. In view of the close attention we were being instructed to pay to health and safety issues that day I suggested that the MCU plan to allow a robust Muslim group to tackle a violent and extremist one with the Met Police ready to pick up the pieces would hardly win approval with our new health and safety conscious management![119]

In fact MWH and MAB officials went one step further than simply guarding against loose talk in the Muslim cafes around Finsbury Park and proactively monitored the movements and conduct of Abu Hamza's supporters.[120] MAB members conducting this work in the days leading up to the day of takeover at the mosque would report back to a manager—very much in the manner of MPSB surveillance or enquiry officers reporting back to their supervising officer.[121] At one level this meant cultivating a discreet relationship with a caretaker at the mosque to establish which of Abu Hamza's supporters were present in the building on a regular basis and generally discover the mood and atmosphere inside the building. Most importantly of all, this was the best way of determining whether Abu Hamza's supporters had any notion that a challenge to their control of the building was imminent. Other monitoring methods included phone calls to close contacts of the mosque occupiers, again on the basis that discreet enquiries might elicit news of any current issues inside the mosque that might bear upon their plans. All of which had been undertaken by the previous management prior to their abortive attempts to regain control but the difference was that it was now being done with greater skill and tradecraft.[122]

Thus every effort was made to prevent Abu Hamza's supporters from becoming aware of these confidential negotiations. Naturally after such a long time of exploiting a weak management regime at the mosque Abu Hamza's supporters had become confident in their own ability to monitor the situation closely. To be sure, had they become aware of plans to evict and exclude them they would have been inclined to consolidate their presence inside the building and potentially barricade themselves inside and resist any attempts to remove them.[123] This was precisely the kind of scenario that we identified as posing a threat to our plans and that required careful contingency planning to counter. During the course of these planning discussions the full extent of the partnership relationship became evident. Again one of the key MAB officials explains:

Working with the police and the other agencies was a good experience. We had confidence in their judgment and I think they came to respect ours. When they suggested reclaiming control of the mosque on a Friday we went away and thought about the implications. From a tactical point of view we thought it would be better to do it on a Saturday. We came back and explained our thinking on this point. They listened and agreed with us.[124]

Before proceeding to give an account of the actual eviction of Abu Hamza's supporters from the mosque on Saturday 5 February 2005 it will be helpful to examine the background of the MWH and MAB officials who executed it. That is the purpose of the next chapter.

5

FINSBURY PARK ISLAMISTS

I first visited officials at the MWH in November 2001 before the MCU was formally launched and before I met the trustees at the Finsbury Park Mosque. Although it was pouring with rain and I had no umbrella such was the close proximity of the building to an exit from Finsbury Park underground station that I barely got wet. It was very much a fact-finding visit to help formulate ideas about the way the MCU might best focus its attention. The visit was arranged by the same community police officer who introduced me to the trustees at the neighbouring Finsbury Park Mosque. She was one of several local police officers who had formed an exceptionally high regard for the skill and integrity of the management and staff at the MWH and at the allied MAB which had its offices in the same building. Indeed, she was the first person to suggest the common sense of what would finally transpire in February 2005: the key role of the MWH and the MAB in the removal of Abu Hamza and his supporters from the Finsbury Park Mosque.

After introductions I asked Fadi Itani, the manager then of the MWH, if Abu Hamza had ever sought to take control or exert influence at their centre. He replied that Abu Hamza and his close supporters had once approached the centre with a view to holding circles there but had been refused. I was left in little doubt that Abu Hamza and his hench-men would have found it difficult to intimidate officials at the MWH in the way they had done in the Finsbury Park Mosque on the other side of the railway. During the course of regular visits during 2002 I came to share my Islington police colleagues' positive assessment of the MWH and the MAB at 233 Seven Sisters Road as a centre of excellence in terms of constructive civic engagement and the provision of welfare services for local people. Itani and his colleagues also evinced the necessary confidence when seeking to tackle problems of the kind posed by Abu Hamza and his supporters. Later on I would be able to contrast this quality with its erosion among the Finsbury Park Mosque trustees where years of attrition with Abu Hamza had taken their toll.

The reclaiming of Finsbury Park Mosque from the *de facto* control of violent extremist supporters of Abu Hamza on 5 February 2005 is the single event that epitomises the outcome of partnership work between MCU officers and their Finsbury Park Islamist partners at 233 Seven Sisters Road (MWH and MAB). It is also an event that crystallises the arguments in opposition to the partnership. The Muslim partners consist of an identifiable group of Muslims who have had an important presence in the Finsbury Park neighbourhood for over thirty years. That presence became synonymous with a poorly repaired office building and outbuilding at 233 Seven Sisters Road that served as both a mosque and London headquarters for the MWH from 1977 onwards and later as the headquarters for the MAB as well. In fact their combined presence in Finsbury Park can be dated from 1975 when Muslim students purchased and occupied student accommodation at 86 Stapleton Hall Road to the east of Finsbury Park underground station.[1] The later MWH presence at 233 Seven Sisters Road continues today whereas the MAB office moved to 124 Harrowdene Road in North Wembley in 2005. Individuals who commenced this Muslim presence in Finsbury Park as students in the 1970s did so at a time before 'Islamist' had become a pejorative term but was then simply an indication of an active rather than passive regard for the politics many Muslims believed was inherent to their religion.[2] Generally speaking they remained sanguine about referring to themselves as Islamists throughout the study period even though the term had become a weapon in attacks against them by opponents who regarded them as sectarian and subversive.

Significantly, the Islamist presence in Finsbury Park pre-dates the opening of the Finsbury Park Mosque, a new and imposing purpose-built mosque at 7—11 St. Thomas Road opened in 1994. On that happy occasion Prince Charles was guest of honour yet only two years later the mosque came under the influence of a khatib[3] hired by the trustees to improve relations with local youth—Abu Hamza.[4] Between 1994 and 2004 there was barely any dialogue between officials at the

MWH and MAB and the mosque notwithstanding their close proximity and an offer of support from the former to their new neighbours. During the same period Abu Hamza ensured the mosque became known internationally as the UK's most vilified centre of violent extremism and al-Qaeda-inspired propaganda. MCU officers found a lack of neighbourly co-operation explicable:

Everywhere we went in London we found mosques close by each other where there was little or no contact. In Waltham Forest for instance it took a council meeting after the arrests [terrorist arrests regarding a conspiracy known as 'the airline plot'] in 2006 to introduce different mosque trustees to each other even though they had been in same area for over ten years.[5]

In my research study the most important data arises from interviews and participant observation with the Muslim partners themselves but valuable insights are also derived from interviews and observations with MCU and other MPS police officers and Muslim community representatives in Finsbury Park and further afield. An analysis of texts, most especially transcriptions of talks often delivered and recorded in Finsbury Park Mosque by street leader and al-Qaeda apologist Abu Hamza prove illuminating especially when contrasted with the views of his Islamist neighbours at 233 Seven Sisters Road. By asking the Muslim partners how they conceived the al-Qaeda threat to London, counter-terrorism policing, Muslim communities and the London partnerships my study repeated questions asked by MCU officers in their own assessment both prior to and after entering into a partnership with them. This link between the study's data analysis and a professional assessment by MCU officers is crucial because it helps to answer a central research question—how did the police and community partners conceive legitimacy and effectiveness in their partnership work? Just as prior experience is significant for MCU officers so valuable prior experience gained by Muslim partners in Finsbury Park was brought to bear during the period January 2002 to October 2007.

The Muslim partners had a presence in Finsbury Park that can be traced back to the 1960s and 1970s. Both the nascent MAB and the newly formed MWH chose Finsbury Park as a London base, the latter starting business in the capital as early as 1970. Both organisations would emerge in the 1990s and 2000s as leading UK Islamist centres of religious and political activity and after 2002 as key partners of the MCU. Throughout the 1970s and 1980s a small number of exiled and immigrant Arab Muslims from the Middle East and the Maghreb settled in the area. The leading figures amongst these émigré communities tended to be prominent figures in the Muslim Brotherhood in Egypt and its allied and affiliated groups in the Maghreb and Middle East. While many have since moved away from the immediate Finsbury Park neighbourhood most still live in adjoining North London boroughs.[6] Many, however, continued to travel to Friday jumma prayer in the prayer hall at the rear of the MWH as they did throughout the 1990s. Since February 2005 they also prayed at the Finsbury Park Mosque after they played a decisive role in reclaiming control of the mosque from Abu Hamza's supporters.[7]

By 1991 the MWH had become an established focal point for Arab Muslims in North London, especially those who supported or sympathised with the Muslim Brotherhood. As well as providing a traditional meeting place for Friday prayers and congregation thereafter it also became a recognised centre for support services that were greatly valued by Muslims newly arrived in the UK. The MWH established links with local councils, charities, voluntary services and police so as to help new arrivals acquire skills and training necessary to enhance their employment prospects and status as citizens. Typically a Muslim family arriving in the area from abroad would be able to get practical support from the centre and to be able to access the services and training most applicable in their cases. All of this was financed by charitable donations from members of their own community and undertaken in isolation from the work of the Finsbury Park Mosque that was situated just a short distance away—separated only by a railway bridge that carries express trains departing and arriving at King's Cross mainline station. Because the neighbouring Finsbury Park Mosque was run by and initially catered for Muslims with backgrounds in the Indian subcontinent the gap between the two establishments was at first quite pronounced.

As elsewhere in Muslim London it would take several decades to dissolve the cultural and religious differences that Muslims with different mother tongues and different religious understandings brought from their countries of origin. Ironically, it was the extremist Egyptian Islamist Abu Hamza—a West Londoner—who would by-pass the Muslims ensconced in the MWH and make a direct connection with the management of the Finsbury Park Mosque in the mid-1990s. It would then fall to the MWH and MAB to help their Muslim neighbours finally rid the mosque and the area of Abu Hamza's negative West London influence much later in 2005. Although it is therefore an arbitrary point from which to chart the development of the Finsbury Park Arab Islamist community (alongside its Indian sub-continent Muslim neighbours), 1991 is an appropriate date given that it marks the beginning of the period when the immigrant Muslim community began to put down roots in the area, raising families that would grow up to be British Muslims as opposed to immigrant Muslims. It is also a date that marks a concerted effort by its leading figures to expand a programme of community support and provision that was modelled on their experience to date in the UK and also their prior experience abroad. That experience was largely, although not exclusively, modelled on and connected to the activities of the Muslim Brotherhood in the Middle East and countries in the Maghreb.

When asked why Finsbury Park was first chosen as a venue interviewees recalled that it was simply a case that the area had the advantage of being a fifteen-minute tube journey from central London and it was also one of the few parts of London where the less affluent could afford to rent property to live and work. The premises at 233 Seven Sisters Road that the MWH rented to use for prayer and administration were therefore extremely cheap. Faulty radiators, water leaking through the roof and the noise of the adjacent railway and main road provided a constant reminder of the venue's shortcomings—especially so for émigrés used to the warmer climes of the Middle East and North Africa. Nevertheless, the advantages of operating in a country where they were free to live according to their understanding of Islam for the first time in their lives provided an incentive:

Some of us whose families had been evicted from our homes in Palestine had grown up in exile and in refugee camps in Jordan, Lebanon and Kuwait where we would be under the constant surveillance of the Muhabarat.[8] Sometimes family members were picked up and held for months at a time.... Finsbury Park was sometimes wet and cold but we experienced freedom for the first time.[9]

That sense of freedom from intrusive security attention was even more pronounced for Islamists who had experienced torture at the hands of security services and police in countries such as Egypt, Algeria and Tunisia.[10] This escape from torture helps establish London as an important centre of refuge for exiled political activists of all kinds over a long period. Being used to providing support for political refugees who faced ongoing threats of state-sponsored political violence in

115

London as part of our routine MPSB duties we were conscious of the important role of London as a safe haven from repression and violence abroad. This was the experience that made me concerned once the war on terror necessitated the government forging close ties with the security services of the very same despotic regimes many of our new Islamist partners had escaped from. I would become even more alarmed when the government adopted so much of Melanie Phillips' account of Islamist London as *Londonistan*—an enemy of Britain instead of the partner I proposed.[11]

Typically, to illustrate, a middle-aged North African who still suffers acute pain and disability from the torture that police in his home country inflicted on him when he was a young and ardent political activist, found London a safe haven in both the physical and psychological sense.[12] His only crime as a young adult was to believe that the Muslim country where he grew up in North Africa should be ruled according to Islam. For expressing such a view within the imperfect sanctity of a university he was forced to endure the removal of flesh and the rupture of vertebrae by security officials highly practiced in the clinical art of maximising pain and injury.[13] Another North African exile recalls how his torturer would break off from his work to pray and eat before returning to the clinical task in hand.[14] Yet another evokes the same sense of torture as a routine business when recalling how the police officer who had inflicted significant pain and injury on him subsequently joked with him that it was not personal, that he (the torturer) would happily carry out the same activity on his behalf (the victim) if the victim ever came to power, as an Islamist.[15] This attitude is evidence of systematic torture that has simply become a habitual practice, not always pretending to have the purpose of eliciting guarded information but merely the necessary response of a dictatorship to any nascent challenge to its authority. That at any rate was the familiar method of policing against which members of the Metropolitan Police would be compared by the Islamists in their new North London home.[16]

Once released from prison the physical and psychological impact of the torture that had been inflicted on some of the London émigrés ensured that the subsequent interactions they had with police officers in their home countries were imbued with menace and anxiety.[17] Although they had become used to the routine production of identification papers and questioning about their movements before their arrests these same interruptions to their pedestrian movements slowly became intolerable. One recalls how he felt physically sick when he found himself in the same café as his torturer.[18] Although they had been told that the police and security services in London did not resort to such tactics they were surprised to find just how respectful the new police were towards them. To be able to explain the same political views that had led to their torture to MPSB police officers who instead took a genuine interest in their safety represented a significant transformation in their fortunes. Typically, for one interviewee, to be treated fairly and decently after such degrading and humiliating treatment at the hands of police in their native countries served as a spur to their subsequent partnership with the MCU:

When I first arrive at Heathrow Airport in 1985 and saw a police officer wearing a turban I was baffled and pleasantly surprised—I didn't know he was a Sikh. In Egypt police never wore beards because any sign of religious adherence was actively discouraged. It was widely understood that to get on in the police and government you had to drink alcohol and generally avoid the impression of being a practicing Muslim. My first positive impressions of London police were confirmed when I got to know the police in Finsbury Park. Most times they were always genuinely courteous.[19]

Broadly speaking, getting used to their new surroundings was a positive experience for the émigrés. Although the lack of local community spirit was apparent:

We came to like Finsbury Park. It was a poor area made up of many different nationalities and we were not looked at as being different. Some of us first arrived when we were students and we had rooms in Stroud Green Road. I found many of the people who had lived in the area all their lives to be very friendly. But actually at first what surprised me was how isolated most people were. Lots of young working people living in bed-sits and council flats and not having much sense of community. This was a big contrast for those of us who had grown up in tight knit family oriented Muslim communities abroad.[20]

For new arrivals and local police officers Islington is a borough of two halves: the affluent southern half where Tony Blair lived before he became Prime Minister in 1997 and the poorer northern half that includes the MWH and Finsbury Park Mosque. One community police officer who first had dealings with the MWH in the 1990s recalls how impressed he was by their sense of civic duty:

Really nice people. Always very respectful and helpful. I soon got to know them really well and considered them among my most reliable contacts. They were always prepared to help with routine policing issues. Once we needed to keep observation on nearby premises being used to supply crack cocaine and the management let us use one of their rooms for two weeks without any problems. Of course once we started to get problems with Abu Hamza and his crowd they were always prepared to help. Unfortunately, the old management at the Finsbury Park Mosque were never willing to accept help. Otherwise Hamza and his thugs would have got sorted out much sooner I'm sure.[21]

Another police officer who served as a detective in the Finsbury Park area in the 1990s recalls how the Arab Islamist management of the MWH played a supportive role in a street robbery case where a suspect wrongly sought to use the centre as an alibi:

I was impressed with the authority the Muslim Welfare House managers had. At one meeting I explained to them that the suspect in this case was a member of a violent gang that might threaten them if they gave evidence against him. They took it seriously but did not hesitate for one minute to help the police. This was unusual to say the least. We had a spate of bad cases connected to this gang and it was great to find potential witnesses who would help us. Later on I had another case where one of their staff helped on an identity parade. And another one where they helped translate some Arabic documents for me. That's what they were like.[22]

In more general conversations with police officers in canteens at Holloway Road and Islington police stations a picture emerged of the MWH as a community centre that stood out as model of excellence in a part of the borough where crime and disorder problems often ran high.[23] By the end of the period under review one community police officer had forged particularly close links with MWH and her liaison work resulted in police officers taking part in training days for Muslim youth who were undergoing courses in learning skills to enhance their employment prospects and citizenship awareness.[24] Long before 9/11 and 7/7 the MWH, an Islamist centre just a stone's throw from the notorious Finsbury Park Mosque, was training Muslim youth to be fit and useful British citizens who would respect the law and work productively with the police and local social services. As their quietly effective work became more widely known, government representatives would visit the Islamist management to acknowledge their major contribution in an area that was otherwise blighted with anti-social behaviour.[25]

Finsbury Park sits at the intersection of three North London boroughs; Islington, Haringey and Hackney. However, the bulk of the neighbourhood is located within Islington and more specifically Islington North—the UK's smallest yet most densely populated voting constituency.[26] A decade before 9/11 the Finsbury Park Islamists cemented what would prove to be a long and productive relationship with their local MP, Jeremy Corbyn who had been elected to parliament in 1987.[27] For those Islamists with traumatic family backgrounds in the West Bank and Gaza it was enormously reassuring to find that an MP who was an ardent campaigner on behalf of the Palestinian cause represented them.[28] More generally, having come from exile in countries where political protests and political campaigning was often heavily curtailed they were excited to find that they were able to express their concerns about Israel's policy towards Palestine without fear of reprisals and in company with British allies like the Palestine Solidarity Campaign (PSC) introduced to them by Corbyn.[29] PSC was founded in London in 1982 and supported 'the right of the Palestinian people to self-determination' and called 'for an end to the Israeli occupation of the West Bank, East Jerusalem and Gaza' and advocated for 'Palestinians' civil, political and human rights, in accordance with international law'.[30] As they began to establish Finsbury Park as their London hub the Islamist émigré community was delighted to affiliate itself to a campaign that argued that 'the suffering of the Palestinians will not end unless there is a just and lasting resolution of the conflict' and hence 'supports the Palestinians' legitimate right to resist, by focusing on political campaigning and educational awareness raising'.[31] Significantly this empathy with the Palestinian cause laid the groundwork for later collaborations that culminated in the Stop The War (STW) campaign.[32]

Whereas Andrew Murray and Lindsey German's history of the STW movement highlights the commencement of partnership work with MAB in 2002[33] it is important to note that a coalition between Finsbury Park Islamists and left-wing activists pre-dates this high-profile venture by several years in the form of *ad hoc* pro-Palestinian campaign activity work where Corbyn served as an interlocutor.[34] This is significant because the extent to which Islamists generally have been integrated into an important aspect of traditional London protest activity is poorly understood. The extent to which prominent Islamists such as Mohamed Sawalha, Azzam Tamimi and Anas Altikriti became familiar and comfortable with left-wing London politics helps explain their willingness to join the STW coalition in 2002.[35] It also helps to explain how important contacts had already been made so as to facilitate strong partnership activity with Ken Livingstone and the Greater London Authority when he became London mayor in 2000. As with

119

Corbyn, Livingstone had been a staunch campaigner on behalf of the Palestinian cause from the 1970s onwards.[36] While for most politicians leading Finsbury Park Islamists Azzam Tamimi and Mohamed Sawalha were beyond the pale because of their reported links to Hamas,[37] for Livingstone and Corbyn that was no bar to engagement. For them the contours of the Palestinian case were analogous to the republican Northern Ireland case and the African National Congress (ANC) struggle against apartheid in South Africa, which were both campaigns they had been active in for a number of years.[38]

In August 2009 the extremist Islamist group HT was typically quick to seize on comments made by David Miliband, the British Foreign Secretary, in a BBC radio interview in which he was understood to retrospectively license terrorism committed by the ANC.[39] While talking about the life of Joe Slovo, a member of the armed wing of the ANC in apartheid South Africa Milliband was asked if there were circumstances in which terrorism was the right response.[40] After consideration, he replied that there were circumstances in which terrorism was justifiable and effective.[41] HT spokesman Taji Mustafa said the comments showed 'a spectacular double standard' coming from a British Foreign Secretary, 'who condemns Muslims in Palestine who suffer under the apartheid Israeli occupation'.[42] 'If a Muslim had made similar comments about resisting occupation', Mustafa continued, 'they may have found themselves arrested under anti-terror laws made by Mr Miliband's government against the glorification of terrorism'.[43] While Mustafa's immediate concern was to bolster membership and support for his fringe organisation his penetrating analysis exactly matched the narrative repeated endlessly for two decades on the streets of Muslim London by Abu Hamza and his cohorts. Not, to be clear, the notion of a British double standard that was on the streets in any event—but rather the al-Qaeda narrative that licensed reciprocal terrorism against Britain, whereas for HT it helped license abstention from British politics.

In contrast, for the Finsbury Park Islamists at 233 Seven Sisters Road the double standard prompted closer engagement in British politics following the path of Corbyn and Livingstone. Moreover, for old Labour politicians like Corbyn and Livingstone, being politically active had always meant traipsing the streets of central London on Saturdays and Sundays on demonstrations against political oppression whether in Palestine, South Africa, Northern Ireland or South America. Along with other familiar campaigners like Tony Benn and George Galloway they were isolated figures during the Thatcher years but would become ever more out of kilter with the new Labour government of Tony Blair first elected in 1997. Indeed, it would be hard to present a greater contrast of political behaviour within the same party than on a typical weekend in 2003 when the Prime Minister and his inner circle were planning the UK's contribution to the 'war on terror' at Chequers and Corbyn, Livingstone and Tony Benn were marching down the Edgware Road to speak in Hyde Park against it.

Not that a willingness to march through London on cold, wet winter weekends was ever confined to the Labour Party. This after all is an arena where fringe groups like the Socialist Workers Party (SWP) and the Revolutionary Communist Party (RCP) rubbed shoulders with *ad hoc* campaigning groups dedicated to single issues. Betty Hunter, a stalwart PSC activist, epitomises the dedication that prompts attendance at countless demonstrations and pickets in support of a cause that attracts neither high-profile media attention nor any sense of political traction. However, Palestinians themselves were impressed to find dedicated supporters willing to stand shoulder to shoulder with them.[44] Thus, important links were made that again introduced Finsbury Park Islamists to left-wing activism.[45] Notwithstanding the religious imperative that guided the Islamists' activity—and which was generally absent in street level left-wing London politics—a shared belief in social justice became a shared focus and a point around which trust could be built.[46] The presence in London of powerful Islamist voices in favour of democracy of the kind that old Labour politicians related to was of great significance. For instance, like many of his Islamist supporters, Sheikh Rachid Ghannouchi had been forced to leave Tunisia and had been granted residence in the UK.[47] His analysis of world politics was little different from Jeremy Corbyn's and helps illustrate how a bond grew between the two groups. It was no co-incidence that it was Azzam Tamimi's biography of Ghannouchi that introduced several old Labour activists to his work.[48] In fact the book was based on Tamimi's PhD thesis, and also served to introduce Labour and other politicians and activists to a wide range of Islamist thinking via his centre, the Institute for Islamic Political Thought.[49]

Undoubtedly the most contentious area of agreement between the Finsbury Park Islamists and their new left-wing London allies was that part of their political analysis that dealt with US support for Israel.[50]

There was complete agreement that Zionist influence in the US was determined to paint Islamism as a threat to US interests, sufficient to replace communism after the end of the cold war. Ghannouchi cites as an example the visit of former Israeli Prime Minister Yitzhak Rabin to Washington in the early 1990s:

During that visit, Rabin demanded that the United States support Israel in its war against the Islamists, 'the enemies of peace, who threaten the regimes of Algeria, Egypt, Tunisia, and other countries in the region.... The Arab world and the entire world will pay dearly if this Islamic cancer is not stopped.... Today we the Israelis truly stand in the firing line against fundamentalist Islam. We demand all states and nations to focus their attention on this huge threat inherent in Islamic fundamentalism'.[51]

This mutual view of the Islamist cause being undermined throughout the 1990s by a powerful alliance of Zionist support within the US and Israel was the basis for agreement on wider initiatives that would culminate in the STW. It was also the basis for partnership work that was generally carried out under the banner of tackling Islamophobia.[52] Increasingly throughout the 1990s London Muslims from many different backgrounds could unite on the common ground of shared experiences of anti-Muslim sentiment. This in turn led to a sharing of memories of important events from their respective communities' different colonial pasts.[53] When Newham Muslims with families in Kashmir listened to Finsbury Park Muslims with families in the West Bank and Gaza there was an inevitable and shared empathy based on a sense of political grievance. This process acknowledges that 'senses of injustice and perceptions of agency' emanate from a 'repertoire of myths, memories and symbols' that can be 'a causal factor in the transformation and radicalisation of collective political action'.[54] Indeed, Jonathan Githens-Mazer's model of social movement radicalisation in an Irish republican context is especially pertinent in Finsbury Park where Jeremy Corbyn was well qualified to make a link between Irish republican and Arab Islamist experience of colonialist violence and oppression.[55] Moreover, academic and popular notions of politically active campaigning groups like MAB as the smiling faces of a concerted Islamist attempt to take control of Europe[56] become difficult to sustain when examined at close quarters. HT might aspire to such success but like their secular counterparts the SWP they have little appetite, skill or resources to convert aspiration into reality.[57]

During 2002 the top floor of 233 Seven Sisters Road became a hub of political protest activity that united Muslims and non-Muslims. As

Richard Phillips' research highlights MAB became well known throughout Muslim communities as a result of its work in the STW coalition.[58]
Most notably MAB organisers played a major role in galvanising
unprecedented Muslim participation in London's largest modern demonstration on Saturday, 15 February 2003.[59] Muslims from a range of
backgrounds joined with Campaign for Nuclear Disarmament activists
and hundreds of thousands from 'middle England' to produce a peaceful and integrated demonstration against the war in Iraq. Fuad Nahdi
captures the hugely positive impact the event had on social cohesion:

On February 15th Britain came together like at no other time in contemporary
history. Pakistani women shared pakoras and cucumber sandwiches with women
from the shires in the biggest anti-war march ever—a postcard image of race
relations that no Home Office initiative could ever dream of achieving.[60]

Regrettably, Nahdi noted, the demonstration was ignored in Westminster and the ensuing war in Iraq had a hugely damaging impact on
social cohesion. By April 'Britain's 1.6 million Muslims [were] living
on a diet of death, hypocrisy and neglect' that was 'traumatising and
radicalising an entire generation':[61]

Mosques up and down the country are for peace, but also for the defeat of the
invading coalition forces. And—having watched on satellite TV the images of
Iraqi civilian casualties—nobody is horrified by the suicide attack by an Iraqi.
While the outcome of the war in Iraq remains uncertain, there is little hope in
the fight for the hearts, minds and loyalty of British Muslims. While the anti-
war Ken Livingstone is invited to mosques, senior government ministers now
struggle to get picture opportunities with credible grassroots Muslim groups.[62]

In consequence the MAB office was a hive of activity working around
the clock galvanising and harnessing Muslim community anger positively and constructively.[63] However, a follow-up demonstration on Saturday 22 March, the day US troops advanced towards Baghdad, saw a
smaller more sombre anti-war march through central London to Hyde
Park—200,000 was still an impressive figure for a short-notice event.
Downstairs on the first floor MWH colleagues reported that Abu
Hamza and his supporters had been rebuffed in their attempts to spread
their violent messages from the Finsbury Park Mosque into the MWH.[64]
Organising national peaceful protests and countering violent extremism
locally characterised work at 233 Seven Sisters Road and provided a
solid basis for partnership work with MCU police officers.

Whereas trustees at the Finsbury Park Mosque did not really understand the nature of Abu Hamza's politics, our new partners at the

123

MWH and MAB were expert interpreters of his prodigious recordings which his supporters circulated through their networks around Britain. Many of the tapes were recorded in his office on the first floor of the mosque. Reference to over a hundred hours of Abu Hamza's recorded talks and to interviews with members of his audiences confirms the recurring nature of his theme of a Muslim duty to undertake jihad against the USA and against Israel. Talks and welfare support were only part of a process that would culminate in outdoor training exercises where group bonding could develop, just as it would be intended to do in the military. As Marc Sageman has suggested the business of developing a strong 'in-group' identity is crucial but in Abu Hamza's Finsbury Park circles it was a process that benefitted from being organic, unstructured and flexible. Interestingly, on this point, an interviewee with first-hand experience of Hamza's circles recalls how outdoor training sessions were intended to separate young men with real potential to endure hardships from those who were intimately attached to their home comforts.[65] Again a phenomena familiar to army recruit training officers and one that also militates against the applicability of the notion of 'self-radicalisation' in a terrorist context.

The same witness speaks to Abu Hamza's belief that he was fighting a world Zionist conspiracy. Terrorist attacks might only be symbolic but they were hugely important in propaganda terms, to encourage Muslims to believe that they were not powerless, and to show the Jewish American enemy that Islam would fight back. Abu Hamza was therefore especially pleased to refer his young supporters in private to the model of what was then the only attack on the WTC in 1993. In public he would confine his comments to support for the blind Sheikh Omar who was imprisoned in the USA. Like Osama bin Laden he was fascinated by the idea that the enemy could be hurt financially by terrorism. Implicit in his thinking appeared to be the negative stereotype of the Jew as a moneylender to the Christian who could be damaged by financial ruin. Had he known that his Islamist neighbours at the MWH were engaged in inter-faith dialogue with Christian and Jewish leaders he would have happily used such information as ammunition in an effort to undermine their credibility with youth audiences.[66]

In contrast, notwithstanding their unflinching criticism of Israel's policy towards Palestinians the Finsbury Park Islamists were acutely aware of a need to establish good relations with all their London neighbours.[67] This included the orthodox Jewish community at nearby

Stamford Hill and the wider Jewish community in North and East London. When police reported to the MWH that attacks had taken place at a local Jewish cemetery they were anxious to help.[68] It struck them that Islamophobic attacks on Muslims and anti-Semitic attacks on Jews might provide a platform for joint action and closer co-operation.[69] That view was shared by police who sought to broker meetings on that very theme. In the event the perception in some Jewish communities that the MWH was stridently anti-Semitic itself proved a handicap.[70] However, the very idea of such co-operation was intolerable to Abu Hamza whose supporters were reasonably suspected of having been involved in attacks of this kind.[71] From Abu Hamza's perspective the divide between Muslims and non-Muslims was insurmountable. It provided the license for Muslims to attack non-Muslims:

If anybody ask you now outside the difference between Muslim blood and non-Muslim blood you will not know. ....And shall I tell you ...the bottom line of the Muslim blood that it is preserved that it is protected. The Muslim blood to start with is protected by Allah (SWT) untouchable. This is the bottom line just the start line of Muslim blood the Muslim owner the Muslim money. And the starting point of the *kafir* blood or the apostate that their blood is allowed and sometime it is a must to go and get it. And their owner is for everybody who can get it and their money is for whoever can get it, if there is no Islamic State. If there is an Islamic State then it becomes the duty to make sure their money is distributed among the believers that their women are distributed amongst the believers and their blood is spilt. This is clear, this is Islam. You don't like it you leave Islam.[72]

During the course of participant observation key figures in the Finsbury Park Islamist firmament discussed this Abu Hamza's comment in some detail.[73] Apart from commenting on his poor grasp of Islamic scholarship they expressed deep concern at his unscrupulous exploitation of young audiences, many of whom would be susceptible to his purpose of facilitating al-Qaeda recruitment and support.[74] More generally, however, the talk reminded them that a trickle of young people had come to them at the MWH after attending Abu Hamza's talks and that they were able to disabuse them of his teachings. Not that it was an easy process. Invariably Palestinians themselves would be crucial in explaining that legitimate lawful protest activity was the way to help— not to follow Hamza's violent route map. They were able to point to clear cases where their Islamist approach served to act as a countermanding influence to Abu Hamza's. In doing so they adopted a different approach to their salafi counterparts at the Brixton Mosque (see

Brixton, Part Three) relying less on a religious corrective and more on a legitimate outlet for expression of political grievance. What they shared with their Brixton brothers was a high level of street credibility. Both groups enjoyed a reputation for physical presence; to be willing and able to stand up to the bullying tactics employed by supporters of Abu Hamza, Abdullah el Faisal and Abu Qatada. This was, according to MCU officers, absolutely vital.[75]

A former Lebanese citizen took over as director of the MWH in 2000 and played a key role in introducing MCU officers to the centre's work during 2002. The new director inherited a centre that had established a thoroughly deserved reputation for integrity and responsibility in a challenging neighbourhood.[76] It would, however, be fair to say that he displayed the kind of flair and business skills that took the centre onto a more professional level thereafter.[77] In tandem with the MWH national director, the local director developed a strategy that saw increased liaison with the local council and other local voluntary agencies.[78] The centre became a resource more for the borough than purely for the Arab Muslim community alone. This change of management also marked the first serious discussions between the MWH and the management of Finsbury Park Mosque with a view to helping the mosque tackle ongoing problems posed by Abu Hamza and his supporters. In 2002 the MAB joined MWH at 233 Seven Sisters Road by making use of three offices on the top floor. Closely inter-related in terms of membership both groups shared a strong attachment to charitable work. MCU officers became regular visitors to the address and got to know management and staff very well at both offices.[79] We were also able to see how much local community work MWH staff did for the local community, noting an open-door policy that allowed local people to attend and receive all the kind of advice that might be dispensed at a Citizen Advice Bureau.[80]

MCU officers became regular contributors to citizenship programmes at the MWH where they were able to use police and council contacts to help local citizens with problems.[81] Transparent too, centre staff were pleased to announce that they were working closely with the MCU and the MSF to address several community concerns.[82] Issues included hate crimes often involving attacks on women where typically the victim would have her hijab violently pulled off while travelling on a bus or in another public place.[83] In 2002 this made many Muslim women in Finsbury Park and other parts of London fearful and hesitant to use public transport and to keep their public outings to a minimum.[84] This concern to support victims of hate crime became characteristic of the MCU approach—seemingly a long way from conventional counter-terrorism yet wholly familiar to experienced MPSB officers who had taken part in similar ventures in Brixton and Tottenham in the wake of the Brixton riots in 1981 and the Broadwater Farm riot in 1985.[85] Between 2002 and 2007 MCU officers worked closely with local community police officers to help combat the influence of activists such as Abu Hamza and his supporters at the Finsbury Park Mosque, just as they had done as MPSB officers in respect of small pockets of violent political extremism in Brixton in 1981–83 and Tottenham in 1985–87.[86] What each scenario had in common was the sense that genuine local grievances against police and government provided fertile soil for violent extremists who wanted to drive a wedge between police and minority communities.[87] Although Abu Hamza was different in that he would use what he claimed to be Islamic license for keeping the community at odds with the authorities his tactics and purpose were no different to street leaders of small groups of anarchists and revolutionary communists who enjoyed brief local status in the 1980s and 1990s.[88]

Again this was an area where MCU officers ignored prevailing notions of an 'exceptional al-Qaeda threat' and 'new terrorism' and instead called on prior MPSB experience to help assess a complex situation in Finsbury Park just as they did in Brixton.[89] Opposite the MWH in Seven Sisters Road was a gloomy, cavernous, rundown public house the *Sir George Robey* where a decade earlier individuals collected money for PIRA, at that time a common occurrence at several other pubs in the neighbourhood as well.[90] Then MCU officers learnt to distinguish illegal financial support for terrorism of this kind from legitimate fundraising activity that took place by groups such as the Troops Out Movement and various prisoner support organisations.[91] It was reasonably well understood that while PIRA might seek to exploit lawful organisations like the Troops Out Movement that shared some of their political aims if not their methods and that it was lazy and generally counter-productive to conflate one with the other.[92] However, in practice, it was often difficult to disentangle lawful from unlawful. Junior MPSB officers arrived at a better understanding of how to do so by learning complex intelligence assessment skills from senior colleagues in ways that Flyvbjerg, Kenney and Hamm describe as necessary to expert learning.[93] Significantly much of this learning took place in communities, often talking to community contacts in pubs and cafes, and relied less exclusively on covert human and technical intelligence than would become the case in the war on terror.[94] It was a learning process where the importance of local community context was axiomatic. As one MPSB interviewee noted, 'you didn't get a course certificate at the end of it'. Office-based intelligence analysts and other office-based staff had key support roles to play as well but the 'view from the street' was always afforded precedence—not least because it was key to accurate community impact assessments that went hand in glove with effective and legitimate counter-terrorism operations.[95]

MCU officers attending meetings at the MWH and MAB offices in 2002 were used to attending community meetings while being privy to current ongoing operational intelligence concerning the al-Qaeda terrorist threat in London and beyond.[96] Thus for instance if an MCU officer was aware of a car index number that was of current interest in a local operational context and he happened to see it parked in a nearby street on his way to a meeting at 233 Seven Sisters Road he would be able to report the sighting immediately by mobile phone to colleagues. None of which impacted directly or indirectly on the MCU officer's meetings but which illustrates the nature of local street-focused MPSB work. It was also an approach that would subsequently enable MCU officers to show photographs of terrorist suspects to community contacts in an effort to secure identifications. Second nature to MPSB officers this was an approach to intelligence gathering that was alien to detectives new to counter-terrorism intelligence gathering who came from a different policing culture where only strictly controlled relationships with informants were permissible.[97]

After a series of corruption cases mainstream CID officers had come to accept new regulations aimed at ensuring relationships with criminal informants were more tightly controlled and did not ever rely on personal relationships. The same regulations governed counter-terrorism informants which was an added reason why MCU officers differentiated their partnership work from the necessary and vital business of 'source handling' (i.e. running informants). For MCU officers effective relationships with representatives of community organisations like the MWH and MAB relied wholly on personal relationships and patient trust building that was antithetical to source handling but considered essential by Thomas and Inkson to establish cross-cultural partnerships.[98]

A typical MCU meeting with three community contacts and two police officers discussing local and international politics might often be viewed as wasteful from a mainstream CID vantage point. The MPSB notion of building trust as a precursor to gaining intelligence was increasingly out of kilter with a harder more systematic approach to intelligence gathering. In addition, an MPSB management notion of trusting officers to have the skills and experience not to inadvertently let slip operational intelligence to community contacts was challenged by new managers suspicious of so much autonomy being granted to officers and the risks that went with such practice. Thus MCU officers in Finsbury Park in 2002 found themselves working at the end of one culture of counter-terrorism policing and the beginning of another that was far more risk averse.[99]

In 2002 utilising prior experience MCU officers began to assess two very different kinds of fundraising in Finsbury Park.[100] Dealing in larger sums than now passed over the counter in the *Sir George Robey* opposite, MWH staff could rely on generous responses to charitable appeals that took place according to the strict dictates of the Islamic calendar.[101] Thus, all members of the MWH and MAB communities made *zakat* payments on a scale determined by their incomes and financial assets as elsewhere in practising Muslim London.[102] Not least because of a significant Palestinian presence much *zakat* money was earmarked for support of Palestinians suffering hardship in the occupied territories and in refugee camps in Jordan, Lebanon and more widely.[103] MCU officers anticipated scope for exploitation by terrorists but over a period of time came to be impressed with the efficiency of MWH and MAB fundraising in this arena.[104]

This positive assessment is important when considering the legitimacy of the MCU partnership in Finsbury Park. Allegations that Islamist charities often serve as a cover for terrorist support have become deeply embedded in media and academic thinking.[105] To be sure, as Jude McCulloch and Sharon Pickering highlight in an article that sits in the emerging critical studies on terrorism school, 'measures targeted at the financing of terrorism gained great momentum' after 9/11.[106] In fact, as they recall, Bush's 'first strike on the global terror network' shortly after 9/11 'involved freezing assets and blocking financial transactions of those allegedly involved in terrorism'.[107] Thus combating the financing of terrorism became a 'key tool in the war on terror' that led to at least one optimistic assessment that the war on terror might be 'won by the destruction of cheque books instead of on the battle-field'.[108] Ehrenfeld illustrates a prevalent view when he suggests that 'money is often provided to terrorists through legitimate businesses and institutions such as NGOs or even international aid organisations and through various charities'.[109] It is not, however, necessary to endorse McCulloch and Pickering's assessment that 'the suppressing of financing of terrorism measures' are 'reminiscent of the coercive strat-egies of an earlier colonial period' to acknowledge that it is a field where valuable community work like that carried out at MWH can too easily be conflated with unlawful activity in support of terrorism.[110]

The same was true just five miles away in an old warehouse in Crick-lewood Lane, in a similar state of disrepair to 233 Seven Sisters Road, that served as the headquarters for the Palestinian charity Interpal, a prime beneficiary of *zakat*[111] collections at the MWH and across Mus-lim London. Many Muslim Londoners held Interpal in high regard and were deeply troubled when the charity was regularly singled out for criticism in the media as being linked to terrorism.[112] MCU officers first met Interpal officials at their office in 2002 when they were the subject of death threats and criminal damage to their office.[113] Like leaders in MAB, Interpal's indefatigable leader Abu Yusef, otherwise Essam Mustafa, had a family background in Palestine and then in exile that inevitably meant he knew several individuals that would grow up to become members of Hamas.[114] Rather than see this kind of association in a negative light MCU officers observed the positive value of passion-ate advocates of support for Palestinians like Abu Yusef who had expe-rienced family losses at the hands of Israeli military action.[115] When Abu Yusef denied the right of Abu Hamza and other street leaders to licence al-Qaeda attacks against the UK because of support for Israel it carried weight in the same audiences targeted by Abu Hamza.[116] In making this assessment MCU officers were following recognised approaches in other areas of crime prevention where effective voices needed street credibility.[117]

Observing the role of Interpal, MWH, MAB and other Muslim char-ities in London MCU officers became aware of a fallacy in accounts that suggested *zakat* money might end up in Hamas' hands notwith-standing the best efforts of British charities.[118] What, MCU officers asked, would the outcome be if Interpal and similar charities were shut down? Firstly, MCU officers cautioned, Muslim community confidence would be shaken.[119] Secondly, Abu Hamza and his followers would win more support for their claim that they were the better recipients of *zakat* for donors who wanted their money to reach victims without red tape. As far as possible therefore MCU officers worked closely with Interpal to ensure that their important work was not undermined by accusations of terrorist funding that were premised more on 'guilt by association' than any hard evidence of malpractice. This involved multi-agency partnership work not least with the Charity Commission that resulted in a fair and penetrating assessment of Interpal's legitimacy. It also enabled MCU officers to observe the scrupulous nature of Interpal and other Muslim charities' book-keeping for themselves. As they became aware of the significant extent to which al-Qaeda influence in London was predicated on widespread community empathy with the plight of Palestinians in the West Bank, Gaza and the refugee camps, MCU officers assessed that Interpal and other charities were a valuable and legitimate conduit whereby Muslims discharged their religious obligations that consequently offered no vacuum for Abu Hamza and others to exploit. By virtue of their close links this also validated *zakat* collections at the MWH and elsewhere in London from which Interpal and the victims it supported benefitted.[120]

I considered that many beneficiaries of Interpal aid (and indirectly aid from the MWH) would be the children, siblings, parents, relatives, friends and associates of Hamas members. I took the view that humanitarian support of families in conflict zones was a necessary precursor to conflict resolution. In London I was equally keen to encourage police colleagues to limit the adverse impact of terrorist arrests and searches on innocent family members because by so doing it would reduce potential grievances for Abu Hamza and others to exploit. In the same way sensitive family support would, I assessed, also facilitate a better understanding of the context of the offences being investigated. Most importantly of all, I assessed, if police conducted anti-terrorism operations in consultation with the MSF (of which the MWH was a leading member) then when they were carried out well MWH and other members could demonstrate the value of working in partnership with police to their communities. When, however, counter-terrorism operations were perceived to be disproportionate or ill-conceived then partnership with police would be questioned, especially by youth communities who were at high risk of stop and search policing measures that would often have an alienating effect.

Andrew Hind, Chief Executive of the Charity Commission, concluded the most recent favourable review of Interpal by noting that 'charities working in high-risk situations make a hugely important contribution to communities in desperate need'.[121] 'The risks and challenges involved in these areas' he adds, 'require difficult and often finely-balanced judgments by charity trustees, as well as a greater effort in the development, implementation and monitoring of their humanitarian work'.[122] This and other positive reports from the Charity Commission helped balance the adverse impact of a decision in 2003 by the US Treasury to include Interpal in a list of charities with links to terrorism, specifically that it aided Hamas.[123] The publication of the US Treasury list led to Interpal's assets being frozen and an investigation by the Charity Commission that cleared Interpal of any illegal activities. When the Board of Deputies of British Jews repeated the allegation Interpal issued civil proceedings and following an out-of-court settlement the Board of Deputies apologised for referring to 'terrorist organisations such as Hamas and Interpal' and made clear that it 'should not have described Interpal in this way'.[124] However critics of Interpal insist that a series of validations by the Charity Commission are superficial and poorly focused.[125]

In contrast MCU officers viewed partnerships with Muslim charities like Interpal and the MWH as having the added benefit of undermining violent extremists like Abu Hamza who were desperate to convince Muslim Londoners that police and government agencies were enemies and never potential partners.[126] For Abu Hamza's purposes, if the UK adopted Daniel Pipes' recommended approach to the issue of *Zakat*, al-Qaeda's recruitment prospects would have increased dramatically.[127] For the majority of academics researching the issue from a top-down vantage point there remained a tendency to conflate all Islamist charitable work with terrorism. Thus, in one of the better argued accounts in this canon Shawn Teresa Flanagan posits the notion that the kind of 'ties that unite diaspora communities' (presumably like the ones represented by the MWH and MAB) 'not only compel them to become involved in charitable activities that affect other members of their community, but often to become involved in contentious politics'.[128] 'In many cases terrorist organisations use charitable service provision' she continues 'as a tool to move community members in a rightward direction along this continuum of acceptance', a view that is supported by a 'number of scholarly articles and media accounts'.[129] In contrast, on the streets of Finsbury Park, Abu Hamza and his supporters were in no doubt that Interpal, MWH and MAB seriously inhibited their efforts to collect money for operations and activities inspired by al-Qaeda.

It is difficult to quantify just how small a percentage of Islamic charitable activity in the UK would be of any operational interest to counter-terrorism policing but it is unlikely to be any more than the small amount of criminal interest that surrounds the entire edifice of UK charitable activity.[130] That is to put Flanagan's concerns into perspective. The overwhelming amount of Islamic charitable activity in the UK—as exemplified by Interpal, MAB and MWH's contributions—has been as free from criminal activity as any other area overseen by the Charity Commission, yet singularly stigmatised by academics, think-tanks and journalists.[131] Flanagan's single narrative really does obscure the reality on the ground:

Much political violence originates from the fact that groups are excluded from political and social participation in mainstream society. Interestingly, charity by minority groups is often motivated by similar exclusion.[132]

On the contrary, there has been no sign of exclusion in the overwhelming majority of cases that MCU officers came into contact with, not least Interpal, a Palestinian charity so often the focus of unwarranted adverse media attention.[133] The MWH director's exemplary career in Islamic charity work in the UK was typical. In 2000 he developed his interest in charitable work by moving to the MWH where his focus shifted to support work in London for newly arrived Muslims. 'I wanted to do something at the grassroots level with the community in this country' he said, 'especially addressing the needs of new communities'.[134] After making over a hundred visits to Interpal, MAB and MWH during 2002—2003 it became increasingly clear to me that treating Muslim charities with the same broad brush of suspicion as Muslim communities was unwarranted, counter-productive and was likely to have the same unintended consequence of reducing much needed Muslim support for counter-terrorism.[135]

The overwhelming weight of investigative academic, think-tank and media attention was concerned above all else with charitable work in connection with Palestinian support and the risk that charitable donations might end up in the hands of Hamas.[136] In contrast Jonathan Benthall and Jérôme Bellion-Jourdan are two researchers who have taken time to look at the issues from the perspectives of the charities themselves.[137] They offer an alternative perspective on Islamic aid by examining the social and political history of *zakat* and unpick many negative stereotypes in the process. Their account also helps to indicate how the Palestinian case is unique in important respects, in particular the extent to which empathy with the Palestinian cause has been negligently conflated with both support for terrorism and with anti-Semitism. No insistence on the difference between anti-Zionism and anti-Semitism will reduce the impact of accusations that are generally endorsed at the highest level of government. As even the Prime Minister's wife Cherie Blair found out to her cost when she expressed an understanding of the plight of young Palestinians who became suicide bombers, the pressure to enforce conformity to uncritical support for Israel can be significant.[138] Therefore, the fact that the Finsbury Park Islamist community generally and both the MWH and MAB in particular had a prime connection to the Palestinian cause meant that expressions of empathy with them would be confined to the politically brave or politically naïve.[139]

6

RECLAIMING THE MOSQUE

There is such a dramatic contrast between the police raid on Finsbury Park Mosque in 2003 and the MAB-led multi-agency operation to reclaim it from Abu Hamza's supporters two years later that it is worth exploring the comparison. In the first operation local Muslim community perspectives were subordinate to an operational imperative that government intended to use to demonstrate British commitment to the war on terror to US allies. In the second Muslim-led operation the government said nothing and declined to publicly support the new trustees of the mosque after they successfully removed Abu Hamza's supporters from the mosque. Equally noteworthy, the first operation resulted in significant damage to the mosque whereas the second operation left the building intact. Lastly, while the first operation made no dent in Abu Hamza's support and may indeed have served to increase his stature, the second operation seriously curtailed his influence and replaced it with an emphasis on British political protest as a response to grievances as opposed to isolation and violence. In general terms, the first entry to the mosque consisted of a top-down imperative while the second was a bottom-up local community approach.

Whereas Prime Minister Blair used the raid on 20 January 2003 to promote the war in Iraq he was conspicuously silent about the operation to reclaim the mosque on 5 February 2005. So too the media. According to a senior police source quoted in *The Suicide Factory*:

At the meetings [in 2003] we had with the security services in Downing Street Mr. Blair was always asking why we weren't taking action against these people—Hamza and three or four others. He was getting rather fed up with being told they were being monitored. It took the trigger of the ricin inquiry and the murder of DC Oake to actually do it [carry out the raid on the mosque].[1]

In a detailed summary of the police raid on the Finsbury Park Mosque on 20 January 2003 Sean O'Neill and Daniel McGrory highlight the tensions between an operational imperative to search the building in connection with a terrorist investigation known as the ricin plot and the need to take account of Muslim community sensibilities.[2] What this account fails to capture, however, is community concern about the scale and method of the search that was the topic of heated discussion at the MSF in the aftermath of the police operation. At the time most Muslim community representatives were prepared to accept that an operational imperative justified the raid but they questioned the need for 200 hundred police officers, helicopters and forced entry. What, they asked, was the point of the MCU establishing good relations with the mosque management if they could not be trusted to facilitate discreet entry to the building so as to avoid damage? The other major concern expressed by community representatives was the extent to which police appeared to be in collusion with government in allowing the case to be used as propaganda in support of the looming war in Iraq.

To trace this second concern it is necessary to return two weeks before the raid. On 7 January 2003 Home Secretary David Blunkett and Health Secretary John Reid issued a joint statement stating that traces of the poison ricin had been found by counter-terrorism police at a flat in Wood Green in North London. 'Ricin is a toxic material which if ingested or inhaled can be fatal' the statement announced, 'our primary concern is the safety of the public'.[3] Blair was quick to latch onto this development linking it to the dangers posed by weapons of mass destruction claiming that 'the arrests which were made show this danger is present and real and with us now. Its potential is huge'.[4] As Peter Oborne notes 'within weeks the ricin case was being cited around the world as further justification for the war in Iraq':[5]

US Secretary of State Colin Powell told the UN Security Council of a direct link between the British 'Ricin Plot' and an alleged al-Qaeda 'poison camp' in Iraq. The following day Tony Blair endorsed these remarks, ...adding that 'it would not be correct to say there is no evidence linking al-Qaeda and Iraq'.[6]

In late March 2003, US commanders in Iraq claimed to have destroyed a 'poison factory', though, as Peter Oborne notes, 'no chemicals or laboratories were found'. The US commander-in-chief, General Richard Myers, claimed it was the 'site where people were trained and poisons were developed that migrated into Europe' adding 'we think that's probably where the ricin in London came from'.[7] Such blatant political exploitation of a terrorist case by politicians who were determined to justify war in Iraq was viewed with deep dismay by the Finsbury Park Islamists who took the view that the invasion of Iraq would only exacerbate the problems posed by al-Qaeda and al-Qaeda-inspired terrorism. As one of them recalled in interview:

We were holding a Stop the War planning meeting a few days after the raid on the Finsbury Park Mosque. The atmosphere was very tense. We felt Tony Blair was adding to the fear of the situation to justify the war in Iraq but the link was tenuous and the policy misguided. Later it became clear that the whole ricin plot had been grossly exaggerated and that made the government's position even more sinister.[8]

There was another factor in the ricin plot case that would emerge as contentious: torture. Having absconded from the UK, Mohammed Meguerba was arrested by Algerian police on 16 December 2002. After being interrogated and tortured for two days he 'allegedly revealed a poisoning plot in north London naming the Algerian Kamel Bourgass as ringleader and other Algerians as co-conspirators':[9]

Meguerba's information led police to a flat in Wood Green where they arrested several men though Bourgass was not there. The police did discover recipes for ricin, a mortar and pestle and castor beans from which it is possible to extract ricin. On 14 January while on the hunt for another terror suspect the police raided a flat in Crumpsall, Manchester. By chance they found Bourgass and another alleged conspirator. After a violent struggle Bourgass murdered DC Stephen Oake and wounded other police officers.[10]

That the investigation should then move to the Finsbury Park Mosque came as little surprise to regular mosque users who had been used to seeing Bourgass working and residing there with his Algerian friends. For the mosque trustees the police raid gave them an opportunity to reclaim the building from Abu Hamza and his supporters. Unfortunately, however, the extent to which the government sought to use the ricin plot as a basis to bolster the case for war in Iraq served to undermine the credibility of Muslims who were prepared to work with the authorities against the likes of Abu Hamza. As a result MCU officers spent a great deal of time seeking to explain to senior management and civil servants how the plans for war in Iraq were serving to alienate the kind of credible Muslim community support that was needed to help reduce the influence of Abu Hamza (along with Abu Qatada, Abdullah el Faisal and other such propagandists and apologists) in those sections of the community that were susceptible to it. Our message tended to fall on deaf ears. There was always a stock answer along the lines that police could not alter international politics. My response at the time was that government should understand the likely consequences of its actions. Standing shoulder to shoulder with George Bush in a war in Iraq would, I suggested, play into al-Qaeda's hands in the UK. There seemed to be insufficient appreciation of the extent of al-Qaeda influence in the UK and how going to war in Iraq would increase it further. The police, I argued, had a duty to assess the likely outcomes of actions in terms of the terrorist threat to the UK.

In a speech delivered at Policy Exchange in 2007 Peter Clarke, head of the Metropolitan Police CTC, confirmed the official police line that in 2002 'the perception was that if there were a threat to the UK, its origins were overseas'. In that year, Clarke recalled, 'the spectre of a home-grown terrorist threat was not yet with us'.[11]

Whereas the MCU was trying to promote a street-level view of the problem Clarke offers an investigator's perspective:

During that year, 2002, we focused on groups of North Africans, mainly Algerians, to find out whether they were engaged solely in support, fund raising and the like, of terrorism overseas, or whether they posed a real threat to the UK itself. We followed a trail of petty fraud and false identity documents across the country. Eventually that trail took us to Thetford where, in the unlikely surroundings of rural Norfolk, we found the first real indication since 9/11 of operational terrorist activity in the UK—recipes for ricin and other poisons. That led us eventually to Wood Green and the chemicals, the Finsbury Park mosque and of course the terrible murder of Detective Constable Stephen Oake in Manchester in January 2003.[12]

There is no recognition here that intelligence leading to the search of the Wood Green address may have been obtained by the torture of Mohammed Meguerba by Algerian police. Instead, Clarke makes an oblique and passing allusion to the legal difficulties raised in 'international terrorist conspiracies':

That case taught us many things, not least about our ability to operate across borders, both within the UK and overseas. It showed us the difficulties that international terrorist conspiracies pose for our domestic judicial system.[13]

No recognition, then, of the negative impact close collaboration with the Algerian police might have in winning Muslim community support for UK counter-terrorism in an area like Finsbury Park. No recognition, either, of the damage done to the Muslim community's confidence in UK counter-terrorism by the government's cynical use of the ricin plot. Instead, Clarke highlights the damage caused to police credibility by allegations that the terrorist threat had been exaggerated:

For the police, it also marked the beginning of our understanding of the impact that the emerging distrust of intelligence in early 2003 would have on our relationship with the media and therefore the public. This was the first time, in my experience, that the police service had been accused of exaggerating the threat posed by terrorists in order, it was alleged, to help the Government to justify its foreign policy.[14]

In contrast, in 2003, I was concerned to highlight the damage government policy was doing to Muslim community confidence in counter-terrorism. Increasingly, I gained a reputation for speaking out on this issue at meetings such as the MSF held monthly at NSY. In consequence the MCU won a degree of respect from Muslim community groups including the Finsbury Park Islamists while at the same time it became a marginalised voice in an inherently conformist ACPO counter-terrorism police culture. Close partnership working also evolved between the MCU and the local MP Jeremy Corbyn, a leading critic of the war on terror in general and the war in Iraq in particular. It became part of my assessment that politicians like Jeremy Corbyn and Ken Livingstone were better able to build confidence with Muslim groups who had the capabilities to counter al-Qaeda influence than those like Tony Blair who had become closely identified with a neo-conservative anti-Islamist Washington agenda.

Throughout December 2004 and January 2005 Corbyn played a key role in negotiating a transfer of stewardship of the mosque from trustees who had fought valiantly but in vain against Abu Hamza's influence to a new group of trustees with the local credentials necessary to accomplish the task. In essence this meant a transfer of power to ardent critics of the war in Iraq which was why nominal mosque trustee Khalid Mahmood, a staunch Blairite, was uncomfortable with the plan. In several tense meetings in Finsbury Park and in Portcullis House, Westminster, Corbyn needed to call on all his experience and considerable mediating skills to keep all key stakeholders on board. That the plan came to fruition was a tribute as well to the efforts of a dynamic local partnership marshalled by MCU officers and supported by the Charity Commission. Right up until the day of an operation to reclaim the mosque it was uncertain and contingent on a number of local factors that it would go ahead.

Early on Saturday morning on 5 February 2005 up to a hundred supporters of the MWH and MAB began to assemble at 233 Seven Sisters Road. Public order-trained Metropolitan Police officers assembled a mile away at the little used Highbury Vale police station. According to an Islington police officer who was on 'early turn' (6 am start) that morning there was no discernable evidence of major organised activity taking place in the area:

It was only because I was aware of what was happening that I noticed groups of Arab and Asian men parking their cars in the side streets behind Seven Sisters Road and walking in small groups towards the Muslim Welfare House as early as 7am. They were parading nice and early for a briefing just like us![15]

There was also a sense in which both sides of the London partnership were using their experience, their street skills and tradecraft to avoid sending out any warning signals to any of Abu Hamza's supporters or allies that something significant and dramatic was being planned for later that morning. The same interviewee notes:

Some others involved [Muslim Welfare House and MAB members] stayed in their cars, like they were waiting in reserve and others made their way to the Turkish café behind the station for a coffee. Really, just like us! Quite funny. Very switched on. What a contrast. Compared to the times the old guard tried to re-assert control at the mosque. Embarrassing. Not their fault. Just a question of horses for courses.[16]

Again there were similarities in the police and community briefings that were commented upon at the time by an MCU officer:

Clear objectives; attention to timing; readiness to adapt to circumstances as they unfolded; contingency planning, what ifs; clear division of responsibilities and sub briefings; communication protocols; primacy to intelligence gatherers; on the spot intelligence assessment to inform decision making; media strategy; community strategy. Impressive.[17]

By 10 am up to a hundred MWH and MAB supporters were deployed in the vicinity of the Finsbury Park Mosque each paying close attention to their individual instructions and to their mobile phones for orders.[18] Some were watching the mosque itself so as to monitor and report movements. Key MAB figures on the top floor of 233 Seven Sisters

Road received and disseminated intelligence concerning the situation inside the mosque. Two MCU officers and two Islington police officers worked in an office next to the room where the community operation was run and acted as a liaison point:

There was a major concern about entering the building without forcing entry. Great detail went into planning entry with consent but at the same time there was contingency planning in the event of resistance. On the one hand the new trustees had lawful ownership but the civil law of property gave no right to force entry against unlawful occupiers without an injunction. Police powers too were circumscribed and restricted to preventing a breach of the peace. The key issue was therefore lawful peaceful entry and then any claims Abu Hamza's supporters believed they had to occupancy could be settled in the courts—with them on the outside and the new management on the inside. There was concern that if they were barricaded in they would be difficult to dislodge.[19]

MCU officers inside 233 Seven Sisters Road were in close contact with colleagues in their office at NSY. Similarly uniformed police officers running the policing support operation in Finsbury Park were in close contact with colleagues at the public order control centre in NSY. This was important because it enabled police to monitor and assess the operation as it unfolded and also to monitor a series of risks including the possibility that far-right extremists might descend on Finsbury Park Mosque to stage an impromptu protest as they did from time to time. From the perspective of officers running the public order control room the operation at the mosque was one of several police deployments that would be overseen and serviced on a typically busy Saturday. Contingency planning was well rehearsed so that in the event of disorder at Finsbury Park police re-enforcements could be dispatched quickly. Equally, if disorder arose elsewhere in the capital then officers might be redeployed from Finsbury Park. Overall the cost of the policing operation was far less than would have been the case if instead of supporting this community-led operation police were supporting an attempt by the former trustees and the Charity Commission to enforce a civil injunction seeking to evict Abu Hamza's supporters.[20] Not only was the financial cost reduced but so too was the risk of adverse community impact. Abu Hamza's supporters were adept at manipulating community anger and would be bound to exploit the situation if police were seen to be entering the mosque by force as they did in 2003.[21]

Partnership provided a safe space for learning lessons from experience during the course of a shared contingency planning process in the

141

weeks leading up to the operation. For instance, when the mosque was searched in an anti-terrorist operation in 2003 local Muslims were told that arrangements had been made in advance with the MWH to enable them to pray at 233 Seven Sisters Road while the mosque was closed. This was a minor inaccuracy that had a major negative impact on the MWH at the time because it suggested, wrongly, that the centre was part of the planning for the raid or was at least aware of it. In the event use of helicopters and forced entry to the mosque in 2003 led to a local Muslim community perception that the operation was disproportionate and heavy-handed. In contrast, in 2005, a multi-agency partnership operation in which the MWH and MAB would lead on local community communications instead of police.

Inevitably during high-risk operations partners who have previously only talked together come to see the calibre of their opposite numbers. MCU officers were certainly impressed with the way their community partners handled the pressure in the hour leading up to a decision to enter the building immediately. The decision followed careful assessments of intelligence and was followed by an evaluation of options that mirrored police procedures. The decision was premised on establishing the optimum time in terms of minimising resistance and conflict. After discussions with Barry Norman's deputy and the MCU, the new mosque management team entered the Finsbury Park Mosque without resistance and took control of the building before 12 noon. Their supporters followed them into the mosque in an orderly fashion. Abu Hamza's supporters had been caught completely unawares and were mostly away from the building at their homes in West and South London. That satisfactory state of affairs was partly the result of good planning, careful assessment but also as always in these kinds of situations a slice of good fortune.

After several hours on the streets and after mounting tension and suspense in the days leading up to the operation there was immediate excitement in both MAB and police camps when entry to the building was gained and secondly when an immediate search of the building found it to be unguarded.[22] According to one MAB activist:

We were pleased. You never know what to expect. You hope for the best but plan for the worst. This mosque had been a big problem for the community and now we had a chance to put things right. And you know, we had never been given a chance before. We knew the police had trusted us and we had respect for them.[23]

Within minutes, however, mobile phones were buzzing and Abu Hamza's supporters became aware that the mosque had been entered by a large group of people.[24] Under the leadership of Abu Abdullah, Abu Hamza's deputy, they formed a group and approached the mosque at 2 pm. MCU officers assessed that they would be surprised to see no police presence at the mosque. Instead, they were cordially invited into the building by the new management. Visibly shocked to see that their long-term headquarters had been taken over they noted that access to the first floor and to the basement had been boarded up. They also noted the presence of a strong physical presence quietly demonstrating control. They were asked to enter the main room on the ground floor and encouraged to discuss the situation.[25] Abu Hamza's supporters were further wrong footed by the complete absence of trustees who they had grown used to bullying and intimidating. Instead their predilection for violent confrontation was muted. Two of their team had gone to the rear of the building and reported by mobile phone that entry was blocked.

Suddenly the dynamics had changed. The building that had become a second home, a place that gave them a sense of pride, had been snatched from their control. They recognised faces from MWH and MAB and knew from experience that they were now facing tough opponents. Nevertheless anger got the better of one of Abu Hamza's henchmen who punched and injured a supporter of the new management team:

This man was very angry. We said calm down, we will listen to you. He shouted and pushed and we said be calm and talk. He said we were working for George Bush and we should be ashamed. Then we ignored him because his colleagues were calmer. Angry like him but not so bad. Then he just hit our brother and so we escorted him out of the mosque and our brother needed some medical treatment but really it was a small incident. The main friends of Abu Hamza they started to talk to us. We offered them some tea and we were relaxed but alert. But *yany* all the time they were looking and thinking if they could overpower us. Yes, to hit us and push us out. But really *yany* they could see they could not do it.[26]

The new managers soon controlled the situation and discussions were conducted in a civil if formal manner. Abu Abdullah, Abu Hamza's deputy, sought to make it clear that he and his supporters had a rightful claim to a presence in the mosque. However, it became apparent to him and his supporters that the old management regime had been replaced by one that would not be intimidated in the same way. Indeed, Abu Abdullah knew precisely who it was he was talking to and was visibly taken aback to find that the mosque had effectively passed into the control of the *Ikhwan*. An MCU officer explains:

Kamel el Helbawy is a very respected figure even outside his own Arab circle. His background is well known and his presence at the mosque during this difficult negotiation was crucial. He also has a deep booming voice which commands attention as well which comes in handy at times like these! Plus many in the MAB group have a strong physical presence so as to be able to stand up to bully boys like Abu Abdullah. Like all bullies they are the first to realize when they are facing tougher opponents and to back off.[27]

Throughout the day, MCU officers watched developments unfold from a vantage point at the operational hub, an upstairs office on the top floor at 233 Seven Sisters Road. We were able to offer advice to the individuals leading the operation and communicate with police colleagues who were being held in reserve in the event of problems arising. At one key point an MCU officer was asked for advice about the timing of the move to enter the mosque. This was a critical juncture and witnessed the only small tactical difference between community and police perspectives. As noted earlier the same issue arose regarding the best day to opt to carry out the 're-occupation' of the mosque. As on that occasion police deferred to expert community knowledge when their thinking was explained. Here an MCU officer's long-term rapport with the community leadership was instrumental in communicating between the two partners. At this key moment the value of the partnership having built trust and mutual confidence over a long period proved invaluable. As one MCU officer explained:

We had seen many public order situations where senior police lacked sufficient confidence in a community group to be prepared to allow them to take action when the risks were high. This would often be a decision taken in the heat of the moment. Here the risks were pretty huge and the tension was starting to build up. There was no certainty that the mosque would be empty nor that Abu Hamza's group hadn't found out about the plan. We were concerned that Abu Hamza's group might have their own plan to defend the building. It was certainly pretty clear that they would have defended it if they had got wind of the new management and what was happening.[28]

This was the first time experienced police officers had ever seen a community group execute such a plan. Indeed, in a series of earlier contingency planning meetings when the old Mosque management regime was in place it had become clear to police that their ability to cope with the pressure and the intimidation was severely limited. That lack of resourcefulness had become evident during the two earlier abortive attempts to re-open the mosque in 2004. An issue of leadership also emerged. On the police side Barry Norman was prepared to assess, manage and take risks. The same MCU officer notes:

Barry showed confidence in the MCU officers and community voices to help him assess the situation. Other senior police officers in his position would not have invested time and trust building to the same level. Least of all to empathise with community views. It's like in any other high pressure policing situation when it comes to making decisions you want to be confident in the people who are advising you and the ones who are going to carry it out.[29]

Later on the Saturday afternoon Abu Hamza's supporters, led by Abu Abdullah, were obliged to leave the mosque without securing any compromise from the new management team. Instead, they were politely asked to reflect on their position over the next few days. On the following Tuesday evening Abu Abdullah asked to meet the new management team again and the meeting took place away from the mosque. Abu Abdullah was accompanied by a small group of Abu Hamza supporters and at first he sought to negotiate a space for his group under the new management regime. This was a significant climbdown from his initial response to the takeover a few days earlier. However, he continued to argue that if a compromise could not be reached he would have recourse to legal proceedings against the new trustees. None of this cut any ice with a new management regime that was confident of its ability to face down the bullying and thuggish behaviour of Abu Hamza's supporters let alone any weak claim to lawful occupancy. That said, they knew that they would have faced insoluble problems if they had not secured entry to the building on the preceding Saturday. They were now negotiating from a position of strength. Neither the civil nor criminal law would have helped them immediately had Abu Hamza's supporters retained physical possession of the mosque. Indeed, at this meeting the new trustees were even more emphatic in describing the new terms of engagement:

The mosque was now open to everyone. There would be no more intimidation. Anyone committing acts of violence or intimidation would be handed over to the police. Anyone wishing to dispute the authority of the trustees should report their concerns to the Charity Commission. They [Abu Hamza's supporters] would be allowed to pray in the mosque so long as they followed the new ground rules. However, they would no longer be allowed access to any facilities at the mosque, least of all office space. Neither would they be allowed to lead prayers, make speeches, distribute leaflets or organise events.[30]

Behind the scenes much work was undertaken by MCU officers, Islington Police, the Charity Commission, Islington Council and Jeremy Corbyn to ensure the new management team had every support in securing the mosque against any attempts by Abu Hamza's supporters to reclaim it or to undermine the new regime.[31] Close co-operation with Islington police, of the kind that had been in place with the neighbouring MWH for over ten years, was established so that any criminal activity could be reported immediately. Police and local authority were also able to provide expert advice and support in relation to the safety and security of the building. Difficulties that the previous management regime faced in providing the necessary resources to staff the mosque adequately were finally overcome.[32] The kind of expertise that had been in evidence at the MWH and MAB over a long period was now brought to bear at Finsbury Park Mosque. In addition, the absence of neighbourly support between the two establishments was now replaced by active co-operation and mutual support.[33]

On the following Friday the new management team were able to proclaim their success publicly at Friday prayers.[34] Again they had a very sizeable presence at the mosque to help deter any would-be protestors from causing a disturbance. As on the previous Saturday policing was held in reserve and Barry Norman and a small team of officers were present in the street outside the mosque to oversee events and talk to the media. One of the MAB local organisers was the most visible face at the entrance to the mosque. Smiling broadly and smartly dressed in a grey suit and tie he shook every one entering the mosque by the hand and conveyed a reassuring presence for police and public. He said later it was one of the proudest days of his life:

Look this was a very big day for us. We were doing a very important thing in Islam, doing good for the community, for community relations and for security. And for me personally. In Egypt I got big trouble from the police. Torture. Now I was working with Barry [Norman] with Jeremy [Corbyn] with the Muslim Contact Unit and all the authorities in a very nice way. This was the right way.[35]

For an Islington police officer who had witnessed events at the mosque over the preceding five years it was also a memorable day:

I must admit I kept expecting to see Abu Hamza's supporters coming along the road to try and reclaim the mosque and cause trouble. Bear in mind they were perfectly free to do so....on previous occasions when the old management tried to keep them out they just waltzed in. But this day was different. The new management team looked confident even though they were probably nervous. They had a really strong reassuring presence and behaved just like we would do [in the police] when you want to send a strong signal to people who might want to provoke trouble.[36]

In addition, Jeremy Corbyn was on hand to encourage and support the new management regime. Whereas previously his presence inside the mosque had been challenged by Abu Hamza's supporters who did not want any *kafir* inside their domain, the new management provided him with the space to hold monthly surgeries at the mosque. Corbyn announced his pleasure:

I am delighted that the Finsbury Park Mosque is now fully reopened, with its members showing a determination to build its support in the local community and in cooperation with everybody else. It has been a great day. I thank the trustees, staff, and local police for all their help and support in ensuring this peaceful transition coming about.[37]

Predictably, the only dampener on proceedings was the activity of Murdoch journalists who were determined to detract from the success of the new management regime by highlighting the alleged historical links of one of the trustees, Mohammed Sawalha, to Hamas. As Mohammed Sawalha left his home that morning to attend the re-opening event he was doorstepped by a *Sunday Times* journalist who put the allegation to him. The following report resulted:

A Muslim leader appointed to help to run the recently reopened Finsbury Park mosque in north London is a former military commander of Hamas, the Palestinian terrorist organisation. Mohammed Kassem Sawalha is one of five trustees appointed to give the mosque a fresh start.[38]

The same journalist later met Barry Norman and questioned him about working with extremists and this was reported in the same article:

Barry Norman, the Metropolitan police chief superintendent who has been working closely with the trustees, said: 'I am aware of the background, but if I took the view that I'm not working with this or that person I'd end up spending my whole life in my office'.[39]

Corbyn was especially helpful in defending the new management against these kinds of charges. As a highly regarded constituency MP he was able to articulate the importance of encouraging Palestinian grievances against Israel to be expressed in democratic ways. He was also able to argue that historical allegations of the kind being made against Mohammed Sawalha should be weighed against the value of the work he was doing on behalf of the local community. Corbyn had long experience of similar allegations being made against his constituents in connection with PIRA that were later found to be unfounded. Therefore he argued that this previous experience was relevant:

It is incredible news that the British Prime Minister has given an apology on behalf of the government to the families of the Guildford Four. What happened in 1974 was appalling, and what followed was a grotesque miscarriage of justice wherein four people were imprisoned for nearly two decades, and those of us who campaigned for their innocence were routinely abused by the popular press, notably the *Sun* and the *Daily Mail*. The families continue to suffer the trauma they went through, having had their loved ones in prison for a crime they did not commit. I welcome the apology. One should not however forget that Paul Hill [a former Finsbury Park resident] was the first person to be arrested under the Prevention of Terrorism Act and I feel that the control orders and other aspects of anti-terror legislation recently gone, or currently going through parliament, may well lead to identical miscarriages against people, and possibly Muslims in the future.[40]

However, after 7/7 MCU support for the Finsbury Park Islamists became even more problematic. The government launched an urgent dialogue with Muslim representatives that was premised on an entirely different understanding of the problem. Whereas MCU officers urged partnerships with expert Islamists and expert salafis the government sought out Muslim partners who tended to lack the same street awareness. When the Prime Minister announced that 'the rules of the game have changed' and explicitly equated 'a suicide bomber in London' with 'a suicide bomber in Tel Aviv' it became clear that an important group of London Muslims recently responsible for successfully tackling and removing al-Qaeda ideology from Finsbury Park Mosque might become problematic counter-terrorist partners in view of their politics.[41] Indeed, under proposed new counter-terrorist legislation it became conceivable that these experts in countering al-Qaeda terrorist propaganda and recruitment in Britain could themselves face prosecution for their support for what they called Palestinian resistance to an illegal occupation abroad.

The Finsbury Park Islamists had proved themselves to be effective in the fight against al-Qaeda terrorist influence in London. While other Muslim community groups lacked the will or the resources to tackle the problem, senior figures at the MWH and MAB bravely reclaimed the notorious Finsbury Park Mosque, London's embarrassing centre of violent extremism, from a bunch of dangerous thugs who brazenly supported and promoted al-Qaeda ideology. The Finsbury Park Islamists' parallel condemnation of US/UK policy in the war on terror and support for Palestinian resistance was key to the community credibility they needed to tackle violent extremists in unlawful control of the mosque.[42] The very qualities that made them uncongenial political allies in Westminster served Londoners well in the street fight against violent supporters of al-Qaeda. That at least was an MCU perspective—an increasingly marginalised viewpoint post-7/7.[43]

The assessment certainly raised a dilemma for police which might be posed in the following terms: can police abandon or curtail successful partnerships with effective opponents of al-Qaeda because of their politics or their religious practice? Inevitably this became a fraught situation for MCU officers. From a community policing perspective, however, there appeared to be a legitimate basis to continue to engage in partnership with the Finsbury Park Islamists. To begin with there was a prime police duty to prevent or reduce threats to the capital. That purpose was clearly well served by a partnership between MCU officers and the Finsbury Park Islamists. Equally, MCU officers could point to MWH willingness to engage sympathetically with Jewish community representatives in London in an effort to build bridges as evidence that went some way to rebutting allegations that fierce criticism of Israel's Palestinian policy equated to anti-Semitism. In addition the fact that MAB worked effectively with Jewish, Christian, and gay activist participants in STW provided a sound basis for encouraging young British Muslims to express their political grievances through legitimate protest and not through terrorism or sectarianism. MAB officials were also clear that young British Muslims should not seek to emulate Hanif Asif and Omar Sharif who carried out a suicide bomb attack for Hamas in Tel Aviv in 2004. MAB members were clearly shocked when it became clear that the attack had been carried out in the name of Hamas. In consequence, MWH and MAB members were active in persuading young British Muslims that political grievances should be channelled through the ballot box and in lawful protest. In the same way, they were active and effective in restraining young British Muslims from fighting 'jihad' in Iraq.[44]

Ken Livingstone, the London mayor, tackled the issue head on. He identified 'real parallels between what happens in Israel-Palestine today with the bombing campaign run by the ANC against the white apartheid regime 20 years ago in South Africa'.[45] 'Would the supporters of Nelson Mandela have been thrown out of this country' he asked, 'because they were supporting the bombing campaign against the apartheid racist regime in South Africa?'[46] In fact, Livingstone went on to deal with another controversial but critical case: that of the leading international Muslim scholar, Sheikh Yusuf Al Qaradawi who he endorsed as 'probably the most respected, progressive Muslim cleric in the world' and warned that banning him from entering Britain would be 'incredibly divisive'.[47] The mayor concluded, 'there will be very few Muslim scholars or leaders who will ever be admitted to Britain (if Qaradawi was to be excluded under new government proposals) because the vast majority of Muslims identify with the struggle of the Palestinian people'.[48]

Consequently a tension of perception and premise arises at the very outset of what government and senior police officers intended to be a tougher and more targeted approach to counter terrorism and Muslim community support in the wake of 7/7. Moreover, a second related tension emerged between government and Muslim community representatives concerning the nature of terrorist recruitment and its connection (if any) to a process of radicalisation. A leaked Home Office paper 'Young Muslims and Extremism' advised:

The aims of policy to prevent British Muslims, especially Young Muslims, from becoming attracted to extremist movements and terrorist activity should have two main points: (a) isolate extremists within the Muslim community, and provide support to the moderates, equipping and encouraging them to oppose the extremist threat within their communities (it is important to identify moderates correctly—some of those who are influential in the extremist world purport to be moderates), (b) help prevent young Muslims from becoming ensnared or bullied into participation in terrorist activity.[49]

Crucially, then, the question arose: which side of the new extremist line did the Finsbury Park Islamists fall? Were they 'with us or against us'? If the answer was negative then the position of the MCU became untenable. Not surprisingly MCU officers encountered major reservations from the Finsbury Park Islamists (as with other community groups) about the negative impact the proposed anti-terrorist measures would have on their own grassroots efforts to tackle terrorist propaganda and recruitment. Particular concern surrounded two proposals: for new anti-terrorism legislation creating (i) 'an offence of condoning or glorifying terrorism' to be 'applied to justifying or glorifying terrorism anywhere, not just in the UK'; and (ii) the proscription of HT.[50] Given that the history of emergency anti-terrorist legislation introduced in response to terrorist outrages often showed resultant community alienation rather than proactive support MCU officers thought it was important that these concerns be taken seriously.[51] While HT was an organisation with few friends in the wider Muslim community it was fair to say that their non-violent politics was a long way removed from violent extremism. That was why other Islamist groups opposed a ban against them—they feared it could be the thin end of the wedge. Concerns about 'justifying or glorifying terrorism abroad' related for the main part to Palestinian suicide bombers. Clearly, *real politic* demanded government respond in a way that satisfied a strong sense of popular retributive justice in the wake of 7/7. For their part, Finsbury Park Islamists were relieved to see that the human rights issues attaching to emergency anti-terrorist legislation were thoroughly debated in parliament, most especially the House of Lords. Those with family backgrounds in the Middle East and North Africa compared that regard for the rule of law favourably with politics in their home countries.

I argued that the Finsbury Park Islamists had successfully tackled al-Qaeda terrorist recruitment, propaganda and support (as had the Brixton salafis) and to dismiss or sacrifice their efforts in pursuit of a new 'moderate' community partnership that excluded them as extremist was counter-productive. Moreover, sufficient evidence emerged to provide a sound basis for arguing that the partnership initiative which resulted in the removal of Abu Hamza's supporters and influence from Finsbury Park Mosque had helped to re-direct young Muslims previously under Abu Hamza's influence into mainstream political activity.[52] At the end of October 2007, I concluded that there was real substance to the notion that the Finsbury Park Islamists had set an example of legitimate political jihad that served to undermine the illegal and terrorising jihad of Abu Hamza and his supporters.[53] One former Abu Hamza supporter is very clear about the positive impact the Muslim partners have had in his case and amongst his counterparts:

We used to like Abu Hamza's talks. He introduced us to the history of Muslim oppression and that got us very angry. Then we wanted to get trained for jihad. But listening to Azzam Tamimi and Jeremy Corbyn has convinced us that Muslims have good friends who understand the injustice in places like Palestine. Now we are active politically as British Muslims, not fighting Britain.[54]

PART THREE

BRIXTON

7

CORRECTING ERRONEOUS BELIEF

I was in Feltham[1] for street robbery. Same as Richard Reid.[2] Later [than Reid].[3] Same call from Faisal.[4] Sounded good to me. Rob the *kafir*. Could have got me killed. Or back in prison. Stupid. Three years with that erroneous belief till I came to Mr. Baker's khutbah.[5]

'Erroneous belief' and 'erroneous call' are two of a handful of stock terms in the Brixton salafi counter-extremism lexicon that have been used to good effect over the last fifteen years.[6] The interviewee here had switched his allegiance from Abdullah el Faisal and Osama bin Laden to Abdul Haqq Baker and the Brixton salafis and adopted a new vocabulary as well as a new sense of citizenship.[7] Used repeatedly throughout interviews and discussions with Brixton salafis the terms serve to underscore their dual motivations in life—correcting a false call to Islam and helping local youth to become responsible citizens, often having previously been involved in extremism or street crime themselves.

Just as earlier chapters highlight the significance of prior experience for the MCU and their Muslim partners in Finsbury Park so valuable prior experience gained by the Brixton salafis was brought to bear in their partnership with the MCU during the research period January 2002 to October 2007. By tracing the development of a new salafi community led by three Londoners in the early 1990s and examining their encounters and clashes with three London-based al-Qaeda apologists and propagandists, Abu Qatada, Abu Hamza and Abdullah el Faisal it becomes possible to assess the basis on which MCU officers placed such high value on their street skills. Which is not to suggest that either the three London salafis or the three London resident al-Qaeda propagandists and apologists were without close colleagues who played important roles as well, but rather to present these six individuals as playing especially important roles that serve an explanatory and illustrative purpose well.

Moreover, if 'al-Qaeda' only emerged as a familiar descriptive term after 9/11, three factors combine to prompt the use of the term to depict the growing influence of the three named al-Qaeda propagandists and apologists from the early 1990s onwards: the continuity of thought and purpose shown throughout by the three men that culminates in express support for al-Qaeda attacks including 9/11; their long-term commitment to educate British Muslims about their duty to actively support Muslims fighting abroad, such as in Bosnia during the early 1990s;[8] and the sense in which their tacit support for the first attack on the WTC in New York in 1993 pre-figured and characterised their active endorsement of the second attack in 2001.

A central focus on three leading members of a new salafi community in Brixton is important because the three men would subsequently be approached by MCU officers to form a partnership towards the end of 2002. Largely negative interaction with police during the period 1991–2001 therefore predates the formation of the MCU and to a certain extent helps explain the rationale for forming the unit. In addition, by tracing the three Londoners' development from secular to religious lifestyles it becomes possible to comprehend the motivation for their bravery in tackling violent extremists with no support from police or other outside agency before 9/11. By highlighting examples of outstanding and unrecognised bravery by the Brixton salafis in confronting violent extremism during this period it also becomes possible to grasp how they won the admiration and respect of MCU and other police officers. In this way the participants' understanding of the legitimacy and effectiveness of the London partnership between the MCU and the Brixton salafis aimed at countering al-Qaeda propaganda and recruitment activity in London is elucidated.

While the prime research material for this chapter necessarily involves participant recollection, that potential deficit is compensated wherever possible with scrupulous cross-referencing to extant contemporary records. For example when Brixton salafi interviewees talked about their confrontations with Abdullah el Faisal in 1995 and 1996 I was able to check their accounts against MCU interviewee and other community interviewee accounts from other parts of London. It is also important to stress that the contemporaneous nature of the participant observation serves to corroborate and amplify much of the partici- pants' recollections of their work in the same arena in an earlier period. This is important because the division of Brixton salafi experience between pre- and post-MCU engagement is a necessary but arbitrary device. Moreover, long before any counter-terrorism practitioners and terrorism studies scholars came to identify the extent of the influence of the three London-based al-Qaeda propagandists and apologists the Brixton salafis diagnosed the problem themselves and embarked on a course of community inoculation. Of course 'inoculation' may be a problematic analogy in some respects but it is useful because it is the one used by the Brixton salafis themselves to describe their work—and it properly denotes their view of *takfiri* ideology as a deviant position with a long history. Broadly speaking, a *takfiri* is a Muslim who prac- tises *takfir*, which is to accuse other Muslims of apostasy.[9] The term *takfir* derives from the word *kafir* and describes a declaration that a person's claim to be a Muslim is impure.[10] Indeed, for the Brixton salafis the task of protecting communities from a strain of deviant thinking promoted by Satan—*Shaytaan*, a *jinn*[11]—involves following a lead set by the true followers of the prophet Muhammad ever since the *Khawarij*[12] demonstrated a destructive sectarian impulse in Islam's first century. As one of the three leading Brixton salafi explains:

Even though we were still new Muslims once we understood clearly from trusted scholars in Saudi and Jordan that they [Abu Qatada, Abu Hamza and Abdullah el Faisal] were giving a false call to Islam we sought to discharge our duty to protect new and existing Muslims from their influence. This was our clear Islamic duty. We were dealing with the same problem as the Khawarij. This meant we would try and speak to everyone they spoke to. So, for instance, when we heard that Abu Hamza had spoken to a group of students in say Leeds we would make it our business to go the same student society and deliver the correct message within the next week or two.[13]

Why did MCU police officers attach value to this minority salafi perspective?

We could see they had potential. Our first job was to assess them. They did the same with us. Who could blame them? They had ten years of poor service from the Met, to put it mildly. We had to deliver and so did they.[14]

As an experienced MPSB officer why think of the Brixton salafis as partners instead of informants?

They were like us. They monitored the street. They kept a finger on the pulse. And they had a sense of civic duty. Not many people have that. Not many informants have that. Most other Muslims we met were out of touch with the street, they might be in touch with local mosque politics, or national politics, but not with the street.[15]

An MCU colleague made a different point:

It's true what [officer's name] says about their [Brixton salafi] civic duty. But for the handful of people who get involved in police consultative groups and the like that generally means attending a meeting one evening a month. And getting paid expenses. These guys do it every minute of the day, 24/7, its their whole lives. No payment. Just a reward at the end of the day, insha'Allah.[16]

When academics and think-tanks address terrorism from a top-down perspective it is generally to locate the phenomenon in a broader context of international politics.[17] On the fewer occasions when academics and think-tanks address terrorism from a bottom-up perspective it is almost always to interrogate the psychology and dynamics of groups of participating individuals.[18] MCU officers adopted a bottom-up vantage point as well but instead interrogated the experience of eye-witnesses to terrorist recruitment and influence at close quarters in a specific community in London—Brixton.[19] Our purpose was to assess the suitability of the Brixton salafis as partners in a counter-terrorism initiative.[20] Similarly, my research study seeks to evaluate preliminary evidence concerning the authenticity and value of the eye-witnesses' community experience, most especially their knowledge of a handful of young men who have become involved in terrorism and violent extremism. Crucially this community perspective reveals interplay and inter-dependence between street crime and terrorism that is otherwise often neglected.[21]

For insider observers on the sometimes violent streets of Brixton in South London it is axiomatic that petty drug dealers operate in the lowest and most vulnerable places within an intricate global network of organised crime.[22] Their commercial relationship with the commodity they trade in is often compromised by their own dependency on it. According to a former Brixton drug dealer with convictions for drugs-related crime it was 'stupid street kids' like him 'who took the risks and got prison and the men in suits who kept clean and made lots of money'.[23] As such the lives of petty drug dealers are far removed from the lives of the global strategists who manipulate their day-to-day livelihoods. Similarly there is an appreciation on the Brixton street that

many foot soldiers in the global network of al-Qaeda-inspired terrorism lead lives equally far removed from those of the global strategists
who provide the rationale and propaganda for their actions. On the
Brixton street it has also become clear that petty drug dealers and
other servants of organised crime have sometimes become involved in
al-Qaeda-inspired terrorism as foot soldiers. While from one stand-
point that might be seen as swapping one low status high-risk occupation for another it would appear that the individuals concerned see it
differently—believing that al-Qaeda-inspired terrorism affords them
high status and religious rewards. It is not, however, intended to suggest a strong link between the two types of criminal activity, merely to
emphasise three key points: that petty criminals and terrorist foot soldiers share similarly distant relationships with the strategists that deter-
mine their high-risk criminal activities; that circumstances exist in
which the street skills of petty criminals are likely to be valued and
deployed in terrorist scenarios;[24] and that petty criminals may be
attracted to terrorism in the belief that it affords status and dignity that
their lives have otherwise lacked:

Although we talk about the Brixton street its mainly the estates where the
gangs operate. Loughborough Road estate, Myatt's Field estate [nicknamed
'Baghdad'], Angell Town estate, Stockwell Gardens estate, Stockwell Park
estate, [all in the London Borough of Lambeth], North Peckham estate [in
neighbouring Southwark].[25]

On the Muslim Brixton street Abu Hamza and Abdullah el Faisal
emerge as two prominent propagandists who sought to inculcate the
belief that Islam welcomed and rewarded young men who had committed crimes like street robbery and drug dealing in ignorance but
who after becoming Muslim might quickly aspire to criminal activity
in the name of Islam instead. For some members of gangs like the Muslim Boys[26] Abu Hamza and Abdullah el Faisal had replaced Rastafar-
ian Jamaican gangsters as role models.[27] As a result they warned young
Muslims not to trust the police and especially not to trust Muslims
who worked with the police but to understand that their Islamic duty
to perform jihad (as they described it) placed them above the petty
constraints of man-made laws and its enforcers. Both men evinced a
strong empathy with petty criminals who had not enjoyed the benefits
of a settled family life or decent education. Abu Hamza would trade
on his pre-practising days as a bouncer in the West End to win credibility amongst young men involved in street crime. Abdullah el Faisal

would purport to have been involved in criminal activity on the tough streets of Jamaica so as to win respect with the same audiences. Although neither man resided in Brixton, but rather in Shepherds Bush (West London) and Stratford (East London) they became regular visitors to the neighbourhood where they held talks and 'study circles' often in booked meeting rooms or homes. More importantly they drew likeminded people from different parts of the capital and places like Luton together and developed networks of support. So for example it would become commonplace for supporters in Brixton to travel by tube to Finsbury Park to attend an Abu Hamza circle there or a meeting in Willesden if Abdullah el Faisal was speaking. Their ability to instil a sense of value and respect amongst young men who they encouraged away from drug abuse (often in demanding circumstances) often won them grudging admiration from Muslim elders who applauded their results while agonising over their methods. According to one community elder Abdullah el Faisal was known to have invested inordinate energy in helping a very serious drug dealer to 'become a good Muslim':

To be honest at first I could only see good in the man. He was powerful and had a great way of getting through to youth who were involved in drugs and much more. They took notice of him. Then he had a softer side too and would take a boy under his wing and help him get off drugs even when it was very difficult. But most of all he brought young men to Islam. And we were delighted with him.[28]

Another interviewee thought it important to highlight the number of reformed petty street criminals who went on to become reasonably competent teachers themselves—having learned skills from Abu Hamza and Abdullah el Faisal amongst others.[29] One example he gave was Mohammed Hamid who came to public attention when he was convicted and imprisoned for 'training men in secret camps in the Lake District and New Forest' in 2008.[30] The interviewee, himself a reformed street criminal, recalls meeting Hamid for the first time in or about 1997:

He was part of this broad Abu Hamza group and he was about the same age but he was his own man as well. He was a regular caller at Speaker's Corner in Hyde Park and everyone knew him. He was really someone who had done some bad things in his youth but who came through it and wanted to help the youth not make the same mistakes. He loved the outdoor pursuits and was a good organiser of events. You knew he was reliable unlike some others. He was a comedian too.[31]

Certainly there is a basis for describing Hamid as having absorbed and adapted the rhetoric of Osama bin Laden and other iconic figures in ways that was never envisaged or intended by the al-Qaeda strategists. Thus, using the calypso tune of *The Banana Boat Song*, the trial heard how Hamid adapted the lyrics to become: 'Come Mr Taliban, come bomb England, before the daylight come, you wanna see Downing Street done'.[32] Much to the outrage of *The Sun* and other newspapers BBC journalists Phil Rees and Nasreen Suleaman had paid for Hamid to take another group paintballing for a BBC television documentary called *Don't Panic I'm Islamic* which was screened in 2006:

At Hamid's trial Phil Rees, who produced the show, told the court that he was impressed by Mr Hamid's sense of humour while looking for someone to appear in the documentary. He said: 'I think he had a comic touch and he represented a strand within British Muslims. I took it as more like a rather Steptoe and Son figure rather than seriously persuasive. I saw him as a kind of Cockney comic'.[33]

According to a Brixton salafi interviewee Hamid is typical of individuals who have maintained some of the bravado and street culture that went hand-in-hand with their pre-practising and criminal lifestyles.[34] The outcome was a kind of hybrid identity where Islamic imperatives were blended with street culture. This is most pronounced, they say, in cases where the *takfiri* licenses street crimes against *kafir* victims on the basis that it is acceptable in Islam. When Hamid was subsequently convicted one interviewee was shown the following BBC news report and asked to comment on it:

A man said to be one of the most important recruiters for Islamist extremism in the UK has been convicted at the end of a major trial. Mohammed Hamid, 50, of east London, was found guilty of training men in secret camps in the Lake District and New Forest to prepare them to fight abroad. Among those to have passed through Hamid's camps were the four failed suicide bombers of 21 July 2005. All four of the men responsible for the failed bombings were friends of Hamid. The conviction marks a major success for counter-terrorism policing with Hamid regarded as a key figure in extremist networks. Police say Hamid played a crucial role in grooming young men for terrorism and possible training overseas. Hamid's training came in the form of camping trips around the UK and late night talks in the living room of his home. Prosecutors said he sought to groom impressionable young men, a process that had only intensified after the July 2005 suicide bombings.[35]

His first impression, the interviewee said, was one of amazement at the massive contrast between the incredibly serious interpretation the police put on Hamid's behaviour post-7/7 and 21/7 and what he said was their complete disinterest when Hamid was doing exactly the same things for years beforehand:

Personally I don't think Hamid was a big player. I think he is being talked up for the jury and the media. Loads of us have been on his paintballing trips, you can't say we were all being groomed. But fair enough he got away with things for a long time and then because of 7/7 and 21/7 he gets hit. He can't argue with that.[36]

Reading the BBC report also prompted the interviewee to comment on Hamid's motivation:

You know what he was doing was wrong but it doesn't always take a sledge hammer to crack a nut. This kind of report will get them more supporters. You have got to speak to the same youth and put them straight about where Hamid and the others are wrong. But not any Muslims can do that. It needed the Brixton brothers to spot what was wrong with his call. Honestly in the 1990s it was only Abdul Haqq (Baker) and his salafi brothers in Gresham Road who were calling Abu Hamza, Hamid and the others extremists. No one else seemed to know what was going on or care about it.[37]

In an interview on BBC television two of Hamid's co-defendants, Mousa Brown and Hamid Ahmet, were anxious to denounce the prosecution in the wake of their acquittals. Brown, for his part, sought to ridicule the notion that serious terrorists would have been so open about their outdoor activities and suggests they were unfairly targeted by police and security services to become informants:

Referring to allegations prosecutors made about his own activities, Mr Brown said the picture painted bore no resemblance to reality. He had ended up in the dock, he said, because of his Muslim beard and the leisure activities he enjoyed. 'This is because of legislation which says that I'm a terrorist because I went paintballing and look the way I look', Mr Brown told the BBC after his release. 'It was blatantly obvious to the police that I was innocent', he said. 'They knew [from the beginning]. They knew after I was charged'. Mr Brown said officers from MI5 approached him after police had charged him with involvement in Hamid's camps, and had offered him a deal. 'They said to me that they knew that I'm not a terrorist and "we can help you"', he said. 'They wanted me to become an informant in the community. I will never forget that. 'They would have known that I was innocent because of the surveillance—they would have heard my views on terrorism. 'I have condemned it outright in conversations that they taped'. Mr Brown said he believed he had gone into the trial like a football team '15 points behind' at the start of the season, thanks to police and media attention to the case.[38]

The same interviewee also knew Brown and other defendants in the case. He was asked to comment on Brown's BBC interview as well:

Look that stuff about being pressured to be an informant rings true. That's no different to the way police might put pressure on you to be a grass in drugs and ordinary crime. No different really just bigger pressure, bigger stakes. But at the same time Mousa Brown is not talking straight about their views. They do support bin Laden but generally it's all talk. You feel sorry for them because they like to think they are important but they are not. Ok some got off but others ended up going to prison for a few years as though they are serious terrorists but really they are just playing games. But that's just the same as when they were doing robberies and drugs deals. They were small time then and the real criminals and the real terrorists just think of them like dirt.[39]

The interviewee was asked if the presence of 21/7 terrorists at one of Hamid's training camps made any difference because that was clearly a key factor in Hamid's conviction:

Not really. The fact is you might get serious people looking at these kind of events to see if they can find new recruits. Now maybe that's how the people got found and chosen for 21/7. I can't say but it's true the people for 21/7 were well known to us as well and that did not make us responsible for them. To be honest we have held outdoor training events and not been able to vouch for everyone. And let's not forget they couldn't get things right on 21/7. They were failures in crime and next they were failures in terrorism.[40]

What emerges from these and other interviews with former street criminals who have converted to Islam as a way of renouncing their former lifestyles is a sense of the importance of the influence of authoritative figures who have themselves become devout, practising Muslims after previously leading morally corrupt and criminally punishable lives.[41] If the influence comes from individuals like Abdul Haqq Baker and his colleagues then the outcome is likely to be beneficial for the individual and the communities he interacts with.[42] When, however, the influence is provided by the likes of Abu Hamza, Abdullah el Faisal or Mohamed Hamid then the outcome is far less certain and may, as evidenced by 21/7, end in terrorism.[43] The interviewee's point that many individuals attending paintballing and other 'training camp' events with Hamid were not or were resistant to 'grooming' may appear commonplace but should not be overlooked. Certainly for informed insiders in the Brixton salafi community the question of why some youths went paintballing with Hamid and did not get 'radicalised' while others did is no different to a similar kind of question they would ask about their own influence when they organised their own paintballing events. They have a different purpose to Hamid but they show similar skills when interacting with their youth groups. Like all teachers or youth leaders in a wide range of training scenarios they have learnt to accept that for a host of contingent reasons beyond their control some youths will come under their influence and others will not. Another Muslim community leader who organised weekend outdoor pursuit sessions for young Londoners in East London between 1995 and 2000 highlights a key issue:

When you have got a group of kids together for the weekend you have got an opportunity to make a big impression on them. Especially if you have travelled away from London in a mini bus together and you pitch tents in a remote part of the country. You can get through to them in a way you would never do in their own area. If they are involved in street robberies and drugs then it is vital you talk to them away from their own streets. It's also the best place to tell them what is wrong with Faisal and the others [extremists]. But it is disappointing when someone you thought had listened gets back to their old ways when they get home. You just have to keep giving the true call. And sometimes a youth who you never thought was listening surprises you because they become good Muslims.[44]

The limitless contingencies that surround the issue of youths drifting away from and alternatively being drawn towards youth leaders whether they be Muslim or not raises difficult research issues of the kind identified by Marc Sageman:

The inability of specific factors, singly or in combination, to distinguish future mujahedin from non-mujahedin [Sageman's term for al-Qaeda terrorists] limits our ability to make statements that are specific to terrorists. Identification of variables specific to the creation, maintenance and demise of terrorists requires comparison with a relevant control group of non-terrorists.[45]

So in Hamid's case the picture of his outdoor pursuit activities is incomplete if attention focuses solely on those individuals who are known to have become terrorists. It is necessary to illuminate the narratives of over two hundred young Muslims who had attended the same and similar events to gain any meaningful understanding. Just as an imam who had six terrorists in his weekly congregation of 1000 worshippers for Friday prayers is clearly not a 'terrorist associate' in any pejorative sense. Nevertheless, bottom-up narratives from community witnesses to the process of propaganda and recruitment make a valuable contribution to Sageman's call for a control sample. In a discussion with Brixton salafis in 2007 a similar point was made in connection with Mohammed Siddique Khan the leader of the 7/7 London bombers:

> He was a trained youth worker. Everyone who had worked with him was shocked when they saw he was a bomber because they knew how good he was helping young people. Well there you have it. It's the same skills. It's just how you are using them. That's the only difference.[46]

In the same discussion there was a bleak recognition that someone as skilled as Khan would have been able to infiltrate a local government project aimed at tackling violent extremism had it suited his purposes to do so—such was his ability 'to tick all the right boxes' with officials.[47] Consequently academics have found it far more fruitful to investigate the motivations and rationales of terrorist movements rather than the personalities and motivations of the individuals who collectively comprise a whole. Nonetheless, in each individual case of recruitment to a terrorist movement there will be coherent, complex and compelling reasons *why* and *how* that individual became a terrorist. Such are the obvious constraints concerning access to active and imprisoned terrorists that empirical research in this field is extremely limited. However, such research that exists reinforces the notion of ordinary people performing extraordinary roles, often in extraordinary circumstances.[48]

To put the Brixton salafi experience into context it is worth quoting Mehmood Naqshbandi, not least because it is an extract from a booklet that was written in response to a request from MCU officers for a reliable guide to Muslim communities for police officers:

> Since the 1980s there has been an increasing awareness among Western Muslim youth of their identities as Muslims as distinct from their ethnic identities, which have become diffused in younger generations. As specifically Muslim issues have become topical, these have focussed youngsters' attention on Islam. At the same time, these generations have an inability to connect with the obscure factionalism of their parents, and they have available to them high quality literature in Western European languages that challenges conventional Islamic authority and propagates concepts about returning to the roots of Islam, the *Salaf*. These influences have combined to produce an influential and growing body of young Muslims who have adopted a spectrum of practices ranging widely from militant hostility to full participation in Western society, and coming under a broad umbrella generally known as salafi-ism.[49]

The Brixton experience is indeed largely a convert story. Abdul Haqq Baker emerges as a pivotal figure and documents the first in-depth convert Brixton salafi perspective himself.[50]

At the beginning of the 1990s he was one of three close friends who were contemplating giving up secular young black Londoner lifestyles and becoming strictly practising Muslims.[51] At the end of 2001 they were established managers of the Brixton Mosque facing tough questioning from the police and the media about their connections to the al-Qaeda shoe-bomber Abdul Raheem, otherwise Richard Reid.[52] They would face similar questions about their connections to Zacarias Moussaoui subsequently convicted of terrorism offences connected to 9/11.[53] Such was one outcome of the dramatic transformation in their lives occasioned by their enthusiastic embrace of a new religion.[54] At no point then or subsequently did they regret the decision they made to give up their former lifestyles—on the contrary, they had acquired an unshakeable belief in the precepts of their new religion and therefore in their own eyes their greatest accomplishment was to have played key roles in the conversion of hundreds of young men to Islam.[55] On reflection, for MCU officers, this fact neatly described the different but compatible motivations the Brixton salafis and the MCU brought to the London partnership: a religious imperative to proselytise and correct error on one side of the partnership and a duty to prevent harm on the other.[56]

In changing their lifestyles the new Muslims never actually departed from the Brixton street scene they knew so well.[57] Instead they deployed their street skills in what was often a strenuous and demanding fight against violent criminal and extremist elements, the most dangerous masquerading as Muslims themselves.[58] In using their street credentials to encourage young black Londoners to become Muslim they were behaving no differently to their evangelical Christian neighbours whose conduct was enthusiastically supported by police.[59] For the MCU to support their efforts at tackling violent extremism was therefore both pragmatic and consistent.[60] When asked to recall the compelling moments in their initial conversion process the three Brixton salafis suggest they responded positively to overtures from a handful of black Londoners who had already embraced Islam as a way of enhancing their self-esteem.[61] No one was more instrumental or encouraging than Sheikh Mohammad Kamaludin who together with Hamid Abdullah formed Ansaru Allah, the forerunner of the Brixton Mosque located in a house in Stockwell in 1976:

One of the crucial things we learned from Sheikh Kamal was the importance of civic duty. Sheikh Kamal was the first Muslim prison imam in London.

Every day he would go into prison with the sole purpose of helping men who were in serious trouble. Men who had made a mess of their lives. We could see that he was doing what a Muslim had to do. There was never any question for us that being a Muslim was somehow private or spiritual. It was about being active in the community. Trying as hard as could to promote good and right behaviour. Sheikh Kamal also taught us we could work for the civil service— no basic conflict with being a Muslim.[62]

For his part Sheikh Kamaludin was delighted that a younger generation was converting to Islam and bringing with them new skills and energy:

I could see [the three Brixton salafis] were going to build on the foundations we laid. It was a good feeling. Like me they were from the streets. But they were focused. They knew the Nation guys [Nation of Islam] and the others were on the wrong path and were good at sorting them out.[63]

Having himself given up the un-Islamic pleasures of Brixton street life in the 1970s when becoming Muslim, Sheikh Kamaludin could empathise with the new Brixton salafis as they came to terms with the enormity of a sudden cultural disjuncture in their lives. For instance when they gave away their precious musical instruments and records they were following in the Sheikh's footsteps—he had been immersed in Jamaican music as the UK road manager of reggae star Jimmy Cliff prior to conversion. Another experience Sheikh Kamaludin spoke about foreshadowed some of the negative responses the Brixton salafis would encounter throughout the study period:

I was proud of my role in the prisons. It was a pioneering role. I had a fine record for fifteen years. But when I retired there was no recognition. Nothing. That disappointed me.[64]

When pressed to reflect on why he had failed to receive any official recognition for his services Sheikh Kamaludin concluded that it was probably his salafism that had caused problems for Prison Service management once they came under the influence of mainstream Deobandi and Sufi-oriented Barelvi Muslims. That problem would certainly recur for the Brixton salafis during the course of the study period.[65] In any event, Sheikh Kamaludin's personal introduction to Islam proved decisive for one of the new Brixton salafi leaders.[66] That said, it is notable that for most of the fifty plus black London Muslim converts I met during the course of participant observation highlighted the powerful impact of hearing and reading the actual words of Allah as written in the Qur'an.[67] The appeal of this direct and simple connection to their creator appears crucial to the conversion process. Later the salafi converts would want to hear and understand the words of their new religion in their original Arabic—but initially it was a life-changing experience to be connected so clearly to their creator, even in language that was a translation from the original. Christianity, those with traditional religious upbringings recalled, could not compete with that clarity.[68]

Two related factors also played a part in prompting them to think about Islam and becoming Muslim. One was their ongoing interest in black American politics and the influence of two iconic figures, Mohammed Ali[69] and Malcolm X, who had both embraced Islam.[70] As in Mohammed Ali's case it was not orthodox Islam but the Nation of Islam that had achieved a small but significant presence in Brixton, as elsewhere in black London. Malcolm X, on the other hand, was known to have moved from the Nation of Islam to an acceptance of orthodox Islam. One of the founding Brixton salafis comments on the significance of Malcolm X in his own conversion to Islam:

I read Malcolm X's autobiography in 1991 and it made a huge impression. What attracted Malcolm X to Islam was absolutely crucial for me as well. It was equality and justice for blacks. When Malcolm X went on hajj to Mecca it was the first time he really experienced a fraternity of people where black, white, yellow, brown didn't matter. He had left the racial segregation of America behind and he found true equality in Islam. We were still facing discrimination in London and we were attracted to Islam for some of the same reasons as Malcolm X. We were also curious about the Nation of Islam but we soon came to see that it was a deviant, false religion with no proper foundation.[71]

Nor was becoming Muslim entirely inconsistent with an established local black community move towards fundamentalist and evangelical Christian practice. Again interviews and participant observation suggest that both local evangelical approaches to Christianity and salafi approaches to Islam appealed especially to sections of the black youth community who had become involved in and wanted to escape from the pervasive influence of street gang—'gangster'—culture where violent crime and the risks of death, injury and imprisonment were high.[72] Islam in general and the salafi rendition of it in particular offered salvation, redemption and the opportunity to 'wipe the slate clean' in much the same way as evangelical Christianity. Islam, however, had the advantage of being linked to an iconic black role model, Malcolm X.[73] If Martin Luther King was remembered as a stereotypical Christian who turned the other cheek when faced with injustice Malcolm X represented a more determined black activism that asserted itself against racism.[74] That at least, may help explain why becoming Muslim has particular appeal for local black youth in Brixton. Thanks to the pervasive influence of black American and Jamaican street culture the Atlantic gap had grown small. Jamaican influence also accounted for the strong presence in Brixton of Rastafarianism—here again, an iconic black figure Bob Marley serving to blend strict religious adherence with political activism and street credibility. According to one local interviewee the only drawback to becoming 'Rasta' for Brixton youth wanting to escape violent crime was that it did not remove them from the same street influences and tended to leave them at the mercy of Jamaican drug dealers.[75]

When recalling the experience of conversion and the early months of being Muslim the Brixton salafi leaders point to the clarity and precision of the salafi creed as being crucial to their personal religious development.[76] This particular recollection is germane:

At first we were happy to accept all these different approaches to Islam taking place under the same roof. Typically we would see Nation of Islam brothers rubbing shoulders with Sufi brothers and agreeing to conduct prayers in different ways. But it was very disjointed. Some of the Sufi brothers from Africa retained folk customs that had nothing to do with Islam. When we started to hear the pure salafi call we were struck by its simple truth and began to feel uncomfortable with talk of Sufi saints and talk of Sufi masters. And even more uncomfortable with all that crazy Nation of Islam stuff. We were drawn to a call that seemed to cut through all the man-made trappings that reminded me of the Catholic Church and get straight to the heart of being Muslim. For us being salafi meant being guided by Allah (swt) and having a very clear, practical role in the community. The Prophet Muhammad (pbuh) and his companions were active community leaders and being salafi meant we should follow that example.[77]

The following year, 1992, Spike Lee's gritty portrayal of the black political icon in the film *Malcolm X* was shown at the Ritzy Cinema in Brixton (as it was all over London) where it attracted significant interest. A combination of black political activism and street presence was immensely popular with local black audiences many of whom had experienced the Brixton riots a decade earlier. For them, the racial prejudice Malcolm X fought against resonated with their personal experience, albeit theirs was on a less dramatic scale. Local black relations with the Metropolitan Police were also far from serene, notwithstanding the wholesale recommendations for improvement made by Lord Scarman in the wake of the Brixton riots.[78] Two years later former world boxing champion, Mohammed Ali, now suffering from Parkinson's disease, attended a local school and members of the new salafi community were overawed to meet another black American hero. Significantly, however, at precisely the same time, a black activist from Jamaica, Abdullah el Faisal was making a name for himself locally as an established Muslim who had the added credibility of having studied in Saudi Arabia. Initially the new Muslims regarded Faisal favourably; his willingness to challenge authority and stand up for black youths against the police appeared wholly consistent with the Malcolm X style of approach they admired so much. Only later in 1993 would his extremism become clear to them.[79]

Prior to their conversion (or as they would say 'reversion') to Islam, the future Brixton salafi leaders were simply three close friends who enjoyed the pleasures of black London street culture. For one of them a memorable transition from youthful secular indulgence to strict salafi religious observance was marked by dancing self-consciously in proto-salafi dress at a *Public Enemy* London gig and smoking cannabis in the precincts of a local mosque.[80] Memorable because they proved to be the final acts of his old secular self. By embracing Islam he and his friends waved goodbye to the trappings of their familiar lives, most notably the musical instruments that were denied them in their new strict, religious identities. At no point, however, did they feel they were distancing themselves from the heartbeat of Brixton as the capital of black consciousness in the UK. This was not a religious conversion that equated to a retreat in any sense. While they may not have signed up to Darcus Howe's politics their conversion to Islam saw them retain the strong sense of black Brixton identity that Howe articulates:

If you walk through Brixton there is Bob Marley Way and Marcus Garvey Way, named after the man who spawned Rastafarianism. Even the names of the streets indicate the presence of blacks in Brixton. I want to add that it is a Jamaican presence. Jamaica has a long tradition of black nationalism for freedom led by Bob Marley. Brixton is a working-class black oasis of revolt and anger. On any day of the week you will meet black people who walk with their shoulders square, heads still and with a quiet presence of black power. There is nowhere else in the United Kingdom where that exists.[81]

In this way salafism came to answer their own growing, nagging concerns about the arcane nature of Sufi practice on the one hand and the idiosyncratic nature of Nation of Islam beliefs on the other.[82] Abdul Haqq Baker and his two close friends were drawn to the notion that human reason was limited and that individuals should not seek to fathom the inscrutable nature of Allah. To them, Sufi claims of 'mystical' knowledge appeared arrogant and elitist. The word of God, they felt, should be accepted on its own terms, not subjected to man-made analogy and invention. Slowly but surely they began to challenge what they saw as the deviant approaches to Islam that were taking place around them. By dismissing pacifist, elitist, quietist Sufi practice on the one hand and *takfiri* insurrection on the other it felt to them as if they had found the middle ground—itself a defining feature of Islam. Within two years this resulted in them establishing the first ever British-run Salafi mosque in the UK. Power struggles and negotiations characterised their rise from new Muslim adherents to management and control of the mosque. By the end of 2001 they had played a major role in curbing the influence of key al-Qaeda strategists who had targeted the community for al-Qaeda support and recruitment. Not only did this singular achievement go unacknowledged at the time it remained poorly understood and contested until the end of the study period. This is critical because had they followed a Sufi route instead of a salafi course they would have had no credibility in tackling al-Qaeda propaganda. That at least was their own assessment and later the assessment of the MCU.[83] In discussion the Brixton salafi leadership agreed that Quintan Wiktorowicz accurately summarised the essence and implications of becoming salafi for them:[84]

To protect tawhid [the oneness of God], Salafis argue that Muslims must strictly follow the Qur'an and hold fast to the purity of the Prophet Muhammad's model. The latter source of religious guidance plays a particularly central role in the Salafi creed. As the Muslim exemplar, he embodied the perfection of tawhid in action and must be emulated in every detail. Salafis also follow the guidance of the Prophet's companions (the *salaf*), because they learned about Islam directly from the messenger of God and are thus best able to provide an accurate portrayal of the prophetic model (the term 'Salafi' signifies followers of the prophetic model as understood by the companions).[85]

In their formative years as new Muslims one of their key reference points was the work of Ibn Taymiyya (1263—1328) a controversial Muslim scholar, popular with their salafi mentors.[86] In acknowledgement, they re-named the Brixton mosque, *Masjid Ibnu Taymeeyah*,[87] (their preferred spelling) while retaining an English rendition by which it is more commonly known, *Brixton Mosque and Islamic Cultural Centre* (albeit locally it is either referred to as the Brixton Mosque, the Gresham Road Mosque or sometimes the Jamaican Mosque).[88] An important point attaches to their decision to re-name the mosque after Ibn Taymiyya in so far as their understanding of Ibn Taymiyya's texts and the significance they placed upon them ran counter to prevailing wisdom. For many al-Qaeda supporters and allied activists Ibn Taymiyya was a champion for jihad against corrupt rulers. This position had become axiomatic since it was first published in 1981 in a seminal text for violent extremism, *The Neglected Duty* by Abdal Salam Faraj (1954—1982).[89] In fact Faraj distorted Ibn Taymiyya's texts to suit his purpose, an approach that would later be adopted by Shaykh Abdullah Azzam (1941—1989), a charismatic Palestinian leader of the anti-Soviet jihad in Afghanistan. Faraj used Ibn Taymiyya to legitimise the murder of the Egyptian President, Anwar Sadat, and Azzam went on to use the medieval scholar to underwrite a case for repossessing all former Muslim lands, Andalusia included.[90]

In contrast the Brixton salafis developed an understanding of Ibn Taymiyya's texts where forbearance was the required virtue in the face of injustice from rulers:

Among the fundamentals of the truth, which the texts [to which one refers to know the religion] provide proofs of, is that people with a tyrannical and unjust leader are ordered to show patience in the face of his tyranny, his injustice, his oppression, and not to fight him. The Prophet, may God pray over him and grant him peace, has likewise commanded that in more than one hadith. He did not, absolutely, authorise the pushing back of oppression by fighting. Quite the contrary: given that fighting is the source of dissension, he prohibited the pushing back of oppression by this means and ordered patience—Ibn Taymiyya, *al-Istiqama*.[91]

In this respect the Brixton salafis were following the best contemporary scholarship on Ibn Taymiyya, principally carried out by Yahya Michot, an Oxford scholar.[92] In the circumstances it was apposite for Michot to attend the Brixton mosque to lecture on the subject in 2006.[93] Suffice to say, however, the authors of the 9/11 Commission Report chose to dismiss such scholarly approaches and adopt a neo-Orientalist approach by locating Ibn Taymiyya as the root cause of the al-Qaeda phenomena:

The catastrophic threat at this moment in history is [....] the threat posed by Islamist terrorism [...] Osama bin Laden and other Islamist terrorist leaders draw on a long tradition of extreme intolerance within one stream of Islam (a minority tradition), from at least Ibn Taymiyya, through the founders of Wahhabism, through the Muslim Brotherhood, to Sayyid Qutb. It is not a position with which Americans can bargain or negotiate. With it there is no common ground on which to begin a dialogue.[94]

By the mid-1990s Abdul Haqq Baker and his two close friends had become the driving force at a local mosque in Gresham Road, Brixton, by then a bulwark against the growing influence of al-Qaeda propagandists and supporters in the area.[95] After two years they had evaluated the many competing strands of Islamic adherence prevalent locally and decided to follow salafi practice under the guidance of salafi scholars in Saudi Arabia and Jordan.[96] Such familiarity with the leading salafi scholars of the day gave them useful tools with which to refute heavyweights like Abu Qatada who traded on their alleged links to key salafi scholars themselves.[97] Despite a paucity of genuine English language scholarship on salafism the Brixton salafis have been quick to commend Quintan Wiktorowicz and Thomas Hegghammer, from the USA and Norway respectively, as two scholars whose work on leading Saudi- and Jordan-based salafi scholars they regard as being reasonably accurate and impartial.[98] Indeed their discussions with both scholars during the course of participant observation have offered fascinating complementary insights into two distinct 'insider' and 'outsider' perspectives on the same salafi scholars.[99] However, although the Brixton salafi leadership are prepared to accept Wiktorowicz's three-part salafi typology—purist, politico and jihadi[100]—they do suggest important qualifications.[101]

Most importantly, the Brixton salafi position is that the 'jihadi' categorisation for al-Qaeda terrorists is more accurately defined as *takfiri*.[102] Their first-hand experience of dealing with Abu Qatada, Abu Hamza and Abdullah el Faisal and their supporters is that they have deviated from the straight path of Sunni Islam and should not therefore be considered salafi at all.[103] To call them 'jihadi' is, they suggest, to devalue true and authentic jihad. *Takfiri* is used by Brixton salafis to denote extremist groups and individuals who regularly make pronouncements that corrupt Muslim leaders and individuals can be attacked because they have by their conduct become unbelievers (*kafir*).[104] *Takfiri* is also used to denote the way the same extremist groups and individuals sanction and promote attacks against unbelievers without regard for the necessary contexts demanded by Islam's core

texts. Therefore, they argue, *takfiri* more accurately denotes the important sense in which individuals and groups wittingly cross clear religious boundaries in an effort to justify their cause (in this case, violence
against fellow UK citizens in the UK).[105] Thus as soon as it became
clear to the new Brixton salafis that Abdullah el Faisal was licensing
violent crime against *kafirs* on the streets of London they saw that he
was transgressing very clear salafi teachings.[106] This is an important
understanding that formed the basis for the Brixton salafis' later youth
outreach work where they sought to clarify true Islamic teachings. It is
also crucial to establishing the legitimacy and effectiveness of their
youth outreach work. Several Sufi Muslims complained that the Brixton salafis were promoting a version of Islam that looked to narrow-
minded Saudi scholars for direction. In fact, as the Brixton salafis
correctly observe, it was precisely their strict allegiance to Salafi scholars (and disdain for Sufi scholars) that gave them credibility when tackling the *takfiris*.[107]

Ironically, the Brixton salafis turn to an American academic, Quintan Wiktorowicz, for a fair assessment of their religious credentials. In
particular, they agree with Wiktorowicz that the defining characteristics of salafism are a 'puritanical approach to the religion intended to
eschew religious innovation by strictly replicating the model of the
Prophet Muhammad'; a creed that 'revolves around strict adherence to
the concept of tawhid (the oneness of God)'; an 'ardent rejection of a
role for human reason, logic, and desire'; and by 'strictly following the
rules and guidance in the Qur'an and Sunna (path or example of the
Prophet Muhammad)' salafis 'eliminate the biases of human subjectivity and self-interest, thereby allowing them to identify the singular
truth of God's commands'.[108] Success for this approach was demonstrated for the Brixton salafis between 1997 and 2001 when over 1500
young people, mainly from South London, converted to Islam at the
Brixton Mosque.[109] It is notable that most of the fifty plus black London Muslim converts met or interviewed during the course of participant observation highlighted the powerful impact of hearing and
reading the actual words of Allah as written in the Qur'an. The appeal
of this direct and simple connection to their creator appears crucial to
the conversion process. In this respect they have something in common
with early modern London Protestant forebears like the radical Ana-
baptist William Gouge who rejected religious hierarchy in favour of
direct engagement with religious texts.[110]

Why were MCU officers interested in these antecedents of the Brixton salafis? 'It was genuine interest' an MCU officer recalls, 'a shared interest in street politics and a strong feeling of repairing years of mistrust'. He also highlights the importance of trust building:

....it's good to know people you are dealing with are authentic. And it helps to assess expertise, credibility and calibre. You get to meet so many people whose talk is stronger than their actions.[111]

8

CHALLENGING TERRORISTS

The salafi community based in Brixton, South London, provide compelling accounts of their success in combating the propaganda of Abu Hamza, Abu Qatada and Abdullah el Faisal at close quarters over a sustained period from the early 1990s onwards. Initially this community-based work consisted of resistance to the efforts of Abu Qatada and Abdullah el Faisal to win influence in their own communities and to take over control of their mosque (or masjid, as they would prefer to call the building, a former household residence converted to religious use). Indeed, the local salafi leadership was first comprised of relatively new Muslim converts who candidly admitted that for a brief period they were almost seduced by the claims of Abu Qatada to possess legitimate Islamic authority to allow him to assume control of the mosque and leadership of their local salafi community. Similarly Abu Qatada established a regular presence at a youth club (the Four Feathers) near Baker Street and the Regent Park Mosque (officially the London Central Mosque). His lack of fluent English was more than compensated by his reputation as a senior scholar and the willingness of loyal supporters to translate his teachings for eager audiences.

Abu Qatada's outwardly impressive religious credentials were only exposed as sham when the Brixton leadership made enquiries of authoritative salafi scholars in Saudi and Jordan. Later, the same line of enquiries enabled the same local London leadership to rebut the challenges to their authority by Abdullah el Faisal. Suffice to say for the many young British born, British naturalised or British resident Muslims who gathered in circles to listen to the charismatic talks delivered by Abdullah el Faisal (in English) and by Abu Qatada (largely in Arabic at first but with some simultaneous English translations) the absence of religious authority was not apparent. Indeed, like their contemporary Abu Hamza, that lack of 'official' licence was turned to good advantage. Thus, the 'official' salafi scholars based in Saudi and Jordan who denounced them as 'extremists' and to whom the Brixton mosque management deferred were easily dismissed as 'sell-outs', 'dollar-scholars' or corrupt lackeys of the West who were part of the problem of corruption al-Qaeda sought to solve.

By endorsing the so-called 'dollar-scholars' against the subversive influence of such London-based al-Qaeda propagandists as Abu Hamza, Abu Qatada and Abdullah el Faisal the Brixton salafis inevitably sustained the same kind of criticism themselves. While this criticism might undermine them on occasions it was generally something they reckoned on overcoming when they were addressing the same Muslim youth audiences that the al-Qaeda propagandists were seeking to influence. Whether at public meetings, in study circles or in one-on-one counselling sessions, the Brixton salafis were able to offset the charge of subservience to corrupt Arab regimes by strict adherence to mainstream salafi interpretations of Islam that valued public security above political conflict or the exercise of political agitation. When dealing with the widely felt political grievances that al-Qaeda sought to exploit, the Brixton salafis would acknowledge the legitimacy of a sense of political injustice (say for instance in relation to the treatment of the Palestinians by Israel and the West) while adhering to a position of non-intervention on the basis that a British Muslim's primary duty was to attend to his (or her) religious, social and family obligations in the UK. For example, during the conflict in Bosnia, for the Brixton salafis (following the advice of salafi scholars in Saudi and Jordan) there was a duty to provide charitable aid to fellow European Muslims who were facing hardship but no duty to fight jihad with their Bosnian brothers on the front line.

Many London Muslims were exercised by the plight of Bosnian Muslims during the bloody conflict that followed the breakup of Yugoslavia after the collapse of Russian and East European communism. In response, a small but significant number of London Muslims expressed their solidarity through the provision of aid, some travelling personally to the war-torn region to dispense it. During the course of participant observation in August 2007 one seasoned Brixton salafi recalled his own role in the Bosnian conflict:

It started with BBC news reports where barbaric attacks on Muslims soon became commonplace. Then we started to get appeals for help from brothers who had gone to provide support themselves. Brixton did what most other active Muslim centres did—collect emergency aid materials. I drove one lorry load of provisions to Bosnia to try and provide some tangible support myself. I was very tempted to stay and fight but I was not permitted to do so. According to our scholars the position was that the Bosnian Muslims were fighting a legitimate defensive jihad against a violent aggressor. Some Muslims in London thought it was ok to join them in fighting jihad but our position was that we were not permitted to do so as British Muslims. We got some criticism for that.[1]

Al-Qaeda researcher Evan Kohlmann[2] typifies an approach by mainstream terrorism studies' scholars that occasionally overlooked the genuine community concern that existed in London as elsewhere in Europe during the Bosnian civil war. For Kohlmann, this was the period when London-based al-Qaeda propagandists like Abu Hamza sought to mobilise UK Muslims as *mujahideen* in defence of Bosnian Muslims with a view to galvanising a siege mentality so as to facilitate a global jihad against the West. By acknowledging the extent to which ordinary London Muslims travelled to Bosnia to undertake charitable support work on their own volition (without prompting from Abu Hamza or other al-Qaeda propagandists) it becomes possible to demonstrate the opportunistic nature of al-Qaeda terrorism, feeding as it does off community concerns rather than setting new agendas. By the same token it is possible to differentiate between al-Qaeda terrorism and London Muslim community charitable activity so that the latter is not pejoratively conflated with the former without good cause.

A restrained approach by the Brixton salafis stood in sharp contrast to the edicts of Abu Hamza, who consolidated his power base at the Finsbury Park Mosque in North London during the mid- to late-1990s. Here in a transcription of a talk Abu Hamza gave to a circle of supporters in London in 1999, Abu Hamza seeks to demonstrate the superiority of his call to violent action over the responsible approach of his South London neighbours:

Don't you know Allah is happy when a *kafir* is killed? Don't you know that? Don't you know Allah is happy when a Muslim is taken out of his prison by force and you are humiliating the *kafirs* who put him in? Don't you know that? Don't you know that Allah is happy when you stop the evil from every society so the people can have good ears and they go have good listen to the reality of Islam. Don't you know that? Don't you know that the Prophet has praised people who will change people in life so they can change them into janaah also in the hereafter.... I am telling you what the ulama have failed to tell you. Because simply they cannot say this because they have sold the religion of Allah. They are giving you now a very blunt statement everywhere, simply because the money is too sharp in their mind.[3]

Just as Abu Hamza, Abu Qatada and Abdullah el Faisal had leadership qualities and gathered devoted supporters around them so too Abdul Haqq Baker emerged as a leader and spokesman for the Brixton salafis and would often find himself on the front line of heated disputes with the three *takfiris* and their supporters.[4] The first major clash occurred in November 1993 when Faisal and forty supporters entered the Brixton Mosque with a view to seizing control.[5] By this time Faisal had been excluded from the mosque because of his *takfiri* ideology.[6] Instead he had moved a short distance away to lead study circles in the local vicinity and attracted sizeable audiences. Faisal spent considerable time attacking the ideas and practices of the Brixton mosque that had expelled him.[7] In one recorded talk 'The Devil's Deception of the Saudi Salafees' he launches into a tirade against the Brixton Mosque management on the basis of their alleged subservience to the corrupt rulers of Saudi Arabia.[8] Because the Brixton salafis made it their business to monitor Faisal's study circles they became aware that he had decided to break his ban at the mosque and attend the following week with his supporters in a show of strength.[9] News of this potential confrontation spread rapidly throughout Muslim South London.[10] Faisal had chosen his time well because the Mosque management were already dealing with tensions between different groups of mosque users.[11] In interview, Baker recalls that while the mosque management team was ready and prepared to deal with the potential conflict, they were also conscious of the need to avoid overreaction and violence.[12] At a time that would not have been anticipated if the Brixton Mosque management had been less well informed, Faisal entered the mosque with approximately forty supporters. According to Baker:

He proceeded to the main prayer area, sat and began his lecture, despite my presence as mosque leader. My team immediately approached the 'security' around Faisal, and Faisal himself, and left him and his team in no doubt that they had entered without authority and in contravention of the ban—and that we would not allow them to take over. We knew it was likely that some of Faisal's were carrying firearms so we had to take that into account. We were very firm but acted in a calm manner—although we were anxious about the risks involved. We had about twenty close supporters with us and in addition about two hundred other mosque users were present. Faisal made it clear that he intended to deliver an address and positioned himself in front of the microphone—his security or bodyguards forming a semi-circle around him. Faisal started to speak but very soon his voice fell silent—I had instructed a colleague to switch off the public address system. Several of his supporters got very angry but they were restrained by the commanding presence of our own supporters who had a tough reputation.[13]

Other eye witnesses confirm Baker's account and agree that this was a trial of strength that Faisal lost. He also lost face with his supporters. Before he left the mosque in defeat however he tried to deliver his address in another room but was again thwarted by the close physical attention of the Brixton salafis. On departing Faisal tried to save face by saying that he would return soon—he did not. Surprisingly, given their level of hostility and desire to demonstrate ascendancy Faisal and his supporters declined to resort to violence. All the evidence suggests that they chose not to offer violence because they were left in no doubt that it would be met with staunch physical resistance.[14] News of the Brixton salafis victory against Faisal and his supporters spread rapidly around the Muslim streets of South London. For his part Faisal sought to limit the damage to his street credibility by seeking some spurious moral high ground on the dubious basis that he would keep his dignity against a 'bunch of thugs'. This from a man who happily sanctioned cowardly violent street attacks on defenceless *kafirs* in London.[15]

Witnesses to the showdown at Brixton Mosque are convinced that it proved decisive in cementing the Brixton salafis' reputation for strong physical defence of their territory and ability to confront the *takfiris*. As a result they began to receive requests for support from other Mosque managements facing similar problems. One such request did in fact come via third parties from the Finsbury Park Mosque trustees seeking to tackle the adverse influence of Abu Hamza in 1997. In the event they declined this last offer because they felt they would run the risk of arrest and imprisonment in the event of any ensuing violence. 'Talking to contacts in Leyton, Fulham, North Kensington, Croydon, Regents Park and especially Finsbury Park', an MCU officer notes, 'it was clear that the Brixton salafis had earned a reputation for bravery'.[16] 'This is one of the most important qualities you look for in the community' the MCU officer continued, 'groups who are willing and able to take action—a track record. Rare. Why would you get involved in a dangerous arena if you didn't have to?'.[17] Not everyone approved of their robust tactics but there was wide community acknowledgement in 2001 that no other group had stood up so fearlessly to the bullying of Abu Hamza, Abdullah el Fasial, Abu Qatada and their supporters throughout the 1990s.[18] On the contrary, elsewhere in the capital there were examples of extremist bullying being successful, not least at the Finsbury Park Mosque.

By virtue of their actions by the mid-1990s the Brixton salafis had become recognised opponents of Abu Hamza (from Egypt), Abdullah el Faisal (from Jamaica via Saudi) and Abu Qatada (from Jordan), three of the most well-known but by no means the only al-Qaeda propagandists and apologists to have settled in London in the 1990s before being imprisoned in the UK in the following decade.[19] The fact that each of the three individuals has been cited in recent UK terrorism trials as having had an influence on the phenomena of 'homegrown' British Muslim terrorism adds interest to their role as al-Qaeda propagandists in London. By describing them as al-Qaeda propagandists I do not seek to establish conclusive organisational or network links between any one of the three and al-Qaeda's strategic hub, most publicly epitomised by Osama bin Laden and Ayman al Zawarari. Instead, I propose to rely on the evidence of their own speeches and talks—freely available either currently or in the past and used as evidence against two of them in terrorism trials—and on the evidence of Brixton salafis and other London Muslim interviewees who attended their talks and otherwise knew them.[20] In doing so I am following a path trod by the Brixton salafis continuously from 1993 and the MCU between 2002 and 2007. For instance between 11 and 23 January 2004 Brixton salafis and MCU officers studied two tapes by Abdullah el Faisal at great length, sharing interpretations to mutual benefit.[21] With research findings feeding back to the MCU and the Brixton salafis this facilitates a circular and reciprocal learning process building on Flyvbjerg's, Kenney's and Hamm's complementary notions of expert learning.[22]

What emerges with surprising clarity is that each of the three extremists had established reputations at the street level as effective communicators of a narrative that was al-Qaeda's in all but name long before 9/11. By this time Abu Qatada, Abu Hamza and Abdullah el Faisal had become well used to the Brixton salafis countermanding their violent messages.[23] In 1999 Abu Hamza delivered approximately 200 talks to Muslim audiences around the UK.[24] On at least thirty occasions Brixton salafis made it their business to attend the same venues the following week (or within a short period) to challenge his accounts and to reduce his adverse impact.[25] For his part Abu Hamza (as would Abu Qatada and Abdullah el Faisal) associated the Brixton salafis with corrupt 'dollar-scholars' and Saudi sheikhs who could not be trusted to speak uncomfortable truths:

Look at the sheikhs they are giving you a very poor kind of fatwa. Every kind of fatwa to disable you to make sure you gonna be slaughtered .... If you can't protect yourself can you protect Islam? If you can't protect your brother do you expect anybody else to protect you when it comes you turn? If you don't help your brothers do you expect Allah to help you? And if you don't say the word of truth do you expect Allah will even raise your voice when you are humiliated and killed?[26]

At defining moments in the mid-1990s the Brixton salafis confronted Abu Hamza, Abu Qatada, Abdullah el Faisal and their supporters in circumstances where street credibility rather than religious credibility were the important and competing qualities in issue.[27] Suffice to say their staunch adherence to mainstream salafism combined with a willingness to face intimidation with steadfast physical courage earned the relatively young black convert management of Brixton Mosque the respect of local Muslim youth and the grudging regard of their al-Qaeda opponents, who were otherwise used to getting their own way elsewhere in London.[28] Again, this demonstrable street quality helped them offset charges of sell-out heaped upon them by their opponents.[29]

In 1996 Abdul Haqq Baker and colleagues reported their concerns about Abdullah el Faisal to Brixton Police—at the police station just a hundred yards from the Mosque. Their concerns about Faisal's licensing and promoting of violence to non-Muslims (*kafir*) had reached a new level. They had a finger on the local pulse and had become convinced that despite their best efforts Faisal was managing to spread his message effectively through study circles and informal dialogue. This was the position they explained to police but they were not reassured that their concerns had been understood or appreciated. A throwaway comment attributed to police that they had more important things to do than sort out Mosque disputes did not inspire confidence. Eventually police put the allegations to Abdullah el Faisal and he rejected them out of hand. He maintained that the Brixton Mosque management had a vendetta against him and that he wished to make a counter allegation against them on the basis that they had threatened violence and intimidation against him. Suffice to say the matter appears to have rested there, without any further police investigation, certainly leaving the Brixton salafis disillusioned by an apparent lack of interest from police. Witnesses recall forming the impression that Abdul Haqq Baker and Abdullah el Faisal—understood to be fierce opponents in the local salafi community—were viewed by police at the time as being instead rather similar—both Muslim fundamentalists.

Brixton salafi concerns about their own arrests were not without foundation. In 1995 and 1996 occasions arose when leading members and supporters were briefly held in police custody after incidents in which they had become embroiled in conflicts with street gangs. In the event they were not charged with offences but their role as active citizens seeking to prevent young Muslims from getting involved in gang violence and extremist violence was not readily understood or appreciated by police. Certainly, the Brixton salafis were unable to forge a close relationship with the police at this time. On the contrary, relations with Brixton Police became very tense.

Brixton is also an important case study site because Abdullah el Faisal regarded himself as being well qualified to attract black convert Muslims (like himself) to the al-Qaeda flag. As we have already noted he encountered effective opposition from the Brixton salafis. However, it was not difficult for him to operate in the vicinity, away from the direct notice of the Brixton mosque. This is what he did during the second half of the 1990s and right up to his arrest in 2003, attracting black convert Muslims to his wider Muslim youth audiences, many of whom had family backgrounds in Islam, albeit of a significantly different character.[30] Typically, he would license al-Qaeda attacks that his audiences might see on the television and lesser street-level criminality that they might be engaged in. In the latter case it would be commonplace to allow that young street robbers converting to Islam might continue their criminal activity so long as they only robbed non-Muslims, the *kafir*. When the opportunity arose, the Brixton salafis were extremely effective at countermanding this kind of advice to new converts with a background in street crime because they could relate to them on their own terms and put Faisal's erroneous analysis into its proper context. Again in direct street level negotiations between local black salafi leaders (aged in their twenties and thirties during the 1990s) and local black street criminals new to Islam (typically aged between fifteen and twenty) street credibility was crucial and readily understood. Physical presence underscored religious authority.

In 2003 the Brixton salafis and their MCU partners turned their attention to the problem of extremists in prison. Typically, they did not have a formal meeting on the topic but rather a series of discussions as they went about their immediate partnership tasks. Later, in interview, a Brixton salafi leader recalled:

I think we were the only ones who were worried about the influence of Abdullah el Faisal and the others in prison in 2003. First of all we shared our experience of what prison is like. The MCU spoke about the experience of IRA and other terrorist prisoners. We spoke about the experience of young men like Richard Reid who came to Islam in prison. We agreed we needed to help prisoners just like we helped youth on the outside. At the time the prison service were reluctant for us to get involved but with time progress has been made.[31]

It follows that if the Brixton salafis had posed no threat to Abdullah el Fasial's recruitment programme he would almost certainly have ignored them—as he did with all other Muslim groups in the area. The fact that it mattered to al-Qaeda supporters to ridicule their most effective opponents on the streets and in the cafes where they competed for recruits served as a valuable performance indicator for the MCU. How to measure effectiveness in any crime prevention field is notoriously difficult but MCU officers were conscious that effectiveness at the street level required authenticity and street presence that would be assessed on the street on its own terms independently of any outside perspective, least of all one endorsed by 'the authorities'. Abdullah el Faisal attacked the Brixton salafis as being subservient to the Saudi king and the Saudi authorities generally as part of a concerted strategy to undermine their credibility. Had he been able to back that up by some evidence of physical success in terms of confrontation with his opponents then it might have counted for more. This was the same tactic employed by Abu Hamza and Abu Qatada. Interestingly, in the following extract, Abdullah el Faisal makes some sweeping generalisations about the significance of the Brixton salafis being 'African-Caribbean':

Why is it that the African-Caribbean community of Brixton Mosque they are the most vehement in their love of Fahd? [Brixton salafi published response: *Observe Faysal's propaganda here and use of simplistic reasoning in order to incite the audience to agree with him. Masjid Ibn Taymiyyah (Brixton Mosque) is independent and receives absolutely no financial support from Saudi Arabia and never has done, yet due to Faysal's propaganda this has become disseminated around the UK.*] The answer is clear, Umar said that poverty leads to what? To kufr! Poverty leads to kufr. That's why you only find the very rich Arabs in this movement, you don't find Moroccans, Algerians in this movement! Am I lying? Am I lying? I'm talking in this country do you find Moroccans and Algerians in the Salafee movement? If I'm lying tell me. I want to be corrected. There's a few in this country, but the vast majority are they in this movement? Just one and two. The people who are in this movement are the rich Arabs in the Gulf who have something to lose!'[32]

Although the salafi refutation properly addresses the inaccuracy of the description of the Brixton salafi community, Faisal does make a valid point about the vast majority of Algerian and Moroccan Muslims living in London. They have been overwhelmingly poor and disinclined to accept the authority of Saudi or other foreign national government influence. No doubt their own experience of corrupt government activity in their home countries contributed to a mind-set that found the anti-authoritarian rhetoric of Abu Qatada, Abu Hamza, Faisal and their supporters appealing. However, to characterise the Brixton salafis as quietist and subservient to any political regime would be to misrepresent their religious practice.

The Brixton salafis resort to a familiar tactic by placing Faisal and his ilk with the Kharijis, an 'early sectarian group in Islam',[33] a strategy that has proved very effective. Equally effective is the tactic of drawing attention to Faisal's failure to gain influence in the Brixton area:

Faysal picks out and highlights the African and Caribbean community in particular due to Faysal's own failure to generally penetrate the Muslim community of this particular ethnic background with his da'wah. The reality is that due to the Salafee da'wah being accepted and received from reverts and Muslims from Muslim backgrounds of African origin London, the da'wah of Faysal was going extreme and was based on personal failures and frustrations. Faysal's failure in the Brixton area, which is an area which many so-called 'revolutionaries' have tried to gain a foothold for their own desires and designs, led him to oppose the salafees of Brixton the most and accuse them of kufr.[34]

The Brixton salafis are now on very strong ground and can be seen to be on the attack against a weakened opponent:

....Faysal applies a racial stereotype which has its origins with the kuffaar and Faysal has merely accepted it, which is that the Salafees, and those from African and Caribbean origins 'are coming from very poor backgrounds and are hungry' SubhaanAllaah! Not only is this utterly incorrect but it is also an ethnic and racial stereotype that Faysal is regurgitating. From those who attend Masjid Ibn Taymiyyah (Brixton Mosque) are doctors, consultants, self-employed businesswomen and men, civil servants, teachers, youth workers, college and university students, IT experts, university graduates and more! Therefore, we totally reject the racist and stereotypical slanderous descriptions of the *salafees* of Brixton as being 'poor and hungry' and 'unemployed' which constantly dribbles off the dirty tongues of Faysal and those like him from the *takfeerees*.[35]

Similarly, the following extracts are taken from a discussion during participant observation in 2006 in which Baker comments on a talk given by Abu Hamza to a small group of young supporters in 1998. In doing so Baker is engaging retrospectively with issues he was involved in at the time, when he regularly addressed the same audiences as Abu Hamza. The discussion also replicates scores of discussions between MCU officers and Brixton salafis where the former sought to under-stand and evaluate the knowledge, skills and tactics the latter brought to bear on their efforts to tackle terrorist propaganda.

Key: AH = Abu Hamza talk 'Learning from Experience', 1998 recording—ref AH1, see index in chapter 4; AHB = Abdul Haqq Baker (2006); RL = Robert Lambert (2006).

AH   The Islamic news is that the people of Albania and Kosovo, they just need a shake up like Bosnia. Which is some blood to refresh their memory about Islam. And Allah has given them just that. And insh'Allah I think it's working, there is some blood being spilt inside Kosovo.... So everybody knows the Balkans is a very hot area. .... And the people are ready they just need somebody to provoke them or somebody to guide them and to be patient with them for it to be a hot area. Insha'Allah it will be a hot area. And before it's a hot area we want the hot people to make the hot area. So this is the situation. So you keep sharpening your teeth and don't bite your tongue.

AHB   Abu Hamza mentions something very pertinent. He said the Muslims are ready. This is with regards to the Kosovo situation. He is funda-mentally wrong in his assessment. The Salafis know that Muslims like he describes are not ready (even if jihad was legitimate which is another issue altogether). You just have to look around the world at the state of many Muslims and the fact that they are not practising Islam properly and their understanding of the fundamentals of *tawheed* and unification of Allah's worship and lordship is not clear for many of them. They're worshipping graves and going to saints in the graves. They're calling on other people other than Allah which you'll know the fundamental call of all of the Prophets in Islam that is highlighted was to the oneness of Allah. The *tawheed*. So we chal-lenge Abu Hamza at the very beginning because he is wrong to call people to Islam to teach them so that they become 'hot'. When they become 'hot' the region will become 'hot', etc. And you need the 'hot' people to go and teach so the area becomes hot. Now this is provoca-tive because what he is saying is you call the people to Islam and then get them to fight the jihad in that area. You need the people who are equipped to take them to that jihad to fight. Ordinarily that is not such a problem. That's not the final objective looking at the condition of the people of Kosovo. What should be said is we need to go and give dawah, no problem I agree with him on that. Give dawah call the people to Islam. Educate them, strengthen them equip them ok. If the situation then prevails with regards to a situation of jihad and the people are ready, they are educated, they have returned to their religion, they understand what they are saying then yes. That can be the next stage. But again I come back to the point that it's not for Abu Hamza or me to decide or dictate that. That's for someone of knowledge who has been briefed of the situation in detail.

RL   Did you address this at the time?

AHB   All the time. We were on Abu Hamza's trail. Speaking to audiences he spoke to. Having a lot of success. But of course once he took his supporters to small circles then it was difficult. But we would sometimes hear of youth who had been called to his circle and where we knew them we would go and speak to them.

RL   Go to their homes?

AHB   Go to their haunts. Sit down with them in a café. Talk to them. What we still do today. We keep our finger on the pulse.

RL   What about Abu Hamza's views on dawah?

AHB   So far what Abu Hamza is saying there is no contention with and you'll find all the Muslims will agree with what is being said here. That's not the issue. The issue here is what he says in regards to the reference to fighting. You educate them according to *tawheed*. About the oneness of Allah. About the life of Prophet Muhammad (PBUH). About why they're in the situation they're in now because they have left the religion. This is what you educate them about and how to become self-sufficient and stand up for themselves in the point of being proud Muslims. So Abu Hamza at the moment, and this is the case with quite a few extremists. There will use pure rhetoric that is about jihad, jihad, jihad. The wrong understanding about jihad.

AH   So the sheikhs are ignorant about the political map and they don't want to know about the political map. Secondly they don't want to move from their place so they are blind when they give you their advice. Thirdly they are not trustworthy anyway, to be asked. That is known. It is not the fault of the sheikh alone it is the fault of the people who asking the sheikh. You're asking something which he does not know. You go to ask sheikh for example about the premium bonds or something. What he will say to you when you ask him about something he does not know. So you are right you should ask the sheikhs who are there in the front line. Who are sharing their destiny. If the mujahideen themselves are in Bosnia fighting shoulder to shoulder with each other and mujahideen in Afghanistan fighting shoulder to shoulder to each other. ...Then here comes the sheikh. He said 'yeah insha'Allah it's allowed'. If the people waited ten years for him it would not have been called the people waited ten years for him it would not have been called Okorania or Shokorania or something.[36]

RL   Can you comment on Abu Hamza's communication skills?

AHB   Abu Hamza is able to tap into a market like those who know the street culture and the grass root culture, so his way of speaking is very, very effective. That wins over the youth a lot of the time. You'll find that most of us who are successful, it is because of the language that we use and an understanding of the current affairs. So he is speaking about the things in Kosovo much of which cannot be challenged. The information he is getting I dare say a lot of it is accurate. But I would say as well that some of it is spurious. But for those in the audience if they cannot challenge that they've only got what they are getting from the media. It is likely that he is only getting that from the media as well. But with some historical perspectives that he knows, some other incidents like the Bosnian conflict and elsewhere he can see a pattern developing which is perfectly all right. Assume he knows that. With that information the language that he is using and the casual sort of style that he is talking with, this is very appealing. Not using words that are above the heads of the people, talking on that street level. Self-assured. This is the thing, myself and others who can speak effectively to youth will speak in a similar style.

RL   What about his encouragement to ignore the Sheikhs when it comes to jihad?

AHB   Now the Jordanian scholars say no you have to have an *emir*, a leader of a state who orders you to jihad. Other differ with that to an extent that if it is a defensive jihad or the government calls a jihad then you go to fight the jihad. Now Abu Hamza's understanding doesn't even fall into any of those. It is very similar to Osama Bin Laden when he started moving around autonomously without any leadership authority just according to his dictate of where they needed to go and fight. So there is complete independence in that respect for the reasons that he is saying. Not to have dependency upon the Saudi government or any government that say they will support you financially when they have asked you to stop fighting. So what you have is a potentially anarchic group. A group that is bent on anarchy because if then the leadership say we're going to stop and negotiate now for the better peace of the people. It's not for a small group of mujahedeen to say no way and continue roaming around the country and killing enemy when there is a time of truce. You won't find this in Islamic legislature. You'll see that the Prophet (PBUH) might have despatched army units but when he called them back or when he said to make peace or to make a truce then that was exactly what was made.

This extract of a running commentary by Baker on a talk delivered by Abu Hamza highlights the extent to which a dispute about the religious obligations of young Muslims in Britain has been played out to an al-Qaeda agenda in community settings over a long period. It also serves to illustrate the value of shared learning with the MCU:

The most amazing thing about the Abdul Raheem [Richard Reid] case was we were suddenly in the news. Before then no one listened to us. But the media interest was a big problem because our enemies made trouble out of it. We could manage things on the street but we had no experience with national media. Meeting the MCU came at a good time. But it would have been good to have started a partnership sooner. Much better. Might have helped stop him [Richard Reid].[37]

The notion that the combined skills of the Brixton salafis and the MCU might help prevent cases like Reid's became a defining feature of the London partnership in Brixton. However, although the MCU was formed in January 2002 it was not until the end of the year that the unit was finally able to embark in earnest on a trust-building project with the Brixton salafi leadership.[38] The reason for the delay was that the Anti-Terrorist Branch (ATB) had to undertake and complete an investigation into the Abdul Raheem (Richard Reid)[39] and Zacarias Moussaoui[40] cases and that involved interviews with Abdul Haqq Baker, chairman of the Brixton Mosque and his colleagues.[41] According-ing to Baker that experience did nothing to increase his confidence in the police and therefore left the MCU with a legacy of suspicion to overcome.[42] What Baker makes plain, however, is that it was just one aspect of the ATB investigation that he found problematic and that came towards the conclusion of what had until then been a very cor-dial and constructive encounter:[43]

There was a sudden change in tone. I had been helpful and co-operative and they appeared to be appreciative. But then the main detective put it to me that I should think about working for them otherwise I would be a suspect in the case.[44]

Given his prior dealings with police this approach was not entirely foreign to him but it seemed all the more inappropriate in the present circumstances:

I didn't expect that because I was being very transparent. I said look I have been trying to tell you about this problem for the last eight years so don't treat me like a criminal now just because of what has happened. I had been warning this would happen [Richard Reid/Zacarias Moussaoui cases] for a long time.[45]

The frustration was shared equally by the Brixton salafi leadership who had each experienced negative and sometimes confrontational encounters with the police. As one explains:

You have got to appreciate the history of police and community relations in Brixton. The riots. Scarman. Stop and search. We grew up with all of that. In some ways it had got better but there were always incidents that kept it simmering. And big issues for Muslims. Lee Jasper [from the Mayor of London's office] got improvements for people in Brixton. But not for the Muslims. We became the outsiders. And probably the only group in Brixton that couldn't get any government or council funding. We were the poor relations. The council didn't want to know. The police didn't want to know us.[46]

What was the reason for this isolation?[47]

I think we had left the mainstream local community network—where Lee Jasper was well connected—when we became Muslim. That wasn't our choice. You could become Rasta, Christian, Buddhist, even Nation of Islam, anything and still be connected but Muslim was different. At least Salafi was different. People could see we were different. Why were we dressed like that? Council leaders could meet Muslims at the Town hall and they would wear suits and talk to the council agenda. We became the biggest mosque in Lambeth but we could somehow be ignored.[48]

What were relations like with other mosques in Lambeth?[49]

Same thing. We were outsiders. Not trusted. Friction. Why were we praying like that? Who did we think we were? What was wrong with the way they did things? Established communities and established networks. Would they speak against us to the council? Would they call us the extremists? This is what I have been told.[50]

But this situation improved?[51]

Slowly things began to improve, insha'Allah[52]

Returning to the specific issue of police relations. Was it true that efforts to report Abdullah el Faisal to the police had been rebuffed?[53]

Yes. 1996. We had been battling with Faisal for three years. We tried to explain our concerns about his violence. But there was no real interest.[54]

There was one notable exception. In 2000 a local police officer, 'home beat' or 'community' constable began to build the trust with the Brixton salafi leadership that had hitherto been lacking.[55] His willingness to help the Brixton Mosque with a range of problems slowly broke down barriers that had become problematic. Thus, for instance, the police officer would assist with problems created by drug users throwing discarded needles into the Mosque's entrance. There would also be familiar issues like parking problems at Friday prayer times that benefitted from cordial relations between the mosque management and police:

Apart from the help [...] provided it was good to begin to feel that we were not so isolated and that our efforts to help the local community were understood and appreciated.[56]

In addition, because the community police officer enjoyed good relations with other Muslim communities and other faith groups in the neighbourhood he was able to dispel some of the misperceptions that had begun to build up in relation to the Gresham Road mosque. This was the period when the mosque opened its own school—the Iqra school—in a building next door to the mosque. Here again, the police officer was able to assist the school with a number of routine matters that were vitally important in terms of trust building. This officer apart, the Brixton salafis still felt wary about police at that stage and had no constructive dialogue with senior police management prior to 9/11.

For the MCU officers, the community police officer's role was crucial and illustrative:

In the first year [2002] we spent a lot of time visiting local police stations to see if any home beat [community based] officers had built up links with local Muslim communities in the way that [...] had. It was a mixed picture.[57]

Apart from being a great guy [...] was good because he was allowed to stay put. When I walked around Brixton with him everyone said hello. He had been on the same beat for ten years. That wasn't allowed to happen anymore.[58]

Paid off. When John Stevens [MPS Commissioner 2000–2005] wanted to know the score about local drugs strategy and the impact on the street he came to speak to [...] first. Then the Borough commander.[59]

But the new Commissioner [Ian Blair 2005–2008] was keen on neighbourhood policing but less aware of the value of guys like [...] being allowed to stay put. It's not about a new system. It's about giving home beats real status and rewards. Not flooding a neighbourhood with community support officers.[60]

[...] was a dying breed. And so were we! The new management didn't want experts and specialists staying in one place.[61]

Importance attaches to time and commitment in trust-building activity between police and suspicious communities and yet it is often neglected.[62] As one of the Brixton salafi leaders recalls:

When we got a phone call from a police officer at New Scotland Yard saying he wanted to come and talk to us about our views on the problems of terrorism it sounded reasonable enough but you know once bitten twice shy and we were very cautious. What did help was that [...] said we would get the call. So we were not taken by surprise.[63]

This was the inauspicious beginning to what would eventually prove to be an effective and enduring partnership between the Brixton salafis and the MCU. What was immediately clear to the MCU officers was the sense of frustration amongst the salafi leadership that they had been 'banging their heads against a brick wall' [symbolised by Brixton police station across the road from the Brixton Mosque] for a long time and felt isolated.[64] What was immediately clear to the Brixton salafis was that the MCU had an expert understanding of the problem that complemented their own:[65]

With the Anti-Terrorist Branch you understood they have got an investigation and they want to find out who was working with Richard Reid and Zacarias Moussaoui and who else can they charge. Fair enough. And that felt just like any other police investigation only bigger, much bigger. I got the clear impression from them that they were working hand in glove with the FBI on both cases and that seemed to give them an added sense of importance and urgency. Whereas the MCU officers came from another direction altogether. They were genuinely interested in our views on the underlying problems and were not threatening or aggressive from day one. They respected our expertise and we came to respect theirs.[66]

Would they have preferred to deal with [...] concerning Abdullah el Faisal?[67]

No because we dealt with [a community police officer] about local crime problems. It was good to talk to people who specialised in this area. When we spoke about the World Trade Center attack in 1993 we both knew about the people involved. It was the same when we spoke to [...] about the drug dealing in our neighbourhood—we knew the same people. Yes, there are sometimes overlaps. That's why we need to talk to each other.[68]

This was a question the MCU posed themselves that prompted them to visit the Brixton salafis: which sections, if any, of London's diverse and burgeoning Muslim communities had any expertise in tackling al-Qaeda influence?[69] Clearly the Brixton salafis had a wealth of evidence to demonstrate their experience and expertise in this field. Their reluctance to engage with members of a police service who had previously only displayed suspicion and sometimes aggression towards them was gradually overcome by recourse to patient trust-building and a willingness to engage as partners—not to recruit them as informants.[70] The integrity and reputation of the police officers was vital at an early stage in overcoming distrust.[71] Brixton was and remains the touchstone for relations between the Metropolitan Police and London's black communities:

It was very reassuring indeed—and a big surprise at first. To find an experienced detective who was Muslim who understood street crime and extremism and most of all understood what we had been up against in the 1990s was tremendous. We had some deep discussions about the issues and it really helped to cement a partnership approach with the MCU.[72]

There was a balance to be struck between confidentiality and transparency. For better or worse the MCU had decided to forego the security that recourse to the covert methodology surrounding the handling of informants provides.[73] Partnership became stronger, as it sometimes will when faced with adversity:

The MCU was a very small unit which helped in many ways. We got to know four of them as friends. We would ring their mobiles if there was a problem. And when we needed help they were able to come up with solutions and support.[74]

Of some concern to the MCU was the risk that individuals carrying out an informal community intelligence gathering role on behalf of al-Qaeda supporters would seek to capitalise on the issue and stir up community antagonism against the Brixton salafis.[75] This was no idle speculation, again experience of dealing with the PIRA threat taught the officers to appreciate the extent to which terrorist movements sought to embed long-term activists within supportive communities.[76] By the same token, MCU officers were not surprised to see attacks against Baker as a 'grass' and 'snitch' originating from within UK prisons where an increasing number of al-Qaeda suspects were beginning to gather.[77] This inevitably led to an overlap of genuine and legitimate prisoner support activity with terrorist support activity. Often the distinction between the two kinds of activity would not be apparent except to terrorists and well-informed counter-terrorists.[78] Moreover the PIRA used prison as a base for propaganda activity of all kinds, something the MCU soon began to discern was underway within the burgeoning al-Qaeda prison population.[79] This concern is echoed in a policy report published by the think-tank Rand Europe:

Imprisoned members of radicalized and violent organizations have long played a central role in the information and propaganda campaigns run by parent organizations and a wider network of sympathisers. This was true of the Suffragettes, the Irish republicans and the American White Supremacists and it is true today of those embracing violent jihadism. In the modern Irish example, Soairse was an organization created to support Republican prisoners and their families by fund-raising, and to run information campaigns to keep the prisoners in the target community's consciousness.[80]

Since 9/11 Rand has been a prolific publisher of reports on the al-Qaeda terrorist threat yet this is the first one to draw lessons from the experience of countering and studying the PIRA. Significantly, one of the report's authors is—like the MCU founders—steeped in MPSB counter-terrorism experience.[81] Suffice to say PIRA strategists would have considered it remiss if they had not kept themselves fully informed about Soairse membership and activities (as would counter-terrorism). Similarly, it was reasonable for the MCU to assume that al-Qaeda strategists would pay very close attention to the running of support groups like Cage Prisoners[82] and Helping Households under Great Stress, a registered UK charity which was 'set up by British Muslims in response to the new Anti-Terror Legislation ... to provide support and advice to households affected by this legislation' and to raise funds and to encourage voluntary support to assist the families of prisoners and detainees.[83] In 2008 the Rand Europe report was concerned that 'the exploitation of the imprisonment of violent jihadists for propaganda purposes' might 'continue to play a leading role in Islamist propaganda campaigns'.[84] Five years previously the MCU was working closely with salafis and Islamists and facing concomitant threats from al-Qaeda propagandists in prison.[85] In the intervening period a succession of Rand reports have led the field in conflating salafis and Islamists with the al-Qaeda threat. Indeed, particular Rand reports have pointedly identified salafis and Islamists as subversive threats and Sufis as ideal police partners with whom to tackle them.[86] Such double jeopardy—a partnership that was criticised by Muslims susceptible to al-Qaeda recruitment and by think-tanks opposed to salafis and Islamists— became the defining feature of the London partnerships. In its own way it added to the bonding of police and community partners. It certainly did nothing to inhibit the resolve of the Brixton salafis to protect local youth from al-Qaeda influence.[87]

In 2006 the Brixton salafis published a major refutation of the work of Faisal.[88] This refutation incorporated the lengthy experience of Baker and close colleagues of tackling this key extremist over a long period.[89] This remained an urgent task throughout the period under review because of the ongoing circulation of Faisal's recorded talks while he was in prison.[90] After years of approaching and tackling problems in ways they learnt on the street how did it feel when the Brixton salafis first discovered that they had to follow very strict rules of salafi argumentation?

It was odd at first. But it was all part of learning how to conduct ourselves. In Quintan Wictorowicz's article he suggests the salafi method of argument is artificial and dry but I think it's just very logical.[91]

195

The method of refutation highlighted in the following extracts perfectly illustrates the Brixton salafi approach to the problem of terrorist propaganda and recruitment—one that has been successful in tackling it on numerous occasions.[92] MCU officers encountered numerous cases where individuals who were previously under the influence of Abdullah el Faisal (and Abu Hamza and Abu Qatada) later became strictly practising Muslims under the guidance of the Brixton salafis.[93] Cases were also noted during the course of participant observation.[94] Notwithstanding the importance to the Brixton salafis of the scrupulously formulaic salafi framework for refuting the 'erroneous beliefs' of Abu Qatada, Abdullah el Faisal and Abu Hamza, the rhetorical skills of Abdul Haqq Baker (and colleagues) have appeared to be equally important when winning young adherents away from equally charismatic leaders.[95] Indeed, one interviewee who was a strong supporter of Faisal from 1999 to 2001 paid credit to Baker's communication skills:

I first took notice of Abdul Haqq Baker by accident. I was supposed to be recruiting young people from the Brixton Masjid—I had leaflets to give them to attend a talk by Sheikh Faisal [Abdullah el Faisal]. But I got listening to Abdul Haqq Baker's khutbah [talk during jummah prayer on Friday] and what he was saying made sense. He was relating to my life instead of manipulating meanings like Faisal did. Yes he was a better speaker than Faisal and that made an impact too.[96]

This is a recurring theme in the interviews and informal discussions held within the Brixton salafi community.[97] What emerges with striking clarity is that the Brixton salafi leadership was understood on the Brixton street to be so resolutely committed to a particular rendition of Islam as to be capable of withstanding and overcoming attacks from persistent detractors like Faisal.[98] As one interviewee expressed the point, 'the Brixton salafis have stood up to their enemies, taken them on and won, and that's why they have respect'.[99] Therefore, it follows, the street skills and the religious integrity of the Brixton salafis are mutually re-enforcing and present their opponents with a very proactive form of defence. Nonetheless, they are faced with equally resolute opponents who seek to undermine them as 'sell-outs'.

According to MCU officers Baker was right to emphasise the importance of Faisal's ability to 'galvanise' his supporters and his need to counter it.[100] Leadership, for the MCU, was a crucial issue.[101] When it came to giving new Muslims a sense of identity and belonging, both

Faisal and Baker had outstanding leadership skills.[102] Their ability to imbue convert Muslims who had recently been involved in drug-taking and related crime with a new sense of purpose and civic responsibility became well known locally.[103] Indeed, it is worth noting that Faisal subsequently attracted significant followings in Willesden[104] and Edmonton,[105] where again some black convert Muslims were often successfully encouraged to move away from lifestyles revolving around drug and alcohol abuse.[106] One respectable Deobandi Muslim leader in North London was full of praise for Faisal because of his skills in this area and found it difficult to accept the picture painted of Faisal at his Old Bailey trial.[107] According to MCU officers such a blind spot towards extremists like Faisal was not uncommon in the wider Muslim community prior to 7/7 because of the extremists' ability to attract new converts to Islam and to influence them away from drugs, alcohol and 'nightclub lifestyles'.[108] For the MCU the Brixton salafis had a unique role to play in countering al-Qaeda influence because they had a leadership that could match and outperform the extremists in relation to the same target audience.[109]

During the course of participant observation there was considerable evidence of the personal enmity that built up over a long period between Faisal and his supporters on the one hand and Baker and the Brixton salafis on the other.[110] The MCU took this as evidence of the effectiveness of the Brixton salafis in competing for the same recruits or followers. As one MCU officer explains:

By the end of 2002 we had visited over a hundred and eighty mosques and Muslim community groups around London and the kind of expert knowledge we found at Brixton was in very short supply. We drew up a short list of ten mosques and centres where we had found expertise in understanding and refuting al-Qaeda propaganda and recruitment in the capital and Brixton was number one.[111]

It follows that if the Brixton salafis had posed no threat to Fasial's recruitment programme he would almost certainly have ignored them—as he did with all other Muslim groups in the area.[112] The fact that it mattered to al-Qaeda supporters to ridicule their most effective opponents on the streets and in the cafes where they competed for recruits served as a valuable guide for the MCU.[113] How to measure effectiveness in any crime prevention field is notoriously difficult, but the MCU were conscious that effectiveness at the street level required authenticity and street presence that would be assessed on the street on its own terms independently of any outside perspective, least of all one endorsed by 'the authorities'.[114] Faisal attacked the Brixton salafis as being subservient to the Saudi king and the Saudi authorities generally as part of a concerted strategy to undermine their credibility. Had he been able to back that up by some evidence of physical success in terms of confrontation with his opponents then it might have counted for more. This was the same tactic employed by Abu Hamza and Abu Qatada.

During the period 2002 to 2007 MCU officers spent a significant amount of time listening to accounts from a wide variety of Muslim Londoners who had some experience of the street scene—essentially a sub-culture—in which these kinds of debates took place.[115] During this period Baker emerged as the most strident and effective critic of Abu Hamza, Abu Qatada and Abdullah el Faisal.[116] There was recognition that Faisal, Abu Hamza and company achieved the major part of their influence through the force of their personalities and leadership skills.[117] As a result Baker's equally committed and forceful leadership style was increasingly recognised to be an essential counterweight.[118] Moreover his familiar presence on the same circuit as Faisal, Abu Qatada and Abu Hamza ensured that listeners could readily challenge their stigmatisation of him as a Saudi stooge and a police informant:[119]

They have a lot of traffic between people working the dawah and the big belly sheikhs who coming from Saudi Arabia all the time. The red carpet sheikh and the cheap tickets to Umrah. Those who don't agree about this. He informs the police about them. He use every instant to link them to him to put them in trouble. Like what he says if you heard the Radio 4 or in the radio. He said hundreds of people in Britain they are linked to 9/11. Could you believe that? He said it loudly. He said he is afraid for his life because Muslims are after him now. Even the dogs in the street will be after him now. Can you believe a person say this about himself? That he is a police informer.[120]

Inevitably, the important distinction between being a police informant and a police partner would count for nothing in Abu Hamza's eyes.[121] Moreover by becoming key players in the London partnership initiative Baker and his colleagues increased the risks they faced of violent attack from extremists.[122] Generally speaking their reputation for defending themselves stood them in good stead but a significant responsibility also fell to the MCU to safeguard their interests.[123] In addition to the usual risk management regime the Brixton salafis also found that the MCU's growing reputation for opposing Islamophobia and challenging aspects of government counter-terrorism policy was extremely helpful in undermining Abu Hamza's claims that were working against the community.[124] Nonetheless Abu Hamza's attacks were popular amongst his own circle. Next he calls Abdul Haqq Baker an agent provocateur:

[Baker] is probably a police plotter because those people they can plot a crime. They can provoke a crime. Then blame others and inform the police about it. ...they provoke a crime they get simple words from his mouth for the general terms and then they put him inside. The link between this mosque and American mosque east coast mosque are very strong. All of them issue fatwas anybody who against their teachings or attack or criticise the Kings of the Gulf.[125]

Abu Hamza moves seamlessly from the specific to the general—from the possible via the probable to the certain. In the next extract he shows his penchant for humour, something Abdullah el Faisal sought to emulate:

If you read their statements how much this person has tried. So many times he went to the Brixton police station and went to Scotland Yard and telling them it's too late now what the government is doing. It's what he says Sergeant Abdul Haqq or Sergeant what's his name? Bacon. He should be called Bacon. So that sergeant who is a convert from non-Islam to non-Islam.[126]

In a significant number of cases these attempts to ridicule Baker backfired.[127] When new or curious members of an Abu Hamza audience went to listen to Baker themselves they were struck by his powerful presence and the forthright way in which he confronted the claims made against him.[128] In particular Baker has been described as being very adept at dispelling the next allegation made by Abu Hamza, that the Brixton salafis hide behind Saudi sheikhs:[129]

But the people who worship falsehood they will also always try to divert and use the simple minded Muslims against each other. So this is what this man said. So when you see he said this person who was the bomb shoe man which is Mr Ridley [Richard Reid] that brother who was caught in France trying to blow the aeroplane. He said he is a convert and they were giving him sessions like many Muslims who are converted to Islam.[130]

Abu Hamza's failure to explain that Faisal had been largely responsible for subverting Reid from the influence of the Brixton salafis is significant. He continues:

But when people see the beauty of Islam they accept Islam. Once they teach the five pillars of Islam then they obviously start say they are from the West. They said well if you teach me how to read the book I found some ayahs in the book why don't you explain this ayah. No no. don't understand this ayah. This ayah isn't like this. Wait until the sheikh come from Saudi and he will give you his ayah. Or he will tell you what is the meaning of this ayah. This is what they doing. So they fail at then they go against each other and obviously people criticise them they criticise their kings. But as their kings and their scholars do in the Arabia allow kufar in the land of the peninsula. They do the same thing here. They themselves go to the kufar against their own brothers. They grass their own brothers.[131]

In conversation the Brixton salafis accept that Abu Hamza had some success in denigrating them but they remained defiant and experienced in defending themselves.[132]

9

AL-QAEDA RECRUITS

Did the Brixton salafis accept that they had failed to win over Richard Reid and Zacarias Moussaoui and to prevent them becoming terrorists? What did these two cases tell the MCU about the limits of Brixton salafi influence? While in broad terms both the Brixton salafis and the MCU acknowledged that in a high-risk arena there would always be cases where failure would arise, it nevertheless became increasingly clear to both partners that failure of this kind might be limited by devoting more time and resources to the task. That effort was at the heart of the London partnership endeavour. Learning from these two cases would be crucial. Moussaoui, convicted in the USA for al-Qaeda terrorism in connection with 9/11, was like Reid, well known to the Brixton salafis. Baker gave evidence on his behalf in 2006, principally to avoid Moussaoui being sentenced to death—and thereby avoid the erroneous claim that he would become a martyr:

If Zacarias and all his friends had been able to claim he was a martyr then it would have had very bad consequences in the community.[1]

Subsequently Baker gave an interview to the BBC which accords with the account he gave to the MCU:

Moussaoui's lawyers have called witnesses from Britain to try to show how he was radicalised in this country. He spent 7 years living here before he went to America. Abdul Haqq Baker was the main defence witness from Britain. He told the court that when he first met Moussaoui he was an affable man whose behaviour changed when he started attending sermons by extremist preachers.[2]

BBC reporter Nasreen Suleaman (NS) interviews him (AHB):

NS Zacarias Moussaoui arrived in London in 1993 and enrolled at the South Bank University where he began to study for an M.A in Business Studies. Moussaoui was born in Morocco but grew up in France where he was not known as a practising Muslim. His interest in Islam began when he arrived in Britain he started to attend Brixton Mosque in South London. Moussaoui not only prayed at the mosque but was also to sleep there as he had yet to find any accommodation. It was here the chairman of the mosque Abdul Haqq Baker first met Moussaoui.

AHB He was friendly he seemed like a very serious individual but had a sense of humour, quite jovial.

NS How soon after he started attending Brixton Mosque did he start to change?

AHB I'd say it had to be about a year to eighteen months and that's when we were taking a quite firm stance against the extremist's propagation in the area and they moved off to other centres and opened or started renting other premises. I noticed that he started attending those premises and it was then we started seeing conflict about our ideology and practice and their ideology and practice.

I put it to Baker that his account in this BBC interview was at odds with those parts of an account provided by Moussaoui's brother, Abd Saamad Moussaoui in which the influence of the Brixton salafis is seen as the route to al-Qaeda.[3] This was hardly surprising Baker suggested because Abd Samaad Moussaoui had no firsthand experience of the London Muslim scene.[4] It would be perfectly understandable that—from a distance—he would notice the changes to his brother's lifestyle brought about by becoming a practising Muslim at the Brixton Mosque and then blame that change for his subsequent adoption of al-Qaeda's ideology. It is an entirely valid perspective, especially for a brother, but it has negative ramifications when it is applied more widely. To conflate the influence of the individuals who recruited Zacarias Moussaoui into terrorism with the individuals who were best placed to prevent that happening is necessarily problematic.[5] Baker gave this interview in 2006 and despite the fact that he had been telling the media since December 2001 that Faisal, Abu Hamza, Abu Qatada and company had never had control of Brixton Mosque or been imams there, sections of the media continued to repeat the opposite.[6] MCU officers explored these same issues with the Brixton salafis in 2003 and had been able to verify them.[7]

When this much light is shed on a topic in the space of a short radio interview it is not difficult to grasp how much depth and insight might be gained when the Brixton salafis and MCU officers shared experiences of terrorist motivation during the course of ongoing and sustained dialogue. That, surely, is what constitutes expert learning and expert knowledge as described in different ways by Flyvbjerg, Kenney and Hamm.[8] Learning from experience was also a starting point for police partnership. As Baker observes, if he had received support from the police in the 1990s he would have had somewhere to turn when he became concerned about the safety of individuals like Reid and Moussaoui. MCU officers agreed that close liaison then would have resulted in a better intelligence picture at the very least.

When Baker and his close colleagues first heard the news that Abdul Raheem, otherwise Richard Reid, had been arrested for attempting to blow up a transatlantic flight *en route* to the USA at the end of 2001 they realised that the media would be bound to descend on the Brixton Mosque.[9] Although Reid had disappeared from their radar over a year earlier it seemed inevitable to them that his prior association with the Brixton salafi community would be sufficiently well known to ensure they were implicated in the case.[10] It was agreed that Baker would act as spokesman for the mosque. Within hours the media duly arrived and Baker was kept frantically busy dealing with their demands for information.[11] He gave numerous interviews, conducting himself with dignity, providing very clear information that was accurate and truthful, generally while standing in the street outside the mosque in Gresham Road. In interview it was useful to review press cuttings to prompt his recollections of the events:

It was a cold day—as you can see from the pictures, I was wearing a thick jumper and gloves! I knew I would have my work cut out defending the masjid against some stereotyping but on the whole I was pleased with the way it went. I also knew my comments would be seized upon by Abu Hamza, Abu Qatada, Abullah el Faisal and company to say I was collaborating with the enemy.[12]

Richard Reid would later be sentenced to life imprisonment in the USA after admitting that he tried to blow up a commercial flight using a bomb hidden in his shoe. At the time it was thought that he acted alone but it subsequently emerged that another British Muslim, Saajid Badat from Gloucester, had been earmarked by a 'handler', Nazar Trabelsi (a former footballer serving a ten-year prison sentence in Belgium for plotting to bomb a NATO airbase) to take part in the same or a similar attack.[13] Certainly in 2005 Saajid Badat pleaded guilty to a conspiracy to commit a terrorist act with Richard Reid having been found to be in possession of an identical 'shoe-bomb'.[14] While the evidence in the Badat case showed that al-Qaeda operatives had skilfully recruited two British Muslims to carry out a 'suicide bomb' attack prior to 9/11, the initial media reporting that confronted Baker on the doorstep of his mosque was more preoccupied with a story about a 'crazy loner' with a wild-eyed appearance:

It was difficult to get across to the media a clear picture about Reid. They had this notion about him being a crazy fanatic. This was not helpful. He was not the brightest intellectually speaking and he was easily led but he still had good skills. What I would call street skills. He was a good graffiti artist for instance. So he was like a lot of young people in our community. He was part of a youth culture where street crime was normal behaviour. These are useful skills for people like Abdullah el Faisal to exploit. I'm not saying Faisal recruited Reid directly but we lost influence over Reid because of what Faisal and the others were calling.[15]

The son of an English mother and Jamaican father, the so-called 'shoe-bomber' was born in 1973 in Bromley, South London. Reid attended Thomas Tallis secondary school in Blackheath, south-east London, from 1984 to 1989.[16] His father, Robin, told BBC News he had been in prison for most of Richard's childhood. 'I was not there to give him the love and affection he should have got', he said.[17] This is how the key part of his story has been widely reported:

[Reid] fell into a life of petty crime and in the mid-1990s was jailed for a string of muggings, for which he served sentences in a number of prisons, including Feltham young offenders' institution in west London. It was while at Feltham that Reid is said to have converted to Islam. After his release, he followed the path taken by many other Muslim prisoners, to Brixton Mosque, in south London. The place of worship has a reputation for attracting converts and helping ex-offenders re-adjust to life in the outside world. Initially he fitted in well. Taking the name Abdel Rahim, he became known for his willingness to get involved in the workings of the mosque and to learn Arabic.[18]

'In fairness' Baker points out 'the BBC reporting tended to be the most reliable and least sensationalist'. He confirmed that the following extract from a BBC report was accurate:

At some point Reid began to get involved with extremist elements, says the chairman of Brixton Mosque, Abdul Haqq Baker. Reid was 'tempted away' by 'individuals who set up a few years ago away from the mosque', Mr Baker says. 'Their teachings were a lot more militant'. He says extremists worked on 'weak characters' and believes Reid was 'very, very impressionable'. Reid attended external classes and started to question the peaceful philosophy of his teachers.[19]

However, on examining the next extract from the same interview he identifies 'the beginning of what has become a familiar problem', the reduction of complex issues into sound bites:

[Reid's] appearance also changed, says Mr Baker. He went from wearing western clothes to the traditional Islamic thobe—a loose, long-sleeved, ankle-length garment—with a khaki combat jacket on top.[20]

Baker explained his concerns in interview:

Now these two comments were separate. I was not saying that wearing traditional Islamic dress was in any way problematic, or an indication of Reid's extremism. On the contrary, it is more likely to be of concern when an individual switches from Islamic dress to western appearance—like in Zacarias Moussaoui's case. But what I was drawing attention was Reid wearing a khaki combat jacket as an indication of the time when he started to get more militant. The bigger problem is that the media started to describe Reid's adoption of salafi practice as part of his move towards extremism. This became the norm and was very damaging.[21]

In important respects, for Baker, extracts from the following interview with Peter Herbert, a British lawyer, are more insightful. Herbert visited Richard Reid in prison in the USA at the request of Reid's mother. He reports that Reid was perfectly sane, reflective and self-possessed:

I am not crazy as they suggest, but I knew exactly what I was doing', [Reid] said. 'Of course I would have been sad to have those people die, but I knew that my cause was just and righteous. It was the will of Allah that I did not succeed'. His motivation for turning to violence, he said, was the foreign policy of the US government, which, he said, had resulted in the murder of thousands of Muslims and oppressed people around the world from Vietnam to southern Africa to Afghanistan and Palestine.[22]

Another Brixton salafi comments that Herbert has captured an important aspect of the case here. 'Reid', he says, 'was genuinely concerned about US foreign policy. We all were. Just because he hadn't much formal education didn't mean he was stupid.[23] What he misses out though is that Brixton mosque always taught that British Muslims had no Islamic right to carry out attacks of this kind'.[24] So for this interviewee who once spent all night trying to talk Reid away from the teachings of Abdullah el Faisal 'and company' there was a feeling of frustration that the report was missing the most important issues:

It was 1998 when I tried to talk Reid away from the extremists. We were up all night talking. In the end he agreed with me but in those days we had no way of following cases up. Our work was just spontaneous. I guess Reid must have gone back to Faisal's erroneous teaching. Ideally I would have followed up the meeting and kept on his case. But at the time I had no time to do that kind of work. Nor did the brothers. We did the best we could to combat the false calls and we worked long hours doing that.[25]

Again the interviewee is representative of wider Brixton salafi opinion when he argues that the Peter Herbert interview endorses the misapprehension that anger over foreign policy leads inexorably to terrorism. 'This is what al-Qaeda want to suggest, so it has to be countered'.[26] The interviewee is especially critical of the following extract of Peter Herbert's interview with Richard Reid that appears to accept that Muslims are not inhibited from carrying out such actions:

One issue that baffles those trying to counter al-Qaeda is why young men will kill themselves for such a cause. Reid compared himself to the suicide bombers of Hamas. They did not have rockets or tanks or F16 jets to fight with, he said, and had to fight with the tools at their disposal. 'What do you expect people to do?' he added.[27]

The Brixton salafis had always challenged that notion. Equally, however, the interviewee accepts Reid's observation about his political motivation as being critically important when assessing how best to tackle the problem:

We don't disagree that this injustice exists. We don't try and apologise for US or UK government action, but we explain how Islam tells you how to act responsibly. That Osama bin Laden and Richard Reid are falsifying their religion. Coming from us Salafis that is a powerful message.[28]

There was a lot of discussion amongst those who knew him about why Reid's attempt to ignite his bomb on the aeroplane failed.[29] The fact that he appeared to have been so indiscreet about his attempt to ignite the bomb suggested to many of his former associates that he may have been wanting to get caught.[30] This is more than just idle speculation, and has more resonance now that it has emerged that his would-be accomplice Saajid Badat had recently pulled out. The main point, according to one interviewee, being that Reid had an abundance of street-crime craft and would have known to prepare or prime his bomb away from attention—for instance in a toilet—had he been intent on escaping capture.[31]

MCU officers were principally concerned to empower the negotiating skills deployed by the Brixton salafis when engaging with Muslim youth who were vulnerable to al-Qaeda influence.[32] At this point the distance from conventional 'top-down' counter-terrorism is significant. However, nothing in the innovative methodology of the police unit's empowerment approach restricts 'hard' counter-terrorism from pursuing terrorist suspects in more familiar ways. Brixton salafis expressed awareness that any of their youth 'clients' might at any time and unbeknown to them be the subject of a covert terrorist investigation.[33] Indeed in discussions, Brixton salafi youth workers expressed an understanding that if their efforts to remove a young person from terrorist influence were unsuccessful they would be obliged to report the individual to the police.[34] At such a point it becomes clear how this seemingly novel partnership approach to counter-terrorism relies fundamentally on the same traditional 'good cop/bad cop' routine as hostage negotiation and every other conceivable kind of policing engagement with law breakers that takes place in the modern world. It is merely its application to countering terrorist recruitment that is pioneering.

Certainly, MCU officers assessed it to be misleading and counterproductive to endorse the stereotyping, profiling and conflating of salafis with al-Qaeda terrorism.[35] The fact that al-Qaeda terrorists adapt and distort salafi approaches to Islam does not mean that salafis are implicitly linked to terrorism or extremism, still less that individual salafis are likely to be terrorists or extremists. No more, MCU officers reflected, was Catholicism a key pointer to PIRA terrorism. Equally, UK recruits to al-Qaeda terrorism had a range of backgrounds that sometimes included prior affiliation to, or family association with Deobandi, Sufi or Barelvi traditions. However, it was axiomatic that by the time they became al-Qaeda suicide bombers (or other active terrorists) British Muslim recruits had bought into an al-Qaeda world view that subverted and distorted strands of salafi and Islamist thinking. That was why it increasingly occurred to MCU officers that salafis and Islamists often had the best antidotes to al-Qaeda propaganda once it had gained influence. To conflate salafis and Islamists with the problem was therefore potentially to inhibit their willingness to immunise their communities against it.[36]

The shooting dead of the innocent electrician Jean Charles de Menezes by the Metropolitan Police at Stockwell tube station on 22 July

2005 was an unintended part of an unprecedented counter-terrorist response to the suicide bomb attacks on the capital on 7 July and 21 July 2005. Each of the three events had a major impact on the Brixton salafis and their local neighbourhood and their response to each event highlighted the immense value they had brought to the London partnership initiative in the three preceding years. The success of patient trust-building in a partnership can only be assessed when it is put under strain at times of intense community and media pressure and that was certainly the case for both community and police partners during the days and weeks that followed these traumatic events.

One immediate response of the Brixton salafis to the bomb attacks on the London Underground on 7 July, was to highlight how they had been warning of just such a terrorist risk for a long time and to advise government that they had a fundamentally flawed understanding of what the underlying causes of the attack were. Abdul Haqq Baker was especially concerned that Tony Blair's 'shoulder to shoulder' approach to the war on terror with George Bush was unnecessarily fuelling Muslim youth anger and increasing their susceptibility to the propaganda of the *takfiris*. Unfortunately for the MCU their attempts to bring the Brixton Salafi analysis of the problem to the attention of government and even senior police officers was seriously undermined by more powerful voices who had the ear of government. Muslim advisors or gatekeepers within the Cabinet Office, Home Office and FCO were as distant from the Brixton salafi perspective as they were dismissive of it. As a result, Tony Blair and his close advisors made it abundantly plain that they took a very different view of the problem and favoured contrary analyses like Lord Meghnad Desai's that was subsequently set out in his book *Rethinking Islamism: the Ideology of the New Terror*.[37] For both the MCU and the Brixton salafis it was extremely frustrating that their expertise was being ignored when it mattered most:

Instead of listening to experts like the Brixton salafis the government set up an urgent working group with Muslim groups who really had no firsthand experience of the problem. It was the blind leading the blind.[38]

What was most disturbing to the Brixton salafis was the extent to which the government's embrace of 'liberal extremists' only served to empower the *takfiris*:

What I mean by this is that you cannot go from one extreme to another. You cannot tackle extremists like Abu Qatada and his kind by holding up a liberal extremist—someone who claims to be a Muslim but who is known not to be practicing but is liked by government because he wears a suit and says the war in Iraq is ok—and then saying this is the model of Islam we want in Britain. We might as well all go home.[39]

Instead Brixton salafi expertise pointed directly to the long-term influence of Abu Qatada, Abu Hamza, Abdullah el Faisal and their followers in Britain on individuals like the 7/7 bombers. Indeed, the Brixton salafis were part of a national salafi network so it came as no surprise to them to hear from a salafi contact in Bradford that Jermaine Lindsey the black convert Muslim member of the 7/7 cell had come under the adverse influence of Abdullah el Faisal while a student in neighbouring Huddersfield. Moreover, the Bradford salafi narrative was strikingly similar to that of their Brixton counterparts in so far as having endured years of being ostracised by police, local authority and majority local Muslim communities. One Bradford salafi who knew Lindsey put it this way:

Comparing notes with Abdul Haqq Baker I would say the Richard Reid case and the Jermaine Lindsey case have a lot in common. Both men came under the influence of Abdullah el Faisal and the *takfiris*. I could talk Lindsey round and Abdul Haqq could talk Reid round when we had opportunities but you need to spend a lot of time with these individuals otherwise they will go back to the *takfiris* and get more set in their ways. The point is Lindsey could have been prevented getting into that group but you have got to have time and resources to match what the *takfiris* are doing.[40]

It would take another eighteen months before the experience of the Brixton salafis would begin to be taken seriously beyond the MCU. In contrast, because the attempted terrorist attacks on 21/7 and the shooting dead of Jean Charles de Menezes on 22/7 had immediate repercussions in Brixton these two incidents did at least enable the MCU to bring the Brixton salafi voice to the attention of the local police chief. During 2003—2004 it had become possible to begin the sensitive process of restoring trust in Brixton police and a local community police officer continued to play a key role in this endeavour. The Brixton salafis were introduced to a new local police chief, Martin Bridger, who was prepared to commit time to building trust and prepared to take risks (as was his counterpart Barry Norman in Finsbury Park). One important gesture was for Martin Bridger to make this statement outside the Brixton Mosque just as the London *Evening Standard* was describing it as the 'terrorist mosque':

Today once again I witnessed the inner strength of Lambeth's communities, standing together to condemn the recent atrocities which have nothing to do with Islam. We all acknowledge that the days, weeks and months ahead will be challenging for us all but we are determined to work hard together to overcome the evil that is affecting our communities.[41]

The fact that the Brixton salafis and other Muslim groups in Brixton knew members of the 21/7 cell alerted Brixton police to the benefits of the MCU partnership approach and the fact that valuable local intelligence might be gleaned without recourse to the use of informants.[42] While it appeared that the 21/7 terrorists were beyond the reach of the Brixton salafis it was also the case that the young people they came into contact with would need the counselling skills they provided. Referring to failed 21/7 bomber Hussain Osman one Brixton salafi commented:

He was one of Abu Hamza's supporters. We knew he was trouble but apart from the MCU no one was ever interested in what we said. He was like all the other *takfiris* who had never really given up their love of thieving and defrauding. They just thought they were justified now from the teachings of Abu Hamza and Abdullah el Faisal instead.[43]

While Hussain Osman was fleeing the country Jean Charles de Menezes was travelling to work and was fatally mistaken for the terrorist at Stockwell, the next tube stop along from Brixton. Notwithstanding their deep shock the Brixton salafis were able to provide valuable feedback in terms of community anger and response. According to a member of the MCU this was input was crucial:

The Brixton salafis are in touch with the street. When there is real community anger around you need to know how it's playing out. It was the same when there was an angry reaction to the arrest of Baba Ahmed in Tooting in 2003. Local Muslim community leaders who were not in touch with the street told police everything was calm. The Brixton salafis and other street based groups in the capital gave an accurate assessment to the MCU. That was very much the case in the weeks after Stockwell.[44]

Martin Bridger's willingness to support the Brixton salafis was a significant breakthrough and indicated to the MCU that it stood a far better chance of gaining ground at the local level than in Westminster.[45] At the same time the Brixton Mosque won small but significant recognition of its position when the Press Complaints Commission published the following correction:

Our article of 12 April 'Jailed preacher of hate in court battle to stay in Britain' referred to Sheikh Abdullah el Faisal as the 'Brixton Mosque preacher'.

Faisal only preached at Brixton Mosque in the early 1990s and not after the current administration was elected in 1994.[46]

Although the Brixton salafis were developing their own distinctive identity they were also part of a broad and disparate national salafi movement that continued to have an adverse impact on wider Muslim communities. 'Looking back', Baker recalls, 'I think we were sometimes a bit too assertive in our dawah':

You know we could upset some elders because we would not compromise on religious principles. But that's being a salafi. We would tell it to people straight and sometimes they would get upset because they had compromised with Islam and they didn't want to be told. Maybe at times we could have been gentler.[47]

Interestingly, it was a small group of white middle-class English Sufi converts who took particular exception to the salafi rendition of Islam.[48] To a large extent they had converted to Islam on an entirely different understanding of the religion and with wholly different implications. Conversion to Islam, for most British Sufi converts, meant that their religious practice could remain largely in the private sphere and would not require them to forego many of their prior attachments to cherished English pastimes.[49] In general, Sufism appealed to an established English middle-class fascination with mystical and individual religious experience and contrasted sharply with the demands of anti-mystical salafism. More specifically, for leading Sufi commentators the infiltration of salafi discourse into the UK in the 1990s was symptomatic of a failure to curb adverse Saudi influence in the UK.[50] In the immediate aftermath of 9/11 Abdal-Hakim Murad was quick to trace the roots of the attack to 'Wahhabism' (that is, salafism):

The movement for traditional Islam will, we hope, become enormously strengthened in the aftermath of the recent events,[51] accompanied by a mass exodus from Wahhabism, leaving behind only a merciless hardcore of well-financed zealots.... Only a radical amputation of this kind will save Islam's name, and the physical safety of Muslims, particularly women, as they live and work in Western cities.[52]

Murad gives voice here to a tendency that became prevalent during the 1990s but grew apace after 9/11—an attempt on the part of some Sufis to deflect Islamophobia away from their own version of Islam and towards salafis—where they believed it belonged. Given that Islamophobia became a recognised phenomenon in 1990s Britain this is an important aspect of intra-communal tensions.[53] Certainly, the Brixton salafis grew used to sniping from their co-religionists during the period under review, the more so, as they grew in stature. Given that so many of their Sufi critics were white middle-class intellectuals it is not idle to reflect that the attacks would have caused concern had their targets been black working-class evangelical Christians and not salafis.[54] As the Brixton salafis have noted many times, the kind of racist abuse they often received before they became Muslim prepared them well for the more subtle but equally patronising attacks they would receive as salafis from some sufis.[55] However, if 9/11 opened doors for influential Sufis to meet UK policy-makers, 7/7 allowed them unprecedented access to the mainstream UK media, increasingly fixated with 'homegrown terrorism' and the so-called 'radicalisation' process. Thus, in January 2007 Abdal-Hakim Murad explained his concerns about 'Wahhabism' in an investigative television programme, *Undercover Mosque*:

[Wahhabism's] principle is totalitarian, it's highly judgemental, it has no track record of dealing with other sorts of Islam or unbelievers with any kind of respect. If you are outside the small circle of the true believer you are going to hell and therefore you should be treated with contempt.[56]

Thus the Brixton salafis confronted a consistently hostile Sufi presence in the UK that sought to undermine and misrepresent their efforts.[57] One interviewee crystallises the issue in this way:

I was black working class before I became Muslim. Becoming salafi has strengthened my allegiance to the victimised and poor in my community.[58]

One interviewee, a Londoner who converted to Sufi Islam in the late 1980s recalls how the Brixton salafis' arrival on the scene in the early 1990s sent shock waves through the local Muslim order that had begun to establish itself in the preceding two decades.[59] The Brixton salafis were considered anathema by many sections of Muslim London but especially by those Sufis who had come to regard salafism (or Wahhabism as they preferred to call it) as the epitome of discord and disharmony both in the Muslim world and in relations between the Muslim world and the West.[60] In areas surrounding Brixton tensions developed between the salafis and the sufis. According to one of the Brixton salafis this tension had as much to do with a dismissive and patronising attitude towards their black Brixton identity as it did to the strand of Islamic practice they had adopted.[61]

Given the extent to which the English Sufi movement was led by a white, middle-class Oxbridge elite it should come as no surprise that its disapprobation of Brixton and other British salafis would have a marked impact in Whitehall.[62] In government circles in the immediate aftermath of 9/11 sufi voices gained audience and purchase (as Hamza Yusef famously did with George Bush in the USA) to the detriment of salafis who were described as Saudi stooges and threats to the social cohesion of the UK.[63] Therefore, as MCU police officers became familiar with the sterling efforts of the Brixton salafis to tackle violent extremism they took it upon themselves to correct the pejorative account that their rivals had sown in Whitehall.[64] To have the confidence to do so speaks well for the trust developed by the London partnership. That it took the MCU six years to make a modest impact in their efforts to portray the Brixton salafis in a positive light speaks eloquently for the level of fear and suspicion generated by their influential opponents.[65]

However, in 2007 with the support of the MCU key members of the Brixton salafi community launched a new youth outreach scheme called Strategy to Reach, Empower and Educate Teenagers (STREET) that sought to extend their local work to a wider audience.[66] Football and boxing were amongst the regular activities provided for the benefit of young Muslims. Typically, throughout the winter of 2007/8 average crowds of eighty youths attended Saturday evening football sessions in Kennington Park.[67] Unlike most other football sessions in London the players were given a salafi pep talk before kick-off in which they were encouraged to give of their best on the pitch and to treat their opponents with respect for the sake of Allah.[68] Conscious that imprisonment had done nothing to diminish the adverse influence of Abu Hamza, Abdullah el Faisal and Abu Qatada in Muslim communities the STREET leadership sought the facilities and resources to engage in counselling with young Muslims who had come under their extremist influence. Given the inevitable sensitivities that surround this kind of work the MCU played a key role in supporting the STREET project with potential funders in central and local government. Considering the extent of counter-extremist work the Brixton salafi community had been involved in over a long period on an entirely voluntary basis it was thought apposite for central and local government to help fund this more cohesive project. Crucially, MCU support was extended in 2007 to include Brixton police, the venue that in 1996 saw Brixton salafi concerns as mere rivalry or factionalism between local religious groups. At the time of writing the project has achieved outstanding success that has been verified independently.

Notwithstanding a growing appreciation of the Brixton salafi role as a bulwark against al-Qaeda propaganda amongst academics such as Quintan Wiktorowicz and Thomas Hegghammer there was still a tendency to bracket them with the terrorist problem in policy circles. That was largely the case with an influential report from two New York Police Department (NYPD) analysts published in 2007. Interestingly, the Brixton salafis responded to it in detail.[69] This is how their refutation is introduced:

Within the 'war on terror' scenario the *salafi da'wah* and tradition has been seen as a methodology which is the main cause, thrust and impetus for terrorism and political violence and as even promoting such radical views. A large body of research has been authored which seeks to claim that the *salafi* way is indeed an extremist radical belief system which eventually manifests itself with political violence and terrorism. One such report which follows this rather simplistic and incorrect assertion is the latest report by the New York Police Department entitled *Radicalisation in the West: The Homegrown Threat* by two senior intelligence analysts for the NYPD, Mitchell D. Silber and Arvin Bhatt.

The refutation proceeds to defend salafism:

Even though they aimed to understand the process by which Muslim youth become attracted to more extreme understandings and interpretations of Islam, it fell far short of doing the subject any justice and greatly misunderstood much in this regard. One of the more glaring problems with the report is that it rather boldly holds the *salafi* methodology as being the main catalyst for terrorism and then seeks to present examples of what they consider to be 'salafi'. Here is where the problem lies, as the two analysts Silber and Bhatt, make reference to samples which are not 'salafi' in the slightest and are rather *takfeeri, jihadi, ikhwaani (i.e. followers of the Muslim Brotherhood)* and even at times *Tablighi*!? Yet all of it is placed under the poorly defined, by them, rubric of 'salafism'.

Published in 2007 the NYPD report was universally praised by US and European counter-terrorism experts for its insightful and groundbreaking research into the urgent topic of violent radicalisation.[70] The contrasting response of the Brixton salafis came as no surprise to the MCU who had operated in the middle of such opposing analyses for five years. However, coming as it did in 2007 when the MCU had spent much time seeking to convince counter-terrorism counterparts in the UK, Europe and the USA that salafis were neither synonymous with nor a stepping stone towards terrorism it was frustrating for the unit to find such misrepresentations still holding centre stage. For the Brixton salafis it was disappointing to find that the MCU had been unable to dislodge the anti-salafi bias that permeated the wider counter-terrorism world, both academic and practitioner. US Researcher, Scott Atran called for the London police to learn from NYPD on how better to engage with their Muslim communities shortly after the NYPD report was launched.[71] If anything a deep distrust of all things salafi was even more manifest in Europe, especially France and Germany, where partnership approaches with salafis were roundly condemned.[72] In the circumstances the Brixton salafi refutation performs a useful purpose by critically assessing 'some of the claims of Silber and Bhatt and explore the reality of the *salafi* way in regards to issues related terrorism, political violence and extremism':[73]

To claim that the *salafi* way, belief and understanding is one of the indicators or 'signatures' of terrorist-related incidents is absolutely incorrect. So even though Silber and Bhatt claimed that the *salafi* way was a facet of terrorism and violent extremism based on a dozen or so 'case studies'—then their case studies, [painstakingly re-contextualised in the refutation] have not actually shown that any of those involved were *salafi*![74]

To a certain extent the refutation grew out of the Brixton salafis' close relationship with the MCU. Certainly, the reasons given as to why strict salafis were less likely to be recruited into terrorism are ones the MCU had grown familiar with throughout the London partnership initiative:

Strict *Salafis* are religious and not entrenched in political activity, political involvement and rhetoric; let alone terrorism. Politics is not their first port of call, rather to educate and cultivate Muslims upon *tawheed* and adhering to the *Sunnah* of the Prophet Muhammad (*sallallaahu'alayhi wassallam*) along with purifying the beliefs of the Muslims is their focal emphasis.

Salafis frown upon forming political parties and groups which are based on partisan loyalties.

Salafis do not hold secret clandestine meetings in order to put into place a strategic political plan.

Salafis do not pledge allegiance to heads of organisations, groups and political parties.

Salafis hold it to be un-Islamic to stage a revolt or rebellion against the leader of a Muslim country regardless of how unjust and oppressive that leader is, and especially if the Muslims do not have the ability to remove a particular leader from power.

Salafis take into account the benefits and harms of any action which is done in the name of advancing the religion.

Salafis do not agree with the targeting of innocent people in warfare based on the evidences from the Qur'aan and Sunnah.

According to MCU officers all of these points have been evidenced during the course of five years' close engagement of the London partnership initiative. The first point, 'Strict *salafis* are religious and not entrenched in political activity, political involvement and rhetoric; let alone terrorism' is also shown to be accurate during the course of participant observation. However, as Abdul Haqq Baker explains in interview, it is not an approach that should be confused with political quietism:

We do not shy away from the political injustices that the *takfiris* use to call the youth to terrorism. As you know when things were hot after 7/7 my Friday khutbas were very uncompromising about the failure of the American and British policy in Iraq to tackle this problem. This is important for the youth to see that we are not afraid to speak up against policies that are wrong. And it is part of the way I attack the *takfiris* in the same khutbas for thinking they have the right to resort to terrorism. In my khutbas I have to calm the anger of the youth and bring them to understand that Islam does not allow fools like Faisal to make decisions about using violence. The youth have to understand that Islam forbids what Faisal says—whether they like what he says or not.[75]

In addition, the refutation usefully lists those Safalfi scholars 'who *salafis* take their guidance' from:

Imaam 'Abdul' Azeez Bin Baaz, Imaam Muhammad Naasiruddeen al-Albaanee, Imaam Muhammad bin Saalih al-'Uthaymeen (*raheemahumullaah*), Imaam Muqbil bin Haadee al-Wadi'ee and other contemporaries such as Shaykh 'Abdul'Azeez Aali-Shaykh,[76] Shaykh 'AbdulMuhsin al-'Abbaad al-Badr,[77] Shaykh Rabee' bin Haadee al-Madkhalee,[78] Shaykh Saalih al-Fawzaan, Shaykh AbdulMuhsin al-'Ubaykaan,[79] Shaykh AbdulMaalik ar-Ramadaanee,[80] Shaykh AbdusSalaam as-Suhaymee, Shaykh Khaalid al-Anbaree,[81] Shaykh Ali Hasan al-Halabee al-Atharee,[82] Shaykh Mashhoor Hasan Aal Salmaan, Shaykh Saleem al-Hilaalee, Shaykh Saalih Aali-Shaykh,[83] Shaykh 'Abdul'Azeez bin Rayyis ar-Rayyis,[84] Shaykh AbdusSalaam Burjis (*raheemahullaah*) and many others—all of these *salafi* scholars are regarded as the heads of the *salafi* methodology and tradition and are all well-known for their stances against terrorism, extremism, political agitation and the likes, we will mention some of their statements later. Yet Silber and Bhatt did not refer to these *Salafi* scholars whatsoever and merely equated the *salafi* tradition with terrorism and violence—this is inappropriate.[85]

Recent trials in the UK have highlighted the value al-Qaeda terrorists and al-Qaeda supporters attach to training Muslim youth in outdoor pursuits. Paintballing, camping, white water rafting, mountaineering, martial arts and survival skills have all featured as 'innocent' activities that serve to build and bond teams in ways that are wholly familiar to police and army recruits the world over. The fact that the Brixton salafis can offer the same kind of environments in which to offer Muslim youth audiences similar activities while presenting a wholly different account of UK citizenship and responsibility is critical. Needless to say, however, a farmer in the Brecon Beacons may not immediately distinguish between Brixton salafis and al-Qaeda supporters and it is therefore important that a unit such as the MCU can vouch for their London community partners when they venture to remote regions of the UK. This kind of support work by the MCU also helps distinguish their role from that of traditional 'police handlers' and their 'informants'. Policy designed to ensure the efficient police management of informants ('covert human intelligence sources') does not encourage the trust-building and partnership-building approach of the MCU. On the contrary, policy in this field seeks to avoid close relationships of the kind that have secured modest success for the MCU and its Brixton salafi partners.

Although it was a slow process by January 2007 the MCU had provided sufficient opportunities for the Brixton salafis to showcase their skills so as to enable them to become a recognised part of what by then had become a major new government policy development—preventing violent extremism. Firmly grounded in its local experience and expertise the Brixton salafis developed STREET, a youth outreach project that sought to overcome the obstacles they had encountered in their long-term effort to counter the influence of the *takfiris*. Regrettably, despite outstanding success, opponents of salafism would successfully undermine STREET in Westminster in 2011.

PART FOUR

VICTORIA

10

ANGER AND ALIENATION

On more than one occasion my walk from Victoria underground station to NSY was a time to prepare to deliver bad news to senior police management and Home Office officials. For all the exciting developments I saw unfold in Finsbury Park and Brixton between 2002 and 2007 I was often obliged to report stories of anger and alienation from within London Muslim communities. Without wishing to be unduly dogmatic I am inclined to suggest that these negative reports invariably related to the wider war on terror and to the performance of counter-terrorism locally. All were worth listening to. To ignore them was to ignore a central tenet of effective policing. Often, anger and alienation arose because of the way the war on terror was conceived and implemented. Invariably, anger and alienation were reactions that al-Qaeda strategists and propagandists might seek to exploit for the purpose of recruitment and both active and tacit support. My job was to explain to senior management how police might respond to anger and reduce alienation so as to hinder al-Qaeda's purpose and improve the standing of counter-terrorism policing in Muslim communities in London.

I genuinely believed that the adage 'communities defeat terrorism' was well founded but required careful implementation. I took the view that counter-terrorism policing was most likely to win and retain community support when it remained as tightly focused as possible on legitimate terrorist suspects. Support was most crucial in communities where terrorist movements sought recruits and supporters. Unfortunately the war on terror encouraged an opposite approach that risked creating 'suspect communities'. Locally, instances of unfocused, ineffective counter-terrorism policing consisted of unnecessary stop and searches. In the circumstances it made sense to reflect on earlier policing failures to build trust with alienated communities. As the former Labour cabinet minister Peter Hain noted as a researcher before entering parliament, 'Members of minority or marginalised communities were especially prone to poor service from a minority of officers who failed to uphold the highest standards of the police service on this fundamental issue of professional service'.[1] Phil Cohen offers the testimony of Detective Sergeant Holland of West Yorkshire Police giving evidence against Asian political activists in the 'Bradford 12' appeal case in 1981 in support of this viewpoint:

Police officers must be prejudiced and discriminatory to do their job ... to search long-haired youths in bedraggled clothing ... and West Indian youths wearing tea cosy hats and loitering in city centres ... The police are expected to act against those people who, by their conduct, mode of life, dress, associates and transport are most likely to be criminals.[2]

Thus, for instance, while law-abiding white-collar workers are rarely associated pejoratively with white-collar criminals such as company fraudsters there was always a likelihood that law-abiding black Londoners would be stigmatised as street robbers by virtue of their superficial resemblance to black street robbers.[3] As I have already noted many black Londoners who had subsequently embraced Islam would face a new risk of pejorative conflation with al-Qaeda terrorism. However, the risk of unfair conflation with al-Qaeda was most pronounced for friends and associates of suspected al-Qaeda terrorists. This was certainly the case for a number of friends and associates of Binyam Mohammed when he was held in Guantanamo Bay. Al-Qaeda propagandists have always been quick to capitalise on topical issues of particular concern to local communities. In this way they demonstrate a grasp of the vital propaganda link between the global cause—the abused ummah—and local neighbourhood experience. Thus, typically, a report alleging torture against a London Muslim terrorist suspect in August 2005 became powerful material for an experienced al-Qaeda propagandist:

A former London schoolboy accused of being a dedicated al-Qaeda terrorist has given the first full account of the interrogation and alleged torture endured by so-called ghost detainees held at secret prisons around the world. For two and a half years US authorities moved Binyam Mohammed around a series of prisons in Pakistan, Morocco and Afghanistan, before he was sent to Guantánamo Bay in September last year.[4]

Suffice to say, when Clive Stafford Smith, Binyam's lawyer delivered his client's account of torture to the young man's friends and members of his local community in North Kensington it caused immediate shock and outrage:

They cut off my clothes with some kind of doctor's scalpel. I was naked. I tried to put on a brave face. But maybe I was going to be raped. Maybe they'd electrocute me. Maybe castrate me. They took the scalpel to my right chest. It was only a small cut. Maybe an inch. At first I just screamed ... I was just shocked, I wasn't expecting ... Then they cut my left chest. This time I didn't want to scream because I knew it was coming. One of them took my penis in his hand and began to make cuts. He did it once, and they stood still for maybe a minute, watching my reaction. I was in agony.[5]

Presented at Al Manaar, the Muslim Cultural Heritage Centre in August 2005 the case raised the controversial subject of 'extraordinary rendition' that would later become a headline issue for Condoleezza Rice and European leaders in December 2005. The lawyer, Clive Stafford Smith:

This is outsourcing of torture, plain and simple. America knows torture is wrong but gets others to do its unconscionable dirty work. It's clear from the evidence that UK officials knew about this rendition to Morocco before it happened. Our government's responsibility must be to actively prevent the torture of our residents.[6]

In keeping with Asghar Bukhari's admonition to community leaders to channel anger that may lead to terrorism in peaceful ways the Muslim community meeting addressed by Clive Stafford Smith sought to achieve exactly that purpose. Distressing information was delivered in a controlled and supportive setting and, most crucially, offered and encouraged responses to Binyam Mohammed's case in practical and active forms: demonstrations and campaigns. Importantly, it also revealed to associates of a young terrorist suspect how his support was being led by campaigners outside the Muslim community. If it also introduced them to forms of protest that may sometimes infringe public order legislation it should still be viewed in the wider context of activity that gives purpose and direction to a sense of injustice that might otherwise lead to terrorism. None of which entirely dispels the concern that emotive campaigning activity of this kind provides opportunities for terrorist propagandists to exploit the same sentiments that are otherwise being channelled in non-violent protest. The fact that terrorist propagandists will generally seek to capitalise on alleged injustices of this kind with a view to increasing a Muslim community sense of victimisation and alienation should not, however, detract from the positive preventative value that attaches to non-violent protest activity that shares the same grievances terrorists seek to exploit. At the very point al-Qaeda propaganda insists that violence is the only response to the UK's perceived refusal to take Muslim concerns seriously an alliance of UK Muslim and non-Muslim activists demonstrate the alternative purposefulness and potential effectiveness of non-violent protest activity. Very often this is also the point at which ineffective counter-terrorist responses are confined to denial or evasion of the alleged injustice—here an implicit involvement in torture. Greater purpose may often be served by acknowledging and evaluating the value of community action of the kind described.

This is not to deny that harrowing accounts of torture in Abu Ghraib and Guantanamo Bay, as much as in Binyam Mohammed's case, may serve to 'radicalise' sections of British Muslim youth without need for al-Qaeda interventions. However, I do question accounts that seek to describe such 'radicalisation' pejoratively as part of a slippery descent from moderation into dangerous extremism. To demonise and to move against the 'radicalisation' of Muslim youth is to deny the legitimate grievances that give rise to it and serves counter-terrorism ill. Rather, the validity and intensity of much 'radicalisation' needs to be respected, harnessed and protected from the dangerous overtures of al-Qaeda propagandists such as Adam Gadahn:

Britain is the one who taught America how to kill and oppress Muslims in the first place. By drawing on experienced gained during hundreds of years of blood soaked colonial history. Lest we forget Britain is today besides prosecuting its occupation of Southern Iraq, the one heading the NATO occupation of Afghanistan and relieving the bloodied and bruised Americans in the south and east of the country. We haven't mentioned the fact that these actions of the Americans and the British are prohibited by the same international law treaties which they hypocritically claim to uphold and protect; that they impose on others even as they themselves violate them with impunity.[7]

Reports of British Muslims travelling to fight alongside the Taliban in Afghanistan bears testimony to the success of this kind of propaganda. Gadahn continues:

What I am saying is that when we bomb their cities and civilians as they bomb ours; or destroyed their infrastructure or transportation like they did ours; or kidnapped their non-combatants like they kidnapped ours. No sane Muslim should shed tears for them. They should blame no one but themselves because they are the ones who started this dirty war. They are the ones who will end it; by ending their aggression against Islam and Muslims; by pulling out of our region; by keeping their hand out of our affairs. Until they do that neither Forest Gate style police raids. Neither Belmarsh or Guantanamo cells nor the mosque or Imams advisory council will be able to prevent the Muslims exacting revenge on behalf of their persecuted brothers and sisters.[8]

Gadahn's exploitation of genuine community anger in Forest Gate in 2006 was first highlighted to MCU officers by an astute Muslim partner. Effective counter-terrorism should therefore be closely integrated with Muslim community initiatives that seek to channel 'radicalisation' positively away from terrorism. Inevitably this entails close proximity (not close association) with necessarily strong community condemnation of much government foreign and counter-terrorist policy and police and security service counter-terrorist activity. This is not a contradictory position for counter-terrorism practitioners, merely complex.

Throughout the period 2002—2007 Muslim community leaders expressed concern that every instance of departure from established criminal process—such as indefinite detention of suspects at HMP Belmarsh, control orders, extraditions to the USA, reports of the use of information obtained by torture abroad, collaboration with US authorities in respect of detainees held at Guantanamo Bay—increased a sense of alienation and persecution in Muslim communities. More crucially, it increased opportunities for al-Qaeda to exploit the gulf between police and community perspectives. In situations like this police must sometimes take difficult messages to government. This required an appreciation that the war on terror may on occasions work to the detriment of UK interests. Al-Qaeda strategists and allied supporters do not welcome authoritative non-Muslim engagement with credible Muslims campaigning against the war on terror. Nothing, from their perspective, is more damaging to the al-Qaeda narrative than an effective campaigning Muslim-non-Muslim alliance on the very issues where al-Qaeda insists on violent exclusively Muslim action. Thus when credible Muslims took part in academic-activist events such as a Campaign against Criminalising Communities (CAMPACC) London conference examining the community impact of counter-terrorism[9] it unwittingly struck at the very heart of al-Qaeda's exclusivist strategy. By the same token, the al-Qaeda grip on a potential recruit's imagination is also weakened when highly regarded released Guantanamo Bay detainees Moazzam Begg[10] and Martin Mubanga[11] engaged publicly with non-Muslim activists and academics.[12] Moreover when such engagement brings the war on terror within an established secular framework of anti-government analysis it offers Muslims a plausible parallel analysis that addresses and threatens al-Qaeda's version:

...strategies for 'containing' terrorist threats involve counter-insurgency methods against entire populations, which then conveniently become targets for state persecution in their own right. Its 'anti-terror' weapons include bans on organisations, exemplary prosecutions, stop-and-search powers, freezing the bank accounts of Muslim charities, blackmail against refugees to act as police informers, etc....[13]

Anti-war activists in this context become 'unlikely counter-terrorists'[14] and combine with London Irish communities to build cross-community support for Muslim Londoners against a common state oppressor. In this latter respect, Paddy Hillyard has been especially important in bringing the prior experience of 'suspect' Irish communities to the attention of Muslim campaigning groups such as Free Babar Ahmad, Stop Political Terror, the MSF and the IHRC amongst others.[15] The last thing a London based al-Qaeda propagandist wants to see is potential Muslim recruits joining forces in a campaign against the war on terror with non-Muslim activists who cherish a whole range (from the terrorist's perspective) of subversive, secular tendencies. As Abu Hamza—one of al-Qaeda's most efficient London recruiters—was fond of reminding his audiences, 'you must not engage with the doctrines of the West, whether they come from Bush, Blair or Fidel Castro'.[16] Indeed when interviewees explain the lengths terrorists go to in countering the influence of non-Muslim support it becomes apparent how wide off the mark conventional accounts are that brand anti-war on terror political activists opponents of counter-terrorism. Instead, an unlikely alliance of non-Muslims achieves precisely the kind of Muslim community engagement their detractors say is needed to defeat extremism. Returning to a major theme at the *Suspect Communities: the Real War on Terror* conference the following extract takes on its own counter-terrorism complexion:

....critical voices should be heard in their own right as terrorism experts, emphasising the role of multinational companies and occupation forces (e.g. in Palestine, Iraq, Chechnya, etc.) as obstacles to a peaceful world. In countering the partisan expertise of terrorology, we all have a role to play—political activists, academics, lawyers, journalists and many others—especially by supporting each other and working together.[17]

To illustrate the point, one interviewee who escaped from Algeria to Finsbury Park in 1995 recalls being pleasantly surprised when he went to a meeting at the London Metropolitan University in Holloway Road (then the North London Polytechnic) at which Irish republican experience was explicitly linked to Algerian Muslim experience of 'colonial violence'. His surprise, he recalls, turned to fascination when at the same series of student meetings he was also shown a screening of the film *Battle of Algiers* for the first time:

When Colonel Mathieu is shown using torture to extract information from Muslims to find out who is in the FLN this is very familiar to Algerians today. It made me think how our parents won a victory against the French only to allow a dictator to repeat their methods against the Muslims. Now the Algerian government employs police who are as brutal as Mathieu. And as hostile to Muslims.[18]

However, this interviewee is not representative of most Algerians coming to Finsbury Park in the 1990s and 2000s. He was relatively well educated and had sufficient skill and knowledge of English to enrol at college when he first arrived. His Islamist connections also put him in touch with the MWH in Seven Sisters Road. Thus he became part of a vibrant Islamist youth scene that developed articulate expressions of Islamist politics that blended experiences from around the globe in wholly peaceful and democratic ways. In contrast, the vast majority of Algerians arriving in London in this period were drawn to the nearby Finsbury Park Mosque having heard on the grapevine that 'Sheikh' Abu Hamza and his supporters would help them with accommodation and the means to survive in London, if necessary by recourse to false documentation and credit card crime.[19] Needless to say it is this aspect of émigré activity that has been fully documented by the authors of the 'Londonistan' narrative while the positive work of the Finsbury Park Islamists has been ignored or conflated with the influence of Abu Hamza.[20]

Interestingly, the interviewee's interest in the film *Battle of Algiers* also offers an insight into the empathetic nature of the MCU's relationship with the Finsbury Park Islamists. A discussion about the film served as a valuable icebreaker when the prospect of partnership working was first being discussed with the interviewee. From my perspective the film offered penetrative insights into the learning of terrorists and counter-terrorists in a pressurised, community environment and helped to highlight mistakes that were being repeated post-9/11. The film portrays Muslim Algerians employing highly developed skills of covert communication and disguise while planning, planting and detonating bombs that kill and maim French civilians in cafés and bars. In practice terrorist-taught skills like bomb-making are performed in stressful scenarios and street skills are employed simultaneously to ensure a carefully devised clandestine strategy is not thwarted by counter-measures employed by the police.[21] The film demonstrates how the same skills are subsequently developed by counter-terrorists aiming to negate the covert tactics employed successfully by the terrorists. This reciprocal process is described by Mike Kenney as 'competitive adaptation' and to be successful policing organisations (like most other bureaucratic agencies) have to overcome an inherent institutional inflexibility.[22] Thus, in *Battle of Algiers* Colonel Mathieu, leading a crack team of French paratroopers, astutely analyses the strategic and tactical methodology of his terrorist opponents and the failings of his predecessor so as to successfully undermine their power base—the local Muslim community. By torturing members of the community and terrorist suspects he elicits vital intelligence about the concealed identities and covert whereabouts of key terrorists. His consequential justification for such controversial methods is remarkably similar to that offered by political apologists of the 'war on terror', namely that it represents a lesser evil than the one it seeks to eradicate.[23]

Notwithstanding the film's faithful portrayal of Colonel Mathieu's effective use of tradecraft in countering terrorism, it is nonetheless reported to have been screened at the Pentagon to demonstrate to military leaders how the war in Iraq might fail if, like Colonel Mathieu's tactics employed against Muslim civilians forty years earlier, it fails to 'win hearts and minds'. Torture too is acknowledged by at least one US counter-terrorism practitioner to be counter-productive.[24] That lesson necessarily waits until the final scenes of the film when it becomes apparent that the seemingly successful tactics employed by Colonel Mathieu have failed to eliminate the underlying grievance that gave rise to the terrorism in the first place. Where the MCU policing project appears to depart from Pentagon thinking about 'hearts and minds' is in recognising that solutions cannot be imposed from without. Thus the only community group who appear to have had legitimacy in the

Muslim community portrayed in *Battle of Algiers* are the FLN, the very body that resorted to terrorism against the colonial French 'occupiers'. To have won the 'hearts and minds' of the Algerian community Colonel Mathieu would have had to open a dialogue with the very people he chose to torture. To do the same in Iraq from 2003 onwards the Pentagon would need to differentiate between Iraqi insurgents and al-Qaeda terrorists. In the UK the MCU project was aimed at curtailing the kind of al-Qaeda influence that led to 7/7 enlists the skills of salafis and Islamists who share some of the same political and religious background as al-Qaeda. A fact that experienced counter-terrorists involved in the MCU project find unsurprising. A fact, moreover, that community projects aimed at tackling the adverse influence of drugs and gun crime on youth communities recognise as being axiomatic. Credible community voices against terrorism, drugs and gun crime only arise from within communities depending as they do on a kind of street skill that cannot be awarded by outsiders, least of all government officials.

Street expertise provides a nexus between police and community skills that bears directly on the London partnership initiative that the young Algerian discussing *Battle of Algiers* with me chose to join. Axiomatic for both partners is the need to cultivate skills that will enable negotiations to take place with targets of recruitment for dangerous and illegal activity.

Sharing this kind of approach became axiomatic for the London Partnership initiative and is relevant to the 1990s because in Finsbury Park as in Brixton that was when Islamists and salafis tackled the problem on their own. It is also relevant because the Finsbury Park Islamists and the Brixton salafis saw Abu Hamza, Abu Qatada and Faisal sowing the seeds in the 1990s for what would happen on 7/7. Thus, Mohammed Siddique Khan, the leader of the 7/7 al-Qaeda London tube bombers, demonstrated his expert street skill-sets when he was unexpectedly and casually approached by an old school friend in a busy Leeds shopping street just days before he led the first ever suicide terrorist attack in the UK.[23] While taught skills might have reminded him of the importance of 'maintaining cover' at all times only developed street skills allowed Khan to engage happily in small talk for a long period with a non-Muslim he had not seen for several years. So successful was Khan in presenting an alter ego that concealed his all-consuming covert terrorist purpose that his old school friend could not recognise the man he met in the street as the perpetrator of mass killing of innocent civilians days later. Other witness accounts bear consistent testimony to Khan's proficiency in presenting an innocent and plausible face to colleagues, friends and family alike in the months and days leading up to 7/7. Against such skilled performers admonitions from government ministers and police chiefs to communities to report suspicious behaviour are likely to prove fruitless. Which is not to overlook the fact that Khan had by then appeared on the UK counter-terrorist radar in 2004 but rather to illustrate how effectively terrorists may become experts at concealment and deception both through taught procedures and improvised aptitude.

Much the same will be gleaned from perusing the available evidence surrounding the preparations of the 9/11 bombers.[26] Mohamed Atta, like Khan a key player in a carefully managed conspiracy, displays similar expertise that formal teaching alone cannot produce. In both cases it may be reasonable to speculate that al-Qaeda strategists had previously identified exactly this potential in both men—well developed street skills. As such their ability to succeed in such critical tasks was not a matter of chance, rather an indication of expert preparation and recruitment. To allow otherwise would be to deny al-Qaeda the strategic acumen that is essential for the effectiveness and longevity of any significant terrorist movement. Indeed, in important respects, al-Qaeda recruiters are no different to experienced military, security and police trainers who select specialist officers to perform dangerous covert operations against organised crime and terrorist targets. In consequence covert terrorist skill is passed on from teacher to apprentice in the same way that it is done by the very individuals being trained to disrupt them.[27] Moreover, as Kenney highlights, counter-terrorism has much to learn from counter-drugs trafficking expertise that has been forced to develop its own brand of clandestine skill-sets in an attempt to keep pace with the problem it is employed to tackle.[28] Which is not to overlook the fact that organisational learning is a two-way street. To be sure much could usefully be written about counter-terrorists' ability to pass on valuable experience to fellow practitioners in counter-drugs trafficking or counter-gun crime work.

I was involved in a 'novel approach' to counter-terrorism that owed much to counter-drugs trafficking and counter-gun crime fields of experience as well as its own specialist sub-discipline. In particular the MCU was aimed at empowering street skills in Muslim communities against the efforts of al-Qaeda propagandists to subvert and recruit young Muslims to their cause. In important respects the project adapted soft, community policing approaches to drugs problems where susceptible youth are engaged as potential victims and differentiated from unscrupulous traffickers and pushers who are targeted for long-term imprisonment. In 2002 UK counter-terrorism (as elsewhere in the West) there was no precedent for treating young potential terrorist recruits as victims who should be rehabilitated into the community, as opposed to being targeted and prosecuted for serious terrorist offences. To allow credible grassroots Muslim community groups to perform much of this work with minimum supervision was to push well beyond the boundaries of conventional counter-terrorism. Indeed, even in counter-drugs and counter-gun crime policing there is scepticism about the ability of 'soft' community initiatives to rehabilitate offenders or divert susceptible youth away from criminal behaviour. How much more resistance might then be encountered to 'soft' approaches when the subject is the most politically charged of the day—terrorism.

In 2003 I placed myself at odds with government policy on counter-terrorism by endorsing Muslim community concerns that British foreign policy—most especially but not exclusively in respect of the war in Iraq—had an adverse impact on the terrorist threat to the UK. The Blair government was always careful to describe the al-Qaeda threat as existing independently of British foreign policy and as having ideological motivation that pre-dated 9/11.[29] Moreover, Tony Blair, as British Prime Minister, was at pains to describe 7/7 as an 'attack on our way of life' when delivering high-profile media messages that explicitly excluded political grievance from an analysis of the root causes of terrorism:

But, coming to Britain is not a right. And even when people have come here, staying here carries with it a duty. That duty is to share and support the values that sustain the British way of life. Those that break that duty and try to incite hatred or engage in violence against our country and its people, have no place here. Over the coming months, in the courts, in parliament, in debate and engagement with all parts of our communities, we will work to turn those sentiments into reality. That is my duty as prime minister.[30]

In a speech to the World Affairs Council in Los Angeles on Monday, 1 August 2005 Blair described a struggle between 'reactionary Islam and moderate, mainstream Islam'.[31] Rather, the MCU inclined to Peter Bergen's analysis of root causes having far more to do with a violent political response to US (and after 9/11, UK-backed) policies in the Middle East.[32] In consequence whenever the MCU reported and endorsed the views of its community partners that directly contradicted the Prime Minister's analysis it faced the prospect of marginalisation itself.[33] This became particularly acute after 7/7 when ACPO officers became even less inclined to challenge government orthodoxy on the topic.[34] Which raises an additional question concerning MCU legitimacy and effectiveness when the unit's rupture with government policy extended to acknowledging Richard Jackson's claim that the language of the war on terror 'prevents rather than facilitates' the search for solutions to terrorism.[35] This was for the MCU to explain both that government policies and the manner in which they were expressed ran the risk of being counter-productive.[36] Certainly, when discussing the problem with community partners it became increasingly clear that the terrorist threat had to be understood in terms of the war on terror—the killing of civilians by 7/7 suicide bombers alongside 'US helicopter gunships attacking insurgents on the streets of Fallujah'.[37]

I sought to define a significant gap between and within police and community perspectives about effective counter-terrorism policing. For senior police officers wedded to a community impact assessment model intended primarily to measure potential street disorder it was difficult to listen to a new and more elusive message: sections of the community best located to tackle terrorist propaganda were becoming disillusioned with vital aspects of counter-terrorist policing and were liable to adopt a posture of passive disengagement in consequence.[38] The MCU also had to overcome internal organisational resistance to a partnership approach that fell outside traditional investments in covert intelligence gathering activity aimed at disrupting and apprehending suspected terrorists.[39] This organisational resistance took two complementary forms. On the one hand counter-terrorism strategists were sceptical about an investment of specialist resources in an initiative that might be better carried out by community police officers.[40] For their part mainstream police managers questioned the viability of counter-terrorism officers engaging in community partnership work that generally fell to community police officers to perform.[41]

Both areas of concern are evidenced, albeit indirectly, in research commissioned by ACPO in 2004, undertaken shortly before 7/7, and written up in its aftermath.[42] In an article presenting the research findings Martin Innes concludes that 'the long history of difficult relations between many minority communities and the police' results in the likelihood that 'only a comparatively thin form of trust can be cultivated by police'.[43] Properly resourced neighbourhood policing, Innes argues, should carry out this trust-building work—echoing the view of the [then] new Metropolitan Police Commissioner, Sir Ian Blair. In essence this model restricts Special Branch to mainstream, covert counter-terrorism and allows neighbourhood policing to 'foster and develop the trust that is required for people to provide information to them'. Commenting on this observation one MCU officer noted:

This sums up the problem we faced after 7/7. ACPO was impressed with the trust we had built with Muslim communities but didn't want to see that work being done by Special Branch for two reasons. One there was a long-term organisational antipathy towards MPSB on the basis that it had operated independently for too long—and it was going to be wound up. Two, there was a clear strategy that the new Commissioner would make his name by introducing the first fully resourced form of neighbourhood policing. The MCU didn't fit in on either count. Just as plans were being made to wind up MPSB we started to hear that the MCU would be 'mainstreamed' which was to say our idea would be re-branded outside of Special Branch. Crucially that would allow partnerships with problematic partners to be replaced with less controversial ones.[44]

By championing neighbourhood policing Innes' report proved vital to ACPO policy implementation. Here the report identifies strategic shortcomings that should be remedied by adopting a national Neighbourhood Policing model, without reference to the MCU:

The community intelligence accessed may not generate the hard leads of the sort provided by other more traditional covert methods. But it may overcome the problem of the diffusion of information by developing indicators of suspicion about individuals, groups, and locations that the police should examine more closely. What local policing potentially provides is an ongoing sensitisation to the normal state of a community and thus may detect early signs that risks have increased in some manner.[45]

Curiously, despite the fact that he quotes from an interview where an MCU officer explains the complexities that exist in Muslim communities,[46] Innes reckons that 'subtle intricacies of and nuances of this kind are not the kind of things that police have been especially well tuned to in the past'.[47] This failure to recognise the extent to which his interviewee was evidencing precisely the kind of expertise that had been expected of MPSB officers for decades is revealing. Given the extent to which the report articulates and reflects government and police management thinking about the strategic direction of counter-terrorism and community (or neighbourhood) policing during the period under review it helps to explain why the MCU initiative failed to convert community approval into organisational achievement. The significance of that gap between approval and achievement is also highlighted at various points where the MCU accomplished important tasks that neither conventional counter-terrorism nor mainstream community policing had the appetite or aptitude to do so.

In addition at a fundamental level MCU officers worked to a different set of objectives than the US-led, UK-backed global war on terror launched in the aftermath of 9/11. Again this is in marked contrast to ACPO and their own Strategic Contact Unit that always scrupulously avoided any criticism of the war on terror and accepted the government's diagnosis of the problem. In contrast, the MCU demonstrated a dual concern: to reduce the influence of al-Qaeda propaganda and recruitment in communities that are susceptible to it and to empower community groups that have the skills and willingness to counter it. In doing so the unit relied on prior counter-terrorism experience, most notably in respect of PIRA, where a failure to win the battle for hearts and minds of Irish republican youth proved costly. In doing so, however, MCU officers offered an interpretation of counter-terrorism experience that sat at odds with prevailing 'top-down' accounts that focused instead on the relationship between the PIRA leadership and the British government—first protracted violent conflict then negotiation leading to resolution. Instead, the MCU officers focused on Irish Catholic communities in London that had at times been alienated by aspects of counter-terrorism policing experienced by them as disproportionate and stigmatising.[48] As a result the PIRA stood to gain potentially invaluable recruits on 'the mainland', increased tacit support in the communities concerned, both to their operational benefit and the concomitant detriment of counter-terrorism policing. In consequence, MCU strategy was aimed at minimising the risks of counter-terrorism policing alienating sections of Muslim communities so as not to increase the risk of young London Muslims becoming terrorists or sections of the community becoming hubs of tacit terrorist support. While performance measurement here is inevitably elusive sufficient empirical evidence of success has been generated to afford a wider quantitative and qualitative analysis. Moreover, by contrasting the London partnership initiative with aspects of the war on terror that have clearly boosted al-Qaeda recruitment it is possible to open up a rich seam of future counter-terrorism research.

Nonetheless, the MCU made a small and sometimes negative impression on those two established and well-resourced policing models—counter-terrorism and community policing—but a larger and more positive impression on the Muslim community groups it developed partnerships with. Indeed, wider police negativity towards the MCU was at times compounded by a significant investment in establishing a closer direct relationship between counter-terrorism policing and community policing.[49] That centrally driven initiative helped to restrict the MCU to a marginal role between 2002 and 2007. Conversely, however, the London partnership initiative demonstrates how that sense of exclusion from the mainstream has sometimes been turned from a deficit to advantage. On the community side, both salafi and Islamist partners are described as representing practising, minority communities within a burgeoning and diverse Muslim London. In important respects salafi and Islamist partners can be seen as representing communities that have been marginalised by more powerful majority elements in the mosaic that is Muslim London. Consequently, the London partnership initiative covers two areas of partnership engagement—police with salafi partnerships and police with Islamist partnerships—where all three parties have often had to overcome the disadvantage of marginalisation. In addition, according to MCU counter-terrorism experience, both salafi and Islamist partners represent communities at increased risk of unintended stigmatisation by counter-terrorism policing and a concomitant increased risk of susceptibility to terrorist recruitment or support. Here Andrew Silke's argument that poorly focused, retaliatory counter-terrorism activity may be counter-productive is germane:

The US aggressively chasing down al-Qaeda and its affiliates throughout the world, may find that a last resolution to the chase eludes it, regardless of how much energy and military force it invests in the campaign.... If past experience is anything to go by, defeating or diminishing the overall threat of terrorism is not something that either small—or large-scale retaliations have yet been able to achieve.[50]

The development of the partnerships relied on the skills and experience of MCU and Muslim community partners who challenged prevailing wisdom about the way to tackle al-Qaeda at virtually every turn. If mainstream counter-terrorism acknowledges the need for community support it is principally as a prerequisite for community intelligence that will allow terrorist activity to be identified in time for it to be disrupted.[51] MCU officers took this objective a stage further and posited the notion that counter-terrorism will fail to win the support it needs if it is perceived to care more about intelligence than the fair and proportionate treatment of Muslim communities.[52] Community concern here is shown to extend across all areas of counter-terrorism, from approaches to recruit informants to the alleged mistreatment of British Muslim terrorist suspects at home and abroad.[53] In particular MCU officers examined Muslim community concerns about the treatment of British Muslims at Guantanamo Bay and at multiple venues during the course of what the US authorities have termed extraordinary rendition. In both instances MCU officers challenged the notion that UK counter-terrorism can be arbitrarily separated from the acts of its US partners in the war on terror, still less from the actions of its own military partners in Iraq and Afghanistan. Throughout the first six years of its existence, the London partnership initiative appreciated the importance of acknowledging these concerns in an effort to reduce the risk of al-Qaeda propagandists mobilising community disquiet as a vehicle for recruitment and support. In doing so it aligned itself to stern critics of the war on terror. At this point the distance from conventional counter-terrorism looms large.

MCU officers had extensive experience of covert intelligence gathering including what is called the handling of covert human intelligence sources, i.e. police informants.[54] Their decision not to employ this tactic for engagement with Muslim community representatives was of fundamental importance to them:

It was always clear that source recruitment would need to continue. What was equally clear was that the benefits of treating community representatives of all kinds as partners was being overlooked. That the MCU should create space for partnerships and not get involved in handling informants. You can't do both anyway.[55]

Another MCU officer expands the observation:

Overlooked in our world [i.e. counter-terrorism]. But look what had been happening under John Grieve's command [the MPS Racial and Violent Crime Task Force]. Community leaders who were vocal critics of police were being approached to work with police as partners. Not as informants. John Grieve could overcome [police] sceptics because of his record. He would explain how it was harder to win community support than to recruit informants but more satisfying and more beneficial in the long run. But one didn't preclude the other.[56]

The discussion continues, demonstrating the kind of on-the-job learning that characterised the MCU:

That is the important bit. Working *with* not *for* the police. Dave Veness under-stood that as well. I think he had the idea that Muslim community groups could engage with police in the same way the Community Security Trust (CST) did representing Jewish community interests.[57]

That was the thinking behind the Muslim Safety Forum (MSF). But whereas the CST would give police a pretty unified and pre-packaged position on any number of topics the MSF would often give conflicting opinions and demon-strate the diverse nature of Muslim views.[58]

MCU officers also developed a partnership approach with members of the MSF:

When you recall in 2002 the *Muslim News* was running a story about MI5 and Special Branch officers harassing Muslims—trying to intimidate them. We were asked about that at an MSF meeting. Was the MCU recruiting informants? Were we part of that harassment? [name supplied] had a copy of the *Muslim News* at the meeting.[59]

I was asked the same question more than once. It was the same when the *Guardian* ran a story about the MCU spying on Muslims.[60]

[Muslim community leader] was extremely upset about that. He knew one of the families that had been visited. He introduced us to the idea that it could also undermine his position in the community when he was known to attend the MSF and meet police. What was he doing about it? What did he get for the community from meeting police?[61]

MCU officers empathised with community leaders when they com-plained about intrusive methods of intelligence gathering in cases like this one where the *Muslim News* story ran under the headline 'MI5 and Special Branch officers have visited the homes of over 30 British Muslims since May':[62] Described in the paper as 'fishing' expeditions that were 'part of a new strategy to collect information on possible ter-rorists' in which 'no one was arrested'. The Home Secretary, David Blunkett, was reported to have apologised to some of the Muslims interviewed, 'I am sorry' he is quoted as saying, 'that anyone inter-viewed was distressed by the experience'.[63] It is instructive to quote further from the *Muslim News* report:

We felt intimidated. 'They alleged that our names and addresses were found in the Tora Bora region of Afghanistan', one Muslim from Blackburn was quoted as saying. Most of those visited preferred not to be identified....All the Mus-lims said they co-operated with the security services and answered their ques-tions. Some of them said they reluctantly agreed to talk to the Special Branch as they were 'too frightened' to say 'no' as they were not aware of their rights and thought that 'if we had refused to talk to them, they would have suspected that we had something to hide.[64]

Coming as it did at exactly the time MCU were beginning to approach Muslim community representatives it is hardly surprising that the [then] two officers staffing the unit should have been questioned about it.[65] Naturally, the report was widely known and it created fear and suspicion that MCU officers were actually just an extension of this intrusive approach. Then, as throughout the period under review, the MCU was able to explain its role to the MSF and that at least went some way to reassuring key representative groups that partnership engagement was at least intended to be qualitatively different to source recruitment (that is the recruitment of informants or what is described above as 'fishing expeditions').[66] Set up shortly before the MCU the MSF met police at NSY on a monthly basis and had far more community credibility than the Diversity Directorate's Independent Advisory Group.[67] Key MSF members soon became close allies of the MCU and assisted the MCU in carrying out its role.

On the critical issue of how police should approach community leaders the MSF expressed outrage and disbelief when it was reported in 2003 that a senior Muslim scholar Sheikh Yusuf Motala had missed an important flight departing from Heathrow Airport because he had been questioned by Special Branch officers who apparently wanted the kind of information about his role as principal of the Darul Uloom seminary in Bury that was freely available, or available on request at less inopportune moments.[68] When complaining about the indignity caused to the Sheikh at an MSF meeting, the Muslim Council of Britain (MCB) representative likened the incident to the Archbishop of Canterbury being questioned by police about his work at Lambeth Palace and being forced to miss an important flight in consequence:

Anger. Phone never stopped ringing. What was going on? What was the point of having an MCU if this kind of thing happened? Did the Commissioner know how much upset this had caused?[69]

Luckily we had a boss then who took it very seriously. That saved the day. Prepared to visit the Sheikh and apologise.[70]

The important point is that you can ask the Sheikh anything any time, you don't have to button hole him at the airport.[71]

Although MCU officers had experience of a partnership approach being adopted within MPSB in earlier counter-terrorism contexts they found the wider MPS organisational memory to be lacking.[72] Moreover, there did not appear to be the political will to adopt the practice in 2002—hence the MCU operated in a vacuum and on a shoe-string. Here an MCU officer reflects on the problem:

We were trying to adopt the Operation Trident[73] model but without the buy-in outside of MPSB. Trident was about treating black community leaders as partners for the first time—giving them some respect for the first time. With some of the Met's fiercest critics—community leaders who had been hostile to the Met for years encouraged to take part by Lee Jasper.[74] Lee put his own credibility on the line to broker a partnership with police. To do the same with Muslim groups in 2002 we would have needed John Grieve's leadership and the same political buy-in. It was never going to happen.[75]

The same strand of MPSB experience also tended to show that a community leader was more likely to impart sensitive information to police when he has established a significant level of trust.[76] Thus if a community partner had concerns about individuals becoming involved in al-Qaeda-inspired terrorism he might be more inclined to report it when he knows the information will be handled fairly and responsibly.[77] More regularly, however, MCU partners would become involved in youth education and training and acquire a track record of success in producing responsible, engaged London Muslim citizens—a situation that would not have flourished if instead of being treated as police partners community leaders had been treated as informants.[78]

As well as being significant for the founding members of the MCU the crucial importance of Irish Catholic community experience was also highlighted by a police interviewee who came from an Irish Catholic community in London. He was anxious to point out that the London counter-terrorism maxim 'communities defeat terrorism' was often undermined in his experience when both Anti-Terrorist Branch and Special Branch detectives wilfully or negligently failed to distinguish between legitimate terrorist suspects and the communities where the terrorists sought to rely on tacit support:

There were two kinds of problem. One was the regular suspicion Irish Cathloic families would encounter when travelling through Heathrow Airport and other airports. This constant fear of arrest or detention would engender widespread feelings of antipathy for the police and sometimes lead indirectly to increased tacit support for the Provisionals. The other problem was more serious and arose when a terrorist suspect was arrested and detectives chose to arrest many known associates without having any evidence of their involvement. This kind of approach was very counter-productive. It certainly did nothing to help get Irish Catholic communities to work with the police against the IRA.[79]

Interestingly, one Muslim community leader who rejected an approach from detectives to become an informant has commented on the pervasive nature of what he calls the 'informant culture' in policing.[80] On the one hand his prior experience of resisting what he describes as a concerted attempt to recruit him as making him wary of entering into a subsequent partnership relationship with MCU officers. On the other hand he describes how one senior police officer who formed a local partnership with Muslim community groups continued to adopt a management rather than a partnership style in his discussions with community representatives.[81]

In some ways the MCU has broken police stereotypes. When I was growing up we had a few meetings with the CID. Some of them really did behave like they were in *The Sweeney*. And I had one friend who got pressured into being an informant and he was always regretting it. Instead of making him feel safe, it made him feel anxious all the time. So when detectives wanted to recruit me I was experienced enough to say no. But I had to be very firm and stand up for myself. So I was initially very wary of the MCU partnership thing but I could see it was different and was prepared to give it a chance. And it has been unusual to be listened to so much. It's been good to be a real partner.[82]

Essentially, MCU officers sought to foster a climate where the suspicion and anxiety that haunts the daily life of an informant is replaced by a healthy atmosphere where the temptation informants sometimes feel to 'guild the lily'—to embellish information—or to act as an *agent provocateur* are removed.[83] For operational reasons specific MCU successes in alternative partnership intelligence approaches are omitted.[84] To create a space for success of this kind identifying and separating al-Qaeda propagandists from the communities they sought to recruit from was a clear MCU objective from inception.[85] This was especially important for officers who recalled how PIRA propagandists would covertly embed themselves in organisations in London that supported their prisoners and their political cause. In one particular case the MCU officers recalled how a convicted PIRA London bomber had spent a decade successfully masquerading as a committed anti-fascist street activist in London.[86] As such he had regular meetings with police as an organiser of demonstrations and meetings. While media attention rightly focuses on the kind of threat al-Qaeda infiltrators might pose to the police or the security services,[87] MCU experience taught of the preventative value of trusted Muslim community leaders who might offset the risk. As one MCU officer remarks:

It was always the purpose of the Provisional IRA to infiltrate well-meaning campaigns in London such as the Troops Out Movement so as to maximise support and identify potential recruits. Incidents of alleged police brutality against Irish republican terrorist suspects or mistreatment of their families when their homes were searched were always good recruiting material. The same situation was bound to arise in respect of al-Qaeda.[88]

Not that the two officers belonged to a police department that was noted for its empathy with London's minority communities—or indeed its commitment to community policing. On the contrary, Special Branch had become synonymous with the covert monitoring of subversive political threats in London.[89] Infiltration rather than community partnerships were the popular hallmarks of an elite police department first established in 1883 to combat the threat to the capital posed by Irish republican bombers.[90] Nonetheless, that prime Special Branch purpose of protecting the capital from terrorist bombs was the motivation for the establishment of the MCU.[91] In fact, the MCU was based on a long tradition of Special Branch partnership engagement with leaders and representatives from minority London communities that had received virtually no public recognition.[92] For instance, in the 1980s Special Branch officers would meet Sikh community representatives in London to discuss the terrorist threat posed by Sikh extremists. Such meetings would be treated confidentially but would not place the community leaders in the category of informants. Rather, they would be treated as 'community contacts' and both police and community representatives would enjoy a cordial relationship based on mutual respect and common interest.[93] One Special Branch veteran recalls:

We had regular meetings with Sikh community leaders in London. First they would discuss local policing issues with the local police. Then we would meet them to discuss the current terrorist threat and how it was impacting on their community. They tended to be broad ranging discussions about the strategies and tactics of the extremists and especially about the way the local communities were reacting to terrorist propaganda. We shared the same concern. Wanting to prevent young Sikhs being recruited into terrorism.[94]

Several Sikh leaders became good friends of MPSB officers and those friendships outlasted the terrorist threat that had first introduced them.[95] None of which prevented the recruitment of informants in Sikh communities for intelligence gathering purposes. This was important

241

because there was a tendency otherwise to think that a 'community contact' was less valuable than an informant.[96] There was also an organisational bias towards informants because then a higher level of control and direction could be maintained.[97] However, this strand of MPSB experience introduced the notion that important strategic and tactical intelligence could be obtained without recourse to covert, intrusive methods. As the same officer explains:

Our job was to figure out who were the community leaders in the know. The ones with credibility. With a finger on the pulse of the community. Often that meant they were sympathetic to the terrorists' cause. One Sikh community leader was far more reliable with intelligence than the informants who were being paid to provide it.[98]

Implicit in the officer's recollection is the concept of valuable information being provided to police, not for payment, not from any sense of coercion,[99] but from what may best be termed a citizen's obligation. In fact, this approach to intelligence gathering remained a minority interest within MPSB and was virtually consigned to history by the time the two officers decided to revitalise the approach for the MCU.[100] In the intervening period misdemeanours by detectives and their informants in the criminal world had prompted legislation and guidelines that imposed rigorous management control over the relationship between police and informants.[101] Inevitably under the new management regime the practice of meeting community leaders on a casual basis declined. Indeed, such was the move away from 'contacts' and towards 'covert human intelligence sources' that it became difficult for the MCU to re-establish the notion of regular, informal meetings with community leaders as a prime source of community intelligence. According to the same officer the 'best picture of the terrorist threat was generally obtained from a Sikh community leader' who never became an informant.[102]

Throughout the period 2002 to 2007 the partnership's two-way cultural empathy and trust-building stands in marked contrast to prevailing attitudes of confrontation and suspicion variously explicit and implicit in the wider war on terror.[103] One Muslim community leader in East London compares the courteous partnership approach of the MCU with his degrading treatment at the hands of immigration and security officials at a US airport where he was detained overnight in a cold cell pending further enquiries into his visit (both to lecture and to see his son at university).[104] When he was asked at 2 am whether he had any tattoos by a security official with a form to fill in it struck him that he was unwittingly on the wrong side of a war between 'us and them'—a thought that has occurred to London Muslim community leaders on numerous occasions.[105] Subsequently on his return to the UK the MCU sought to explain the community leader's value as a community partner against al-Qaeda to US officials but with limited success.[106] Attempts to broker a meeting between US officials and the community leader were unsuccessful. In this case as in so many others the MCU partnership approach towards Muslim figures with uncompromising religious and political beliefs failed to inspire confidence in the wider war on terror.[107] In consequence MCU officers became concerned that their ability to win over suspicious community leaders would be undermined. As one MCU officer notes, 'It is hard to think of someone less likely to have a tattoo and less important in persuading local Muslim youth that al-Qaeda is the wrong way to go'.[108]

In much the same way the partnerships' bridge-building stands in sharp contrast to al-Qaeda propaganda that condemns Muslim community efforts to thwart its terrorist activity as betrayal. Indeed, salafi and Islamist partners face disapprobation from a far wider circle of community opinion where proactive counter-terrorism engagement with police is often seen as a step too far. This position might be characterised as 'active hostility' and was demonstrated by the activist and media pundit Yvonne Ridley when she called on fellow Muslims to be wary of the police in the aftermath of the controversial Forest Gate raid in 2006 in which an innocent Muslim youth was shot and injured.[109] One community leader characterised a more prevalent position for Muslim communities and their representatives as 'passive disengagement' capturing the sense in which the full impact of the war on terror militated against active participation with its agents.[110] A Muslim community leader in West London voiced his frustration with the situation in 2005 in these terms:

I have struggled continuously to convince young members of the community that they should help the police to fight extremism. They believe George Bush is fighting a war against Islam not a war against terrorism and I have given up trying to disabuse them of this idea. Instead I try to reassure them that the British police have got a difficult job to do and should be supported when they are investigating terrorist attacks like 7th July. Unfortunately there have been too many occasions when the British authorities have been seen to be puppets of the US for my words to be heeded. It has become a very difficult issue.[111]

Interestingly, there are examples of precisely the same partnership activity where, on the one hand, salafi or Islamist partners have faced community criticism as 'sell outs' for engagement with police and, on the other, police partners have faced criticism from mainstream media commentators for 'appeasing Muslim extremists'. Not surprisingly, attacks from opposite ends of the spectrum are shown to have bolstered a sense of unity and purpose on both police and community sides of the London partnerships. In consequence, both police and community partners exhibit an awareness of the importance of language in framing the work they are engaged in—'al-Qaeda', 'terrorism', 'war on terror', 'salafi', 'Islamist' are key terms in a long list of contested meanings that are better understood in their wider political context. To this end, Richard Jackson's thoroughgoing analysis of the specific use of language in the war on terror and Stuart Croft's study of its domestic cultural context serve as valuable guides.[112] Both analyses help set the context for a cross-cultural partnership initiative where salafi and Islamist community perspectives were at considerable odds with mainstream media accounts of the war on terror.[113] Moreover the London partnerships were concerned to illustrate the importance of language as a communication tool both in the delivery of propaganda aimed at boosting al-Qaeda support and recruitment and in the community partnership activity aimed at countering it.[114]

One point of consensus emerges in respect of the critical value for both MCU and community partners of trust and confidence building and the importance of reciprocal acts of support in achieving it. MCU officers are shown to have won considerable trust by helping vulnerable members of their partners' communities to pursue criminal charges after suffering physical or verbal abuse—anti-Muslim hate crimes, more commonly known as Islamophobic attacks.[115] Confidence has also been gained when MCU officers have been able to reduce the risk of community partners being questioned at length at airports.[116] For their part community partners are shown to have won the trust of MCU partners by calming community anger in the wake of incidents with potential to cause public disorder.[117] Significantly, salafi and Islamist community partners have proved themselves to be far better placed to effectively monitor and assess community tensions than so called 'strategic' community partners employed by diversity policing.[118]

In addition, participant observation allowed access to intimate day-to-day interaction where trust and confidence is seen to increase as traditional cultural barriers are slowly broken down and mutual ignorance is diminished.[119] Sharing knowledge of partners' families and favourite football teams, for instance, is one of many mundane exchanges outside the partnership endeavour that appears to have helped cement trust and confidence over a sustained period.[120] This is significant because it runs counter to protocols that govern police conduct in dealing with informants.[121] In that arena personal friendships are discouraged in favour of a controlled relationship that focuses solely on the community member's ability to deliver valuable intelligence.[122] Moreover, according to both sides of the partnership, increased mutual respect has been achieved during the course of demanding, sometimes dangerous, proactive engagement. As one community partner explains:

I got a phone call from someone I didn't know very well asking me to help with their son who had joined Abu Hamza's circle. It didn't sound altogether genuine and it just made me concerned that it might be some kind of trap. I went to the house at 9pm but on the way I let the MCU know what was happening and agreed to phone later if everything was ok. As it turned out everything was genuine but it was reassuring to know I had support if I needed it.[123]

11

EXPERIENCE, EXPERTISE AND CIVIC DUTY

In part MCU partnerships in Finsbury Park and Brixton developed because of limited resources. Always part of a small unit, MCU officers would focus narrowly on what they perceived to be centres of community experience and expertise with regard to tackling al-Qaeda influence in the community. This also entailed placing reliance on their own wide MPSB experience and expertise with regard to international terrorism and a willingness to challenge ACPO strategy. In consequence, MCU officers were engaged in a process of ongoing assessment concerning their aims and tactics. Central to that process was a concern for legitimacy and effectiveness. As Muslim MCU officers made clear, their legitimacy and effectiveness in the community would be irretrievably damaged if the MCU was perceived to be engaged in spying on communities instead of supporting them.[1] Similarly, legitimacy and effectiveness were interlinked. MCU officers enjoyed hard-won reputations for achieving results in a specialist department dedicated to intelligence gathering.[2] To retain legitimacy and credibility in that environment while discarding its most notable tools was akin to a Wild West sheriff policing Dodge City without a gun. To attempt to do so was to take a risk that was not commensurate with their pay scale, nor in keeping with new managerialism in mainstream policing where risk aversion had become an important inhibitor.[3]

Quite how this initiative took place beneath the radar of the war on terror until 2005 only becomes explicable when considering the small scale of the MCU and especially when viewed from a bottom-up perspective. Primary data has revealed the extent to which the MCU was operating to a discarded MPSB model that was out of kilter with new ACPO thinking and the wider war on terror. 'Special Branch was already in receivership and about to be wound up' an MCU officer recalled, 'we were yesterday's men'.[4] That is the organisational context in which engagement between the MCU and minority Muslim communities took place between 2002 and 2006.

As noted earlier, during 2005 I became the focus of criticism in the media which helped to focus my attention on issues that went to the heart of the legitimacy and effectiveness of the MCU and the London partnerships.[5] For the main part this criticism was specifically concerned with the MCU's partnership with the Finsbury Park Islamists and Islamists in general, but at certain points it also impacted adversely on the MCU's partnership with the Brixton salafis as well. Critics included journalists, academics, think-tanks and bloggers but their arguments have been most cogently articulated in a series of articles and reports produced by members and associates of Policy Exchange between 2005 and 2009. Given their political influence, it is unsurprising that their criticism should have been taken very seriously by policy-makers and ACPO. MCU work with the Finsbury Park Islamists first led the MCU to be criticised by Policy Exchange in these terms:

Members of the Met's Muslim Contact Unit, one of the weirder parts of the force, extol the work of the Muslim Association of Britain…' [the Islamists at Finsbury Park] thereby revealing themselves to be suffering from 'a kind of ideological 'Stockholm syndrome', the psychological state whereby hostages start viewing the world through the eyes of their captives.[6]

Perceptively Godson is immediately echoing concerns that were expressed about MCU officers 'going native' by a handful of ACPO officers outside of MPSB. Within MPSB there was considerable experience of the empathetic role played by MCU officers. Since 1883 countless outstanding MPSB officers had withstood far more severe challenges to their professional objectivity than might ever arise in an average day on the MCU. Nevertheless, it was a shrewd observation and signalled Godson's empathy towards a small number of ACPO officers who shared some of his concerns about the role of the MCU.[7] Godson sees MCU partnership with the Finsbury Park Islamists as being emblematic of an 'unselfconfident…modern British State [that] has great difficulties setting its own standards' and 'has to bring in dodgy Islamist outsiders to do its dirty work—and then only on Islamist terms'.[8] Such appeasement 'carries a high price' he warns.[9]

In another article dealing with the West Midlands Police, Godson suggests that appeasing Islamists is akin to asking Nick Griffin, the BNP leader, to help combat violent behaviour by Combat 18 extremists on the basis that Griffin has street credibility with alienated skinheads.[10] His point is that Griffin's ostensible non-violence should not be a basis on which police wittingly or unwittingly give legitimacy to his unpalatable politics. Thus, Godson would almost certainly not object if Griffin was employed by police for the same purpose as an informant. That kind of relationship would not grant legitimacy to Griffin's politics—and it would be intended to remain covert.[11] If, hypothetically, MCU officers agreed that Godson was wholly or broadly correct to make a comparison between Islamists and the BNP then they would have abandoned a partnership with the Finsbury Park Islamists and other Islamists. Instead MCU officers argued that Godson wrongly conflated extremist Islamists like Abu Hamza—whose hate-filled rhetoric might well bear comparison with Nick Griffin's—with mainstream Islamists like Anas Altikriti, whose Cordoba Foundation, Godson attacked as 'sectarian'. So far as MCU officers were concerned Altikriti was the antithesis of Griffin, an outstanding community leader who had spoken out against sectarian extremists in the Muslim community for many years and had been assaulted for his trouble. Rather, from an MCU perspective, Altikriti was a typical mainstream Islamist who was probably best characterised by his willingness to risk his life trying to intercede on behalf of the London Christian peace activist Norman Kember when he was held hostage in Iraq in 2005.[12]

In contrast, relying on considerable operational experience of dealing with subversive threats, MCU officers took the view that a non-violent extremist Islamist group like HT might very well be sectarian and subversive in the way Godson suggests. On that basis the MCU never entered into a partnership relationship with HT, regarding them as armchair revolutionaries rather like the Revolutionary Communist Party had once been assessed to be. Continuing the analogy I argued that just as political commentators in the 1980s understood that old Labour socialists like Tony Benn and Jeremy Corbyn were not subversive and should not be conflated with revolutionary communists like Claire Fox[13] so too should they distinguish between mainstream Islamists like Anas Altikriti and khalifate revolutionaries like Majid Nawaz.[14] I was also keen to point out that just as subversives like Fox and

Nawaz were likely to mature into reactionary scourges of their younger selves, generally speaking, mainstream socialists and mainstream Islamists like Tony Benn, Jeremy Corbyn and Anas Altikriti tended to stay true to their political principles throughout their mature years.

There might be a moral argument that the al-Qaeda threat to London was such that the MCU was entitled to enlist the support of anyone who could help tackle it.[15] The philosophical notion of 'dirty hands' provides an analogy of a serious fire when the political views of fire-fighters are of less concern than their willingness to put the blaze out.[16] Instead, I insisted that the views of our Islamist and salafi partners were not incompatible with UK interests and generally not as their detractors portrayed them. Godson acknowledges the need for police to meet Islamists and salafis in the course of their work but insists that it be done 'in a dark alley'.[17] Significantly, he does so in the knowledge that he has the support of key ACPO police officers[18] and more crucially the ear of leading politicians.[19] In the circumstances it is noteworthy that he should begin to engage with the MCU in 2005—once it became clear to him that the unit was working closely with Muslim groups he regarded as a subversive threat. Instead of the MCU partnership approach he wanted to see a counter-insurgency model adopted against the same groups:

During the Cold War, organisations such as the Information Research Department of the Foreign Office would assert the superiority of the West over its totalitarian rivals. And magazines such as *Encounter* did hand-to-hand combat with Soviet fellow travellers. For any kind of truly moderate Islam to flourish, we need first to recapture our own self-confidence. At the moment, the extremists largely have the field to themselves.[20]

Essential therefore to have reformed Islamists like Majid Nawaz and Ed Husain, co-directors of the Quilliam Foundation, heading such counter-subversion initiatives.[21] As Tom Griffin notes Godson's approach to fighting radical Islam 'has significant parallels with a US Department of Defense proposal from 2002', which called for 'efforts to discredit and undermine the influence of mosques and religious schools that have become breeding grounds for Islamic militancy and anti-Americanism across the Middle East, Asia and Europe'.[22] Developing Godson's view a subsequent Policy Exchange report co-authored by a specialist terrorism studies academic and another reformed member of HT finds that the MCU strategy in relation to Finsbury Park Mosque was neither legitimate nor effective.[23] Moreover, the report's overwhelmingly negative assessment of the MCU is presented by the UK's most influential think-tank[24] as compelling evidence that is adduced to influence British counter-terrorism policy in an opposite direction in the future.[25]

According to Maher and Frampton, authors of this Policy Exchange report, the MCU was launched to work with radicals like Abu Hamza on the basis that 'radicals [like Hamza] can be controlled, and that they, in turn, can control angry young men'.[26] This has been a recurring theme in criticism of the MCU and involves an incorrect assumption about the antecedents of the MCU. MCU officers became frustrated that this inaccuracy was never challenged or corrected by ACPO. It can be traced to influential literature on 'Londonistan' a place where government, civil servants, MI5 and MPSB are accused of turning a blind eye to the behaviour of Abu Hamza and other extremists prior to 9/11 (or indeed prior to 7/7) in the cynical belief that it would reduce the risk of terrorist attacks in the UK.[27] Clearly much of this material grossly misrepresents and exaggerates the problem but it has a kernel of truth. There can be little doubt that successive Conservative and Labour governments in the 1980s and 1990s wrongly allowed extremists such as Abu Qatada to enter the UK. Ironically, in the circumstances, the MCU was founded by MPSB officers who had long argued that Abu Hamza, Abu Qatada, Abdullah el Faisal and other violent extremists should be prosecuted. Far from condoning them the MCU was set up by two MPSB officers with the express purpose of disrupting them and assisting Muslim communities to stand up to them.

Unwittingly, therefore, the Policy Exchange report highlights the potential and original value of my insider perspective. Maher and Frampton's claim that the MCU colluded with Abu Hamza is sufficiently contradicted by the primary data produced in my research as to expose a serious credibility gap in the existing literature. By explaining how the London partnerships worked consistently against—not with— Abu Hamza (and London-based extremists like him) my study elucidates a perspective that has been consistently misrepresented and distorted by powerful lobbyists over a sustained period. This is not, therefore, merely an insiders' corrective to a competing outsider analysis of events but a wholly different account of events in which the insiders were themselves key actors.

I do not intend to suggest that all outsider accounts misrepresent the aims and objectives of the MCU as significantly as this Policy

Exchange report. But the example does serve to highlight the need to accurately presents the participants' own accounts of what they did, when they did it and why they were motivated to do so. Without such data being presented and analysed there will be a gap in the literature and a serious risk that historians of counter-terrorism policy and practice in London during the war on terror will be forced to rely on 'expert' evidence that is at best distant and at worst, on occasions, seriously flawed. Moreover, without an accurate account of the participants' own perspectives on the legitimacy and effectiveness of the London partnerships it is hardly possible to gauge the merits or demerits of outsider critiques, especially when they misrepresent the motives or actions of key actors. This is not, however, to claim that my insider perspective has a superior claim to an accurate analysis of its own legitimacy and effectiveness. On the contrary, it seems clear that the primary data might be subjected to more rigorous scrutiny by academic researchers in the future who have no connection with it. But those same researchers would be disadvantaged if they were denied access to the actors' own interpretation of their own actions in the way this study seeks to present them. As such my research is already of interest to academics who are concerned to empower bottom-up community and practitioner voices in an arena otherwise dominated by top-down perspectives.[28]

Significantly, when the Department for Communities and Local Government (DCLG) launched its preventing violent extremism agenda in 2006 it chose to marginalise the work of the MCU working to empower Muslim community groups against al-Qaeda propaganda and recruitment since 2002.[29] Instead DCLG embarked on a new course of engagement—one recommended by Policy Exchange. Although the MCU initiative was commended in a research report written by the think-tank Demos and commissioned by DCLG[30] it was studiously ignored by Ruth Kelly and her advisors when formulating their own strategy.[31] Muslim groups who had no legitimacy in the field of combating violent extremism so far as the MCU was concerned were embraced as DCLG's key partners.[32] In contrast, Muslim groups who had impressed police with their skill and bravery in tackling al-Qaeda propaganda at close quarters were excluded.[33] Two years later the reasons for DCLG's partnership strategy was brought into sharp focus when key MCU community partners were declared outcast and government declined to support a major exhibition in London called

Islam Expo. In a speech at Policy Exchange DCLG secretary Hazel Blears made clear that government regarded specific Muslim figures involved in the organisation of Islam Expo as extremist who she hoped 'to isolate and expose' and thereby 'ensure they were not part of the event next year'. 'Our policy' she said, was 'designed to change behaviour'.[34] Change, it should be noted, in exactly the way recommended by Policy Exchange. Whereas two relatively junior MCU officers who embarked on an initiative to empower Muslim community groups against al-Qaeda in the aftermath of 9/11 were guided by the policing principle that minority communities should be respected as they are—not as politicians and pundits might seek to mould them.

When the war on terror finally began to give way to a 'hearts and minds' approach in 2006 and 2007 the MCU was seen to be out of kilter with UK government and local government strategies where a wholly different set of Muslim community groups were engaged and mobilised against a significantly wider problem—'radicalisation'.[35] Indeed, when the DCLG launched a Muslim community engagement initiative in 2006 aimed at curbing radicalism[36] it appeared to sit at odds with the MCU approach at a fundamental level.[37] While the MCU pointed to the long experience of its salafi and Islamist partners in tackling al-Qaeda activity in London the DCLG initiative was concerned to promote groups like the Sufi Muslim Council (SMC)[38] who lacked any such experience and who sought instead to reduce salafi and Islamist influence.[39] Subsequently, it appeared that DCLG and ACPO interest had shifted from the SMC to the Quilliam Foundation, a self-proclaimed centre of excellence for countering al-Qaeda influence.[40]

From 2006 to 2009 DCLG had a social cohesion agenda that was inimical to counter-terrorism yet had a significant impact on it.[41] The Muslim groups and individuals DCLG promoted as champions of social cohesion were the very ones least capable of delivering success in sections of the community susceptible to al-Qaeda propaganda and recruitment activity.[42] This becomes especially problematic, from an MCU perspective, when the DCLG initiative is described as 'preventing extremism' or 'counter-radicalisation' and MCU community partners are cast in the role of extremists.[43]

Charles Moore, *Daily Telegraph* columnist and chairman of Policy Exchange, invoked the image of arch subversive Arthur Scargill when warning an audience in 2008 of a threat to democracy posed by Islamist and salafi groups including those who had worked in the London partnerships.[44] Moore claims that a subversive threat licenses a coun-ter-subversive strategy every bit as clandestine and ruthless as the alleged threat it seeks to undermine.[45] Now as then when combating communists like Scargill, embedded supporters within the enemy camp would, Moore believes, be crucial players in efforts to undermine 'the extremists'. Thus Moore identifies Ed Husain playing a similar role to Frank Chapple, a 'moderate' trade union leader who was willing to tackle Scargill:

One of the most powerful lessons from Ed Husain's remarkable book, *The Islamist*, is that the people most intimidated by Islamist extremism in this country are Muslims themselves.... We need to realise that every time the wider society enters into dialogue with the extremists we are not only dealing unwittingly with bad people, we are also empowering them against good people.[46]

By signalling the arrival of the Quilliam Foundation as a new coun-ter-subversion force in Muslim communities Moore highlights the extent to which the London partnerships' low-profile, bottom-up pro-jects developed organically by low-ranking specialist police officers working with representatives of minority Muslim communities, had been successfully challenged, undermined and eclipsed by the end of 2007 when I retired. However, for nearly six years the London part-nerships swam against the tide of the war on terror and the influence of Policy Exchange. To ask how London police officers and Muslim Londoners conceived legitimacy and effectiveness in their work is, therefore, to ask the architects and managers of the initiative to explain their rationale for a dramatic departure from prevailing wis-dom. Indeed, it is reasonable to assume that only a strong attachment to notions of legitimacy and effectiveness in the first place could explain such a departure in an arena that generally demands conform-ity of action.

MCU officers were frustrated when a Policy Exchange research report *The Hijacking of British Islam* accused the Al-Manaar Muslim Cultural Heritage Centre of selling and distributing extremist litera-ture.[47] Having visited the centre at least once a week over six years MCU officers knew this to be wholly inaccurate and ill-founded and they were puzzled how a team of 'specialist Muslim researchers' could have reached such an obviously erroneous conclusion. Indeed, having witnessed Abdulkarem Khalil, the director of Al-Manaar, take brave, unstinting action against extremism over the six years they worked in partnership with him MCU officers understandably felt aggrieved when an apparently authoritative research report, allegedly 'the most comprehensive academic survey of its kind ever produced in the UK', and 'based on a year-long investigation by several teams of specialist researchers' caused so much unnecessary harm to the centre's reputation.[48] Suffice to say a belated apology from Policy Exchange to Al-Manaar only followed civil litigation initiated by Al-Manaar.[49] Policy Exchange was also forced to make an apology to Mohammad Abdul Bari, chairman of the East London Mosque, in respect of another inaccuracy in the same report.[50]

If as some academics, commentators and politicians have suggested Policy Exchange reports have sometimes been flawed by research born of ideologically pre-conceived findings then I must guard against the very same danger.[51] At least the time and distance between the simultaneous conclusion of my dual roles as participant in and observer of the London partnerships in October 2007 and the process of analysing the data between January 2008 and September 2009 proved helpful in creating a space for reflection and consultation. That reflective space also facilitated a changing perspective away from a practitioner's focus towards the conceptual demands necessary to make a meaningful research contribution in the academic arena. It was also the space that encouraged the subtle but significant shift from an intelligence officer's role as collector and analyst of data to a researcher's role as collector and analyst of data. Although intelligence data and research data might sometimes consist of the same information one important difference between the two analytical roles is that the latter role is less tied to predetermined objectives. Thus data derived from a talk by Abu Hamza to a small group of his supporters inside Finsbury Park Mosque in November 2001 in which he commended the 9/11 terrorists would have immediate operational and evidential interest to an intelligence analyst. That kind of practitioner interest can be noted with reference to subsequent criminal proceedings at the Central Criminal Court in London when Abu Hamza faced charges of incitement to murder based largely on talks like this one that he wrote, recorded, delivered and discussed in Finsbury Park and elsewhere in the UK over a long period. In contrast, from a researcher's perspective the same material forms part of a wider analysis of the community context in which Abu Hamza was able to spread al-Qaeda influence in Finsbury Park and beyond.

It was during the long transitional process of reading, assessing, 'memoing'[52] and digesting a large amount of primary data that the central importance of experience, expertise and civic duty emerged as core qualities on which the legitimacy and effectiveness achieved by the London partnerships had been built. Of course it was reasonably clear at the outset of my research that these were qualities valued by the participants, but it was a sustained reflection upon the data analysis that helped explain why such crucial importance was placed upon these qualities by the participants themselves. Experience, expertise and civic duty, it became clear, were valued highly because they were the qualities most likely to inform successful decision making and activity in the London partnerships. In a word MCU and community participants in the two London partnerships studied were involved in dangerous and demanding work and found that these three qualities offered what they valued most: reliability.

Reliability has been associated with experience and expertise by intelligence analysts for a long time and is hardly an original research finding. Reliability in relation to civic duty, however, is an entirely original concept. So too the specific finding that reliability was an outcome of the London partnerships where police and community experience and expertise was afforded equal status. Both findings provide a sound basis for future research in the emerging study of community-based approaches to counter-terrorism. Data analysis is very clear about the improved reliability of intelligence when it is delivered by a partnership that includes police and community experience and expertise and is driven by civic duty and not by financial reward as is often the case with covert human intelligence. Moreover, this is a topical research issue as Muslim partners are being re-cast as Muslim suspects and Muslim informants by influential academics and think-tanks. Experience, expertise and civic duty were also qualities that played an important part in building trust and mutual respect between police and community partners who might otherwise have worked independently of each other or on another basis.

Virtually without exception, primary data confirms that the participants in the London partnerships, consciously and sometimes implicitly, shared a strong sense that their own and each other's experience, expertise and civic duty provided them with legitimacy and effectiveness in their work to counter al-Qaeda influence in local communities. Without being at all reductionist these are therefore the three core qualities that the participants are shown to believe empower them to perform the work they do. As such they fit Flyvbjerg's, Kenney's and

Hamm's complementary models of experts and expert learning.[53] Whether the partners were right, wrong or right in parts will not be decided here but at least by analysing and clarifying their own notions of legitimacy and effectiveness it is possible to make an original and distinctive contribution to wider research that is developing on the topic and the conceptual issues it raises.[54] That at least is my aim. It will, however, only succeed if the attempt to collect and analyse data has been carried out as scrupulously and rigorously as intended and as Breen-Smyth argues is vital in insider projects of this nature.[55] Again, whether the research succeeds in this regard will be for others to decide. Certainly it may not succeed in allaying the concerns expressed by Maher and Frampton but it may at least help clarify the basis on which those concerns appear to be held.[56]

The qualities of experience, expertise and civic duty therefore serve as benchmarks when making cumulative research findings according to the three broad themes that have emerged during an analysis of the conceiving data: conceiving al-Qaeda influence in Muslim London; conceiving responses to al-Qaeda influence in Muslim London; and conceiving legitimacy and effectiveness in the London partnerships. It will help to illustrate the findings with reference to developments during the period the study was being written up and discussed with participants in the London partnerships. In doing so, interesting points of concurrence and synergy between the two case study sites—Finsbury Park and Brixton—have emerged. For instance, whereas other research studies have highlighted and amplified points of dissonance and tension between Islamist and salafi perspectives[57] my study discerns areas of mutual respect, mutual support and common purpose between representatives of both minority perspectives in Finsbury Park and Brixton that have hitherto been neglected. This finding highlights the importance of a genuine bottom-up perspective and the importance of an effective and original role performed by MCU police officers. As a result the findings avoid the risk of re-enforcing notions of legitimacy and effectiveness that encourage counter-subversion or counter-insurgency policies of 'divide and rule' rather than healing and building bridges in a way that became the hallmark of the London partnerships.

This is an approach that benefits from ongoing reflection on the primary data in five phases: during a long practitioner role; during interviews and participation; during data analysis; during consideration of the case studies; and during discussion of the completed case studies with participants. It was during the final phase that examples were discussed and agreed that would serve as models or exemplars to highlight the importance of experience, expertise and civic duty. Significantly too it was also during this final research phase that I was able to engage with participants in the London partnerships solely as a researcher and not as a police officer and partner for the first time.

At the outset, to conceive al-Qaeda influence in Muslim London, is to depart from mainstream academic and practitioner definitions of the al-Qaeda threat which focus on membership, in-groups, conspiracies and proactive support on the one hand[58] and tacit support on the other.[59] To conceive al-Qaeda influence in Muslim London is also to depart from academic and think-tank accounts that develop a notion of radicalisation as a conveyor belt upon which individuals may travel towards terrorist activity.[60] From the London Muslim street where my research was carried out both those approaches appear top-down and disconnected even though they sometimes address issues at the personal and local level. For example from a top-down perspective Omar Bakri Mohammed, former leader of HT and currently the exiled head of al-Muhajiroun, appears to have played a significant role in the 'radicalisation' of several young British Muslims who have become involved in terrorist conspiracies inspired or organised by al-Qaeda.[61] As an interviewee who worked closely alongside Omar Bakri between 1995 and 2003 observes after 9/11 his achievements as a self-publicist far exceed any real success he might have claimed to have achieved on behalf of al-Qaeda influence in Muslim London.[62] From a street perspective Omar Bakri's leadership qualities were found lacking over a long period and he never acquired street credibility beyond his small group of followers.[63] According to the same interviewee Omar Bakri tried very hard to capitalise on 9/11 and to portray himself as being linked retrospectively to al-Qaeda, but his opportunism never really cut ice with those who valued action over talk.[64] Omar Bakri was, according to this and other street sources, widely understood to be what Marc Sageman calls a fabulist, an academic term for a bullshit artist.[65]

Furthermore, in Omar Bakri's case as in others, the study benefits from a combination of street perspectives from Muslim and police interviewees and participants. Apart from serving a valuable triangulation purpose for the methodological integrity of the study, this approach also illuminates the ways in which community and police perspectives combined experience and expertise to become the stock-in-trade of the London partnerships. Thus I was able to compare my own earlier practitioner experience interviewing Omar Bakri at length when he was under arrest at Edmonton Police Station in 1991 for incitement to murder with the account of his long time close associate in a research interview in 2007. The circumstances of the first interview were well known to the research interviewee because it was a high-profile arrest. Omar Bakri was arrested after taking part in a London demonstration in which he lead chants of 'death to John Major'—a reference to the British Prime Minister—during a HT march in Whitehall in protest against the Gulf War.[66] In this case as in others it became clear that credibility and legitimacy would eventually be denied to would-be leaders like Omar Bakri by their potential street supporters when they were perceived to lack the moral and physical courage they often demanded of their followers. Exactly the same kind of calculation was made in the police canteen. The street assessment that determined Abu Qatada's, Abu Hamza's and Abdullah el Faisal's ascendancy over Omar Bakri in terms of street credibility was no different, in essence, from the police canteen assessment that afforded ascendancy to John Stevens, John Grieve and David Veness over some of their successors. Both assessments are rooted in their own sub-cultures and tend to remain impervious to top-down attempts to influence them in ways that Tilly conceptualises and the MCU sought to capitalise on.[67]

Another finding here is that academic researchers may sometimes be as vulnerable to fabulists (to borrow Sageman's term) as the investigative journalist Shiv Malik whose book, co-authored with Hassan Butt, *Leaving al-Qaeda*,[68] based on Butt's exaggerated claims to al-Qaeda status, has yet to be published, following an investigation by the Greater Manchester Police (GMP).[69] Up to this point Malik was held in high regard by think-tanks and academics for providing what was widely hailed to be an insightful investigation into the background of the 7/7 bombers in Beeston.[70] However, had Malik investigated the reliability of Hassan Butt on the Muslim street he might not have begun writing a book based on Butt's claims to have been involved in terrorism. Not that Butt's plausibility was ever in doubt, either before or after conversion. Thus, speaking before 7/7: 'I would rather be a traitor to Britain than to my religion'; 'I have direct responsibility for the British recruits'; 'it is my job to get them into the training camps here [Pakistan] where they prepare for war'; [speaking as Omar Bakri Mohammed's agent in Pakistan in 2002] 'If they do return, I believe they will take military action within Britain'.[71] Then, in striking contrast, in 2007 with an eye on the publication of his book: 'what I've come to realise is that killing for the sake of killing, and killing in the name of Islam for the sake of killing, is completely and utterly prohibited'.[72]

By way of explanation, my interviewee claims Butt easily persuaded investigative journalists and commentators that he was an authentic al-Qaeda terrorist recruiter because he was telling them what they wanted to hear—in essence that Butt's role as Omar Bakri Mohammed's man on the ground in Pakistan after 9/11 placed him at the hub of al-Qaeda radicalisation and recruitment activity.[73] Certainly, Nick Cohen spoke to this script when he launched an attack on GMP for questioning Butt's credentials:

Hassan Butt is a member of a group you are going to be hearing a lot more from: Muslims who come out of jihadism and find an almost patriotic belief in the best values of Britain. They cajole and they warn. They help steer British Muslims away from violence while teaching wider society that radical Islam is not a rational reaction to Western provocation, but a totalitarian ideology with a life of its own.[74]

Cohen was right that Butt's story would become ubiquitous. Just as acclaimed journalists saw Butt developing the trend set by Husain's book *The Islamist*, so too did influential academics who conceived al-Qaeda as the violent end of a subversive Islamist threat.[75] While the UK Government's Preventing Violent Extremism programme has yielded many positive benefits in terms of proactive community work, one potential deficit has been the emergence of individuals like Butt claiming to have expertise in this complex and dangerous arena. As a leading Al-Muhajiroun figure (deferring only to Omar Bakri and Anjem Choudary) my interviewee ridiculed Butt's claims to have any meaningful connection to al-Qaeda. He spent two months with Butt in Pakistan when both were there on behalf of al-Muhajiroun and is candid about it being a publicity stunt dreamt up by Omar Bakri Mohammed to try and get some reflected kudos for al-Muhajiroun by being seen (falsely) as providing a conduit for terrorist recruitment. In fact, his first-hand account of Butt as an opportunist (much like his leader Omar Bakri Mohammed) has since been vindicated by an investigation by GMP.[76]

Without intending to suggest anything like the same level of disingenuousness, MCU interviewees highlight a similar authenticity problem with counter-terrorism experts who become contacts for journalists and academic researchers—the latter often anxious to make inroads into the elite circle of counter-terrorism and security officialdom. By way of example one so-called expert with an established media profile was known by MCU officers to have failed to make the grade in MPSB long before 9/11. Another familiar media terrorism expert was known to have never spent one day in thirty years' police service involved in counter-terrorism work. Other cases are less striking but no less telling in regard to the importance of genuine and relevant experience in this arena.

Of course, as Tilly and Tarrow highlight, reputations, credibility and the legitimacy that flows from them are fluid and not fixed in the trust networks in which they are formed,[77] but they are generally more easily lost than retrieved. Having asked exactly the same kind of questions of informants over many years in MPSB participant, MCU officers were struck by the greater clarity and honesty Muslim London partners provided on such topics when the discussions took place instead on a transparent and non-coercive, non-profit basis. By way of example four MCU officers with a combined total of eighty two years' MPSB experience discussed the cases of Abu Qatada, Abu Hamza, Abdullah el Fasial and Omar Bakri Mohammed (amongst other topics) with four Muslim London partners who had cumulative experience of dealing first hand with the same men for in excess of forty years.[78] In and of itself that experience and expertise might not have become greater than the sum of its parts. The key to multiplying its impact was the presence at the same meeting of experienced Muslim police officers who joined the unit to add a key interpretative quality between police and community perspectives.[79] Significantly, selection of the Muslim officers for the MCU was based on their knowledge of the Muslim London street and their own credibility on it. Also noteworthy, these informal collaborative meetings had enormous value for the MCU and stood in sharp contrast to the strict rules of engagement that govern the meeting of one informant at a time by police.

Evidence from MCU police officers, Brixton salafis, Finsbury Park Islamists and other Muslim Londoners coalesces around the roles of Abu Qatada, Abu Hamza and Abdullah el Faisal as examples of credible street leadership figures (in marked contrast to individuals like Omar Bakri Mohammed and Hassan Butt who merely simulate authenticity and legitimacy) who have effectively promoted al-Qaeda influence in local communities over a long period. This gives rise to a new typology that attaches significance to street leaders who have influence in their circles or sub-cultures (and those that aspire to it). At this point the study breaks new ground. It complements but differs from Sageman's research that interrogates court proceedings against British Muslims convicted of terrorism offences since 9/11.[80] It provides context for Sageman's work by establishing a local street context for the phenomenon of al-Qaeda influence in London and outside the capital city. In the cases that Sageman is studying, convicted terrorists may have come into contact with a host of Muslim voices before becoming immersed in a terrorist conspiracy. Were any of these voices influential? That will always be a question to be assessed in each case study on its merits but it will be illuminating to have a clearer view of the credibility and legitimacy of Muslim voices from a Muslim street perspective. To accept the notion that credibility in street politics is conferred from the bottom up is axiomatic in all other areas so it is timely to establish the same notion of street leadership and street influence in Muslim London as elsewhere.

At no point has the evidence been used to establish organisational links between the three men and any individual or group of individuals who are associated with the leadership of al-Qaeda. Even less does it rely on any operational intelligence to suggest that the three men are al-Qaeda terrorists, propagandists or supporters. On the contrary the evidence allows divergence from strict adherence to al-Qaeda policy and strategy at key points in all three cases. Rather, the cumulative evidence reveals the three men opportunistically employing al-Qaeda rhetoric and propaganda at intervals to promote their own agendas. At other points the evidence suggests that al-Qaeda propagandists like al-Suri may have utilised their own experience of the Muslim London street to borrow from effective voices like the three under study.[81] Moreover, all the evidence emerges from publicly available talks the three men gave over an extended period in and out of London, some of which was adduced in evidence against two of them in separate trials for incitement to murder at the Central Criminal Court in 2003 and 2005.

All of which might lead other analysts to dismiss some or all the three men as being disconnected to al-Qaeda. However, that would be to fail to grasp the importance of street leaders especially for young people who have been influenced by them. It would also overlook the likelihood that at some point a genuine al-Qaeda recruiter or strategist will disguise himself as a street activist rather in the way that Pat Hayes did very effectively on behalf of the PIRA for many years in London before his terrorist role was discovered.[82] Hayes was in fact an able talent spotter for the PIRA while simultaneously operating effectively and credibly as an organiser for Red Action, the most violent affiliate to the violent street activist umbrella group Anti-Fascist Action.[83] Hayes demonstrates an interesting connection between street violence and terrorism that is replicated in the Brixton case study site and which gives rise to a new research focus on the nexus between street crime and terrorism. In referring to the case of Hayes it is also intended to break down the unhelpful conceptual barrier between old and new terrorism and the consequent value of the continuity MPSB officers brought to bear on the MCU role. Interestingly, two community interviewees said they had passed information to the MCU about an individual who they believed was carrying out precisely this kind of clandestine recruitment role for al-Qaeda in London. While it is outside the parameters of the study to offer any police view on the information that was supplied to the MCU it does highlight the way in which the effectiveness of the London partnerships can be assessed in exactly the same way as other police partnerships with community groups.

The evidence leads to a new analysis of al-Qaeda. Previously, at one end of a continuum top-down accounts describe al-Qaeda according to the religious and political imperatives that are assessed to drive or licence its ideology.[84] At the other end of the continuum academics focus on the tactics employed by al-Qaeda.[85] In addition a growing body of literature investigates the relationship between al-Qaeda and individuals who become involved in terrorist conspiracies that appear to have been inspired by al-Qaeda, what Sageman describes as push and pull factors in relation to a terrorist in-group.[86] Sageman and others at the cutting edge of this research have tended to diminish the role of street leaders because they have no connection to al-Qaeda—albeit Abu Qatada is often described as an exception in this regard, hence he is understood to be more significant. The primary data in my study suggests that street leaders may have an influence that is in proportion to the credibility they enjoy. Interviewees cite Omar Bakri Mohammed as a street leader who did not share the same legitimacy or credibility as the other three during the study period. What determines influence in this regard? Experience and expertise appear to be the answers just as they are for counter-terrorists. This finding is in accord with Kenney's research into the importance of street skills for both parties.[87] Just as street credibility is afforded by street supporters so too is police credibility won in the police canteen not in the management meeting.

It may therefore be possible to describe the evidence as pointing to the significance of street leaders like Abu Qatada, Abu Hamza and Abdullah el Faisal specifically in relation to the influence they have in communities or sub-cultures. This raises the prospect that street leaders may not have been given due significance in the literature to date. While there has been increased attention afforded to Sageman's push and pull factors in relation to the progress of individuals towards (or away from) al-Qaeda 'in-groups', there has been a tendency to overlook the impact of street leaders because they lack organisational or networked roles.

The London partnerships developed organically from the work of the MCU as part of what has sometimes been favourably described as a new community-based approach to counter-terrorism.[88] Supportive academics and researchers have suggested that the MCU approach to counter-terrorism was often a counter-intuitive as well as a novel approach.[89] I have described responses to terrorist attacks like 9/11 and 7/7 as counter-intuitive when they avoid knee-jerk reactions that unwittingly play into the terrorists' hands.[90] Yet the overwhelming weight of evidence that emerges from the study points to MPSB experience and expertise guiding and informing the actions of MCU officers at every turn and consequently having a major impact on the London partnerships. Far from being new or counter-intuitive this is counter-terrorism based on a rich and unparalleled source of specialist knowledge that has been learnt and taught for over a hundred years in offices, classrooms, pubs, cafes, tube trains, on foot, and in cars and on motorbikes on the streets of London.[91] What provides an unbroken thread to MPSB learning from 1883 to 2006 is the clear and unchanged purpose of protecting all Londoners from the threat of terrorist bombs and political violence. Just as the intended victims of violent street activists have often been the beneficiaries of this experience and expertise, so too have numerous terrorist conspiracies been disrupted to enhance the well-being of all Londoners.[92]

As Kenney has insightfully noted it is the street skill of MPSB officers that will distinguish a successful colleague from one who has failed to make the grade and has consequently returned to uniformed police duties.[93] Alternatively, if an officer failed to make the grade on London streets but had analytical or organisational skills that could be used in support roles at NSY then an MPSB career might still blossom behind a desk. That said, in June 2009, when I attended the retirement party of an MPSB officer who was universally regarded as one of the best of his generation it was his street skills that were lauded not any skills taught in a classroom or on a training course. The officer's experience and expertise had led directly to the arrest of major terrorists and violent political activists over a long period of time. After listening to glowing tributes to his professionalism from colleagues, two younger police officers present remarked that although they had worked closely with the retiring officer for five years they had never known before about his role in cases they heard about for the first time that evening. Their lack of prior knowledge should be attributed to the retiring officer's discretion that was a hallmark of MPSB professionalism. The happy occasion was however marred by the realisation that the officer was one of the last of his kind and that the decision to subsume MPSB into the CTC in 2006 had effectively ended the MPSB role and in particular its unique approach to street craft. The long thread of on-the-job teaching that stretched back to 1883 was at an end. Junior officers at the event bemoaned the fact that under a new management regime it was no longer possible to carve out a specialist career in intelligence gathering in terrorism and political violence in the way that MPSB officers had done in the past. There was also a sense of regret that the new management regime had not recognised the outstanding skills the retiring officer had possessed. Thus while the MCU might continue after the study period closed the MPSB skills that had informed it were no longer valued and were being phased out.

Quite why the Security Service and the Home Office would support and sanction the Commissioner's decision to close the most experienced and effective counter-terrorism department in Europe in the wake of 7/7 is beyond the scope of this study.[94] What is significant, however, is the prevailing view that MPSB belonged to an earlier era and that new terrorism required new thinking and a new structure of counter-terrorism policing, revealing a synergy between academic, think-tank, political and practitioner perspectives. To be sure, the dismantling and closure of MPSB in 2006 did have a profoundly adverse impact on the MCU and hence the London partnerships. As one MCU officer noted when the Finsbury Park Islamists were coming under fire for inviting Sheikh Yusuf al Qaradawi to London in 2004 the Commander of MPSB was on hand to offer support to them and their guest.[95] In contrast, in 2007 when the Finsbury Park Islamists were being denounced as sectarian subversives and the MCU as their appeasers there was no corresponding support from new managers without MPSB experience.[96] The new management appreciated the need for positive relations with Muslim communities but when Ed Husain of the Quilliam Foundation was invited to give the keynote address to a prestigious ACPO conference in 2008 it was clear that MCU influence had declined or changed dramatically and been replaced by an alternative approach. Significantly, it was the National Association of Muslim Police (NAMP) who complained to ACPO about the choice of the Quilliam Foundation as a suitable partner for police.[97] In their reply ACPO showed no sign of recognising that the Quilliam Foundation campaigned stridently for the exclusion of key members of the MSF and MCU partners who were at the forefront of pioneering work in the Prevent strand of Contest, the UK's counter-terrorism strategy.[98]

Before 7/7 the influence of MPSB experience and expertise remained strong—both within the MCU and within MPSB more generally. For the MCU founders it was crucial to balance their own proclivities for street skills with management skills so as to harmonise the work of the London partnerships with wider MPS goals. This was an area that demanded negotiation skills as well as patience. Here again MCU officers were heirs to a formidable legacy of negotiation skills that had been honed over many years at partnership meetings between MPSB, intelligence agencies and civil servants across Whitehall. As a result security of secret files and a readiness to argue on behalf of the MPS had become second nature. In fact the high calibre of MPSB negotiating, analytical and intelligence gathering skills was regularly commented upon favourably by Her Majesty's Inspector of Constabularies (HMIC). In 1998, for instance, MPSB was singled out by HMIC for producing an outstanding intelligence analysis and also for having the best record of supervisory staff appraisals in MPS Specialist Operations.[99] This latter point is significant because the two MCU founding officers could rely on an effective MPSB personnel and administrative support system that allowed them to cross-check their own knowledge of officers they wanted to head-hunt to join the unit against accurate records that would confirm the qualities and calibre they were seeking.[100] Thus although the unit remained very small it was staffed by officers with outstanding records in respect of skills that were valued by MPSB managers and colleagues alike. Thus the unit enjoyed legitimacy within MPSB where its officers were also known to be effective.

Experience and expertise are often best analysed by insiders in counter-terrorism no less than in other fields.[101] To an outsider a mature long-serving senior police officer standing beneath the revolving 'Metropolitan Police' sign at the entrance to NSY talking authoritatively to camera in the aftermath of a major terrorist incident may appear to be both experienced and expert. Increasingly, however, after the retirement of Sir John Stevens as Commissioner and Sir David Veness as Assistant Commissioner Specialist Operations (MPS) (ACSO) in February 2005, the likelihood was that their replacements would often lack both qualities in terms of counter-terrorism. Certainly MPSB interviewees reflected the NSY canteen view that some of the communication mistakes that arose in connection with the handling of the Jean Charles de Menezes affair would have been far less likely to arise had Stevens and Veness remained in post for another six months.[102] Neither man won a reputation for effective counter-terrorism policing by relying on the kind of communication systems or procedures Andy Hayman believed were crucially lacking and partly to blame for management failures on 22 July 2005.[103]

With experience and expertise comes legitimacy and credibility. Senior and junior officers would follow the directions of Stevens and Veness willingly and confidently because of the hard-won credibility they enjoyed.[104] They had, in parlance, 'been there, done it, got the t-shirt'. In an abortive attempt to create that kind of 'street-cred' Blair was reported as having tried unsuccessfully to embellish a history of counter-terrorism by reference to a close involvement in the Balcombe Street siege—a famous terrorist incident in London in 1975.[105] In the event junior police officers involved in the incident were quick to discredit his account.[106] For his part, Hayman candidly admits that he failed to communicate effectively with Blair so as to correct a damaging false impression that a man shot dead by counter-terrorism police at Stockwell tube station was a terrorist suspect.[107] 'But in the fog of the most complex operation ever undertaken by the Met', Hayman reflects, 'I decided to play it safe and leave it for others to speculate'.[108] On further reflection he recognised this 'created a big void' that was 'deeply damaging' and regrettable.[109] The mistake would have a significantly negative impact on the credibility and integrity of the MPS in the eyes of the public and media.

Neither Blair nor Hayman were imbued with the culture of security and counter-terrorism that career MPSB Commanders enjoyed until 2003. Moreover, although Hayman is also self-critical for not challenging Blair's commitment to dismantling detective specialisms in the centralised Specialist Crime Directorate[110] he did exactly the same himself by dismantling MPSB while simultaneously heading the 7/7 investigation. Again he regrets that his failure to challenge Blair's refusal to support a specialist detective's assessment of how best to respond to new operational demands may have resulted in a surge of knife and gun crime in London.[111] However, whereas his predecessor took the view that it was 'unprofessional to move officers back and forth between conventional crime fighting and internal security'[112] Hayman again supported Blair in bringing to an end a century-long tradition in which police officers built specialist careers in countering terrorism and political violence in MPSB.[113] In contrast, for Veness a failure to separate and empower counter-terrorism professionalism resulted in both specialist and mainstream policing being performed 'at best, less effectively than they should be and, at worst, poorly'.[114] In setting out his post-9/11 policing vision Veness called for 'longer-term resourcing' of 'long-term intelligence-led counter-terrorism'.[115] 'It is wiser' he argued, 'to employ one expert to detect a terrorist before an attack than to employ twenty patrolling officers to combat an unknown attacker'.[116]

Hayman's denial of the need for separate MPSB or other long-term counter-terrorism specialisms appeared to fly in the face of Veness' powerful recommendation and his own reflection in regard to street crime. When challenged by an experienced MPSB officer that the MPSB performance had been of such a high standard over a sustained period that the name 'Special Branch' carried international cache and should not be abandoned lightly Hayman disagreed.[117] In his experience, he explained, only two London police names mattered abroad: *Metropolitan Police* and *New Scotland Yard*.[118] Experienced counter-terrorism officers were baffled and dismayed by this response.[119] Hayman had a new organisational plan for counter-terrorism and the accumulated experience and expertise of MPSB that gave rise to the MCU did not feature in it.[120] It was apposite then that Muslim community partners should no longer be chosen by the MCU for their street skills in countering al-Qaeda influence but by ACPO on an entirely different basis.[121]

Similarly, although supportive of its aims Sir Ian Blair did not regard the MCU role as belonging to MPSB.[122] Rather he took the view outlined by the criminologist Martin Innes that 'high' and 'low' policing should be linked but not cross-contaminated.[123] Over and above any other considerations he wanted to focus attention on the potential benefits of his neighbourhood policing plan supporting counter-terror-ism.[124] Rather than endorse Veness' call for long-term specialists Blair promoted neighbourhood policing and gave the example of a local authority caretaker who identified the flat that three 21/7 terrorist suspects had used as a bomb factory.[125] Crucially, for Blair, if his neighbourhood policing plan had been in place the caretaker might have understood and reported the terrorist significance of the discarded dozens of empty peroxide bottles in the waste bins.[126] 'It will not be a Special Branch officer at Scotland Yard' he suggested, 'who first confronts a terrorist but a local cop or a local community support officer'.[127] 'Thus', he concluded, 'national security depends on neighbourhood security'.[128] MPSB interviewees had years of experience of working productively with community police officers in the way Blair suggests yet they were puzzled that he seemed so unaware of the impressive track record of MPSB surveillance officers who had spent whole careers on the streets of London in the close proximity of suspected terrorists and individuals suspected of political violence.[129] In any event, interviewees asked, why not value both MPSB and neighbourhood policing as specialist skills in a counter-terrorism tool kit?[130]

Not surprisingly MCU officers found it difficult to inform Whitehall thinking. Although we became adept in the art of 'arcing' (a police term to denote communications that circumvent strict rules of hierarchical reporting protocols in which a series of line managers will normally check and minute a report before forwarding it 'up the food chain' to be read by a succession of senior managers and disseminated to government agencies where appropriate) we were nevertheless hampered by our relatively low police ranks and a developing shift away from MPSB influence in the MPS.[131] More importantly our key messages were regularly countermanded by influential Muslim advisors in Whitehall.[132] Thus, without endorsing its specific provenance MCU and community participants in the London partnerships reckoned that a government document leaked to *The Sunday Times* in 2004 provided a valuable example of this failure to introduce bottom-up thinking into Whitehall.[133] When, according to the report, 'Whitehall's top mandarins gathered around a table in the Cabinet Office' on 19 May 2004 'to plan a secret project to thwart Al-Qaeda in Britain' the experience and expertise of the MCU and the London partnerships which by then were yielding excellent results was not on the agenda.[134] Instead, the meeting discussed a new counter-terrorism strategy called Contest, 'one of the most ambitious government social engineering projects in recent years' for the first time.[135] The aim of Contest was to 'prevent terrorism by tackling its underlying causes' and its method was to create 'a blueprint to win the hearts and minds of Muslim youth'.[136] A senior civil servant noted that 'Islamic extremism' might be a 'symptom of disaffection'.[137] 'The same disaffection' he suggested, that 'previously surfaced during the riots that shook Oldham and Bradford in 2001'. Contest, it followed, aimed to address 'discrimination, disadvantage and exclusion suffered by many Muslim communities'.[138] At the same time Home Office analysts suggested there may be 'between 10,000 and 15,000 British Muslims who actively support Al-Qaeda or related terrorist groups'.[139] An ICM poll published in March 2004 found that 13% of British Muslims thought that further terrorist attacks on the USA would be justified.[140]

Furthermore, according to the leaked documents, intelligence officers were 'already drawing up profiles of the typical Muslim recruited by Al-Qaeda'.[141] Muslims most at risk of being drawn into extremism and terrorism were said to fall into two groups: 'well-educated with degrees or technical/professional qualifications, typically targeted by extremist recruiters and organisations circulating on campuses'; and, 'underachievers with few or no qualifications, and often a non-terrorist criminal background—sometimes drawn to mosques where they may be targeted by extremist preachers and in other cases radicalised or converted whilst in prison'.[142] The leaked papers showed that MI5 was 'drawing up a detailed description of the terrorist career path'.[143] The aim was to identify the 'specific actions taken by individuals on the path from law-abiding citizen to terrorist'. On the basis of this assessment ministers were said to be planning to 'intervene at key trigger points to prevent young Muslims from becoming drawn into extremist and terrorist activity and action'. 'We need to understand the evolution of the terrorist career path ... to enable us to turn people from the path'.[144]

Notwithstanding a failure to acknowledge the extent to which al-Qaeda was exploiting pre-existing and widespread political grievances that had been heightened by the war in Iraq interviewees felt that there was still a basis on which the London partnership approach might have been incorporated into this new government policy.[145] However, the seeds for the subsequent marginalisation of the MCU and the London partnerships can be gleaned by analysing the Contest plans for 'winning hearts and minds'. The leaked papers revealed that dozens of officials were 'now working across Whitehall on plans to improve relations with the Muslim community' with the 'strategic aim' of winning 'the hearts and minds of those who might otherwise be diverted by Al-Qaeda recruiters on to a terrorist career path'.[146] Spiritual leaders including Hamza Yusuf, 'an adviser to President George W Bush' described as the 'rock star of the new Muslim generation' and fellow American convert Suhaib Webb were cited as key partners who could help persuade British Muslim leaders 'to adopt a more positive, pro-government line'.[147]

This was an approach straight from the pages of Rand and Policy Exchange reports that ignored the key issues of credibility and legitimacy in communities. It was also the approach that would lead to a fully-fledged counter-subversion strategy with the launch of the Quilliam Foundation four years later. I attended talks by Hamza Yusef in London, Bristol and Bradford in 2002 and 2003 and was left in no doubt as to his popularity and positive influence with young people.[148] However, Muslim youth who supported al-Qaeda were not in the audience, not even to heckle. To think that Hamza Yusef could influence al-Qaeda supporters was, a Brixton salafi suggested in 2003, as unlikely as Alex Ferguson successfully appealing to Liverpool supporters to defect to Manchester United.[149]

It was an approach that signalled the demise in influence of Britain's most established and respected Muslim community umbrella organisation, the MCB. No organisation had done more since 1997 to highlight and help the first New Labour government tackle the very issues that were being identified (wrongly in the view of the London partnerships) in these leaked government papers as root causes of the al-Qaeda threat to the UK.[150] Although the papers note that the MCB wrote to Islamic clerics and community leaders urging them to co-operate with police in the fight against 'any criminal activity including (the) terrorist threat' it was the MCB's steadfast opposition to the war in Iraq and the manner in which the war on terror more generally was being conducted that would lead finally to their isolation in 2006.[151] This exile was also widely understood to be a tribute to the impact of Martin Bright's Policy Exchange report *When Progressives Treat with Reactionaries* in which the MCB was re-cast as extremist, sectarian and subversive.[152] Members of the London partnerships took the view that if the MCB was to be stigmatised as 'extremist' then there 'might be no end to the problem'.[153]

Critically too at this point the MCU argued in vain that to exclude the MCB was to exclude an organisation that had done much to tackle Islamophobia, another issue highlighted in the leaked papers as being important for government to address so as to win Muslim community support in the 'battle for hearts and minds' with al-Qaeda.[154] Far from doing so government instead funded and supported the counter-subversive Quilliam Foundation that sought to diminish the problem of Islamophobia in the same way as Kenan Malik:

The trouble with Islamophobia is that it is an irrational concept. It confuses hatred of, and discrimination against, Muslims on the one hand with criticism of Islam on the other. The charge of 'Islamophobia' is all too often used not to highlight racism but to stifle criticism. And in reality discrimination against Muslims is not as great as is often perceived—but criticism of Islam should be greater.[154]

In contrast, Muhammad Abdul Bari, secretary general of the MCB, claimed in 2007 that Islamophobia had become so endemic and institutionalised in the UK as to make reminders about Nazi Germany worthwhile:

Every society has to be really careful so the situation doesn't lead us to a time when people's minds can be poisoned as they were in the 1930s. If your community is perceived in a very negative manner, and poll after poll says that we are alienated, then Muslims begin to feel very vulnerable. We are seen as creating problems, not as bringing anything and that is not good for any society.[156]

Consequently MCU officers became increasingly involved in support work for individual victims of hate crime in London.[157] This was not conventional counter-terrorism work but it was axiomatic to MPSB-trained officers, that if community groups supported police in their own time at no cost to keep the city safe then the least police could do was to support them when faced with anti-Muslim bigotry and hate crimes.[158] Significantly this notion of reciprocity did not feature in the reams of Home Office and ACPO policy papers that emerged in what would become the 'Prevent' strand of Contest.[159]

The London partnerships responded to al-Qaeda influence in communities in fundamentally different ways to government strategies that emerged between 2002 and 2007. Initially those differences were most pronounced when Whitehall followed the Pentagon in sanctioning unprecedented military action against all perceived elements of an evil ideology including a licence to diminish or disregard the human rights of terrorist suspects because of an exceptional threat.[160] I often regarded the Whitehall approach as counter-productive and sought instead to isolate al-Qaeda by building links with communities in London where the terrorist movement sought recruits and support. A willingness on the part of police officers to empathise with the community grievances al-Qaeda sought to exploit was inherent in this partnership approach. In 2002 domestic Muslim communities were conceived in entirely different ways too. To a significant degree Whitehall again followed the Pentagon by regarding domestic Muslim communities as one homogenous 'suspect community' within which an 'evil ideology' had gained root.[161] The MCU conceptualised domestic Muslim communities as minorities that deserved empathetic support in the terms established by a post-Macpherson diversity policing paradigm.[162] When Whitehall widened its perspective of domestic Muslim communities it was to embrace quietist Muslims as advised by Policy Exchange and other influential voices. In consequence, engagement with Muslim communities was undertaken on a wholly different premise. Whitehall sought to identify and engage with Muslims who supported the war on terror against an 'evil ideology'. MCU officers sought to identify and engage with Muslims who had experience of the al-Qaeda phenomenon and expertise in countering its influence in local communities.

Relying almost exclusively on the specialist professional experience and expertise they acquired over three decades in MPSB, the founders and managers of the MCU assessed their Muslim partners in Brixton and Finsbury Park to have performed an outstanding public service on behalf of Londoners, both before and during their respective partnerships with the MCU. The assessment of an outstanding prior performance in the decade before 9/11 was crucial in prompting the MCU's early decision to work as closely in partnership with the Brixton salafis and the Finsbury Park Islamists as they did. Objections to the suitability of the Brixton salafis and the Finsbury Park Islamists as partners for police do not challenge this MCU assessment but rather question salafi and Islamist commitment to democracy and secular society.[163] In turn that challenge forms the basis for questioning the legitimacy and effectiveness of the London partnerships and the role of the MCU.[164] The same MPSB experience and expertise helped the MCU to counter that claim to some degree in both cases but was notably insufficient in the case of the Finsbury Park Islamists, who became subject of a concerted negative media campaign after they took control of the Finsbury Park Mosque.

To be sure, both the Finsbury Park Islamists and the Brixton salafis are shown to deploy high levels of experience, expertise and commitment in their civic duties, most especially in the area under examination—countering the influence of al-Qaeda propaganda and recruitment in their communities. Notwithstanding the obvious differences between the environments where the police officers and their community partners gained their experience and expertise, key similarities emerge in terms of the way they assess the credibility, capability, reliability and integrity of the individuals they engage with. For the Brixton salafis it is an approach to learning that has been honed in a street environment where mistakes cost lives and where reputation is hard won and has to be protected. For the Finsbury Park Islamists it is an approach to learning that has been nurtured in torture rooms and refugee camps in the Maghreb and Middle East and later in the contested arena of activist Muslim politics in London. For MCU officers it is an approach to learning developed in the course of operational counter-terrorism duties in London, where poor assessments of these key qualities of individuals and groups can have serious adverse consequences.

Therefore, following Kenney, each of the three groups have successfully cultivated street skills to the extent that they have demonstrated confidence in their own judgements and a consequent willingness to take calculated risks.[165] In doing so each partner has demonstrated what Flyvbjerg suggests is common to all expert activity, intrinsic reliance on 'intimate knowledge of several thousand concrete cases in their areas of expertise'.[166] Thus expertise in countering al-Qaeda influence in sections of the community where it has taken hold relies wholly on 'context-dependent knowledge and experience' of salafi or Islamist knowledge and local street culture which for Flyvbjerg is of a type that sits 'at the very heart of expert activity'.[167] Moreover, as Flyvbjerg suggests, this type of knowledge and expertise operates at the centre of each case study as a 'research and teaching method or to put it more generally still, as a method of learning'.[168] This is what separates the case study participants—Islamist, salafi and MCU police officers—from the wide body of outside commentators who critique their partnership activity: close engagement with the al-Qaeda phenomenon. As Flyvbjerg insists, 'It is only because of experience with cases that one can at all move from being a beginner to being an expert'.[169] If, alternatively, 'people were exclusively trained in context-independent knowledge and rules, that is, the kind of knowledge that forms the basis of textbooks and computers, they would remain at the beginner's level in the learning process'.[170] This is to posit the dependence of the case studies on expertise that relies on intimate familiarity with its subject and exposes the contrary 'limitation of analytical rationality' that is, according to Flyvbjerg, consequently 'inadequate for the best results in the exercise of a profession, as student, researcher, or practitioner'.[171]

Broadly speaking, a common strand of solidly grounded street expertise tested and found sufficient in the most rigorous field conditions emerges from the research study. Measurement of that success is as elusive in this field as it is in all crime prevention initiatives but no more so. On the specific occasions that the London partnerships demonstrated effectiveness by established policing yardsticks it was acknowledged by MPSB managers. It is not proposed to list all of these cases but instead to highlight a unique Commissioner's commendation awarded to an MCU officer and a Muslim community leader for outstanding skill and bravery while tackling al-Qaeda influence for the benefit of Londoners as an example of outstanding and unheralded success in the tradition of MPSB. By the time of these awards it had become axiomatic that *Daily Mail* readers would read of the MCU approach as a sign of subversion and lunacy at NSY.[172] Indeed, evidence of tangible success contrasts sharply with a lack of experience and expertise in the wider Muslim community and is assessed to be sufficient for policy makers to invest in a comprehensive evaluation programme. A level of expert community intervention against the adverse influence of al-Qaeda propaganda aimed at inspiring more terrorist attacks on London is sufficiently clearly delineated so as to provide an affirmative and provisional endorsement. This positive assessment sits at odds with prevailing accounts of radicalisation and counter-radicalisation.

12

LEGITIMACY AND EFFECTIVENESS

Cumulatively my case study approach provides compelling evidence that endorses the legitimacy and effectiveness of the MCU partnership initiatives in Finsbury Park and Brixton. At the same time, however, by presenting the partnerships on their own terms the experience and goals of its partners is better understood and helps inform a consideration of legitimacy and effectiveness by others. For my part, I am the first to concede that the legitimacy of the partnerships would have been seriously undermined if claims that the MCU's Muslim partners were as antithetical to social cohesion as the BNP were well founded. Again, specialist professional experience emerges as the basis on which both the Brixton salafis and the Finsbury Park Islamists were assessed to be wholly distinct and distinguishable from the BNP. Whereas the BNP's hatred of Muslims in the period under review had been preceded by hatred of ethnic minorities no evidence emerges in the study of either Muslim group exhibiting or harbouring hatred towards any non-Muslims. On the contrary, both groups were at the hub of partnership work with police that was aimed at tackling hate-crime and their success was noted by their Muslim opponents who were imprisoned for that offence.

In 1993 Sir Patrick Sheehy, chairman of BAT Industries, a tobacco conglomerate, was asked by Conservative Home Secretary Kenneth Clarke to subject policing to corporate scrutiny for the first time.[1] Although his report was largely rejected as a result of a typically well-orchestrated Police Federation protest[2] the imprint of the Sheehy Report's new managerialism nevertheless had a lasting impact on the culture of ACPO.[3] When the Police Federation's Alan Eastwood complained that under Sheehy's proposal's 'police would be turned into a commodity', 'cynically hired and learning to cynically serve', 'semi-casualised', becoming mere 'units of manpower'[4] he was anticipating concerns that would become commonplace in the police canteen during my research study.[5] 'Will units of manpower take the same risks?' Eastwood asked rhetorically.[6] With the advent of blogging fifteen years later police officers' dismay at having indeed been reduced to 'units of manpower' and subjected to a stifling 'health and safety culture' that discouraged risk taking became well known outside the canteen and served as evidence of Clarke's covert and long-term cultural success.[7] For MPSB officers Clarke's negative legacy was two-fold because his other major contribution to policing as Home Secretary was to strip MPSB of its national responsibility for the PIRA and related Irish republican terrorism and pass responsibility to MI5.[8]

For MPSB interviewees the closure of MPSB in 2006 was the final act in a process initiated by Clarke that failed to recognise the value of specialist experience and expertise when tackling terrorism no less than other crimes.[9] One MPSB veteran was anxious to explain that this was not an elitist position and illustrated his point by recalling how MPSB officers attended a Police Federation meeting in 1993 in support of other specialist officers who were also being threatened with a loss of status and reward by the 'new managerialism' in the wake of Sheehy.[10] Indeed, on that occasion the MPSB Police Federation representative supported the specialism of uniformed patrol and community police officers against the new management notion that police officers were generalists who could be posted from one role to another.[11] In opposition Tony Blair had been quick to attack the Sheehy Report on the basis that police reform was only justified if it helped 'to cut crime', and make 'our communities safer', and not simply to allow 'the Treasury to cut corners' or satisfy 'some mistaken political dogma'.[12] However, in office, he was closely associated with the new managerialism that led his namesake to close MPSB and bring the notion of a police career in intelligence gathering and analysis of terrorism and political violence to an end. In the circumstances it is fitting that the specialist risk taking of the MCU that gave rise to the London partnerships should have been one final MPSB initiative.

'It will come back after a decent interval' an interviewee predicted of MPSB, 'but called something else and dressed in new clothes'.[13]

Another MPSB veteran was more cautious, pointing to the anomaly of the closure of MPSB. 'Why' he asked, 'was the original Special Branch closed down and every other Special Branch [in the UK] left intact?' 'Because' he said answering his own question, 'provisional SBs developed without any of the history, autonomy, responsibility or resources of MPSB so were always in the pocket of ACPO and Box [MI5]'. Certainly evidence for the significance of this divide between metropolitan and provisional counter-terrorism policing perspectives can be found in Dean Godson's insights into his friend Colin Cramphorn's key role in introducing the changes at ACPO level that led to MPSB's demise.[14] More broadly, Godson's and Cramphorn's shared experience in, and views on Northern Ireland suggests a present and future Special Branch role that is more closely aligned to the Royal Ulster Constabulary (RUC) model which was perforce strongly wedded to informant handling and unable to develop civic partnership approaches in the way suggested by MPSB and MCU officers in this study.[15]

By way of final confirmation, in the week before my research study was submitted to the University of Exeter, Godson invited General Petraeus, Commander of the US military's Central Command (known as Centcom)[16] to deliver the fourth Colin Cramphorn memorial lecture on the topic of military strategy in Afghanistan and its purported importance for containing the terrorist threat in the UK.[17] Perfectly illustrating the subordination of a 'hearts and minds' policing approach to military-led counter-insurgency and counter-subversion strategies, General Petraeus re-enforced high-level military messages delivered elsewhere in London on the same day[18] that set the scene for the re-invention of RUC and colonial Special Branch policing models as conceived and approved by Kilcullen and Nagl.[19] Petraeus linked US and UK military strategy in Afghanistan to the al-Qaeda and al-Qaeda related domestic terrorist threats in the US and UK.[20] Thus, by ensuring that 'al-Qaeda and other transnational groups do not re-establish safe-havens' in Afghanistan, US and allied military strategy, he argued, aimed to make us 'less vulnerable at home'.[21] General Sir David Richards, newly installed UK military Chief of the General Staff, spoke at Chatham House on the same day on the same topic and made the same connection.[22] At the same time a newly appointed UK military counter-insurgency expert with a new co-ordinating role in Afghanistan explained how a 'hearts and minds' approach would embrace colonial Special Branch experience as it sought to implement a 'hearts and minds' counter-insurgency strategy.[23]

In contrast to this military model, the London partnerships developed from the community outreach work of the MCU, a bottom-up, local initiative. After the successful removal of Abu Hamza's supporters from Finsbury Park Mosque in February 2005 local police chief Barry Norman said the community-led operation and the partnership work that facilitated it was a major highlight in his eventful police career.[24] Within months, however, Sir David Veness retired as ACSO and his replacement commenced the task of dismantling MPSB while Godson, a neighbour to NSY, began an energetic lobbying campaign seeking to ensure the MPS never partnered with Islamists or salafis again.[25] On Thursday, 17 September 2009, the same day Godson invited General Petraeus to speak at Policy Exchange, Lorenzo Vidino circulated his latest research paper *Europe's New Security Dilemma* in which he uses the MCU partnership with the Finsbury Park Islamists to illustrate Godson's winning argument that the legitimacy such partnerships clearly bestow upon Islamists is counter-productive and ineffective.[26] Familiar with the MCU and the arguments in this study about the importance of street credibility in determining legitimacy and effectiveness in Muslim London communities Vidino highlights his discussions with security officials in the UK and across Europe where the MCU approach has been assessed and found wanting, precisely on the basis first highlighted by Godson four years earlier.[27]

Publication in the prestigious *Washington Quarterly* imbues Vidino's article with gravitas and influence. These qualities are further enhanced by reference at the beginning of the article to Vidino's academic role at the Belfer Center for Science and International Affairs at Harvard University and references in it to his meetings with senior government officials during the course of his research.[28] Following if not referencing similar findings by Pantucci,[29] Vidino acknowledges that the Islamist takeover of Finsbury Park Mosque in 2005 was effective and successful in removing and reducing the influence of Abu Hamza and his core supporters.[30] However, he appears to agree with the security officials he interviews who point to the long-term deficit of legitimising Islamists in such a process.[31] These deficits are the ones identified by Rand, Middle East Forum and Policy Exchange and their acolyte academics throughout the study period: namely that the Finsbury Park Islamists are best defined by their antecedents with an allegiance to the Muslim Brotherhood which in turn should be viewed as a subversive and sectarian organisation. Vidino's government interviewees helpfully articulate the defining characteristics of subversion and sectarianism in the case of the Muslim Brotherhood: opposition to the three non-negotiable political principles—democracy, freedom of religion and sexual equality.[32]

Vidino quotes Alain Chouet, 'former head of France's counter-intelligence service Direction Générale de la Sécurité Extérieure', to explain that al-Qaeda 'is only a brief episode and an expedient instrument in the century-old existence of the Muslim Brotherhood' and that 'the true danger [was] the expansion of the Brotherhood, an increase in its audience'.[33] Moreover, dissimulation and deception were inherent to the Muslim Brotherhood: 'the wolf knows how to disguise itself as a sheep' Chouet explained.[34] From this top-down perspective it followed that MCU officers or London politicians like Ken Livingstone and Jeremy Corbyn were naive to argue that members of MAB and MWH did not exhibit signs of opposition to democracy, freedom of religion and sexual equality. This was to underestimate Muslim Brotherhood skills in deception and disguise. MCU officers encountered the same perspective from European and US counterparts on a regular basis especially in respect of Tariq Ramadan when he moved from Geneva to London having been banned from moving to the USA in 2005. The notion that Ramadan was guilty of 'doublespeak' became common coinage in practitioner and academic security circles at the same time.[35] Whereas in contrast for activist Muslim Londoner Naima Bouteldja, Ramadan followed 'in the footsteps of revolutionary thinkers like Franz Fanon and Malcolm X' and quite transparently established 'the universal values of Islam within the framework of western societies'.[36]

Gwen Griffith-Dickson suggests a more realistic benchmark for counter-terrorism partnership work might be to ask whether a Muslim is 'hostile to co-operation with non-Muslims' and 'how far is the person or group willing to co-operate with non-Muslims in areas of shared concern?'[37] Throughout the period 2002—2007 the Brixton salafis and Finsbury Park Islamists consistently demonstrate a willingness to co-operate in this way, just as Ramadan recommends they should.[38] Vidino, however, is concerned with other benchmarks and refers to 'the positive radical flank effect', a conceptual term used by social movement theorists,[39] to explain 'why the emergence of al-Qaeda and other jihadist groups... led European governments to see nonviolent Islamists more benignly'.[40] Thus, for Vidino, the notion of a positive radical flank effect illuminates Chouet's account of the 'emergence of a severe and prolonged terrorist threat' leading 'European governments (but not his own) to lower the bar of what is accept-

COUNTERING AL-QAEDA IN LONDON

able and endorse extremist organisations as long as they oppose violence in Europe'.[41] Far from providing new insights this analysis repeats the 'Londonistan' analyses with which we are now so familiar. Instead Vidino seeks to suggest that European governments have come to this analysis of their own volition as a result of experiences like the Finsbury Park Mosque case.

Central to their case against the Islamists is that they are not truly representative of Muslims. Moore considers it apposite to quote Edmund Burke's description of revolutionary agitators as a 'half-a-dozen grasshoppers under a fern [who] make the field ring with their importunate chink, whilst thousands of great cattle, reposed beneath the British oak, chew the cud and are silent'.[42] Godson compares Islamists who challenged the MPS handling of the 'Forest Gate raids' in 2006 with members of the Militant Tendency in the 1980s who Frank Chapple, Moore's counter-subversion model for Ed Husain,[43] dismissed in the following anecdote:

Ere, boy, know what these Trots are like? They're like the Red Indians surroundin' the 'omestead in those early cowboy films. The camera flits from one window to the next and it looks like there's 'undreds of 'em. In fact it's the same three geezers runnin' round'.[44]

In fact the evidence suggests that the Finsbury Park Islamists and the Brixton salafis (and most other London Islamists and salafis) had more community legitimacy and support than either Militant Tendency or Policy Exchange and their respective allies in two separate periods of London politics. Sharing an elitist top-down vanguard approach to politics Militant Tendency and Policy Exchange are perfectly matched ideological opponents, both lacking experience of real urban street life. Indeed, it is perhaps inherent to this kind of top-down political thinking that it is considered legitimate for a small, elite group of Cambridge graduates to forge a counter-subversion strategy against their political opponents. Such was the strength and resources of their trans-global alliances[45] that they appeared to be sufficiently confident to embark on a counter-subversion project without the express support of US or European governments or their security services. Clearly the MCU partnerships with Islamists and salafis in London represented an insider threat that they needed to undermine and remove.

The only study to examine MAB and London Islamist involvement in the STW campaign supports the finding that the numbers of activists in Islamist politics and their relationship with the wider communities they represent is no different to what would generally be found in Labour, Conservative, Liberal Democrat or other London street politics.[46] Phillip's article corroborates this study's finding that MAB and its Islamist allies represented and enabled Muslim and non-Muslim community anger at the war on terror in Iraq legitimately and effectively, perhaps better and more representatively than all three mainstream political parties in Britain.[47] For his part Vidino characterises the entire panoply of the war on terror as reasonably repressive policies and aggressive methods that gave way in due course to a counter-insurgency 'hearts and minds' approach 'to prevent the radicalisation of scores of potential new militants'.[48] At no point do he or his government interviewees allow that any aspect of the war on terror may have exacerbated the terrorist threat in the UK.[49] As such they have no inclination to accept that credible and effective opponents of the war on terror might have been equally effective opponents of al-Qaeda apologists in London—a central research finding in my study.

Instead Vidino offers a solution to what he describes as 'a new security dilemma'.[50] In fact, the solution he offers for police and security services to treat Islamists and salafis as informants and not as partners is exactly the response offered consistently during the research period by Godson and his acolytes to the same problem.[51] Vidino reports that government officials have now adopted this strategy and say it is necessary 'to preserve a harmonious and cohesive society' and also that it allows for 'occasional co-operation' [with Islamists and salafis] that might be necessary 'in emergency situations'.[52] Although the article's major focus is on the democratic deficits of Islamists, Vidino makes it sufficiently clear that salafis should be treated in the same way, thus not only echoing Godson and Moore but also an influential US military report that acknowledged the distasteful but necessary business of engaging salafis for a specific counter-insurgency purpose.[53] Such an unrealistic notion as 'occasional co-operation' could only arise from the kind of top-down thinking that helps to distinguish the bottom-up approach of my study and its contrary findings. Vidino's final question serves to conclude my study as well.

Do European governments achieve their interests by engaging with nonviolent Islamists [and salafis]? 'If the state interest is the marginalisation of extremist and anti-integration ideas among young European Muslims, then many [policymakers]', Vidino reports, 'believe that partnering with nonviolent Islamists is counterproductive'.[54] On this basis, 'short-term and occasional forms of cooperation with nonviolent Islamists [and salafis] can be used to achieve gains against jihadists, but such tactical partnerships should not develop into a permanent strategy'.[55] This is an accurate reflection of UK government policy that marks the eclipse of the MCU and the London partnerships it gave rise to largely as a result of the efforts of an unelected transatlantic elite lobby group.

Nowhere in the wealth of data collected in my study is there any evidence to support what Vidino and his government interviewees take as given: that non-violent Islamists and salafis are unfit for partnership because they hold views that are threats to social cohesion. On the contrary there is clear evidence that points to Brixton salafis and Finsbury Park Islamists (and the many Muslim Londoners they exemplify) serving as antidotes to the terrorism and hate crimes promoted by Abu Hamza, Abu Qatada, Abdullah el Faisal and their supporters. Non-Muslims, Jews, gays and women who might sometimes feature as victims of hate crimes licensed by these extremist Muslims were regularly protected from the risk of attack by the work of both groups in their communities over a long period. More specifically Brixton salafis worked against a secular street gang culture where gays were routinely identified and targeted for particular vilification. If the Finsbury Park Islamists continually campaigned against what they described as Zionist Israel they did no more or less than their local elected MP with whom they worked in partnership to remove Abu Hamza's violent extremist supporters and the al-Qaeda influence they encouraged. What the Brixton salafis and the Finsbury Park Islamists shared was what MCU officers valued most: skill, courage, experience and long-term commitment to the well-being of all Londoners.

The arrival of Vidino's article coincided with my final reflections and consultations with former partners about the research study. It served to highlight the extent to which government policy continued to shift away from the MCU and the London partnership approach and towards the position developed by Policy Exchange and its US, UK and European allies. My reading of Vidino's article also coincided with opinion polls predicting a comfortable victory for the Conservative Party in 2010.[56] Moore and Godson would have been optimistic that the counter-subversion project they appear to have embarked on would be formalised and implemented by a new government whose counter-terrorism policy they have shaped.[57] Similarly their populist ally Melanie Phillips would be anxious to ensure that an era of 'lunacy at the Yard' was finally over.[58] Based on Policy Exchange recommendations police would still be encouraged to engage in the kind of cross-cultural partnerships recommended by Thomas and Inkson[59] but only with partners who conceive al-Qaeda to be part of a wider Islamist or salafi threat. In exceptional cases where there is a need for police to engage with Islamists or salafis it should be in strict accordance with the rules governing dealings with informants and subversives. That outcome would see trusted partners of police become members of suspect communities instead and, on the evidence of this study, consequently provide a propaganda coup for the al-Qaeda apologists they spent two decades opposing in London. In the circumstances the study supports Hillyard's argument that counter-terrorism lessons learned before 9/11 and 7/7 might still be relevant.[60]

By the time my research was completed sufficient time had elapsed to judge the long-term success of the work undertaken in Finsbury Park and Brixton. On Friday 5 February 2010 police officers, politicians, council officials, community leaders, faith leaders and local citizens began to arrive at the Finsbury Park Mosque. They were the guests of the mosque trustees who were holding a celebration event to mark the fifth anniversary of a successful community-led operation in which the nine-year occupancy and influence of al-Qaeda inspired violent extremist Abu Hamza and his hardcore supporters was brought to an end. Barry Norman, the local police chief in 2005 and since retired from the Metropolitan Police, commented on the dramatically changed atmosphere on approaching the mosque. He recalled how after nightfall in the days of Abu Hamza's reign the venue and surrounding streets were often dangerous places for individuals who were not part of Abu Hamza's circle. Now, he noted, an atmosphere of calm and order prevailed.

Visible change, however, was most notable inside the mosque. Sanitation, order, comfort and cleanliness had been restored. The discourtesy, intimidation and disorder that characterised Abu Hamza's tenure had been replaced by a welcoming and orderly regime that restored the mosque to its original purpose and prestige. Most significantly, the first-floor office in which Abu Hamza directed his criminal operations was now used by Mohammed Kosbar to organise activities for local Muslim youth that helped them become active and responsible London citizens instead of becoming terrorists, violent extremists and criminals. The office no longer housed the collected master tapes of Abu Hamza's inflammatory talks for which he was convicted of incitement to murder but instead contained leaflets introducing young Muslims to their civic duties and responsibilities as Londoners. On the main mosque notice board local Muslims who had problems to resolve were encouraged to attend a regular surgery held inside the mosque by their local MP Jeremy Corbyn. This was highly significant. Abu Hamza's supporters were indignant and outraged when Jeremy Corbyn had entered the mosque during their residency and threatened him with violence. So far as Abu Hamza had been concerned the greatest threat to his legitimacy and effectiveness came from the progressive alliance between his Muslim neighbours at the MWH and left-wing politicians like Corbyn. Abu Hamza was right to be worried. He had correctly identified and anticipated the key players who would reclaim the mosque and replace his dangerous influence with one that was wholly benign and conducive to good London citizenship.

I was delighted to take part in this fifth anniversary celebration of a unique community-based partnership operation that finally restored the mosque to its rightful position in the local community. It was a chance for me to highlight the outstanding work of former police colleagues, especially one police officer who had worked quietly and tirelessly over a long period to support and empower both old and new mosque trustees to peacefully reclaim the mosque from the violent extremists. Their efforts had not been in vain. The experience, skill and vision of the new trustees and their new management team provided the sound foundation on which their unheralded five-year success had been built. Most especially, the new trustees' experience in the STW coalition and in Palestinian solidarity campaigns ensured that the genuine political grievances Abu Hamza and his hardcore supporters exploited for the purpose of al-Qaeda-inspired violent extremism were now channelled into traditional, mainstream London politics.

However, with the exception of Transport Minister and London Muslim MP Sadiq Khan politicians attending the celebration were limited to the local neighbourhood. Khan, for his part, indicated that he had been persuaded to attend the event by his colleague Jeremy Corbyn. With government ministers eager to locate and promote the success of community intervention projects against violent extremism it was significant that they should—with the exception of Khan—spurn the golden opportunity provided by this event. Significant but not surprising given the prominence and influence of a contrary account in which the five-year success story at Finsbury Park Mosque was described instead as a story of appeasement in which power was transferred from one group of extremists to another, 'effectively a Hamas takeover of a British Mosque'.[61]

Typically, Blairite MP, Khalid Mahmood—a mosque trustee—in 2010 sided with the mosque's powerful critics.[62] Given its role in publishing pejorative and negative accounts of events at the mosque it was fitting that *The Times* should claim erroneously that Khalid Mahmood had been brought in to 'reclaim the mosque for moderate Muslims' in a 'deal backed by David Blunkett, then Home Secretary, and Tony Blair'.[63] Instead the claim reflects a readiness on the part of *The Times* to diminish the outstanding work of the new mosque trustees and management. It was therefore consistent for *The Times* to present a pejorative view of the mosque trustees' libel claim against the think-tank Policy Exchange whose research director Dean Godson had criticised the mosque trustees and their partnership with police in *The Times* in 2006.[64]

Similarly, there was visible evidence in 2010 of ongoing success for the Brixton salafis in their efforts to reduce the influence of al-Qaeda-inspired violent extremism in and beyond their neighbourhood. Just as they first demonstrated a robust response to Abdullah el Faisal's attempts to takeover their mosque in 1994 so they continued to present a powerful defence of their community against the blandishments of violent extremists. Their street reputation for standing up to the bullying tactics of violent extremists had been further enhanced on Saturday 25 April 2009 when Anjem Choudhury led his group Islam For The UK (an offshoot of al-Muhajiroun) to Brixton to launch what he called a Shari'ah Roadshow. Hoping to attract new recruits and supporters Choudhury employed tried and tested tactics by exploiting genuine and widespread Muslim community concerns about Islamophobia in the media. Specifically, Choudhury sought to suggest that his group represented a fearless defence of Islam in the face of increased hostility to Islam and Muslims in the media. The first topic for the ambitiously titled 'roadshow' was Shari'ah Law and Choudhury's argument was that it was under attack by the media, the UK government and its Muslim 'stooges' and should be defended at all costs by true Muslims. Not unlike BNP leader Nick Griffin at the opposite end of an extremist spectrum Choudhury sought to exploit genuine community grievances for a radical purpose.

Like Abu Hamza and Abdullah el Faisal, Choudhury regarded convert Muslims as especially valuable recruits and that explained his decision to launch this campaign in Brixton. However, also like Abu Hamza and Abdullah el Faisal in the 1990s, he failed to take account of the ability of the Brixton salafis to stand up to his group's hectoring and bullying tactics. In a heated confrontation outside the local underground station Choudhury's group were out-talked and out-muscled by the Brixton salafis to an extent that diminished the extremists' limited street credibility further still and enhanced the Brixton salafis' legitimacy and effectiveness. Like their Finsbury Park neighbours the Brixton salafis were demonstrating street skills and civic responsibility in 2010 that pre-dated the government's Prevent strategy by over a decade and which appeared destined to continue long after Prevent became consigned to a history of ill-conceived Blairite responses to the influence of al-Qaeda terrorism.

Notwithstanding vital differences between Finsbury Park Islamist and Brixton salafi interpretations of their civic duties as Muslim Londoners which this study illuminates, these latest demonstrations of street success in North and South London highlight perfectly what they have in common: an unshakeable Islamic imperative to promote and instil good citizenship in Muslim youth communities. As this study shows they devote their own free time to this task and in doing so offer a role model for a free voluntary sector that places a lesser burden on the public purse.

At the time of going to press a coalition government dominated by the Conservatives is reviewing its counter-terrorism policy. It is the pivotal finding of my research study that success in Finsbury Park and Brixton was based on experience, expertise and a strong sense of civic duty—rare qualities valued and appreciated by their police partners. In contrast, many projects funded by the government's Prevent programme have lacked these essential qualities and consequently failed to acquire the legitimacy and effectiveness necessary to achieve success in a dangerous and demanding environment.

Research work I have undertaken with Jonathan Githens-Mazer since completing my PhD study suggests that the failure of so many Prevent projects to acquire the legitimacy that is a prerequisite for effectiveness in this arena rests squarely on a familiar failing in New Labour government strategies: a blinkered determination to impose top-down solutions against the grain of grassroots reality. With a small but significant Liberal Democrat presence in the new coalition government it was reasonable to anticipate a greater emphasis on local voluntary civic duty that would allow belated recognition of the success achieved in Finsbury Park and Brixton against al-Qaeda influence. Such reasonable optimism increased when noting the appointment of Brent Central MP Sarah Teather as Minister of State for Children and Families in the new coalition government. Like Jeremy Corbyn she shared platforms with politically active London Muslims in 2009 to highlight the desperate plight of children and families in Gaza. In this and in her campaign against Guantanamo Bay and in support of her constituent, the Guantanamo Bay detainee Jamil al-Banna, she demonstrates the effectiveness of a cross-cultural alliance for social justice that Abu Hamza recognised was a major threat to his legitimacy and consequently a powerful antidote to al-Qaeda inspired violent extremism.

On 5 February 2011 UK Prime Minister, David Cameron, addressed a security conference in Berlin and signalled that the approach to counter-terrorism I have been associated with since 9/11 was being abandoned. Writing in the *Times*, columnist David Aaronovitch applauded Cameron's decision to exclude salafis and Islamists from a partnership role in preventing violent extremism in the UK. 'Cameron' he argues, 'comes down hard on one side of an argument about how best to combat "home-grown" terrorism' that has 'gone on since 2001, and sharpened after the 2005 bombings'.[65] Clearly, Teather has been powerless to moderate the influence of key supporters of the war on terror in the same coalition government. If the latter are allowed free rein to implement their recommendations in this arena the outstanding counter-terrorism work at Finsbury Park and Brixton will be undone and replaced by a draconian counter-subversion programme. Under such a regime many of the Muslim Londoners who worked effectively in partnership with police will be re-cast as subversives and monitored—placed in the same 'suspect' category as the terrorists and violent extremists they have bravely tackled over two decades.

APPENDIX

RESEARCH METHODOLOGY

This is an outline of the theoretical and practical considerations that helped shape the methodology I used to collect and analyse primary data so as to answer my PhD research question: how did the participants in the London partnerships conceive legitimacy and effectiveness in their work—countering al-Qaeda influence? To provide insightful answers research methodology is necessarily concerned to draw out and analyse the participants' motivations, strategies and actions.[1] This is what Colin Robson refers to as 'real world research' where the aim is to evaluate an 'intervention, innovation, service or programme' that is often concerned with 'action or change'.[2] Thus cafes, mosques, homes and police stations in Brixton and Finsbury Park were the places where 'some of the issues and complexities involved' in sometimes 'messy' real life situations were played out in the research study.[3]

Given the London partnerships operated at a street level it is reasonable to assume that the issues of legitimacy and effectiveness would not always have been expressly or consciously addressed by the participants at important times.[4] In consequence participants' unwitting testimony is as important as their self-conscious accounts and therefore places value on accounts of London partnership activity and the activity and experience of the participants.[5] Participants' explanations in 2007 of their motivations, strategies and actions in, say, 2003 may be coloured if their legitimacy and effectiveness was called into question in the intervening period. Research methodology therefore needs to take account of the vested interests of the research subjects, not least the researcher himself.[6]

The research study analyses data to establish the 'meaning that actions have for agents' so as to produce results that consist of 'one interpretation of the relationship between the social phenomena studied'.[7] My research methodology can be categorised as anti-foundationalist in so far as it does not look for 'causal relationships', nor to 'produce 'objective' and generalisable findings' in the manner of most positivist research.[8] The overriding purpose of the study's methodology is to facilitate a coherent analysis of how three sets of participant in the London partnerships—the MCU in separate partnerships with the Brixton salafis and the Finsbury Park Islamists, the Brixton salafis in partnership with the MCU and the Finsbury Park Islamists in partnership with the MCU—conceived the legitimacy and effectiveness of their joint endeavours to counter al-Qaeda influence.

My role as head of the MCU throughout the study period required careful consideration so that it did not impair the validity of the study's findings. It was therefore decided that participants in the London partnerships would be consulted about the research proposal and that the study would only proceed if the participants were in agreement. In addition Muslim community representatives who worked in partnership with the MCU in other parts of London whose work is not featured centrally in this study were also consulted. This was the first stage in a process of transparency that Marie Breen-Smyth suggests is vital for integrity in all terrorism-related research[9] but especially when it is conducted by insiders.[10] The second stage was to discuss the primary data with participants in the London partnerships both during and after participant observation, again an approach recommended by Breen-Smyth.[11] The third stage was to show them draft versions of the PhD and to invite comments. Warm approval from participants, however welcome, leads on to the next set of hurdles posed by this particular insider study.

Gillespie highlights dilemmas with participant research concerning judgements about the validity, veracity and status of research data.[12] In particular Gillespie focuses on tensions between the subjectivity and objectivity of the researcher; intimacy and distance, i.e. 'how researchers handle the intimacy required to understand social lives and the distance required to stand back and analyse them'; 'relations of power between researchers and researched'; and 'wider questions about the politics and ethics of doing fieldwork and writing ethnography'.[13] Other key questions that bear upon this study: 'How does the researcher position [himself] in relation to [his] subjects and fellow researchers?'; 'Who is speaking for whom or on behalf of whom with what kind of authority?'; 'What kinds of obligation and responsibility does a researcher have towards her research subjects?'; 'How are issues of trust, truth and reciprocity dealt with?'.[14] Gillespie's own response is apposite:

It is perhaps best to see ethnography not so much as a prescribed set of methods but as an ethos of reciprocity and respect which depends on the goodwill of people to reveal themselves, and to be revealed.[15]

In important respects the fact that both police and community participants were well known to me placed particular demands on what Flick identifies as the basic principles of ethical research.[16] Thus when seeking the informed consent of participants in the London partnerships to interviews and the researcher's participant observation it was important to ensure that each individual had a genuine chance to decline.[17] Consent might be an unproblematic issue if my perspective of the voluntary nature of a partnership relationship with the community participants was sufficient. However, given the extent to which police officers have been seen to dominate and control partnerships with community groups the quality of the consent should not be taken for granted.[18] Informed consent from police participants is no less problematic in principle. As both a researcher and serving police officer of a senior rank to a police interviewee or participant in the London partnerships then informed consent places a severe onus on me to satisfy the rule that consent is entirely voluntary.[19] Alternatively, if consent is voluntary there is a risk of re-enforcing the insider bias inherent in favour of the London partnerships.[20] However, policing culture is understood to be insular and long-term participant observation may be an appropriate method for examining the 'inner reality of police work' not least in a partnership setting.[21]

In any event, all participants were supportive of the project and many chose to engage in lengthy and informal discussions which provided the researcher with additional ideas for conducting the research. In fact, the initial idea for the research study came from discussions with the leader of the Brixton Salafi community, Abdul Haqq Baker, who simultaneously began a parallel research study (also under the supervision of Bill Tupman).[22] In addition discussions about risks of harm were not unfamiliar to those participants whose work in the London partnerships was subject to regular threat assessments. Anonymity was granted to all participants so as to mitigate risks of harm except in instances where their role was a matter of public record and their consent was forthcoming. No amount of empathy, however, can dispel the risk of ethical compromise for the research study as a whole or the individual interviewees in particular. It is reasonable for police and community partners to willingly take risks in the course of the London partnerships' initiative and yet wholly inappropriate for the research study itself to amplify or re-enforce the kind of risks that accompany inherently dangerous counter-terrorism work.

I should therefore acknowledge a privileged and a handicapped position. While long-standing partnership engagement with the interviewees largely precludes spontaneous and unexpected disclosures the same intimacy allows for a developed discussion of the research question. Similarly, while my counter-terrorism role imposed certain legal parameters to discussions this limitation is often offset by a professional skill in empathising with both community and practitioner perspectives. Moreover, because trust, reciprocity and mutual respect was often established with interviewees over a long period of time it would be naïve to disregard it and artificial to create a new basis for research discussions. The inevitability of complementary and mutually re-enforcing viewpoints is a hurdle that has to be negotiated. As Robson cautions, 'Objectivity can be seen to be at risk from a methodology where the values, interests and prejudices of the enquirer distort the response'.[23] According to Robson, relatively prolonged involvement with the study helps reduce both reactivity and respondent bias.[24] In his view the development of a trusting relationship between researcher and respondents helps ensure the latter are less likely to give biased information.[25] On the other hand, he notes, 'there can be greater researcher bias with prolonged involvement as the researcher identified more with the respondents—a kind of researcher Stockholm syndrome',[26] a relevant concern.[27]

Reflection has been conceived as the process through which researchers examine their research approaches acknowledging the extent to which their work can sometimes reproduce identified social problems, for example, in relation to racism and sexism.[28] Some researchers have argued that perspectives within criminology and terrorism studies have often failed to take sufficient account of minority voices, including Muslim and other faith identities.[29] It follows that critical reflection helps reduce this risk when dealing with minority Muslim communities.[30]

Although critical perspectives within academia address counter-terrorism, little academic work has yet specifically addressed engagement issues with Muslim communities.[31] Police and government engagement with Muslim communities post-9/11 has been rather hurriedly conceived and led by government imperatives, containing normative assumptions about Muslim identities.[32]

I have therefore been involved in reflexivity and reflection, a research approach that is more concerned with generating opportunities for understanding, rather than about generating truths.[33] Thus, following Alvesson and Sköldberg, reflective research has two basic characteristics: 'careful interpretation' where all 'references to empirical data are the results of interpretation'; and 'reflection' which focuses attention 'inwards' towards 'the person of the researcher' and 'the relevant research community'.[34] Central to a reflective approach, is a concern to explore and document participants in the London partnerships' own experiences, perceptions and understandings of their work, thereby giving access to voices that have largely been overlooked by the welter of policy-driven terrorist and counter-terrorist discourse post-9/11.[35] In a post-9/11 world, Muslims are often viewed with suspicion by the media, politicians, the security services and by agencies of the criminal justice system.[36] Moreover, particular minorities within the Muslim population, notably salafis and Islamists, are viewed as problem groups.[37] It may be the case that an inclusion of Muslim voices—not least Muslim police officers—in research may help to forge new approaches within social science research, in the same way that a focus upon 'race'/ethnicity, and indeed gender, has carved out new pathways within research.[38]

As John Gerring suggests a 'definitional morass' surrounds the use of case studies in research.[39] It is, however, due in large part to Gerring's critical thinking that the core components of a viable case study—employed in this research study—emerge with a reasonable degree of conceptual clarity: 'its method is qualitative, with a small number of subjects; the research is holistic, thick and a more or less comprehensive examination of the phenomenon; it utilises a particular kind of evidence (e.g. ethnographic, participant-observation); its method of evidence gathering is naturalistic (a real life context); the topic is diffuse (case and context are difficult to distinguish); it employs triangulation (multiple sources of evidence)...'.[40] Robert Yin usefully summarises a case study as 'an empirical enquiry that investigates a contemporary phenomenon within its real life context'.[41]

Case study design therefore provides a flexible framework and focus for a description and analysis of London partnership activity that contributes answers to the research question. Three case study sites have been created: King's Cross, Finsbury Park and Brixton. The three sites highlight significant differences between participants in the three components of partnership activity: the MCU, the Finsbury Park Islamists and the Brixton salafis. For instance, while each group demonstrates expertise in tackling al-Qaeda propaganda, their individual rationales and methodologies are shown to be very different. A three-site case study format also demonstrates a privileged MCU role: a separate partnership relationship with each community group that the two community groups do not have with each other. The study aims to avoid conflating the concepts of legitimacy and effectiveness but rather presents and analyses original primary data concerning each of the three participants' approaches to both issues separately except when they choose to address legitimacy and effectiveness as interdependent or overlapping issues themselves.

Case study design draws heavily on ethnographic enquiries that have engaged with similarly marginalised urban communities. Notable in this regard are Whyte's study of a street corner gang in a Boston slum,[42] Pryce's study of Afro-Caribbean community activity in Bristol[43] and Wacquant's account of boxing in a black ghetto in Chicago.[44] A participant observer will normally have to invest time, energy and ingenuity in building trust and empathy with his host community so as to be able to carry out a demanding role effectively. To illustrate the point, Loic Wacquant describes the significant effort he was required to make to 'carve out [for himself] a small place in the fraternal world [of boxing]' he sought to enter in a poor black ghetto in Chicago.[45] This was necessary if he was to succeed (as he eventually did) in establishing with the members of the gym he was studying 'relationships of mutual respect and trust' so as thereby 'eventually [to] carry out [his] field investigation of the ghetto'.[46] By contrast, I merely carried on working at the hub of the London partnerships where I had begun to build trust on a 24/7 basis in 2001.

Peter Burnham and his co-authors note that case study design is 'closely associated with historical study and with anthropology'.[47] On a standard account a case study consists of the 'detailed examination of a single example of a class of phenomena' that 'cannot provide reliable information about the broader class'.[48] However, as Bent Flyvbjerg notes, this description is 'indicative of the conventional wisdom of case study research, which if not directly wrong, is so oversimplified as to be grossly misleading'.[49] Significantly, Flyvbjerg lists commonplace misunderstandings about case study design: (i) 'general, theoretical (context-independent) knowledge is more valuable than concrete, practical (context-dependent) knowledge'; (ii) 'one cannot generalize on the basis of an individual case; therefore; (iii) the case study cannot contribute to scientific development'; (iv) 'the case study is most useful for generating hypotheses, that is, in the first stage of a total research process, whereas other methods are more suitable for hypotheses testing and theory building'; (iv) 'the case study contains a bias toward verification, that is, a tendency to confirm the researcher's preconceived notions'.[50] Flyvbjerg's challenge to these 'misunderstandings' raises the prospect that a case study approach will achieve its purpose in the present case.

Following Flyvbjerg, it is argued that the role of case studies in terms of human learning is not reducible to formulaic mediation. Human learning is of critical importance at the three case study sites in King's Cross, Finsbury Park and Brixton where expertise and experience are of prime importance. As Flyvbjerg argues, what all experts have in common is 'that they operate on the basis of intimate knowledge of several thousand concrete cases in their areas of expertise'. On this basis the thesis relies on case studies where, according to Flyvbjerg, 'context-dependent knowledge and experience are at the very heart of expert activity'.[51] It is also central to the study's research strategy to endorse the theoretical implications of Flyvbjerg's innovative intervention:

It is only because of experience with cases that one can at all move from being a beginner to being an expert. If people were exclusively trained in context-independent knowledge and rules, that is, the kind of knowledge that forms the basis of textbooks and computers, they would remain at the beginner's level in the learning process. This is the limitation of analytical rationality: it is inadequate for the best results in the exercise of a profession, as student, researcher, or practitioner.[52]

It follows, in the present case, that an adequate explanation of partnership activity that relies heavily on the experience of its police and community participants cannot be gleaned by what Flyvbjerg calls 'analytical rationality' alone. Rather, the case study seeks to demonstrate how context-dependent knowledge is applied and shared within an in-group so that new recruits can learn from more experienced members. As Kenney points out, this kind of learning is necessarily 'on the job' training and resistant to formalised teaching.[53] To do it justice participant observation and semi-structured interviewing needs to be particularly attentive.

The case studies were commenced in earnest in August 2006 when participants in the London partnerships agreed that the researcher should be allowed to use his own participatory role for research purposes, to make notes on it, both concurrently and retrospectively and also to conduct interviews with them. It is the researcher's practitioner role from 2001 onwards (and prior experience) that facilitates a retrospective analysis. The study therefore rests on in-depth, long-term engagement with the main actors in the London partnerships. Twenty-one key participants in the London partnerships between 2001 and 2007 were interviewed at length (five MCU officers, eight Brixton salafis and eight Finsbury Park Islamists). Whereas in most conventional qualitative research studies a key player will be interviewed once, perhaps for as long as two hours, this study has conducted semi-structured interviews with pivotal participants on an ongoing basis over an extended period creating cumulative interview records that exceed twelve hours in length in some cases. More crucially, the same interviewees have also been central players in the researcher's participant observation thereby providing high-quality primary data in terms of a daily display of the validity and authenticity of their approaches to the legitimacy and effectiveness of their contributions to the London partnerships. In addition another thirty police and Muslim community contacts of the MCU were interviewed as well for shorter durations. Following Kenney, interviewees were chosen for their expertise rather than their representativeness.[54] Participant observation took place in Brixton, Finsbury Park and other parts of London on 220 days between September 2006 and October 2007 for a cumulative total in excess of 1400 hours. Both the participant observation and the majority of interviews were conducted while I was employed as head of the MCU. All of the interviews and the recording of participant observation notes were carried out in my own time.

Semi-structured interviewing and participant observation both involve what criminologist Mark Hamm calls 'a methodology of attentiveness (or criminological *verstehen*)' otherwise 'an engaged ethnographic process wherein researcher and subjects of study come to share, at least in part, in (the interviewees) lived reality...'[55] Whereas

Hamm's research involves interaction with violent far-right extremists this research study involves interaction with community representatives who are combating a similar phenomenon—albeit some of them are described as extremists themselves. I share Hamm's belief that life experience can be helpful, in the present case pointing to extensive prior professional experience of close proximity to terrorists and political extremists engaged in violence over a long period of time. Additionally, by highlighting the value of close engagement with his research subjects Hamm suggests valuable benchmarks for this study. An empathetic field-worker approach is helpful when seeking to gain meaningful access to sub-cultures and marginal or suspect communities. Moreover, just as this study distinguishes between 'field' counter terrorism practitioners and colleagues necessarily cocooned from their target communities so does Hamm differentiate the work of 'field' criminologists from colleagues exclusively preoccupied with theoretical considerations.[56]

Normally participant observation would not additionally require semi-structured interviews with the same participants. It is generally considered that the thick descriptions available to a participant observer are sufficient to provide insightful data about the activity being scrutinised—not least in this case where I have been an actual participant for the entire duration of the period being studied in addition to being a participant researcher for a shorter period. However, semi-structured interviews have been conducted with key participants in the London partnerships for four purposes: to probe their notions of legitimacy and effectiveness in relation to the London partnerships; to analyse their actions in relation to the London partnerships where this sheds light on the issues of legitimacy and effectiveness; to provide transcripts of discussions that illuminate important and relevant aspects of their roles in the London partnerships; and to establish the significance of observations that were made as a participant.

Wherever possible I took contemporaneous notes during interviews and participant observation but on many occasions this was not possible owing to the prevailing operational environment. As a rule notes were written up within twenty-four hours and regularly checked and discussed with participants. Recorded interviews were transcribed by a Muslim MCU officer while he was on protracted sick leave from the MPS with an injured back.[57] His knowledge of context and idiom enhanced the quality of the transcriptions. The same officer brought the same skills to bear on transcriptions of audio taped recordings of talks by Abu Hamza. Following Kenney's method, the researcher double-checked the accuracy of transcripts by listening to the audio tapes while reading the transcripts, stopping to ponder inaudible comments before sometimes discussing them with the transcriber or participants.[58] As Kenney suggests this two-staged transcription work is time-consuming but 'essential to ensure the reliability and integrity of critical primary source data'.[59] Again following Kenney, in interview transcriptions respondents' 'false starts, filler syllables, pauses, run-ons, and verbal fragments' ('er', 'um', etc) are removed so as to make them easier to read, 'without changing the content of what was said during interviews'.[60]

At particular points in certain interviews documents are discussed. Examples include recordings and transcripts of talks by Abu Hamza and reports written and published by interviewees. In these cases documentary analysis follows the same criteria applied to an analysis of participant observation and interviews—that is to say, the texts 'do not speak for themselves' but acquire significant meaning when situated within a context set by vigorous analytical and methodological assumptions'.[61] Texts, like interviewee's recollections of events, are therefore located in a political, community and chronological context in an effort to authenticate them. However, as Peter Burnham and his co-authors caution, 'the most serious challenge facing users of documentary sources concerns their response to questions of representativeness and meaning'.[62] Every effort has therefore been made to ensure that the documents and tapes consulted are 'representative of the totality of relevant documents'.[63] As recommended by Scott, I sought to establish 'as much as possible about the conditions under which the text was produced and, on that basis, make sense of the author's situation and intentions'.[64]

An example will help illustrate the methodology: an interviewee answers questions about the influence of a named al-Qaeda propagandist in the community; during the course of an interview he listens to a tape recorded by the same individual; he comments on the al-Qaeda propagandist's style, method and discourse which enriches an analysis of the same tape; and I ask additional questions based on the interviewees responses to the tape. By such an interactive method a key text is subjected to two levels of analysis—researcher and interviewee—and by recourse to three research devices—documentary analysis, 'live' participation and interview discussion. The text referred to in this example is one of several talks given by Abu Hamza to small groups of young British Muslims where he encourages them to adopt al-Qaeda's view of the world and to understand their personal obligation to fight for it. Each tape recording circulated freely in Muslim London during the study period and some were used in evidence against Abu Hamza at his Old Bailey trial in 2005. For the purposes of this research study the tapes have been transcribed by a Muslim Londoner with an understanding of Abu Hamza's colloquialisms. In turn, I familiarised myself with the tapes and transcripts over a period of five years paying particular attention to Abu Hamza's teaching methods. Following Kenney this has been a repetitive and cumulative process listening to audio tapes for over 100 hours. Abu Hamza's teaching methods are then discussed with interviewees who have been actively challenging his narrative in Muslim communities over a long period.

I also followed Kenney's method by coding primary data after carefully re-reading transcripts and notes line-by-line, 'inductively coding the documents according to themes and concepts', both those he had already identified and those that emerged from the data.[65] By March 2008 I had assembled an index containing thirty categories and eighty sub-categories arising from 'pre-established and newly emergent themes' in the primary data.[66] By March 2009 the index had expanded to contain eighty-two categories and two hundred and ten sub-categories of research themes. During this immersive process I also listened repeatedly to the original audio recordings of Abu Hamza's and Abdullah el Faisal's talks alongside primary data so as to better comprehend similarities and differences in communication techniques between them. This helped me to expand my written notes documenting reflections on the research themes and methodological issues, a process Kenney and other qualitative researchers refer to as 'memoing'.[67] In consequence further amendments, improvements and connections between different themes gradually emerged so as to begin to convert them into what Kenney calls a 'coherent theoretical narrative'.[68] That narrative extends from the specific themes that emerge at each case study site through to a cumulative analysis.

Finally, while writing up the study I analysed his data again, returning to coded themes to extract representative statements from the data, a process that involved ongoing reflection on what the participants in the London partnerships said and how their recorded thoughts related to the research question. While I was attentive to data that supported the legitimacy and effectiveness of the London partnerships, he actively sought evidence that disconfirmed his propositions or suggested new connections among the various themes. In this manner, the researcher immersed himself in the data, deepening his understanding of research themes through repeated analysis, reflection and writing in a manner recommended by Kenney.[69] Unlike Kenney, however, I did not use *NVivo*, or any other qualitative data analysis software program, to assist in handling large amounts of text.[70] Instead I held meetings with police and community participants in the London partnerships to obtain additional interpretations and alternative analyses of the data.

The discussions of ethical and methodological issues surrounding my dual role, reflexivity and reflection, case studies and data analysis contain the practical and theoretical considerations that inform my analysis of the London partnerships. In addition they highlight the extent to which I needed to reflect and respond to the complexities and changes that occurred on the ground during the course of an extended study period.

NOTES

PREFACE

1. I am also mindful of the varied responses of victims of terrorism and the empathetic responses many bereaved relatives have to the loss of loved ones in terrorist attacks. While the media generally focuses on retribution as a response, in reality victims demonstrate a wider range of reactions. See Lambert, Robert, 2011. *Listening to the victims of terrorism.* Centre for the Study of Terrorism and Political Violence (CSTPV), University of St. Andrews. 13 January. http://www.st-andrews.ac.uk/~cstpv/journal/opinion-pieces/opinionpieces/files/listening-to-the-victims.html accessed 14.1.11.

1. LEARNING FROM EXPERIENCE

1. Manzoor, Sarfraz, 2009. Channel 4 documentary, *The Enemy Within*, draws on history to portray radical jihadism. *Guardian*, Monday 12 October 2009. http://www.guardian.co.uk/media/2009/oct/12/channel-4-documentary-muslims accessed 11 January, 2011.
2. See for example, Laqueur, Walter, 1999. *The New Terrorism: Fanaticism and the Arms of Mass Destruction.* New York: Continuum; Laqueur, Walter, 2004. *No End To War: Terrorism in the Twenty-First Century.* New York: Continuum; Duyvesteyn, Isabelle, 2004. 'How New is the New Terrorism?' *Studies in Conflict & Terrorism*, 27, pp. 439–454.
3. Manzoor, Sarfraz, 2009. *op. cit.*
4. *Ibid.*
5. Lambert, Robert, 2008. 'Empowering Salafis and Islamists Against Al-Qaeda: A London Counter-terrorism Case Study', *PS: Political Science and Politics* 41 (1), pp. 31–35.
6. Gates, Stephen, 2011. 'Sidney Street siege resonates even 100 years on'. *Guardian.* 2 Jan http://www.guardian.co.uk/uk/2011/jan/02/sidney-street-siege-100-years?INTCMP=SRCH accessed 4.1.11.
7. BBC News, 2006. Reid heckled during Muslim speech. 20 September. http://news.bbc.co.uk/1/hi/5362052.stm accessed 6.1.11.

8. Kleinig, John, 1996. *The Ethics of Policing*. Cambridge: Cambridge University Press, p. 214.

9. *Ibid*.

10. *Ibid*.

11. The issue of competing loyalties raised by police membership of Masonic lodges became topical during my police service. See for example Davies, Nick, 1998. 'Freemasons in the police', *Guardian*. January. http://www.nickdavies.net/1997/01/01/freemasons-in-the-police/ accessed 6.1.11.

12. 'PC George Dixon (Jack Warner) was the first British copper to tread the TV beat and, running for twenty-one years, the longest lasting. The emphasis in the series, which was reassuringly cosy and quaint even in the fifties, was on small, everyday human experiences, not major-league crime and sensationalism, with Dixon a benevolent father figure to the local community'. http://www.whirligig-tv.co.uk/tv/adults/dixon/dixon.htm accessed 2.10.10.

13. Metropolitan Police, 1977. *Instruction Book*. Introduction, p. 1. Author's copy.

14. *Ibid*.

15. *Ibid*.

16. John Alderson retired as Chief Constable of Devon and Cornwall in 1982. See Alderson, John, 1979. *Policing Freedom*. Plymouth: Macdonald & Evans; and Alderson, 1998. *Principled Policing: Protecting the Public with Integrity*. Winchester: Waterside Press.

17. Interview, 3.2.07. See also, Bill Tupman's University of Exeter webpage: http://people.exeter.ac.uk/watupman/Tupman/ accessed 12.11.10.

18. *Marxism Today*, 1982. Policing in the Eighties. Interview with Chief Constable John Alderson. April, pp. 8–14. http://www.amielandmelburn.org.uk/collections/mt/index_frame.htm accessed 12.12.10.

19. *Ibid*., p. 11; see also Bunyan, Tony, 1977. *The History and Practice of the Political Police in Britain*. London: Quartet Books.

20. *Ibid*., p. 11.

21. Author's participant observation notes, vol. 2.

22. Myhill, Andy, 2006. Community engagement in policing: Lessons from the literature. London: Stationery Office http:/www.crimereduction.gov.uk/policing18.htm accessed 3.5.10.

23. *Marxism Today*, 1982. *op. cit*, p. 11.

24. Reiner, Robert, 1985. *The Politics of the Police*. Brighton: Wheatsheaf, pp. 85–111.

25. Renier, Robert, 1985. *op. cit*, p. 92.

26. Interview, 4.7.07.

27. Hain, Peter (ed.), 1979. *Policing the Police*. Vols. 1 & 2. London: John Calder.

28. Blair, Sir Ian, 2005. The Dimbleby Lecture, London—transcript. http://cms.met.police.uk/news/policy_organisational_news_and_general_infor-

mation/commissioner/the_richard_dimbleby_lecture_2005_by_sir_ian_blair_qpm accessed 11.9.10.

29. Innes, Martin, 2006. 'Policing Uncertainty: Countering Terror Through Community Intelligence and Democratic Policing', *Annals of the American Academy*. 605, May, pp. 1–20.

30. Flvbjerb, Bent, 2006. 'Five Misunderstandings About Case-Study Research', *Qualitative Inquiry*. 12 (2) pp. 219–245.

31. '*The Sweeney* was the top-rated British police series of the 1970s, bringing a new level of toughness and action to the genre, and displaying police officers bending the rules to beat crime'. Museum of Broadcast Communication. http://www.museum.tv/archives/etv/S/htmlS/sweeneythe/sweeneythe.htm accessed 6.1.11; see also BBC home, *Life on Mars* http://www.bbc.co.uk/lifeonmars/characters/gene.shtml accessed 6.1.11.

32. Reiner, Robert, 1985. *op. cit*; 'PC George Dixon (Jack Warner) was the first British copper to tread the TV beat and, running for twenty-one years, the longest lasting. The emphasis in the series, which was reassuringly cosy and quaint even in the fifties, was on small, everyday human experiences, not major-league crime and sensationalism, with Dixon a benevolent father figure to the local community'. http://www.whirligig-tv.co.uk/tv/adults/dixon/dixon.htm accessed 2.10.08.

33. Tupman, W and Tupman, A, 1999. *Policing in Europe: Uniform in Diversity*. Exeter: Intellect.

34. An elite mobile police public order and operational support unit, the Special Patrol Group (1965—1987) came to adverse attention when some of its officers were suspected of involvement in the death of teacher Blair Peach at a demonstration in Southall in 1979. While writing this book a previously withheld police report into Peach's death was published, see Campbell, Duncan, 2010. 'The lessons of Blair Peach', *Guardian*. 27 April. http://www.guardian.co.uk/commentisfree/2010/apr/27/blair-peach-policing-lessons?INTCMP=SRCH accessed 14.1.11.

35. Jackson, Richard, 2008. *op. cit*, p. 295.

36. Blair, Ian, 2009. *Policing Controversy*. London: Profile; Hayman, Andy (with Margaret Gilmore), 2009. *The Terrorist Hunters*. London: Bantam.

37. Keeble, Harry (with Kris Hollington), 2010. *Terror Cops*. London: Simon and Schuster.

38. See for example, Godson, Dean, 2007b. 'Introduction to Peter Clarke's Colin Cramphorn Lecture', *Policy Exchange*. http://www.policyexchange.org.uk/images/libimages/260.pdf accessed 14.8.10.

39. Lambert, Robert, 2010. *The London Partnerships: an insider's analysis of legitimacy and effectiveness*. Unpublished PhD. University of Exeter.

40. See page 318.

41. See Acknowledgements, page 6.

42. The artist has kindly allowed the European Muslim Research Centre to display the two paintings. From 8—13 June, 2010 the paintings were fea-

tured in the *War and Body* exhibition in London, supported and funded by City University.

43. Lawrence, Bruce, ed. 2005. *Messages to the World: The Statements of Osama bin Laden*. London: Verso, p. 234.

44. Schmid, Alex, 2004. *op. cit.*

45. *Ibid.*

46. *Ibid.* pp. 205–6; see also Bueno de Mesquita, Ethan, and Dickson, E. S. 2007. 'The Propaganda of the Deed: Terrorism, Counterterrorism, and Mobilization', *American Journal of Political Science*, 51 (2), pp. 364–81.

47. Duffy, Eamon. *The Stripping of the Altars*. Yale: Yale University Press.

48. Chase, Malcolm, 2007. *Chartism: A New History* Manchester: Manchester University Press.

49. Glasgow Digital Library, 2010. Maxton papers. University of Strathclyde. http://gdl.cdlr.strath.ac.uk/maxlen/maxlen07.htm accessed 1.1.11.

50. *Ibid.*

51. Gates, Stephen, 2011. *op. cit.*

52. Malik, Maleiha, 2006. 'Muslims are now getting the same treatment Jews had a century ago', *Comment is Free: Guardian Online* 2 February. http://www.guardian.co.uk/commentisfree/story/0,,2004258,00.html accessed 20.1.10.

53. *Ibid.*

54. Significantly, in July 2007, breaking with precedents set by their immediate and distant predecessors, Gordon Brown, then a new UK Prime Minister, and Jacqui Smith, then a new UK Home Secretary, responded to al-Qaeda-inspired terrorist incidents calmly and judiciously in tone and in terms that failed to oxygenate public fear and terror in the way the perpetrators calculated and recent precedent suggested they would.

55. Reiner, Robert, *op. cit.* 49.

56. *Ibid.*

57. *Ibid.*

58. Holland, Mary, 2006. 'Commons terrorism debate 1974', *New Statesman*, July.

59. Githens-Mazer, Jonathan and Robert Lambert, 2010. *Islamophobia and Anti-Muslim Hate Crime: a London case study*. Exeter: EMRC, University of Exeter; Lambert, Robert and Jonathan Githens-Mazer, 2010. *Islamophobia and Anti-Muslim Hate Crime: UK case studies*. Exeter: EMRC, University of Exeter.

60. Huguenot Society, 2011. History. http://www.huguenotsociety.org.uk/history.html accessed 7.1.11.

61. London Metropolitan archives, 2010. http://www.cityoflondon.gov.uk/Corporation/online_services accessed 2.9.10.

62. Milne, Seumas, 1994. *The Enemy Within: The Secret War Against the Miners*. London: Verso.

63. Author's research notes.

64. *Ibid.*
65. *Ibid.*
66. Alderson, John, 1979. *op. cit.* pp. 82–83.
67. *Ibid.*
68. Lyons, William, 2002. 'Partnerships, information and public safety: community policing in a time of terror', *Policing: an International Journal of Police Strategies & Management.* 25 (3), pp. 530–542.
69. de Guzman, M.C., 2002. 'The changing roles and strategies of the police in time of terror', *ACJS Today*, 1, p. 13.
70. Bloom, Clive, 2010. *Violent London: 2000 years of riots, rebels and revolts.* Palgrave Macmillan. pp. 223–4.
71. *Ibid.*, p. 245.
72. Whitfield, Diffie and Susan Landau, 2007. *Privacy on the Line.* London: MIT press.
73. Ackroyd, Peter, 2001. *London: The Biography.* London: Vintage, p. 737.
74. BBC News, 2008. 'Fatal wartime crush marked', 2 March. http://news.bbc.co.uk/1/hi/england/london/7273488.stm accessed 29.12.10.
75. Stairway to Heaven memorial, 2010. http://www.stairwaytoheavenmemorial.org/gpage5.html accessed 29.12.10.
76. *Ibid.*
77. BBC News, 2008. *op. cit*; see also BBC, 2004. 'WW2—People's war archive. Interview with Alf Roberts, survivor of Bethnal Green underground station crush', http://www.bbc.co.uk/ww2peopleswar/stories/11/a2964611.shtml accessed 29.12.10.
78. *Ibid.*
79. *Ibid.*
80. *Ibid.*
81. *Ibid.*
82. *Ibid.*
83. *Ibid.*
84. Tulloch, John, 2006. *One Day in July: Experiencing 7/7.* London: Little, Brown.
85. Kingston, Peter, 2007. .Confronting risk', *Guardian.* 3 July. http://www.guardian.co.uk/education/2007/jul/03/academicexperts.highereducation accessed 30.12.10.
86. BBC News, 2006. 'Profile: Shehzad Tanweer', 6 July. http://news.bbc.co.uk/1/hi/uk/4762313.stm accessed 29.12.10; and BBC News, 2007. 'Profile: Mohammad Sidique Khan', 30 April. http://news.bbc.co.uk/1/hi/uk/4762209.stm accessed 29.12.10.
87. BBC News, 2005. 'Blair vows hard line on fanatics', 5 August. http://news.bbc.co.uk/1/hi/uk_politics/4747573.stm accessed 29.12.10.
88. NFO Newsfilm, 2006. Transcript of ITV early evening news, 6.7.06. http://www.nfo.ac.uk/collections/records/0014-0005-4741-0000-0-0000-0000-0.html accessed 29.12.10.

89. Dodd, Vikram, 2010. 'List sent to terror chief aligns peaceful Muslim groups with terrorist ideology', *Guardian* 4 August. http://www.guardian.co.uk/uk/2010/aug/04/quilliam-foundation-list-alleged-extremism accessed 14.10.10.

90. Building Bridges for Peace, 2010. 'Founder's story', http://www.building-bridgesforpeace.org/founders_story.html accessed 29.12.10.

91. See http://www.newhamstory.com/node/2167 accessed 30.12.10.

92. Lambert, Robert and Jonathan Githens-Mazer, 2010. *Islamophobia and Anti-Muslim Hate Crime: UK Case Studies*. Exeter: EMRC, University of Exeter; Githens-Mazer, Jonathan and Robert Lambert, 2010. *Islamophobia and Anti-Muslim Hate Crime: a London case study*. Exeter: EMRC, University of Exeter; http://centres.exeter.ac.uk/emrc/publications/Islamophobia_and_Anti-Muslim_Hate_Crime.pdf

93. Taylor, Matthew, 2010. 'Inside the violent world of the new far right', 28 May. http://www.guardian.co.uk/uk/2010/may/28/english-defence-league-guardian-investigation accessed 30.12.10.

94. Shibli, Murtaza, 2010. *7/7: Muslim Perspectives*. London: Rabita.

2. RESPONDING TO AL-QAEDA

1. Beckett, Andy, 2008. 'What can they be thinking?', *Guardian*. 26 September. http://www.guardian.co.uk/politics/2008/sep/26/thinktanks.conservatives accessed 12.12.10.

2. Bright, Martin, 2006. *When Progressives Treat With Reactionaries*. London: Policy Exchange. http://www.policyexchange.org.uk/images/libimages/176.pdf accessed 3.11.10.

3. Pasquill, Derek, 2008. 'I had no choice but to leak', *New Statesman*. 17 January. http://www.newstatesman.com/politics/2008/01/british-muslim-story-case accessed 29.12.10.

4. Bright, 2006. *op. cit.*

5. Pasquill, Derek, 2008. *op. cit.*

6. Pipes, Daniel, 2003. *Militant Islam Reaches America*. London: W.W. Norton & Company; Vidino, Lorenzo, 2005. 'The Muslim Brotherhood's Conquest of Europe', *Middle East Quarterly* Winter 12 (1). http://www.meforum.org/687/the-muslim-brotherhoods-conquest-of-europe accessed 3.4.10; Whine, Michael, 2005a. 'The Penetration of Islamist Ideology in Britain', *Current Trends in Islamist Ideology* 1 Hudson Institute; Whine, Michael, 2005b. 'The Advance of the Muslim Brotherhood in the UK', *Current Trends in Islamist Ideology* 2 Hudson Institute pp. 30–40.

7. Leiken, Robert S. and Brooke, Steven. 'The Moderate Muslim Brotherhood', *Foreign Affairs*. 86 (2) March/April 2007.

8. Godson, Dean, 2005. 'You'll never guess who's to blame for 7/7', *The Times*. 13 December. http://www.timeonline.co.uk/article/0,,1922518,00.html accessed 2.8.10; Godson, Dean, 2006a. 'Already Hooked on Poison', *The Times*.

8 February. http://www.timesonline.co.uk/article/0,,1072–2029734, 00.html accessed 2.8.10; Godson, Dean, 2006b. ;The feeble helping the unspeakable', *Times online*. 5 April. http://www.timesonline.co.uk/tol/comment/columnists/guest_contributors/article702053.ece accessed 2.8.10.

9. Ibid.
10. Githens-Mazer, Jonathan and Robert Lambert, 2009b. 'The demonisation of British Islamism', *Guardian cif*. 1 April. http://www.guardian.co.uk/commentisfree/belief/2009/mar/31/religion-islam accessed 3.4.10; Githens-Mazer, Jonathan and Robert Lambert, 2009c. 'Quilliam on Prevent: the wrong diagnosis', *Guardian cif*. 19 October. http://www.guardian.co.uk/commentisfree/belief/2009/oct/19/prevent-quilliam-foundation-extremism accessed 17.1.10.
11. Godson, Dean, 2005. *op. cit.*
12. Godson, Dean, 2007a. 'The Old Bill Should Choose its Friends Carefully: What on Earth are West Midlands Police up to?, *The Times*, 23 August; Godson, Dean, 2007b. 'Introduction to Peter Clarke's Colin Cramphorn Lecture', *Policy Exchange*. http://www.policyexchange.org.uk/images/libimages/260.pdf accessed 14.8.10.
13. For references to Lambertism see Reut Institute, 2010. Building a Political Firewall against the Assault on Israel's Legitimacy: London as a Case Study, November pp. 40–41 http://www.reut-institute.org/Publication.aspx?PublicationId=3949 accessed 29.12.10; Khan, Amjad, 2010. A dummy's guide to Lambertism. 22 October. http://hurryupharry.org/2010/10/22/a-dummy%E2%80%99s-guide-to-lambertism/; Lucy Lips, 2010. A depressing little story on the *Sunday Times*. 1 August http://hurryupharry.org/2010/08/01/a-depressing-little-story-in-the-sunday-times/accessed 29.12.10.
14. Pantucci, Raffaello, 2009. 'British Government Debates Engagement with Radical Islam in New Counterterrorism Strategy', *Terrorism Monitor*. 7 (10) 24 April. Category: Terrorism Monitor, Global Terrorism Analysis, Home Page, Military/Security, Europe
15. O'Neil, Sean and McGrory, Daniel, 2006. *The Suicide Factory: Abu Hamza and the Finsbury Park Mosque*. London: Harper Perennial.
16. Blair, Tony, 2010. *A Journey*. London: Random House.
17. Owen, David, 2007. *The Hubris Syndrome: Bush, Blair and the intoxication of power*. London: Politicos.
18. Oborne, Peter, 2006. *The Use and Abuse of Terror: The Construction of a False Narrative on the Domestic Terror Threat*. London: Centre for Policy Studies.
19. Blair, Tony, 2010. *op. cit*, p. 351.
20. Ibid, p. 348.
21. Freeman, Hadley, 2010. 'Tony Blair interviewed by Katie Couric', *Guardian*. 15 September. http://www.guardian.co.uk/news/blog/2010/sep/15/tony-blair-katie-couric accessed 15.9.10.

22. Ibid.

23. Githens-Mazer, Jonathan and Robert Lambert, 2010a. *op. cit.*

24. Lambert, Robert and Jonathan Githens-Mazer, 2010b. *op. cit.*

25. Ibid.

26. Blair, Tony, 2010. *op. cit*, p. 348.

27. This is a theme developed by Michael Kenney, see Kenney, Michael, 2007. *From Pablo to Osama* Philadelphia: Penn State University Press; Kenney, Michael, 2008. *Organizational Learning and Islamic Militancy*. Final Report. School of Public Affairs, Capital College, Pennsylvania State University.

28. Campbell, Alistair and Stott, Richard, 2008. *The Blair Years: extracts from the Alistair Campbell Diaries*. London: Arrow Books.

29. Luton is thirty miles north of London.

30. Interview, 24.5.07.

31. Ibid.

32. Court transcript, p. 170. US v. Omar Abdul Rahman et al; S5 93 Cr. 181. http:/intelfiles.egoplex.com/61HKRAHS-sentencing.htm accessed 7.6.07

33. Court transcript, p. 173. *op. cit.*

34. Lustick, Ian S., 2006. *op. cit*; de Lint, Willem, 2004. 'Neo-conservatism and American Counter-Terrorism: Endarkened Policy?', in Mathieu Deflem, ed. *Terrorism and Counter-Terrorism: Criminological Perspectives*. Oxford: Elsevier, pp. 131–153.

35. Ignatieff, Michael, 2001. 'It's war', *Guardian*. 1 October. http://www.guardian.co.uk/Archive/Article/0,4273,4267406,00.html accessed 3.2.09; see also Ignatieff, Michael, 2004. *The Lesser Evil: Political Ethics in an Age of Terror*. Princeton: Princeton University Press; Lincoln, Bruce, 2003. *Holy Terrors: Thinking about Religion after September 11*. Chicago: Chicago University Press.

36. Wilson, Richard Ashby, 2005. 'Human Rights in the "War on Terror"', in Wilson, Richard Ashby, ed. *Human Rights in the 'War on Terror*. Cambridge: Cambridge University Press, pp. 1–37, p. 12; see also, Hurrell, Andrew, 2002. '"There are no Rules" (George W. Bush): International Order after September 11', *International Relations*. 16 (2), pp. 185–204.

37. *Ibid*; see also Lustick, Ian S., 2006. *op. cit*; Blick, Andrew, Choudhury, Tufyal and Weir, Stuart, 2006. *The Rules of the Game: Terrorism, Community and Human Rights*. York: Joseph Rowntree Reform Trust.

38. *Ibid.*, p. 12.

39. *Ibid.*, p. 12; Ignatieff, Michael, 2004. *op. cit* p. 137.

40. *Ibid.*, p. 12.

41. See for example Laqueur, Walter, 1999, 2004. *op. cit.*

42. Duyvesteyn, Isabelle, 2004. *op. cit.*

43. *Ibid.*, p. 440; see also Spencer, Alexander, 2006. 'Questioning the Concept of "New Terrorism"', *Peace, Conflict & Development*. 8, January, pp. 1–33; Enders, Walter and Sandler, Todd, 2005. 'After 9/11: Is it all Different Now?', *Journal of Conflict Resolution*. 49 (2) pp. 259–277.

44. Lia, Brynjar, 2007. *Architect of Global Jihad: The Life of al-Qaeda Strategist Abu Mus'ab al-Suri* London: Hurst, p. 359.
45. *Ibid.*
46. *Ibid.*, p. 368.
47. Githens-Mazer, Jonathan, 2007. 'Myths of Massacre and Nationalist Mobilisation: Ireland and Algeria in Comparative Perspective', in R. Miller ed. *Ireland and the Middle East* Dublin: Irish Academic Press; see also Githens-Mazer, Jonathan, 2008b. 'Variations on a Theme: Radical Violent Islamism and European North African Radicalisation', *PS: Political Science and Politics.* 41 (1).
48. Lehany, David. 2005. 'Terrorism, Social Movements, and International Security: How Al Qaeda Affects Southeast Asia', *Japanese Journal of Political Science.* 6 (1), pp. 87–109, p. 88.
49. *Ibid.*
50. *Ibid.*
51. Tupman, W.A. and O'Reilly, C., 2004. 'Terrorism, Hegemony and Legitimacy: Evaluating success and failure in the War on Terror', Political Studies Association conference, Lincoln, August 2004, p. 3. http://www.psa.ac.uk/cps/2004/tupman.pdf accessed 4.4.08.
52. Gerges, Fawaz A., 2005. *op. cit*, p. 270.
53. *Ibid.*, p. 270.
54. Louw, P. Eric, 2003. 'The "War Against Terrorism": A Public Relations Challenge for the Pentagon', *Gazette: The International Journal for Communication Studies*, 65, pp. 211–230, 211–212; see also Wolfendale, Jessica, 2006. Terrorism, Security, and the Threat of Counterterrorism. *Studies in Conflict & Terrorism.* 29, pp. 753–770.
55. Wolfendale, Jessica, 2006. *op. cit.*
56. *Ibid.*

3. CHOOSING MUSLIM PARTNERS

1. Thiel, Darren, 2009. *Policing Terrorism: A Review of the Evidence.* London: The Police Foundation.
2. Ibid.
3. Weir, Stuart, 2006. *Unequal Britain: Human Rights as a Route to Social Justice.* London: Politicos. *Passim.*
4. Macpherson, Lord, 1999. *op. cit.*
5. Reiner, Robert, 2000. *op. cit.*
6. Scarman, Lord, 1982. *The Scarman Report: The Brixton Disorders 10–12 April, 1981.* London: Pelican.
7. Reiner, Robert, 2000. 3rd ed. *op. cit*, p. 169.
8. *Ibid.*
9. Pantucci, Raffaello, 2009. 'British Government Debates Engagement with Radical Islam in New Counterterrorism Strategy', *Terrorism Monitor.* 7 (10). 24 April.

10. Spalek, Basia, 2005. 'British Muslims and Community Safety post-September 11ᵗʰ', *Community Safety Journal*. 4 (2), pp. 12–20.

11. Kleinig, John, 1996. *op. cit*, p. 55.

12. Renier, Robert, 1985. *op. cit*; see also Milne, Seumas, 1994. *op. cit.*

13. Oborne, Peter, 2006. *The Use and Abuse of Terror: The Construction of a False Narrative on the Domestic Terror Threat*. London: Centre for Policy Studies.

14. Scraton, Phil, 2002. 'In the Name of a Just War', in Phil Scraton, ed., *Beyond September 11: an Anthology of Dissent*. London: Pluto Press, pp. 216–233.

15. Tilly, Charles, 2004. 'Trust and Rule', *Theory and Society*. 33 (1), pp. 1–30; see also Tilly, Charles, 2003. *The Politics of Collective Violence*. Cambridge: Cambridge University Press. *Passim*.

16. *Ibid.*

17. Tilly, Charles, 2004. *op. cit.*

18. Tarrow quoted in Lehany, David, 2005, *op. cit*, p. 97; see also Tarrow, Sidney, 1998. *Power in Movement*. New York: Cambridge University Press, pp. 47–50.

19. *Ibid.*, p. 97.

20. McCauley, Clark, 2007. 'Terrorist Group Persistence and Dynamics. START research programme', http://www.start.umd.edu/start/research/ accessed 19.5.09.

21. *Ibid.*

22. Clutterbuck, Lindsay, 2006. *op. cit.*

23. Ibid.

24. Veness, David, 2001. 'Terrorism and Counterterrorism: An International Perspective', *Studies in Conflict & Terrorism*. 24, pp. 407–416; see also Veness, David, 2002. *op. cit.*

25. Brodeur, Jean-Paul, 1983. *op. cit*; see also Brodeur, Jean-Paul, 2007. *op. cit*; Brodeur, Jean-Paul and Dupont, Benoit, 2006. *op. cit.*

26. Thiel, Darren, 2009. *op. cit*, p. 3.

27. *Ibid.* pp. 31–34.

28. See for example, Innes, M. 2006. *op. cit*; Innes, Martin, Abbot L, Lowe, T, and Roberts, C. 2007. *Hearts and Minds and Eyes and Ears: Reducing Radicalisation Risks Through Reassurance-Oriented Policing*. London: ACPO; Innes, Martin and Thiel, Daniel, 2008. 'Policing Terror', in Newburn, Tim, ed. *The Handbook of Policing* 2ⁿᵈ ed. Cullompton: Willan. pp. 553–579; Thiel, Darren, 2009. *op. cit.*

29. See for example, Murray, John, 2005. 'Policing Terrorism: A Threat to Community Policing or Just a Shift in Priorities?', in *Police, Practice and Research*. 6 (4), pp. 347–361; de Guzman, Melchor C., 2002. 'The changing roles and strategies of the police in time of terror', *ACJS Today*. 22 (3) p. 8–13; Pelfrey, William V., 2005. 'Parallels between Community Oriented Policing and the War on Terrorism: Lessons Learned', *Criminal Justice Studies*. 18 (4), pp. 335–346.

30. de Guzman, Melchor C. 2002. *op. cit.*

31. *Ibid.*

32. Lyons, William, 2002. 'Partnerships, information and public safety: community policing in a time of terror', *Policing: an International Journal of Police Strategies & Management.* 25(3), pp. 530–542, p. 530; see also, Pelfrey, William V., 2005. *op. cit.*

33. Innes, Martin, 2006. *op. cit.*

34. Spalek, Basia, 2002. 'Religious diversity, British Muslims, crime and victimisation', in Basia Spalek, ed., *Islam, Crime and Criminal Justice.* Cullompton: Devon. pp. 50–71; see also Spalek, Basia, 2006. 'Disconnection and Exclusion: pathways to radicalisation?', in T. Abbas (ed) *Islamic Political Radicalism* Edinburgh: Edinburgh University Press.

35. Sharp, Douglas, 2002. *op. cit.*

36. Scraton, Phil, 2002. *op. cit*; Oborne, Peter, 2006. *op. cit*; Gregory, Frank and Wilkinson, Paul, 2005. 'Riding Pillion for Tackling Terrorism is a High-Risk Policy', in Christopher Browning, ed., *Security, Terrorism and the UK.* London: Chatham House. pp. 2–3.

37. Spalek, Basia, 2005. *op. cit.*; Spalek, Basia, and Imtoul, A., 2007. '"Hard" Approaches to Community Engagement in the UK and Australia: Muslim communities and counter-terror responses', *Journal of Muslim Minority Affairs.* 27 (2); Spalek, Basia and Lambert, Robert, 2007. 'Terrorism, Counter-Terrorism and Muslim Community Engagement post 9/11', *Social Justice and Criminal Justice conference papers* Centre for Crime & Justice Studies, Kings College, London. July pp. 202–215.

38. Deibert, Ronald and Stein, Janice Gross, 2002. 'Hacking Networks of Terror', *Dialog-IO.* Spring, pp. 1–14; Bamford, Bradley W. C., 2004. *op. cit.*

39. Gill, Peter, 2006. 'Not Just Joining the Dots But Crossing the Borders and Bridging the Voids: Constructing Security Networks after 11 September 2001', *Policing & Security.* 16 (1), pp. 27–49; Broader, Jean-Paul and Dupont, Benoit, 2006. *op. cit.* Haggerty, Kevin D. and Kauger, Erin, 2006. 'Review Essay: Intelligence Exchange in Policing and Security', *Policing & Society.* 16 (1), pp. 86–91; Stevenson, Jonathan, 2004. Law Enforcement and Intelligence Capabilities. *The Adelphi Papers.* 44 (367), pp. 47–71.

40. de Lint, Willem, 2006. 'Intelligence in Policing and Security: Reflections on Scholarship (editorial)', *Policing & Society.* 16 (1), pp. 1–6.

41. *Ibid.*

42. Waddington, P. A. J. quoted in Reiner, Robert, 2000. 2nd ed. *op. cit*, p. 10.

43. Souhami, A. 2007. *op. cit.*

44. *Ibid.*

45. *Ibid.*

46. Yacoob, Salma, 2007. 'British Islamic Political Radicalism', in Abbas, Tahir, ed. *Islamic Political Radicalism: A European Perspective*, Edinburgh: Edinburgh University Press. pp. 279–294, p. 279; see also McGee, Derek, 2008. *The End of Multiculturalism: Terrorism, Integration and Human Rights.* Maidenhead: Open University Press.

47. Thomas, David and Inkson, Kerr, 2003. *Cultural Intelligence* San Francisco: Berrett-Koehler. *Passim.*
48. Spalek, Basia, El-Awa, Salwa, and McDonald, Liza Z., 2008. *op. cit.*
49. *Ibid.*, p. 14.
50. Balloch, S. and Taylor, M. eds, 2001. *Partnership Working: Policy and Practice* Bristol: The Policy Press.
51. Tilly, Charles, 2004. *op. cit.* Tarrow quoted in Lehany, David, 2005, *op. cit*, p. 97; Tarrow, Sidney, 1998. *op. cit.*
52. Spalek, Basia, El-Awa, Salwa, and McDonald, Liza Z., 2008. *op. cit.*
53. Ansari, Humayun, 2004.*The Infidel Within: Muslims in Britain since 1800.* London: Hurst.
54. Significantly, in 2008 both officers were aligned to the National Black Police Association (NBPA) rather than the more recently formed National Association of Muslim Police (NAMP).
55. Abbas, Tahir, 2005. *op. cit*, p. 16.
56. *Ibid.*, p. 16.
57. *Ibid.*, p. 17.
58. *Ibid.*, p. 17.
59. Gove, Michael, 2006. *op. cit*; Phillips, Melanie, 2006. *op. cit*; Desai, M., 2007. *op. cit*; Cox, C., and Marks, J., 2006. *op. cit.*
60. Benard, Cheryl, 2003. *Civil Democratic Islam: Partners, Resources and Strategies.* Santa Monica: Rand. The main points in the report are repeated in Benard, Cheryl, 2005. 'Democracy and Islam: The Struggle in the Islamic World—A Strategy for the United States', in David Aaron, ed., *Three Years After: Next Steps in the War on Terror.* Santa Monica: Rand, pp. 15–20.
61. *Ibid.*, p. 27.
62. See Great Britain. Home Office. 2006. *op. cit.*
63. Benard, Cheryl, 2003, *op. cit*, p. 36.
64. By citing Bernard Lewis at this point Benard declares her debt to the *Clash of Civilisations* thesis (the term was coined by Lewis before Samuel Huntingdon made it famous); Benard, Cheryl, 2003, p. 36.
65. For a contrary view to this proposition see Faliq, Abdullah, 2006. 'Interview with Alistair Crooke', *Arches* Cordoba Foundation. Winter, pp. 3–9.
66. Benard, Cheryl, 2005. *op. cit.*
67. *Ibid.*, p. 15.
68. *Ibid.*, p. 47.
69. *Ibid.*, p. 47.
70. Cragan, Kim, and Gerwehr, Scott, 2005. *Dissuading Terror: Strategic Influence and the Struggle Against Terrorism.* Santa Monica: Rand; Rabasa, Angel, 2005. 'Radical and Moderate Islam', Testimony presented to the House Armed Services Committee, Subcommittee on Terrorism, Unconventional Threats and Capabilities on February 16, 2006. Santa Monica: Rand.

71. See for example Manji, Irshad, *op. cit*; Darwish Nonie, 2006. *Now They Call Me Infidel: Why I Renounced Jihad for America, Israel and the War on Terror*. London: Sentinel; Warraq, Ibn, 1995. *Why I Am Not a Muslim*. London: Prometheus.

72. Ghazali, Abdus Sattar, 2005. 'Rand reports attempt to change Islam', *IslamicAwakening.com*. p. 14. http://www.islamicawakening.com/view-article.php?articleID=1214 accessed 12.5.08.

73. *Ibid.*, p. 3.

74. *Ibid.*, p. 3.

75. Souhami, A. 2007. *op. cit.*

76. Abbas, Tahir, 2005. *op. cit.*

77. McCants, William, ed., 2006. *Militant Ideology Atlas: Research Compendium*. West Point: Combating Terrorism Center.

78. *Ibid.*, p. 11.

79. *Ibid.*, p. 11.

80. Souhami, A. 2007. *op. cit.*

81. Maher, Shiraz and Martin Frampton, 2009. *Choosing our friends wisely: Criteria for engagement with Muslim groups*. London: Policy Exchange. http://www.policyexchange.org.uk/publications/publication.cgi?id=108 accessed 20.3.09; Vidino, Lorenzo, 2009. 'Europe's New Security Dilemma', *Washington Quarterly*. October, pp. 61–75.

82. Great Britain, Home Office. 2006. *Covert Human Intelligence Sources: Code of Practice*. London: The Stationery Office.

83. Schmid, Alex P., 2004. 'Frameworks for Conceptualising Terrorism', *Terrorism and Political Violence*. 16 (2), pp. 197–221.

84. Clutterbuck, Lindsay, 2006. 'Countering Irish Republican Terrorism in Britain: Its Origin as a Police Function', *Terrorism and Political Violence*. 18, pp. 95–118.

85. Halliday, Fred, 2002. *Two Hours That Shook The World—September 11, 2001: Causes & Consequences*. London: Saki Books. *Passim*.

86. *Ibid.*

87. Schmid, Alex P., 2004. *op. cit.* pp. 213–218.

88. Gerges, Fawaz A., 2005. *The Far Enemy: Why Jihad Went Global*. Cambridge: Cambridge University Press, p. 270.

89. Clutterbuck, Lindsay, 2006. 'Countering Irish Republican Terrorism in Britain: Its Origin as a Police Function', *Terrorism and Political Violence*. 18, pp. 95–118.

90. National Archives, Kew. http://www.nationalarchives.gov.uk/securityhistory/branch.htm accessed 2.12.08.

91. Bunyan, Tony, 1977. *The History and Practice of the Political Police in Britain*. London: Quartet Books. *Passim*.

92. Grieve, John G.D & Julie French, 2000. 'Does Institutional Racism Exist In the Metropolitan Police Service?', in David G. Green, ed. *Institutional Racism and the Police: Fact or Fiction?* London: Institute for the Study of Civil Society (Civitas), p. 19.

93. *Ibid.*, p. 19.
94. Participant observation notes, 8.3.07.
95. *Ibid.*
96. *Ibid.*
97. Spalek, Basia and Lambert, Robert, 2008. *op. cit.*
98. Balloch, S. and Taylor, M. eds, 2001. *op. cit*; Spalek, Basia and Lambert, Robert, 2008. *op. cit*; Chakraborti, Neil & Garland, Jon, 2004. 'Justifying the Study of Racism in the Rural', in Neil Chakraborti and Jon Garland, eds, *Rural Racism*, pp. 1–13. Collumpton: Willan.
99. Spalek, Basia and Lambert, Robert, 2008. *op. cit*; Lash, S, 1994. 'Replies and critiques', in U. Beck, A. Giddens and S. Lash, eds., *Reflexive modernization: Politics, tradition and aesthetics in the modern social order*, Cambridge: Polity Press, pp. 174–215; McGhee, Derek, 2005. *Intolerant Britain? Hate, citizenship and difference* Maidenhead: Open University Press.
100. German, Mike, 2007. *op. cit.*
101. Police officer interviewee and participant PD: MCU officer 2003–2007; MPSB officer 1986–2007; MPS officer 1982–2007: interview 30.11.06.
102. *Ibid*; see also Githens-Mazer, Jonathan, 2008b. *op. cit.*
103. *Ibid.*
104. Provisional IRA bomb attack on the Grand Hotel, Brighton during the Conservative Party conference in 1984.
105. Police officer interviewee and participant PG: MCU officer 2003–2007; MPSB officer 1989–2007; MPS officer 1985–2007: participant observation notes 25.6.07.
106. Police officer interviewee and participant PB: participant observation notes 25.6.07.
107. Police officer interviewee and participant PE: Muslim MCU officer 2003–2007; MPS officer 1991–2007: participant observation 25.6.07.
108. See also Silke, Andrew, 2003. *op. cit.*
109. Police officer interviewee and participant PD: interview 30.11.06.
110. Researcher's MCU presentation to counter terrorism police officers 2006–7. Participation observation notes 25.6.07.
111. Berman, Paul, 2003. *op. cit.*; Ignatieff, Michael, 2004. *op. cit.*
112. Participant observation notes 12.2.07.
113. The author's presentation to counter-terrorism police officers 2006–7. Participation observation notes 25.6.07.
114. Hillyard, Paddy, 1993. *op. cit.*
115. Interviews, 17 and 20.10.06.
116. Transcript from 'martyrdom video'.
117. Sands, Bobby, 1998. *Writings From Prison.* Dublin: Mercier Press, p. 219.
118. Transcript. *op. cit.*
119. Sands, Bobby, 1998. *op. cit*, p. 220

121. Sands, Bobby, 1998. *op. cit*, p. 220.
122. Transcript. *op. cit.*
123. Sands, Bobby, 1998. *op. cit*, p. 220.
124. Transcript. *op. cit.*
125. Sands, Bobby, 1998. *op. cit*, p. 221.
126. Wiktorowicz, Quintan, 2006. 'Anatomy of the Salafi Movement', *Studies in Conflict and Terrorism*. 29, pp. 207–239.
127. Spalek, Basia, El-Awa, Salwa, and McDonald, Liza Z., 2008. *op cit*; Briggs, Rachel, Fieschi, Catherine and Lownsbrough, Hannah, 2006. *op. cit.*
128. Police officer interviewee and participant PH: MPSB officer 1980–2009; MPS officer 1978–2009: interview 29.8.07.
129. *Ibid.*
130. Participant observation notes, 10.10.07.
131. *Ibid.*
132. *Ibid.*
133. Kenney, Michael, 2008. *op. cit.*
134. *Ibid.*
135. Kenney, Michael, 2007. *op. cit.*
136. *Ibid.*, p. 4.
137. *Ibid.*
138. Police officer PD: interview 7.9.07.
139. *Ibid.*
140. *Ibid.*
141. *Ibid.*
142. Participant observation notes, 19.11.06.
143. http://www.muslimsinbritain.org/index.html accessed 2.2.09
144. See for example Gove, Michael, 2006. *op. cit*; Phillips, Melanie, 2006. *op. cit*; Desai, M., 2007. *op. cit*; Cox, C., and Marks, J., 2006. *op. cit.*
145. Dal Babu, 2007, 'Muslim Police Officers and Counter-terrorism', *Police Review*, October.
146. Police officer interviewee and participant PE: interview 29.11.06.
147. *Ibid.*
148. *Ibid.*
149. Police officer interviewee and participant PF: interview 7.12.06.
150. *Ibid.*
151. *Ibid.*
152. Police officer PH: interview 29.8.07.
153. *Ibid.*
154. *Ibid.*
155. Great Britain. Home Office. 2006. *Covert Human Intelligence Sources: Code of Practice*. London: HMSO.
156. Participant observation notes, 6.6.07.

157. Participant observation notes, 12.1.07.

158. Interviews and participant observation notes.

159. Participant observation notes, vol. 2.

160. Sheikh Qabani is a regular visitor to the UK where he is paraded as a pivotal figure in tackling extremism by the Sufi Muslim Council.

161. Lia, Brynjar, 2007. *op. cit.*

162. Coll, Steve, 2004. *Ghost Wars: The Secret History of the CIA, Afghanistan, and Bin Laden, from the Soviet Invasion to September 10, 2001.* London: Penguin; see also Reeve, Simon, 1999. *The New Jackals: Ramzi Yousef, Osama bin Laden and the future of terrorism.* London: Andre Deutsch.

163. Reeve, Simon, 1999. *op. cit.*

164. *Ibid.*

165. Police officer PJ: interview 19.3.07.

166. *Ibid.*

4. ABU HAMZA IN CONTROL

1. The Finsbury Park Mosque was officially known as the North London Central Mosque until January 2011 when the trustees registered the name by which it has always been known—Finsbury Park Mosque.

2. *Ibid.*

3. *Ibid.*

4. *Ibid.*

5. *Ibid.*

6. Police officer PZA: interview 16.4.07.

7. Community interviewee CZD: interview 9.5.07.

8. *Ibid.*

9. Police officer PY: interview, 13.4.07.

10. Community interviewee CZJ: interview 9.9.06.

11. *Ibid.*

12. Community interviewee CZJ: interview 9.9.06.

13. *Ibid.*

14. *Ibid.*

15. Community interviewee CZE: interview 20.12.06.

16. Police officer PW: interview 23.2.07.

17. Islington Police Borough Commander, 2004–2006.

18. Police officer PW: interview 23.2.07.

19. Police officer PZF: interview 9.10.06.

20. Community interviewee CZE: interview 23.10.06.

21. *Ibid.*

22. Husain, Ed, 2007. *op. cit.*

23. *Ibid.*

24. Community interviewee CZE: interview 23.10.06.

25. Husain, Ed, 2007. *op. cit.*
26. Community interviewee CZE: interview 23.10.06.
27. *Ibid.*
28. O'Neil, Sean and McGrory, Daniel, 2006. *op. cit.*
29. Abu Hamza talk: tape transcript.
30. *Ibid.*
31. *Ibid.*
32. *Ibid.*
33. *Ibid.*
34. BBC News, 2005. *op. cit.*
35. Silke, Andrew, 2003. *op. cit.*
36. Kohlmann, Evan F., 2004. *op. cit.*
37. Abu Hamza talk: tape transcript.
38. *Ibid.*
39. 7/7 bomber.
40. Abu Hamza talk: tape transcript.
41. Community interviewee CZE: interview 23.10.06.
42. Abu Hamza talk: tape transcript.
43. *Ibid.*
44. Abu Hamza talk: tape transcript.
45. Poole, Elizabeth, 2006. 'The Effects of September 11 and the War in Iraq on British Newspaper Coverage', in Poole, Elizabeth and John E. Richardson, eds., *Muslims and the News Media*. London: I.B. Taurus, pp. 96–97.
46. Community interviewee CZE: interview 20.12.06.
47. Poole, Elizabeth, 2006. *op. cit.*
48. *Ibid.*
49. Community interviewee CZE: interview 20.12.06.
50. *Ibid.*
51. Interview 17.9.06.
52. Police officers PA and PE in discussion: participant observation notes 13.12.06.
53. Community interviewee CZE: interview 20.12.06.
54. *Ibid.*
55. Police officers PA and PE in discussion: participant observation notes 13.12.06.
56. Police officers PA and PB in discussion: participant observation notes 5.9.06.
57. *Ibid.*
58. Community interviewee CZJ: interview 9.9.06.
59. *Ibid.*
60. *Ibid.*
61. *Ibid.*
62. Police officers PA and PE in discussion: participant observation notes 13.12.06.

63. Community interviewee CZJ: interview 9.9.06.
64. Police officers PA and PE in discussion: participant observation notes 13.12.06; community interviewee CZJ: interview 9.9.06.
65. *Ibid.*
66. *Ibid.*
67. *Ibid.*
68. Community interviewee CM: interview 4.9.06.
69. Lambert, Robert and Jonathan Githens-Mazer, 2010. *op. cit.*
70. Transcript record.
71. Transcript record.
72. Interview, 7.2.07.
73. Interview, 6.9.06.
74. Community interviewees CZM, CZN and CL: interviews 19.2.07; 22.2.07 and 30.8.07; police officers PA and PE in discussion: participant observation notes 13.12.06.
75. *Ibid.*
76. *Ibid.*
77. *Ibid.*
78. *Ibid.*
79. *Ibid.*
80. *Ibid.*
81. *Ibid.*
82. Malung tv, http://malung-tv-news.blogspot.com/2004/06/barry-boss.html accessed 2.10.09.
83. Malung tv, http://malung-tv-news.blogspot.com/2004/06/barry-boss.html accessed 2.10.09.
84. Malung tv, http://malung-tv-news.blogspot.com/2004/06/barry-boss.html accessed 2.10.09.
85. *Ibid.*
86. Boycott, Owen, 2008. 'Mohammed Hamid and his followers', *Guardian*. 26 February. http://www.guardian.co.uk/uk/2008/feb/26/uksecurity.july7 accessed 20.1.10.
87. Tilly, Charles, 2004. *op. cit.*
88. Police officer PD: interview, 11.12.06.
89. Community interviewee CM: interview 4.9.06; police officers PA and PE in discussion: participant observation notes 13.12.06; police officer PD: interview, 11.12.06.
90. *Ibid.*
91. *Ibid.*
92. *Ibid.*
93. Police officers PA and PE in discussion: participant observation notes 13.12.06.
94. Community interviewee CM: interview 4.9.06; police officers PA and PE in discussion: participant observation notes 13.12.06; police officer PD: interview, 11.12.06.

95. *Ibid.*
96. *Ibid.*
97. Police officers PA and PE in discussion: participant observation notes 13.12.06; police officer PD: interview, 11.12.06.
98. *Ibid.*
99. *Ibid.*
100. Tilly, Charles, 2004. *op. cit.*
101. *Ibid.*
102. Community interviewee CZJ: interview 9.9.06; police officers PA and PE in discussion: participant observation notes 13.12.06; police officer PD: interview, 11.12.06.
103. *Ibid.*
104. *Ibid.*
105. *Ibid.*
106. Police officers PA and PE in discussion: participant observation notes 13.12.06; police officer PD: interview, 11.12.06.
107. *Ibid.*
108. *Ibid.*
109. Community interviewees CZM, CZN and CL: interviews 19.2.07; 22.2.07 and 30.8.07.
110. *Ibid.*
111. *Ibid.*
112. *Ibid.*
113. *Ibid.*
114. Kenney, 2007 and 2008. *op. cit.*
115. See for example Innes, Martin, 2006. *op. cit.*
116. *Ibid.*
117. Police officers PA and PE in discussion: participant observation notes 13.12.06; police officer PD: interview, 11.12.06.
118. Tilly, Charles, 2000. *op. cit.*
119. Police interviewee PN: interview, 6.3.08.
120. Community interviewees CZM, CZN and CL: interviews 19.2.07, 22.2.07 and 30.8.07; police officers PA and PE in discussion: participant observation notes 13.12.06; police officer PD: interview, 11.12.06.
121. *Ibid.*
122. *Ibid.*
123. *Ibid.*
124. Community interviewees CZM, CZN, and CL: interviews 19.2.07; 22.2.07 and 30.8.07.

5. FINSBURY PARK ISLAMISTS

1. Community interviewee CN: interview 4.4.07.
2. *Ibid.*

3. 'Khatib' describes a 'person who preaches the Friday sermon (khutbah) at a mosque'—Esposito, John L. ed., 2003. *op. cit.*
4. See for example O'Neil, Sean and McGrory, Daniel, 2006. *The Suicide Factory: Abu Hamza and the Finsbury Park Mosque* London: Harper.
5. Police interviewee PD: interview 7.9.07.
6. Community interviewees CJ, CK and CL: interviews 19.2.07, 22.2.07 and 30.8.07.
7. *Ibid.*
8. Secret police.
9. Community interviewee CJ: interview 19.2.07.
10. Community interviewees CJ, CK and CL: interviews 19.2.07, 22.2.07 and 30.8.07.
11. Phillips, Melanie, 2006. *op. cit.*
12. Community interviewee CS: interview 4.9.06.
13. Community interviewee CU: interview, 10.3.07.
14. Community interviewee CV: interview, 15.4.07.
15. *Ibid.*
16. *Ibid.*
17. *Ibid.*
18. Community interviewee CS: interview 4.9.06.
19. Community interviewee CU: interview 10.3.07.
20. Community interviewee CJ: interview 19.2.07.
21. *Ibid.*
22. Police officer PY: interview, 13.4.07.
23. Participant observation notes, 7.8.07.
24. *Ibid.*
25. *Ibid.*
26. Jeremy Corbyn MP website http://www.jeremycorbyn.co.uk/ accessed 23.4.09.
27. Community interviewees CJ, CK and CL: interviews 19.2.07; 22.2.07 and 30.8.07.
28. *Ibid.*
29. *Ibid.*
30. Palestine Solidarity website http://www.palestinecampaign.org/ accessed 24.4.09.
31. *Ibid.*
32. *Ibid.*
33. Murray, Andrew and German, Lindsey, 2005. *Stop the War*. London: Bookmarks.
34. Community interviewees CJ, CK and CL: interviews 19.2.07, 22.2.07 and 30.8.07.
35. *Ibid.*
36. Hosken, Andrew, 2008. *Ken: The Ups and Downs of Ken Livingstone*. London: Arcadia. pp. 369–382.

37. Godson, Dean, 2006. *op. cit.*
38. Community interviewees CJ, CK and CL: interviews 19.2.07, 22.2.07 and 30.8.07.
39. BBC News online, 2009. 'Tories condemn "terror" comment. 16 August', http://news.bbc.co.uk/1/hi/uk/8204159.stm accessed 20.8.09.
40. *Ibid.*
41. *Ibid.*
42. Hizb ut Tahrir website, 2009. 'British Foreign Secretary "Glorifies Terrorism" In Radio Interview', 16 August. http://www.hizb.org.uk/hizb/press-centre/press-release/british-foreign-secretary-glorifies-terrorism-in-radio-interview.html accessed 20.8.09.
43. *Ibid.*
44. Community interviewees CJ, CK and CL: interviews 19.2.07, 22.2.07 and 30.8.07.
45. *Ibid.*
46. *Ibid.*
47. *Ibid.*
48. Tamimi, Azzam, 2001. *Rachid Ghannouchi: a Democrat within Islam.* Oxford: Oxford University Press.
49. Institute for Islamic Political Thought (IIPT) website. http://www.ii-pt.com/ accessed 22.4.08.
50. Community interviewees CJ, CK and CL: interviews 19.2.07, 22.2.07 and 30.8.07.
51. Tamimi, Azzam, 2001. *op. cit*, p. 173.
52. Runnymede Trust, 1999. *op. cit.*
53. Githens-Mazer, Jonathan, 2007. *op. cit.*
54. *Ibid.*
55. *Ibid.*
56. Vidino, Lorenzo, 2006. *op. cit*; Phillips, Melanie, 2006 *op. cit.*; Gove, Michael, 2006. *op. cit.*
57. Participant observation notes, 10.11.06.
58. Phillips, Richard, 2008. 'Standing together: the Muslim Association of Britain and the anti-war movement', *Race & Class.* 50 (2) pp. 101–113.
59. Community interviewees CJ, CK and CL: interviews 19.2.07, 22.2.07 and 30.8.07.
60. Nahdi, Fuad, 2003. 'Young, British, and Ready to Fight: New laws and the war have pushed our Islamic radicals underground', *Guardian.* 1 April. http://www.guardian.co.uk/world/2003/apr/01/religion.uk accessed 4.8.09.
61. *Ibid.*
62. *Ibid.*
63. Community interviewees CJ, CK and CL: interviews 19.2.07, 22.2.07 and 30.8.07.
64. *Ibid.*

65. Community interviewee CZE: interview 23.10.06.
66. *Ibid.*
67. Community interviewee CZF: interview 19.2.07.
68. Police officer PY: interview, 13.4.07.
69. Community interviewee CZF: interview 19.2.07.
70. Community interviewee CZF: interview 19.2.07.
71. Community interviewee CZE: interview 23.10.06.
72. Abu Hamza talk: tape transcript.
73. Participant observation notes, 13.4.07, 19.4.07 and 7.8.07.
74. *Ibid.*
75. *Ibid.*
76. Police officer PY: interview, 13.4.07; police officer PZA: interview 15.4.07; participant observation notes, 7.8.07.
77. Police officer PC: participant observations notes, 20.11.06.
78. *Ibid.*
79. Police officer PE: interview 15.1.07.
80. Community interviewee CG: interview 17.8.07.
81. *Ibid.*
82. Police officer PE: interview 15.1.07; community interviewee CG: interview 17.8.07.
83. Police officer PE: interview 15.1.07; community interviewee CG: interview 17.8.07.
84. Community interviewee CG: interview 17.8.07.
85. Police officers PA, PB, PD and PG in discussion: participant observation notes, 12.3.07.
86. *Ibid.*
87. *Ibid.*
88. *Ibid.*
89. *Ibid.*
90. *Ibid.*
91. *Ibid.*
92. *Ibid.*
93. Flyvbjerg, Bent, 2006. *op. cit*; Kenney, Michael, 2007 and 2008. *op. cit*; Hamm, Mark, 2005. *op. cit.*
94. Police officers PA, PB, PD and PG in discussion: participant observation notes, 12.3.07.
95. *Ibid.*
96. *Ibid.*
97. *Ibid.*
98. *Ibid.*
99. *Ibid.*
100. Police officers PA, PB, PD and PG in discussion: participant observation notes, 12.3.07.
101. Community interviewee CP: interview 17.8.07.

102. *Ibid.*
103. *Ibid.*
104. Police officers PA, PB, PD and PG in discussion: participant observation notes, 12.3.07.
105. Pipes, Daniel, 2003. *op. cit*; Benard, Cheryl, 2003. *op. cit.* See also Flanagan, Shawn Teresa, 2006. 'Charity as Resistance: Connections between Charity, Contentious Politics, and Terror', *Studies in Conflict & Terrorism.* 29, pp. 641–655; Burr, J. Millard and Collins, Robert O., 2006. *Alms for Jihad: Charity and Terrorism in the Islamic World* Cambridge: Cambridge University Press; Levitt, Matthew 2004. 'Hamas from Cradle to Grave', *Middle East Quarterly.* 11 (1), pp. 1–12.
106. McCulloch, Jude and Pickering, Sharon, 2005. 'Suppressing the Financing of Terrorism', *British Journal of Criminology.* 45, pp. 470–486.
107. *Ibid.*
108. *Ibid*; citing Ayers, A., 2002. 'The Financial Action Task Force: The War on Terrorism Will not be Fought on the Battlefield', *New York School Journal of Human Rights.* 18, p. 458, pp. 449–59.
109. Ehrenfeld, R, 2003. *Funding Evil: How Terrorism is Financed and How to Stop It.* Chicago: Bonus Books, p. 16.
110. McCulloch, Jude and Pickering, Sharon, 2005. *op. cit.*
111. See glossary
112. Police officer PC: interview 3.6.07.
113. *Ibid.*
114. *Ibid.*
115. *Ibid.*
116. Police officers PA, PB, PC, PD, PG, PL in discussion: participant observation notes, 17.6.07.
117. *Ibid.*
118. *Ibid.*
119. *Ibid.*
120. *Ibid.*
121. Charity Commission website, 2009. Charity Commission publishes Interpal inquiry report. Press release, 27 February. http://www.charity-commission.gov.uk/news/printerpal.asp accessed 7.8.09.
122. *Ibid.*
123. US Treasury Department, 2003. Press release, 22 August. http://www.treas.gov/press/releases/js672.htm accessed 3.9.09.
124. Casciano, Dominic, 2005. 'Top Jewish group "terror" apology', *BBC News Online*, 29 December. http://news.bbc.co.uk/1/hi/uk/4564784.stm accessed 3.8.09.
125. See for example Ware, John, 2009. 'Panorama's Faith, Hate and Charity: standing by the allegations', *Guardian Organ Grinder blog.* http://www.guardian.co.uk/media/organgrinder/2009/mar/03/panorama-stands-by-charity-allegations accessed 3.8.09.

126. Police officers PA, PB, PC, PD, PG, PL in discussion: participant observation notes, 17.6.07.
127. *Ibid.*
128. Flanagan, 2006. *op. cit.*, p. 644.
129. *Ibid.*, p. 645.
130. *Ibid.*
131. Levitt, Matthew 2004. *op. cit*; Flanagan, Shawn Teresa, 2006; Burr, J. Millard and Collins, Robert O., 2006. *op. cit.*
132. Flanagan, Shawn Teresa, 2006. *op. cit*, p. 644.
133. BBC TV Panorama 2006. 'Faith, hate and charity. An investigation by John Ware', http://news.bbc.co.uk/1/hi/programmes/panorama/5209466.stm accessed 8.2.09.
134. MCB 2005. Interview with Fadi Itani, 24 January. See http://www.mcb.org.uk/features/features.php?ann_id=727 accessed 3.5.09.
135. Police officer PE: participant observation notes, 17.1.07.
136. Levitt, Matthew 2004. *op. cit*; Flanagan, Shawn Teresa, 2006; Burr, J. Millard and Collins, Robert O., 2006. *op. cit*; BBC TV Panorama 2006. *op. cit.*
137. Benthall, Jonathan and Bellion-Jourdan, Jérôme, 2009. *The Charitable Crescent: Politics of Aid in the Muslim World.* 2nd ed. London: I.B.Taurus.
138. Saggar, Shamit, 2006. The One Per Cent World: Managing the Myth of Muslim Religious Extremism. *The University of Sussex Lecture*, 16 March; see also Saggar, Shamit, 2009. *op. cit.*
139. Police officers PA, PB, PC, PD, PG, PL in discussion: participant observation notes, 17.6.07.

6. RECLAIMING THE MOSQUE

1. O'Neill, Sean and McGrory, Daniel, 2006. *The Suicide Factory: Abu Hamza and the Finsbury Park Mosque.* London: Harper Perennial, p. 255.
2. O'Neill, Sean and McGrory, Daniel, 2006. *op. cit.* pp. 254–263.
3. Carrell, Severin and Raymond Whitaker, 2005. 'Ricin: the plot that never was', *Independent on Sunday*, 17 April.
4. *Ibid.*
5. Oborne, Peter, 2006. *The Use and Abuse of Terror: The Construction of a False Narrative on the Domestic Terror Threat.* London: Centre for Policy Studies, p. 21.
6. Oborne, Peter, 2006. *op. cit*, p. 21.
7. Oborne, Peter, 2006. *op. cit*, p. 21.
8. Interview, 13.3.07
9. Oborne, Peter, 2006. *op. cit*, p. 24.
10. Oborne, Peter, 2006. *op. cit*, p. 24.
11. Clarke, Peter, 2007. *Learning from Experience.* Colin Cramphorn Memorial Lecture. London: Policy Exchange, p. 20.

12. *Ibid.* pp. 20–21.
13. *Ibid.*, p. 21.
14. *Ibid.*, p. 21.
15. Police officer PZF: interview, 24.3.07.
16. *Ibid.*
17. Community interviewees CZM, CZN and CL: interviews 19.2.07, 22.2.07 and 30.8.07; police officers PA and PE in discussion: participant observation notes 13.12.06; police officer PD: interview, 11.12.06.
18. *Ibid.*
19. Police officers PA and PE in discussion: participant observation notes 13.12.06.
20. *Ibid.*
21. *Ibid.*
22. *Ibid.*
23. Police officers PA and PE in discussion: participant observation notes 13.12.06; community interviewees CZM, CZN and CL: interviews 19.2.07, 22.2.07 and 30.8.07.
24. *Ibid.*
25. Community interviewees CZM, CZN and CL: interviews 19.2.07, 22.2.07 and 30.8.07.
26. *Ibid.*
27. Police officers PA and PE in discussion: participant observation notes 13.12.06.
28. *Ibid.*
29. *Ibid.*
30. *Ibid.*
31. Police officers PA and PE in discussion: participant observation notes 13.12.06; police officer PD: interview, 11.12.06.
32. *Ibid.*
33. *Ibid.*
34. *Ibid.*
35. Community interviewee CZG: interview 7.2.07.
36. Police officer PZC: interview 17.3.07.
37. Corbyn, Jeremy, 2005. 'Jeremy Corbyn report, February', http://www.epolitix.com/Resources/epolitix/MPWebsites/Images/i-l/Jeremy%20Corbyn%20FEBReport.pdf accessed 3.10.08.
38. Fielding, Nick and Abul Tahir, 2005. 'Hamas link to London Mosque', *Times online.* 13 February. http://www.timesonline.co.uk/tol/news/uk/article513868.ece accessed 21.10.07.
39. *Ibid.*
40. Corbyn, Jeremy, 2005. *op. cit.*
41. Police officers PA and PE in discussion: participant observation notes 13.12.06; police officer PD: interview, 11.12.06; participant observation notes, 30.6.07.

42. *Ibid.*
43. *Ibid.*
44. *Ibid.*
45. GLA 2005. Ken Livingstone, Mayor of London, press release. 25 August.
46. *Ibid.*
47. Mayor of London, 2005. *Why the Mayor of London will maintain dialogues with all of London's faiths and communities: a reply to the dossier against the Mayor's meeting with Dr. Yusuf al-Qaradawi.* London: Greater London Authority.
48. Mayor of London, 2005. *op. cit.*
49. Winnett, Robert and Leppard, David, 2005. 'Young Muslims and Extremism', *Times Online.* 10 July. http://www.timesonline.co.uk/tol/news/uk/article542420.ece accessed 3.6.09.
50. BBC News online, 2005. 'Full text of Blair speech on terror', 5 August. http://news.bbc.co.uk/1/hi/uk/4689363.stm accessed 9.2.09.
51. Participation observation notes, 30.11.06.
52. *Ibid.*
53. Participant observation notes, 18.10.07.
54. Community interviewee CZE: interview 4.5.07.

7. CORRECTING ERRONEOUS BELIEF

1. Feltham Young Offenders Institute in the London Borough of Hounslow.
2. Convicted al-Qaeda terrorist Abdul Raheem (otherwise Richard Reid) converted to Islam while in Feltham Young Offenders Institute where he was imprisoned for street robbery in the early 1990s.
3. Community interviewee CJ was imprisoned in Feltham Young Offenders Institute in 1999–2000.
4. Abdullah el Faisal was sentenced to imprisonment in 2003 for incitement to murder at the Central Criminal Court in London; in 2007 he was deported to Jamaica and at the time of submitting this thesis in September 2009 he was reported to be resident in South Africa from where he communicated with his UK supporters from his website.
5. Abdul Haqq Baker's talk at jummah prayer at Brixton Mosque most Fridays 1994–2001; occasional Fridays 2002–2007.
6. Community interviewees and participants CA, CB, CC, CD, CE, CF, CG, CH, CZA; interviews 11.10.06; 17.10.06; 8.11.06; 2.12.06; 16.12.06; 23.02.07; 26.2.07; 3.3.07; 19.5.07; 21.5.07; 25.5.07; participant observation notes 15.10.06 and 5.7.07.
7. Community interviewee CJ: interview 5.10.06.
8. For a typical 'top-down' view of the significance to al-Qaeda of the Bosnian experience, see Kohlmann, Evan F., 2004. *op. cit.*
9. Esposito, John L., 2003. ed. *op. cit.*
10. Kepel, Giles, 2003. *op. cit*, p. 31.

11. Esposito, John, ed., *op. cit*, p. 278.

12. Esposito, John, ed., *op. cit*, p. 172.

13. Community interviewee and participant CC: interview 17.2.07.

14. Police officer PB: interview 4.6.07.

15. Police officer PG: interview 4.6.07.

16. Police officer PC: interview 4.6.07.

17. See for example Carter, Ashton B., 2001. *op. cit*; Cronin, Audrey Kurth, 2002. *op. cit*; Heyman, Phillip B., 2001. *op. cit*.

18. See for example Silke, Andrew, 2004. *op. cit*; Horgan, John, 2005. *op. cit*.

19. Police officer PB: interview 4.6.07.

20. *Ibid.*

21. Hamm, Mark S., 2002. *op. cit*.

22. According to community and police interviewees some of the most violent streets are on council estates.

23. Community interviewees and participants CA, CB, CC, CD, CE, CF, CG, CH, CZA; interviews 11.10.06; 17.10.06; 8.11.06; 2.12.06; 16.12.06; 23.02.07; 26.2.07; 3.3.07; 19.5.07; 21.5.07; 25.5.07; participant observation notes 15.10.06 and 5.7.07.

24. Kenney, Michael, 2007 and 2008. *op. cit*.

25. Community interviewee CG: interview 29.4.08.

26. The Muslim Boys came to police and public attention in 2005. See for example BBC News online, 2005. '"Muslim" gangs target vulnerable', 12 August. http://news.bbc.co.uk/1/hi/england/london/4145198.stm accessed 12.8.09.

27. Community interviewees and participants CA, CB and CC: interviews 23.2.07, 26.2.07; 3.3.07; community interviewee CG: interview 29.4.08.

28. Community interviewee CY: interview 19.9.07.

29. Community interviewee CG: interview 29.4.08.

30. BBC News Online, 2008. 'Top Extremist Recruiter Is Jailed', 26 February. http://news.bbc.co.uk/1/hi/uk/7256859.stm accessed 3.1.09

31. Community interviewee CG: interview 29.4.08.

32. *The Sun*, 2008. 'Osama bin London', 27 February. http://www.thesun.co.uk/sol/homepage/news/article851255.ece accessed 12.12.08

33. *The Times*, 2007. 'BBC took terrorists paintballing', 5 December. http://www.timesonline.co.uk/tol/news/uk/crime/article3001102.ece accessed 12.12.08

34. Community interviewee CG: interview 29.4.08.

35. BBC News Online, 2008. *op. cit*.

36. Community interviewee CG: interview 29.4.08.

37. *Ibid.*

38. BBC News Online, 2008. *op. cit*.

39. Community interviewee CG: interview 29.4.08.

40. *Ibid.*

41. *Ibid.*

42. *Ibid.*
43. *Ibid.*
44. Community interviewee CW: interview 8.5.08.
45. Sageman, Marc, 2004. *op. cit*, p. 69.
46. Participant observation notes 8.11.06.
47. *Ibid.*
48. Horgan, John, 2005. *op. cit.*
49. Naqshbandi, Mehmood, 2006. *op. cit.*
50. Baker, Abdul Haqq, 2009. *op. cit.*
51. Community interviewees and participants CA, CB and CC: interviews 23.2.07, 26.2.07, 3.3.07.
52. *Ibid.*
53. *Ibid.*
54. *Ibid.*
55. *Ibid.*
56. Police officers PA, PB, PC and PG: interviews 5.5.07 and 6.5.07.
57. Community interviewees and participants CA, CB and CC: interviews 23.2.07, 26.2.07, 3.3.07.
58. *Ibid.*
59. Metropolitan Police Authority, 2005. 'Ascent 2000 citizenship centre-request for funding', http://www.mpa.gov.uk/access/committees/cop/2003/030519/05.htm accessed 2.12.08.
60. Police officers PA, PB, PC and PG: interviews 5.5.07 and 6.5.07.
61. Community interviewees and participants CA, CB and CC: interviews 23.2.07, 26.2.07, 3.3.07.
62. Interview with Sheikh Kamaludin (community interviewee CZA) 8.1.08.
63. *Ibid.*
64. *Ibid.*
65. Community interviewees and participants CA, CB and CC: interviews 23.2.07, 26.2.07, 3.3.07.
66. *Ibid.*
67. Participant observation notes, 7.9.07.
68. *Ibid.*
69. Cassius Clay became world heavyweight boxing champion in 1964 when he defeated Sonny Liston. Immediately afterwards he joined the Nation of Islam and changed his name to Mohammed Ali.
70. Participant observation notes, 7.9.07.
71. Community interviewees and participants CA, CB and CC: interviews 23.2.07; 26.2.07; 3.3.07.
72. Community interviewees and participants CA, CB, CC, CD, CE, CF, CG, CH, CZA; interviews 11.10.06; 17.10.06; 8.11.06; 2.12.06; 16.12.06; 23.02.07; 26.2.07; 3.3.07; 19.5.07; 21.5.07; 25.5.07; participant observation notes 15.10.06 and 5.7.07.
73. *Ibid.*

74. *Ibid.*
75. Community interviewee CH, interview 16.8.07.
76. Community interviewees and participants CA, CB and CC: interviews 23.2.07; 26.2.07; 3.3.07.
77. *Ibid.*
78. Scarman, Lord, 1981. *op. cit.*
79. Community interviewees and participants CA, CB and CC: interviews 23.2.07; 26.2.07; 3.3.07.
80. *Ibid.*
81. Howe, Darcus, 2000. 'Why Brixton is a place of pilgrimage for 'black diamonds', *Independent Online*, 20 January. http://www.independent.co.uk/news/uk/this-britain/why-brixton-is-a-place-of-pilgrimage-for-black-diamonds-727745.html accessed 4.7.09.
82. Community interviewees and participants CA, CB and CC: interviews 23.2.07; 26.2.07; 3.3.07.
83. Police officers PA, PB, PG: participant observation notes 20.1.07.
84. Community interviewees and participants CA, CB and CC: interviews 23.2.07; 26.2.07; 3.3.07.
85. Wiktorowicz, Quintan. *op. cit*, p. 209.
86. Community interviewees and participants CA, CB and CC: interviews 23.2.07; 26.2.07; 3.3.07.
87. See the Masjid Ibnu Taymeeyah website at http://www.masjidit.co.uk/index.php accessed 25.2.09.
88. Community interviewees and participants CA, CB and CC: interviews 23.2.07; 26.2.07; 3.3.07.
89. Kepel, Giles, *op. cit*, p. 205.
90. Michot, Yahya, 2006. *op. cit.*
91. *Ibid.*, p. 1.
92. *Ibid.*
93. Participant observation notes, 17.10.06.
94. National Commission on Terrorist attacks Upon the United States, 2003. *op. cit.*
95. Community interviewees and participants CA, CB, CC, CD, CE, CF, CG, CH, CZA; interviews 11.10.06; 17.10.06; 8.11.06; 2.12.06; 16.12.06; 23.02.07; 26.2.07; 3.3.07; 19.5.07; 21.5.07; 25.5.07; participant observation notes 15.10.06 and 5.7.07.
96. Community interviewees and participants CA, CB and CC: interviews 23.2.07; 26.2.07; 3.3.07.
97. *Ibid.*
98. Wiktorowicz, Quintan, 2006. *op. cit*; Hegghammer, Thomas, 2004. *op. cit.*
99. Participant observation notes, 10.1.07.
100. Wiktorowicz, Quintan. *op. cit.* pp. 217–228.
101. Community interviewees and participants CA, CB, CC, CD, CE, CF, CG, CH, CZA; interviews 11.10.06; 17.10.06; 8.11.06; 2.12.06; 16.12.06;

23.02.07; 26.2.07; 3.3.07; 19.5.07; 21.5.07; 25.5.07; participant observation notes 15.10.06 and 5.7.07.

102. *Ibid.*
103. *Ibid.*
104. *Ibid.*
105. *Ibid.*
106. *Ibid.*
107. Community interviewee CA: interview 30.2.07.
108. Wiktorowicz, Quintan. *op. cit*, p. 207.
109. Community interviewees and participants CA, CB and CC: interviews 23.2.07; 26.2.07; 3.3.07.
110. Hill, Christopher, 1991. *The World Turned Upside Down: Radical Ideas During the English Revolution*. London: Penguin, p. 35.
111. Police officers PB, PG: participant observation notes 25.9.06.

8. CHALLENGING TERRORISTS

1. Participant observation notes, 23.8.07.
2. Kohlmann, Evan, 2004. *op. cit.*
3. Transcript. Abu Hamza cassette tape 'Dealing with Israel', p. 5.
4. Community interviewees and participants CA, CB, CC, CD, CE, CF, CG, CH, CZA; interviews 11.10.06; 17.10.06; 8.11.06; 2.12.06; 16.12.06; 23.02.07; 26.2.07; 3.3.07; 19.5.07; 21.5.07; 25.5.07; participant observation notes 15.10.06 and 5.7.07.
5. *Ibid.*
6. *Ibid.*
7. *Ibid.*
8. Faisal's talk 'The Devil's Deception of the Saudi Salafees' understood to have been recorded in London in 1994.
9. Community interviewees and participants CA, CB, CC: interviews 26.2.07; 3.3.07.
10. *Ibid.*
11. *Ibid.*
12. *Ibid.*
13. *Ibid.*
14. *Ibid.*
15. *Ibid.*
16. Police officer PC: interview 28.5.07.
17. *Ibid.*
18. *Ibid.*
19. At the time of writing in July 2010 Abu Hamza was serving a term of imprisonment in the UK for incitement to murder while simultaneously awaiting extradition to the USA to face terrorism charges there; Abdullah el Faisal having completed a term of imprisonment for incitement to mur-

der in the UK was deported to Jamaica in 2007; and Abu Qatada remained in preventative detention in the UK without having faced trial.

20. See also, Lambert, Robert, 2008. *op. cit.*

21. Police officer PC: interview 28.5.07.

22. Flyvbjerg, Bent, 2006. *op. cit*; Kenney, Michael, 2007 and 2008. *op. cit*; Hamm, Mark, 2005. *op. cit.*

23. Community interviewees and participants CA, CB, CC: interviews 26.2.07; 3.3.07.

24. *Ibid.*

25. *Ibid.*

26. Transcript of Abu Hamza talk.

27. Community interviewees and participants CA, CB, CC: interviews 26.2.07; 3.3.07.

28. Police officer PC: interview 28.5.07; community interviewee CT: interview 23.5.07.

29. Community interviewees and participants CA, CB, CC: interviews 26.2.07; 3.3.07.

30. *Ibid.*

31. Interview, 6.6.07

32. Salafimanhaj.com, 2006.

33. Espositi, John, ed. 2003. op cit.

34. Salafimanhaj.com, 2006.

35. Salafimanhaj.com, 2006.

36. Abu Hamza talk: tape transcript.

37. Community interviewee CA: interview 12.12.06.

38. Police officers PA, PB, PC and PG: participant observation notes, 6.2.07.

39. On 30 January 2003 Abdul Raheem otherwise Richard Reid was sentenced to life imprisonment in the USA for attempting to blow up a transatlantic passenger jet en route from Paris to Miami.

40. On 4 May 2006 Zacarias Moussaoui was sentenced to life imprisonment in the USA as a conspirator in the 9/11 terrorist attacks.

41. *Ibid.*

42. Community interviewee CA: interview 12.12.06.

43. *Ibid.*

44. *Ibid.*

45. *Ibid.*

46. Community interviewee CB: interview 17.9.06.

47. Researcher's question.

48. Community interviewee CB: interview 17.9.06.

49. Researcher's question.

50. Community interviewee CB: interview 17.9.06.

51. Researcher's question.

52. Community interviewee CB: interview 17.9.06.

53. Researcher's question.

54. Community interviewee CB: interview 17.9.06.
55. Community interviewee CA: interview 12.12.06.
56. *Ibid.*
57. Police officers PA, PB, PC and PG: participant observation notes, 6.2.07.
58. *Ibid.*
59. *Ibid.*
60. *Ibid.*
61. *Ibid.*
62. Balloch, S. and Taylor, M. eds, 2001. *op. cit*; Spalek, Basia and Lambert, Robert, 2008. *op. cit*; Chakraborti, Neil & Garland, Jon, 2004. *op. cit.*
63. Community interviewee CB: interview 17.9.06.
64. Police officers PA, PB, PC and PG: participant observation notes, 6.2.07.
65. Community interviewee CB: interview 17.9.06.
66. Community interviewee CA: interview 12.12.06.
67. Researcher's question.
68. Community interviewee CA: interview 12.12.06.
69. Police officers PA, PB, PC and PG: participant observation notes, 6.2.07.
70. *Ibid.*
71. *Ibid.*
72. Community interviewee CA: interview 12.12.06.
73. *Ibid.*
74. Community interviewee CB: interview 17.9.06.
75. *Ibid.*
76. *Ibid.*
77. *Ibid.*
78. *Ibid.*
79. *Ibid.*
80. Clutterbuck, Lindsay, Greg Hannah and Jennifer Rubin, 2008. 'Radicalization or Rehabilitation: Understanding the challenge of extremist and radicalized prisoners', Cambridge: Rand Europe http://www.rand.org/pubs/technical_reports/2008/RAND_TR571.pdf accessed 12.4.08.
81. See for instance, Clutterbuck, Lindsay, 2006. *op. cit.*
82. Cage Prisoners http://www.cageprisoners.com/index.php accessed 5.7.09
83. Helping Households under Great Stress http://www.hhugs.org.uk/ accessed 3.2.09.
84. Clutterbuck, Lindsay, Greg Hannah and Jennifer Rubin, 2006. *op. cit.*
85. Police officers PA, PB, PC and PG: participant observation notes, 6.2.07.
86. Benard, Cheryl, 2003 and 2005. *op. cit.*
87. Police officers PA, PB, PC and PG: participant observation notes, 6.2.07.
88. Salafimanhaj.com, 2006. The Devil's Deception of Abdullaah Faysal. http://www.salafimanhaj.com/ebook.php?ebook=45 accessed 26.5.09.
89. Community interviewee CA: interview 30.2.07.
90. Community interviewee CB: interview 1.4.07.
91. Community interviewee CA: interview 30.2.07.

92. Police officers PB, PG: participant observation notes 16.5.07.
93. *Ibid.*
94. *Ibid.*
95. Community interviewees CD, CE, CF: interviews 29.1.07; 30.1.07.
96. Community interviewee CE: interview 30.1.07.
97. Police officers PB, PG: participant observation notes 16.5.07; community interviewees and participants CA, CB, CC, CD, CE, CF, CG, CH, CZA; interviews 11.10.06; 17.10.06; 8.11.06; 2.12.06; 16.12.06; 23.02.07; 26.2.07; 3.3.07; 19.5.07; 21.5.07; 25.5.07; participant observation notes 15.10.06 and 5.7.07.
98. *Ibid.*
99. Community interviewee CE: interview 30.1.07.
100. Police officers PB, PG: participant observation notes 16.5.07.
101. *Ibid.*
102. Community interviewee CE: interview 30.1.07.
103. *Ibid.*
104. Willesden is in the London Borough of Brent—see Table 1.
105. Edmonton is in the London Borough of Enfield—see Table 1.
106. Community interviewee CE: interview 30.1.07.
107. Participant observation notes, 16.1.07.
108. Police officers PB, PG: participant observation notes 16.5.07.
109. *Ibid.*
110. Community interviewees and participants CA, CB, CC, CD, CE, CF, CG, CH, CZA; interviews 11.10.06; 17.10.06; 8.11.06; 2.12.06; 16.12.06; 23.02.07; 26.2.07; 3.3.07; 19.5.07; 21.5.07; 25.5.07; participant observation notes 15.10.06 and 5.7.07.
111. Police officers PB, PG: participant observation notes 16.5.07.
112. Community interviewee CE: interview 30.1.07.
113. Police officers PB, PG: participant observation notes 16.5.07.
114. *Ibid.*
115. Police officers PB, PG: participant observation notes 16.5.07.
116. Community interviewee CF: interview 14.1.07; police officers PB, PG: participant observation notes 16.5.07.
117. *Ibid.*
118. *Ibid.*
119. *Ibid.*
120. Abu Hamza talk: tape transcript.
121. Community interviewee CF: interview 14.1.07; police officers PB, PG: participant observation notes 16.5.07.
122. *Ibid.*
123. *Ibid.*
124. *Ibid.*
125. Abu Hamza talk: tape transcript.
126. *Ibid.*

127. Community interviewee CF: interview 14.1.07; police officers PB, PG: participant observation notes 16.5.07.
128. *Ibid.*
129. *Ibid.*
130. Abu Hamza talk: tape transcript.
131. *Ibid.*
132. Community interviewees and participants CA, CB, CC, CD, CE, CF, CG, CH, CZA; interviews 11.10.06; 17.10.06; 8.11.06; 2.12.06; 16.12.06; 23.02.07; 26.2.07; 3.3.07; 19.5.07; 21.5.07; 25.5.07; participant observation notes 15.10.06 and 5.7.07.

9. AL-QAEDA RECRUITS

1. Community interviewee CA: interview 30.2.07.
2. BBC Radio, Today Programme, interview of Abdul Haqq Baker, 20 April 2006 Radio 4 (7.40am). http://www.bbc.co.uk/radio4/today/listenagain/listenagain_20060420.shtml accessed 22.2.09.
3. Moussaoui, Abd Samad (with Florence Bouquillat), trans. Simon Pleasance & Fronza Woods, 2003. *Zacarias Moussaoui: The Making of a Terrorist.* London: Serpent's Tail.
4. Participant observation notes, 3.10.07.
5. *Ibid.*
6. *Ibid.*
7. *Ibid.*
8. Flyvbjerg, Bent, 2006. *op. cit*; Kenney, Michael, 2007 and 2008. *op. cit*; Hamm, Mark, 2005. *op. cit.*
9. Community interviewee CA: interview 30.2.07.
10. *Ibid.*
11. *Ibid.*
12. *Ibid.*
13. BBC News Online, 2005. Interview Peter Clarke, 28 February. http://news.bbc.co.uk/1/hi/england/gloucestershire/4304223.stm accessed 3.10.08.
14. *Ibid.*
15. Community interviewee CA: interview 30.2.07.
16. BBC News Online, 2001. Richard Reid case. 28 December. http://news.bbc.co.uk/1/hi/uk/1731568.stm accessed 12.1.09.
17. *Ibid.*
18. *Ibid.*
19. *Ibid.*
20. *Ibid.*
21. Community interviewee CA: interview 30.2.07.
22. Dodd, Vikram, 2006. Interview with Peter Herbert. *Guardian online*, 26 August. http://www.guardian.co.uk/world/2006/aug/24/alqaeda.terrorism accessed 23.5.08

23. Community interviewee CB: interview 17.9.06.

24. *Ibid.*

25. *Ibid.*

26. *Ibid.*

27. Dodd, Vikram, 2006. *op. cit.*

28. Community interviewee CB: interview 17.9.06.

29. *Ibid.*

30. *Ibid.*

31. *Ibid.*

32. Participant observation notes, 8.3.07.

33. Participant observation notes, 3.11.07.

34. *Ibid.*

35. Participant observation notes, 8.3.07.

36. *Ibid.*

37. Desai, Meghdad, 2007. *op. cit.*

38. MCU interviewee, 1.2.08.

39. Interview, 1.10.07.

40. Interview, 2.4.07.

41. Lambeth Council website. 2005. 25 July. http://www.lambeth.gov.uk/News/NewsArchive/2005/250705CommunityLeaders.htm accessed 2.1.09

42. Police officers PA, PB, PC, PG: participant observation notes 16.5.07.

43. Community interviewee CF: interview 27.2.07.

44. Police officer PG: interview 5.5.07.

45. Police officers PA, PB, PC, PG: participant observation notes 16.5.07.

46. Press Complaints Commission, 2005. http://www.pcc.org.uk/news/index.html?article=NDc1Mg accessed 2.10.08.

47. Community interviewee CA: interview 30.2.07.

48. 'Sufism—Islamic mysticism, often referred to as the internalization and intensification of Islamic faith and practice. Sufis strive to constantly be aware of God's presence, stressing contemplation over action, spiritual development over legalism, and cultivation of the soul over social interaction' Esposito, John, ed., 2003. *op. cit.*

49. Murad, Abdal-Hakim, 2001. *op. cit.*

50. *Ibid.*

51. 9/11

52. Murad, Abdal-Hakim, 2001. *op. cit.*

53. Runnymede Trust, 1997. *Islamophobia: A Challenge For Us All*. London: Runnymede Trust.

54. Police officers PA, PB, PC, PG: participant observation notes 16.5.07.

55. Community interviewees and participants CA, CB, CC: interviews 26.2.07; 3.3.07.

56. Dispatches, 2007. *Undercover Mosque* Channel 4, UK, first broadcast 15 January. http://www.hardcashproductions.com/recent29.html accessed 27.1.08

57. Community interviewees and participants CA, CB, CC: interviews 26.2.07; 3.3.07.
58. Community interviewee CC: 3.3.07.
59. Community interviewee CZB: interview 7.9.06.
60. *Ibid.*
61. Community interviewee CC: 3.3.07.
62. Police officers PA, PB, PC, PG: participant observation notes 16.5.07.
63. Police officers PA, PB, PC, PG: participant observation notes 16.5.07.
64. *Ibid.*
65. Participant observation notes, 8.3.07.
66. Participant observation notes, 8.3.07.
67. *Ibid.*
68. *Ibid.*
69. Silber, Mitchell D and Arvin Bhatt, 2007. Senior Intelligence Analysts—NYPD Intelligence Division Radicalisation in the West—The Homegrown Threat. http://www.nyc.gov/html/nypd/pdf/dcpi/NYPD_Report-Radicalization_in_the_West.pdf
70. Bruce Hoffman, et al.
71. Research notes, vol. 1.
72. Research notes, vol. 1.
73. Salafimanhaj.com, 2006.
74. Salafimanhaj.com, 2006.
75. Interview, 5.10.06
76. [This is the footnote to the Salafimanhaj publication] The current Muftee of KSA.
77. [This is the footnote to the Salafimanhaj publication] One of the senior contemporary *hadeeth* scholars of Madeenah, he authored a book entitled *Bi Ayyi'Aql wa Deen yakunu at-Tafkeer wa't-Tadmeer, Jihad?* [According to Which Intellect and Religion is Bombing and Wreaking Havoc Considered Jihaad!?]—translated into English by Abu Eesa Yasir Gilani (London: Daarul-Itisaam Publishing, 2004).
78. [This is the footnote to the Salafimanhaj publication] Another senior contemporary scholar of *hadeeth*, he is the main *Salafi* scholar to refute the ideas and writings of Sayyid Qutb.
79. [This is the footnote to the Salafimanhaj publication] A scholar from Riyadh, he has authored many books refuting the contemporary *Khawaarij* and *takfeerees*, such as the book which has been translated into English: *The Khawaarij and their Recurring Ideologies* (Texas: Tarbiyyah Bookstore Publishing, 2005). He has also been outspoken regarding the Iraq situation and opposing those *takfeerees* who call themselves 'Mujaahideen'. See: http://www.arabnews.com/?page=7&section=0&article=53890&d=3&m=11&y=2004. Also refer to these questions put to him wherein he unequivocally advises the Muslims to co-operate with the

police if they are aware of terrorists in the community: http://www.al-athariyyah.com/media/pdf/terrorism/qanda_london_bombings_1.pdf

80. [This is the footnote to the Salafimanhaj publication] Author of the 460-page refutation of the statements, beliefs and ideologies of Abu Qatada and others. He also wrote a book regarding the Algerian crisis entitled *Madarik un-Nadhr fi's-Siyasah: Bayna't-Tatbiqat ash-Shar'iyyah wa'l-Infia'lat al-Hamasiyyah* [Perceptions of Viewing Politics: Between the Divinely Legislated Application and Enthusiastic Disturbances], (KSA: Dar Sabeel il-Mumineen, 1418 AH/1997 CE, 2nd Edn).

81. [This is the footnote to the Salafimanhaj publication] An assistant professor in Saudi Arabia, he was one of the first scholars to warn in the late 1990s about the tribulation of *takfeer*, in his book *Hukm bi-Ghayri Ma Anzala Allaah: Usool ut-Takfeer* [Ruling by other than what Allaah has revealed: Principles of Takfeer]. He has also recently written a book emphasising the Islamic evidences against suicide bombing, *'Iqra' Maseerak Qabl an-Tufajjir* [Read about your end, before you blow yourself up!].

82. [This is the footnote to the Salafimanhaj publication] From Jordan he was one of the first to also warn throughout the 1990s about the tribulation of *takfeer* and is one of the main bulwarks against the *takfeeree da'wah* in the world today. Among the many classical works which he has edited he has also visited many countries conducting lectures, seminars and teaching. He has visited the USA (New York in particular), the UK (Brixton and Luton), Canada, Indonesia and is well-known in the Middle-East.

83. [This is the footnote to the Salafimanhaj publication] The current Saudi Minister of Islamic Affairs, he gives many lectures within KSA. Of his relevant lectures to this topic is *A Warning Against Extremism* which has been translated into English here: http://www.salafimanhaj.com/pdf/warning.pdf Other beneficial lectures by Shaykh Saalih Aali-Shaykh which have been translated into English include *The Fitnah of the Khawaarij*, trans. Abu Az-Zubayr S. Harrison here: http://www.authentictranslations.com/trans-pub/sas_fitnah-khawaarij.pdf

84. [This is the footnote to the Salafimanhaj publication] One of the scholars of Riyadh who has also been thorough in refuting the extremist *takfeerees*, he is known for his detailed refutation of their ideas and probably the best that he has written on this topic is his book *al-Burhan al-Muneer fi Dahd Shubuhaat Ahl it-Takfeer wa't-Tafjeer* [The Clear Proofs for Refuting the Doubts of the People of Takfeer and Bombing]—it has been translated into English here: http://www.salafimanhaj.com/pdf/SalafiManhaj_TakfeerAndBombing.pdf

85. Salafimanhaj.com, 2006. *op. cit.*

10. ANGER AND ALIENATION

1. Hain, Peter (ed.), 1979. *Policing the Police.* Vols. 1 & 2. London: John Calder. http://www.amielandmelburn.org.uk/collections/mt/index_frame.htm

2. Cohen, Phil, 1982. Bradford 12. *Marxism Today.* August. pp. 2–3. http://www.amielandmelburn.org.uk/collections/mt/index_frame.htm

3. A shortcoming immortalised in a satirical sketch on Not the Nine O'clock News (BBC TV 1981) featuring a Metropolitan Police Inspector (Rowan Atkinson) who admonishes Constable Savage (Griff Rhys Jones) for arresting a 'coloured gentleman' for possessing 'curly black hair and thick lips' having arrested the same man for similar offences on numerous previous occasions. Bitingly, Constable Savage's punishment is to be posted to the Met's elite riot squad, the Special Patrol Group, a forerunner of the controversial Territorial Support Group.

4. Stephen Grey & Ian Cobain, 2005, 'Suspect's tale of travel and torture', *Guardian*, 2 August, p. 1; the account became newsworthy again during renewed controversy over 'extraordinary rendition' by the USA in December 2005.

5. Grey & Cobain, p. 1.

6. Grey & Cobain, p. 1.

7. Transcript, author's copy.

8. Transcript, author's copy.

9. The CAMPACC conference, *Suspect Communities: The Real War on Terror*, was held at the London Metropolitan University on 21 May, 2005.

10. Detained Guantanamo Bay 2001–4 described in Begg, Moazzam, 2006. *Enemy Combatant: A British Muslim's Journey to Guantanamo and Back.* London: Free Press.

11. Detained Guantanamo Bay 2001–4.

12. See for example, CAMPACC conference, 21 May 2005; Institute of Race Relations. *Racism, Liberty and the War on Terror* conference, 16 September 2006.

13. CAMPACC, 2005. 'Embedded Experts in the "War on Terror"', London: CAMPACC, p. 4.

14. The phrase was coined by Rachel Briggs and first used in a business partnership context, see Briggs, Rachel, 2005. *The Unlikely Counter-Terrorists.* London: Foreign Policy Centre.

15. Hillyard, Paddy, 1993. *Suspect Community: People's Experience of the Prevention of Terrorism Acts in Britain.* London: Pluto Press.

16. Abu Hamza transcript.

17. CAMPACC, 2005, p. 4.

18. Interview, 5.1.07.

19. Six interviews and participant observation notes, vols. 1 and 2.

20. Phillips, Melanie, 2006. *op. cit*; Gove, Michael, 2006. *op. cit.*

21. The terms have been coined by Michael Kenney. See Kenney, Michael, 2007. *From Pablo to Osama: Trafficking and Terrorist Networks, Government Bureaucracies, and Competitive Adaptation*. Pennsylvania: Pennsylvania State University Press, p. 5.
22. *op. cit*, p. 5.
23. See for example, Ignatieff, Michael, 2004. *The Lesser Evil: Political Ethics in an Age of Terror*. Princeton: Princeton University Press.
24. German, Mike, 2007. *Thinking Like a Terrorist: Insights of a Former FBI Undercover Agent*. Washington DC: Potomac Books, p. 121.
25. BBC report, Mohammed Siddique Khan, October 2006.
26. National Commission On Terrorism Attacks Upon The United States, 2004. *The 9/11 Commission Report: Authorised Edition*. London: W.W. Norton & Company. pp. 215–254.
27. Kenny, *op. cit*., p. 5.
28. Kenny, *op. cit*., chapters 2,3 and 4.
29. Rai, Milan, 2006. *op. cit;* see also Ahmed, Nafeez Mosaddeq, 2006. *op. cit*; Oborne, Peter, 2006. *op. cit*.
30. Prime Minister's statement, Friday, 5 August, 2005. See also Neuman, Peter, 2006. *What precisely constitutes a moderate Muslim?* http://www.madrid11.net/node/114 accessed 2.1.08.
31. http://www.number10.gov.uk/output/Page9948.asp accessed 2.8.09.
32. Bergen, Peter, 2002. *op. cit*, p. 242.
33. Police officers PB, PC and PE, interviews 8.5.07.
34. *Ibid*.
35. Jackson, Richard, 2005. *op. cit*, p. 4.
36. Police officers PB, PC and PE, interviews 8.5.07.
37. *Ibid*; see also Jackson, Richard, 2005. *op. cit*, p. 183.
38. Police officer interviewees and participants PA, PB, PC, PD and PE: participant observation notes 25.9.06.
39. *Ibid*.
40. *Ibid*.
41. *Ibid*.
42. *Ibid*; Innes, Martin, 2006. *op. cit*.
43. *Ibid*.
44. Police officer interviewee and participant PB: participant observation notes 25.6.07.
45. Innes, Martin, 2006. *op. cit*, p. 16.
46. *op. cit*, p. 10.
47. *op. cit*, p. 10.
48. Hillyard, Paddy, 1993. *op. cit*.
49. *op. cit*.
50. Silke, Andrew, 2003. 'Retaliating Against Terrorism', in Andrew Silke, ed. *Terrorists, Victims and Society: Psychological Perspectives on Terrorism and its Consequences*. Chichester: Wiley, p. 230.

51. Innes, Martin, 2006. *op. cit.*

52. Participant observation and interviews with Muslim Safety Forum (MSF) members, 2006–7.

53. MSF meeting minutes, 2002–2007.

54. Police officer interviewees and participants PA, PB, PC; participant observation notes 1.5.07.

55. Police officer PB: participant observation notes 1.5.07.

56. Police officer PA: participant observation notes 1.5.07.

57. Police officer PB: participant observation notes 1.5.07.

58. Police officer PA: participant observation notes 1.5.07.

59. Police officer PA: participant observation notes 1.5.07.

60. Police officer PB: participant observation notes 1.5.07.

61. Police officer PC: participant observation notes 1.5.07.

62. Versi, Ahmed, 2002. 'British Muslims complain of harassment by Security Services', *Muslim News*. 24 August. http://www.muslimnews.co.uk/index/press.php?pr=152 accessed 11.12.08.

63. *Ibid.*

64. *Ibid.*

65. Police officers PA, PB, PC: participant observation notes 1.5.07.

66. *Ibid.*

67. *Ibid.*

68. *Ibid.*

69. *Ibid.*

70. *Ibid.*

71. *Ibid.*

72. *Ibid.*

73. According to the Metropolitan Police Authority website, *Stop The Guns*, 'Trident is an anti-gun crime operation that was set up in 1998 to help bring an end to a spate of shootings and murders among young, black Londoners' http://www.stoptheguns.org/whatistrident/index.php accessed 2.4.09

74. Lee Jasper, Mayor of London's advisor on race and diversity issues during research study, 2002–2007.

75. Police officer PF: interview 7.12.06.

76. Police officer interviewees and participants PA, PB, PC, PD and PE: participant observation notes 25.9.06 and 3.5.08.

77. *Ibid.*

78. *Ibid.*

79. Police officer PK: interview, 23.12.06.

80. Community interviewee CA: interview 9.4.07.

81. *Ibid.*

82. *Ibid.*

83. O'Callaghan, Sean, 1999. *The Informer*. London: Corgi Books.

84. See disclaimer.

85. Police officers PA, PB, PC, PD and PE: participant observation notes 25.9.06 and 3.5.08.
86. *Ibid.*
87. BBC News Online, 2006. *Terrorists bid to infiltrate MI5.* 3 July. http://news.bbc.co.uk/1/hi/uk/5142908.stm accessed 10.10.08.
88. Police officer PD: interview 30.11.06.
89. Bunyan, Tony, 1977. *op. cit.*
90. Clutterbuck, Lindsay, 2006. *op. cit.*
91. Police officers PA, PB, PC, PD and PE: participant observation notes 25.9.06 and 3.5.08.
92. *Ibid.*
93. *Ibid.*
94. Police officer PP: interview 10.2.07.
95. *Ibid.*
96. *Ibid.*
97. *Ibid.*
98. *Ibid.*
99. Bunyan, Tony, 1977. *op. cit.*
100. Police officer PB: participant observation notes 25.6.07.
101. Great Britain, Home Office, 2006. *op. cit.*
102. Police officer PB: participant observation notes 25.6.07.
103. Jackson, Richard, 2005. *op. cit*; Croft, Stuart, 2006.
104. Community interviewee CQ: interview 1.5.07.
105. *Ibid.*
106. *Ibid.*
107. *Ibid.*
108. Police officer PD: interview 5.9.08.
109. BBC News online, 2006. *Call to Muslims over police help.* 7 June. http://news.bbc.co.uk/1/hi/uk/5054600.stm accessed 13.11.08.
110. Community interviewee CW: interview 26.1.07.
111. Community interviewee CX: interview 22.9.06.
112. Jackson, Richard, 2005. *op. cit*; Croft, Stuart, 2006. *op. cit.*
113. *Ibid.*
114. Police officer PD: interview 7.9.07.
115. *Ibid.*
116. Community interviewees CA, CB and CC: interviews 2.2.07; 4.2.07; and police officer interviewees and participants PA, PB, PC, PD and PE: participant observation notes 25.9.06 and 3.5.08.
117. *Ibid.*
118. Innes, Martin, 2006. *op. cit.*
119. Community interviewees CA, CB and CC: interviews 2.2.07; 4.2.07; and police officer interviewees and participants PA, PB, PC, PD and PE: participant observation notes 25.9.06 and 3.5.08.
120. *Ibid.*

121. Home Office, 2006. *op. cit.*
122. *Ibid.*
123. Community interviewee CK: interview 14.3.07.

11. EXPERIENCE, EXPERTISE AND CIVIC DUTY

1. Police officers PC, PE, PF: participant observation notes, 23.5.07.
2. Police officer PH: interview 29.8.07.
3. Police officer PO: interview 27.8.07.
4. Police officer PD: interview 7.9.07.
5. See for example Godson, Dean, 2006a. 'Already Hooked on Poison', *The Times*, 8 February. http://www.timesonline.co.uk/article/0,,1072–2029 734,00.html accessed 2.8.09; Phillips, Melanie, 2008. 'Lunacy at the Yard', *The Spectator*, 15 December. http://www.spectator.co.uk/melanie-phillips/3088576/lunacy-at-the-yard.thtml accessed 4.8.09.
6. Godson, Dean, 2006a. *op. cit.*
7. See for example Godson, Dean, 2007b. 'Introduction to Peter Clarke's Colin Cramphorn Lecture', *Policy Exchange*. http://www.policyexchange. org.uk/images/libimages/260.pdf accessed 12.12.08.
8. *Ibid.*
9. *Ibid.*
10. Godson, Dean, 2007a. 'The Old Bill Should Choose its Friends Carefully: What on Earth are West Midlands Police up to?', *The Times*, August 23. http://www.timesonline.co.uk/tol/comment/.../guest.../article2310437.ece accessed 8.7.09.
11. Great Britain, Home Office, 2006. *op. cit.*
12. BBC News Online, 2006. *Kidnap Envoy meeting Iraqi Sunnis.* http://news. bbc.co.uk/1/hi/uk/4494456.stm accessed 12.11.08.
13. Claire Fox was a leading member of the Revolutionary Communist Party in the 1980s and 1990s before becoming director of the Institute of Ideas in 2000. http://www.spinprofiles.org/index.php/Claire_Fox. accessed 4.8.09.
14. Majid Nawaz was a leading member of Hizb ut Tahrir before becoming a co-director of the Quilliam Foundation. http://www.spinprofiles.org/index. php/Quilliam_Foundation accessed 4.8.09.
15. Kleinig, John, 1996. *The Ethics of Policing.* Cambridge: Cambridge University Press, p. 55.
16. *Ibid.*
17. Godson, Dean, 2007a. *op. cit.*
18. See for example Godson, Dean, 2007b. *op. cit.*
19. Beckett, Andy, 2008. 'What can they be thinking?', *Guardian online*, 26 September. http://www.guardian.co.uk/politics/2008/sep/26/thinktanks. conservatives accessed 12.12.08.

20. Godson, Dean, 2006b. 'The feeble helping the unspeakable', *Times online*, 5 April. http://www.timesonline.co.uk/tol/comment/columnists/guest_contributors/article702053.ece accessed 5.6.09.
21. Kundnani, Aron, 2008. 'Islamism and the Roots of Liberal Rage', *Race & Class*. 50 (2), pp. 40–68; see also Kundnani, Arun, 2007. *The End of Tolerance: Racism in 21ˢᵗ Century*. London: Pluto.
22. Griffin, Tom, 2008. Conrad Black's favourite Commissar. *Spinwatch*, 15 May. http://www.spinwatch.org.uk/-articles-by-category-mainmenu-8/49-propaganda/4908-dean-godson-conrad-blacks-favourite-commissar accessed 12.12.08
23. Maher, Shiraz and Martin Frampton, 2009. *Choosing our friends wisely: Criteria for engagement with Muslim groups*. London: Policy Exchange. http://www.policyexchange.org.uk/publications/publication.cgi?id=108 accessed 20.3.09.
24. Beckett, Andy, 2008. *op. cit.*
25. *Ibid.* pp. 52–3.
26. *Ibid.*, p. 53.
27. Kepel, Gilles, 2005, 'Radical secularism', *The Independent opinion page*, 22 August, p. 12; Kepel, Gilles, 2004. *The War for Muslim Minds: Islam and the West*. London: Harvard University Press; Phillips, Melanie, 2006. *Londonistan: How Britain Is Creating a Terror State Within*. London: Gibson Square; Gove, Michael, 2006. *Celsius 7/7*. London: Weidenfield & Nicholson.
28. Spalek, Basia, Salwa el Awa and Laura McDonald, 2008. *op. cit.*
29. Kelly, Ruth, 2006a. DCLG Secretary. *op. cit*; see also Kelly, Ruth, 2006b. *op. cit*; Kelly, Ruth, 2006c. *op. cit.*
30. Briggs, Rachel, Fieschi, Catherine and Lownsbrough, Hannah, 2006. *Bringing it Home: Community-based approaches to counter-terrorism*. London: Demos.
31. Kelly, Ruth, 2006a. *op. cit.*
32. *Ibid.*
33. *Ibid.*
34. Blears, Hazel, 2008. DCLG Secretary. Speech at Policy Exchange. 17 July. http://www.policyexchange.org.uk/Events.aspx?id=688 accessed 12.10.08.
35. *Ibid.*
36. Kelly, Ruth, 2006a. *op. cit*; see also Kelly, Ruth, 2006b. *op. cit.*
37. Police officers PB, PC and PE, interviews 8.5.07.
38. Kelly, Ruth, 2006c. *op. cit.*
39. Police officers PB, PC and PE, interviews 8.5.07.
40. Quilliam Foundation http://www.quilliamfoundation.org/ accessed 11.10.08
41. *Ibid.*
42. *Ibid.*
43. *Ibid.*

44. Moore, Charles, 2008. 'How To Beat the Scargills of Islam', *The 2008 Keith Joseph Memorial Lecture*. Centre for Policy Studies, 10 March. http://www.policyexchange.org.uk/images/libimages/362.pdf accessed 2.12.08.

45. *Ibid.*

46. *Ibid.*

47. MacEoin, Dennis, 2007. *The Hijacking of British Islam*. London: Policy Exchange. http://www.policyexchange.org.uk/images/libimages/307.pdf accessed 4.1.09.

48. *Ibid.*

49. *Ibid.*

50. *Times online*, 2007. 'Policy Exchange apology to Dr. Mohammad Abdul Bari', 17 December. http://www.timesonline.co.uk/tol/news/uk/article3059 836.ece accessed 23.8.09.

51. Smyth, Marie and Jeroen Gunning, 2007. 'The abuse of research', *Guardian* comment, 13 February. http://www.guardian.co.uk/politics/2007/feb/13/thinktanks.uksecurity accessed 3.6.09.; Kundnani, Aron, 2008. *op. cit*; Clegg, Nick, 2008. 'Clegg attacks think-tank's "underhand" briefing on "Unity" festival', http://www.politicshome.com/Landing.aspx?Blog=4060&perma=link# accessed 4.8.09.

52. Kenney, Michael, 2008, *op. cit*, p. 145; see also Tashakkori, Abbas, and Teddlie, Charles, 2007. *op. cit.*

53. Flyvbjerg, Bent, 2006, *op. cit*; Kenney, Michael, 2007 and 2008, *op. cit*; Hamm, Mark, 2005. *op. cit.*

54. See for example Spalek, Basia, Salwa el Awa and Laura McDonald, 2008. *op. cit.*

55. Breen-Smyth, Marie, 2009. *op. cit*; Smyth, Marie, 2005. *op. cit.*

56. Maher, Shiraz and Martin Frampton, 2009. *op. cit.*

57. See for example Meijer, Roel, 2009. *Towards a Political Islam*. Clingendael Diplomacy Papers No. 22. Netherlands Institute of International Relations, The Hague.

58. Silke, Andrew, 2004. *op. cit.*

59. Saggar, Shamit, 2009. *Pariah Politics: Understanding Western Radical Islamism and What Should be Done*. Oxford: Oxford University Press.

60. Glees, Anthony, and Pope, Chris, 2005. *op. cit.*

61. *Ibid.*

62. Community interviewee CV: interview 3.3.07.

63. *Ibid.*

64. *Ibid.*

65. E-mail from Marc Sageman to researcher, 19.8.09.

66. Participant observation notes, 19.8.07.

67. Tilly, Charles, 2004. *op. cit.*

68. Malik, Shiv and Butt, Hassan, 2008. *Leaving al-Qaeda*. London: Constable. In July 2009 Amazon.com wrongly showed the book as having been

published by Constable in May 2008. On the same website Constable provide this synopsis of the book: '*Leaving Al-Qaeda* charts Hassan Butt's early life and Jihadi career as it leads up to the dark secret at the heart of this compelling book—a full account of terrorist activities that were undertaken in Pakistan. Along with this account of Butt's life, his motivations, evolving beliefs, regrets, guilt, and his later re-establishment of moral purpose, this modern story of repentance re-examines the nature of identity in Western society, the state of multiculturalism in Britain and the inner-workings of the international terror network'. http://www.amazon.co.uk/Leaving-Al-Qaeda-Hassan Butt/dp/1845297237/ref=sr_1_1?ie=UTF8&s=books&qid=1252584868&sr=1–1 accessed 3.7.09.

69. Dodd, Vikram, 2009. 'Al-Qaeda fantasist tells court: I'm a professional liar. Manchester man admits to tricking media into believing he was a jihadi'. *Guardian*. 9 February.
70. Malik, Shiv, 2007. 'My brother the bomber', *Prospect*. 30 June. http://www.prospectmagazine.co.uk/2007/06/mybrotherthebomber/ accessed 2.5.09.
71. BBC News online, 2009. *op. cit.*
72. *Ibid.*
73. Dodd, Vikram, 2009. *op. cit.*
74. Cohen, Nick, 2008. 'Scandal of the persecuted peacemakers', *Observer*, 23 March. http://www.guardian.co.uk/commentisfree/2008/mar/23/islam.uksecurity accessed 6.8.09.
75. See for example Pipes, Daniel, 2005. 'Does a "Covenant of Security" Protect the United Kingdom?', Daniel Pipes.org. http://www.danielpipes.org/blog/2004/08/does-a-covenant-of-security-protect-the accessed 6.8.09.
76. Dodd, Vikram, 2009. *op. cit.*
77. Tilly, Charles, 2004. *op. cit*; Tarrow, Sidney, 1998. *op. cit.*
78. Participant observation notes, 11.11.06.
79. *Ibid.*
80. E-mail from Marc Sageman to researcher, 19.8.09.
81. Lia, Brynjar, 2007. *op. cit.*
82. Seaton, Matt, 1995. 'Charge of the New Red Brigade', *Independent on Sunday*, January. Reproduced at http://libcom.org/library/red-action-ira-london-bombs-independent accessed 2.7.09.
83. Hann, Dave and Tilzey, Steve, 2003. *No Retreat: The Secret War Between Britain's Anti-Fascists and the Far Right*. Lytham, Lancs: Milo Books.
84. Ignatieff, Michael, 2004. *op. cit.*
85. Kenney, Michael, 2007. *op. cit.*
86. Sageman, Marc, 2004 and 2008. *op. cit.*
87. Kenney, Michael, 2007. *op. cit.*
88. Spalek, Basia, El-Awa, Salwa, and McDonald, Liza Z., 2008. *op cit*; Briggs, Rachel, Fieschi, Catherine and Lownsbrough, Hannah, 2006. *op. cit*; Blick, Andrew, Choudhury, Tufyal and Weir, Stuart, 2006. *op. cit.*
89. *Ibid.*

90. Lambert, Robert, 2008. *op. cit.*

91. Participant observation notes, 6.5.07.

92. *Ibid.*

93. Kenney, Michael, 2007 and 2008. *op. cit.*

94. See the introduction to the following article for an account of the first diminution of MPSB responsibilities in 1992, Clutterbuck, Lindsay, 2006. *op. cit.*

95. Police officer PD: interview 8.9.07.

96. *Ibid.*

97. Ahmed, Zaheer, 2008. 'Million miles from reality', *Jane's Police Review*, 21 March.

98. Gargini. Richard, 2008. 'ACPO reply', *Jane's Police Review*, 21 March.

99. Police officer PD: interview 8.9.07.

100. *Ibid.*

101. Flyvbjerg, Bent, 2006. *op. cit*; Scheuer, Michael ('"Anonymous"'), 2003 and 2004. *op. cit.*; German, Mike, 2007. *op. cit.*

102. Participant observation notes, 7.1.07.

103. Cohen, David, 2009. 'Andy Hayman: I deeply regret not challenging Ian Blair on de Menezes', *Evening Standard*, 26 June. http://www.thisislondon.co.uk/standard/article-23711377-details/Andy+Hayman:+I+deeply+regret+not+challenging+Ian+Blair+on+de+Menezes/article.do accessed 27.7.09.

104. *Ibid.*

105. Katz, Ian, 2008. Sir Ian's Siege: a footnote. *Guardian*. 1 December. http://www.guardian.co.uk/uk/2008/dec/01/ian-blair-police-met-balcombe accessed 3.8.09.

106. *Ibid.*

107. Cohen, David, 2009. *op. cit.*

108. *Ibid.*

109. *Ibid.*

110. Cohen, David, 2009. *op. cit.*

111. *Ibid.*

112. Veness, David, 2002. *op. cit*, p. 55.

113. Participant observation notes, 25.4.07.

114. Veness, David, 2002. *op. cit*, p. 55.

115. *Ibid.*

116. *Ibid.*

117. Participant observation notes, 25.4.07.

118. *Ibid.*

119. *Ibid.*

120. *Ibid.*

121. Gargini. Richard, 2008. *op. cit.*

122. *Ibid.*

123. Innes, Martin, 2006. *op. cit.*

124. *Ibid.*
125. Blair, Ian, 2005. 'Richard Dimbleby Lecture', 15 November. MPS website. http://cms.met.police.uk/met/layout/set/print/content/view/full/2682 accessed 3.7.09.
126. *Ibid.*
127. *Ibid.*
129. *Ibid.*
129. Participant observation notes, 25.4.07.
130. *Ibid.*
131. *Ibid.*
132. *Ibid.*
133. Winnett, Robert and Leppard, David, 2004. 'Britain's secret plans to win Muslim hearts and minds', *Times Online*, 30 May. http://www.timesonline.co.uk/tol/news/uk/article436135.ece accessed 2.8.09.
134. *Ibid.*
135. *Ibid.*
136. *Ibid.*
137. *Ibid.*
138. *Ibid.*
139. *Ibid.*
140. *Ibid.*
141. *Ibid.*
142. *Ibid.*
143. *Ibid.*
144. *Ibid.*
145. Participant observation notes, 9.10.06.
146. Winnett, Robert and Leppard, David, 2004. *op. cit.*
147. *Ibid.*
148. Participant observation notes, 9.10.06.
149. *Ibid.*
150. Kundnani, Aron, 2008. *op. cit.*
151. Winnett, Robert and Leppard, David, 2004. *op. cit.*
152. Bright, Martin, 2006. *op. cit.*
153. Participant observation notes, 9.10.06.
154. Winnett, Robert and Leppard, David, 2004. *op. cit.*
155. Malik, Kenan, 2005. 'Multiculturalism has fanned the flames of Islamic Extremism', *The Times*, 16 July. http://www.timesonline.co.uk/article/0,,1072–1695604,00.html accessed 27.1.08.
156. Sylvester, R & Thompson, A., 2007. 'Dr. Bari—Government Stoking Muslim Tension', *Daily Telegraph*, 12 November. http://www.telegraph.co.uk/news/main.jhtml?xml=/news/2007/11/10/nbari110.xml accessed 28.4.09.
157. Police officer PB: interview 4.4.07.
158. *Ibid.*

159. *Ibid.*
160. Ignatieff, Michael. 2004. *op. cit.*
161. Hillyard, Paddy, 2005. *op. cit.*
162. Souhami, A, 2007. *op. cit.*
163. Maher, Shiraz and Martin Frampton, 2009. *op. cit.*
164. *Ibid.*
165. Kenney, Michael, 2007 and 2008. *op. cit.*
166. Flyvbjerg, B. *op. cit.*
167. *Ibid.*
168. *Ibid.*
169. *Ibid.*
170. *Ibid.*
171. *Ibid.*
172. Phillips, Melanie, 2008. *op. cit.*

12. LEGITIMACY AND EFFECTIVENESS

1. Kirby, Terry, 1993. 'Protesting police put on an overflowing show of force against Sheehy report at Wembley', *The Independent*, 21 July. http://www.independent.co.uk/news/uk/protesting-police-put-on-an-overflowing-show-of-force-against-sheehy-report-at-wembley-1486099.html accessed 3.5.09.
2. *Ibid.*
3. Police officer PZ: interview 1.6.07.
4. Kirby, Terry, 1993. *op. cit.*
5. Participant observation notes, 15.9.07.
6. *Ibid.*
7. See for example http://coppersblog.blogspot.com/ accessed 8.8.09.
8. Clutterbuck, Lindsay, 2006. *op. cit.*
9. Participant observation notes, 15.9.07.
10. Police officer PZ: interview 1.6.07.
11. *Ibid.*
12. Kirby, Terry, 1993. *op. cit.*
13. Police officer PZ: interview 1.6.07.
14. Godson, Dean, 2007b.
15. *Ibid.*
16. US Central Command (Centcom), 2009. 'Leadership profiles', http://www.centcom.mil/en/about-centcom/leadership/ accessed 18.9.09.
17. Brogan, Benedict, 2009. 'Gen David Petraeus: "Everything in Afghanistan is hard"', *Daily Telegraph blog*, 17 September http://blogs.telegraph.co.uk/news/benedictbrogan/100010385/gen-david-petraeus-everything-in-afghanistan-is-hard/ accessed 18.9.09.
18. Kirkup, James, 2009. 'General Sir David Richards: Afghans losing patience with Nato "failure"', *Daily Telegraph*, 17 September. http://www.tele-

graph.co.uk/news/newstopics/politics/6203170/General-Sir-David-Richards-Afghans-losing-patience-with-Nato-failure.html accessed 18.9.09.

19. Kilcullen, David, 2006, 2007 and 2009. *op. cit*; Nagl, John A., 2005. *op. cit.*

20. Brogan, Benedict, 2009. *op. cit.*

21. *Ibid.*

22. Kirkup, James, 2009. *op. cit.*

23. BBC Radio 5 Live news interview, 17.9.09.

24. Participant observation notes, 22.3.07.

25. *Ibid.*

26. Vidino, Lorenzo, 2009. 'Europe's New Security Dilemma', *Washington Quarterly*. October, pp. 61–75.

27. *Ibid.*

28. *Ibid.*, p. 61.

29. Pantucci, Raffaello, 2009. British Government Debates Engagement with Radical Islam in New Counterterrorism Strategy. *Terrorism Monitor*. 7 (10).

30. Vidino, Lorenzo, 2009. *op. cit.*

31. *Ibid.*

32. *Ibid.*

33. *Ibid.*

34. *Ibid.*

35. Fourest, Caroline, 2008. *Brother Tariq: The Doublespeak of Tariq Ramadan*. New York: Encounter.

36. Bouteldja, Naima, 2005. 'The source of this hysteria: portraying Muslim scholars such as Yusuf al-Qaradawi and even Tariq Ramadan as extremists is absurd—and dangerous', *Guardian—Comment is Free*, 22 July. http://www.guardian.co.uk/world/2005/jul/22/religion.july7 accessed 10.9.09.

37. Griffith-Dickson, Gwen, 2008. 'Countering Extremism and the Politics of Engagement', *Gresham College lecture*. Allen & Overy, London Docklands, 29 April. http://www.gresham.ac.uk/event.asp?PageId=108&EventId=658 accessed 2.1.09.

38. Ramadan, Tariq, 2004. *op. cit.*

39. Della Porta, Donatella and Diani, Mario, 1999. *Social Movements: an introduction*. Oxford: Blackwell.

40. Vidino, Lorenzo, 2009. *op. cit.*

41. *Ibid.*

42. Moore, Charles, 2008. *op. cit.*

43. Moore, Charles, 2008. *op. cit.*

44. Godson, Dean, 2007. 'Struggle for the soul of British Islam hots up', *Times online*, 15 February. http://www.timesonline.co.uk/tol/comment/columnists/guest_contributors/article1386951.ece accessed 6.8.09.

45. Spin Profiles, 2009. Neocon Europe. http://www.spinprofiles.org/index.php/Neocon_Europe accessed 20.9.09.

46. Phillips, Richard, 2008. *op. cit.*

47. *Ibid.*

48. Vidino, Lorenzo, 2009. *op. cit.*

49. McGhee, Derek, 2008. *The End of Multiculturalism: Terrorism, Integration and Human Rights.* Maidenhead: Open University Press, p. 64.

50. Vidino, Lorenzo, 2009. *op. cit.*

51. *Ibid.*

52. *Ibid.*

53. McCants, William, ed., 2006. *op. cit.*

54. Vidino, Lorenzo, 2009. *op. cit.*

55. Vidino, Lorenzo, 2009. *op. cit.*

56. Porter, Andrew, 2009. 'Gordon Brown support slumps to lowest since polling began', *Daily Telegraph*, 29 May. http://www.telegraph.co.uk/news/newstopics/politics/2050682/Labour-Gordon-Brown-support-slumps-to-its-lowest-since-polling-began.html accessed 19.9.09.

57. See for example Gove, Michael, 2006. *op. cit.*

58. Phillips, Melanie, 2008. *op. cit.*

59. Thomas, David and Inkson, Kerr, 2003. *op. cit.*

60. Hillyard, Paddy, 2005. *op. cit.*

61. 'Lucy Lips', 2010. 'Labour Minister celebrates with Daud Abdullah at Hamas Mosque', 15 March, *Harry's Place blog.* http://hurryupharry.org/2010/03/15/labour-minister-celebrates-with-daud-abdullah-at-hamas-mosque/ accessed 20.4.10.

62. Leppard, David, 2010. 'MP quits radical mosque over forgery', *Times online.* 28 April. http://www.timesonline.co.uk/tol/news/politics/article7078865.ece accessed 12.5.10.

63. Ibid.

64. Godson, Dean, 2006a. 'Already Hooked on Poison', *The Times.* 8 February. http://www.timesonline.co.uk/article/0,,1072–2029734,00.html accessed 2.8.08.

65. Aaronovitch, David, 2011. You don't set a thief to catch a terrorist. *The Times.* 10 February.

APPENDIX: RESEARCH METHODOLOGY

1. Flick, Uwe, 2006. *An Introduction to Qualitative Research.* 3rd ed. London: Sage.

2. Robson, Colin, 2004. *Real World Research.* 2nd ed. Massachusetts: Blackwell, p. 1.

3. *Ibid.*

4. Kenney, Michael, 2007 and 2008. *op. cit.*

5. 'Unwitting testimony' is a term first coined by cultural historian Arthur Marwick to refer to evidence that a researcher may infer from a source

(written or oral) aside from evidence that is wittingly or expressly stated. Haralambos, M., Holborn, M., 2004. *Sociology: Themes and Perspectives*. London: Collins, pp. 748–754.

6. Silverman, David, 1993. *Interpreting Qualitative Data: Methods for Analysing Talk, Text and Interaction*. London: Sage, pp 145–146.

7. Marsh, David and Furlong, Paul, 2002. 'Ontology and Epistemology in Political Science', in David Marsh and Gerry Stoker, eds, *Theory and Methods in Political Science*. Basingstoke: Palgrave Macmillan, p. 21.

8. *Ibid.*, p. 21.

9. Breen-Smyth, Marie, 2009. 'The Challenge of Researching Political Terror Critically', *Arches Quarterly*. 3 (4), p. 69; see also Breen-Smyth, Marie, Jackson, Richard and Gunning, Jeroen, 2009. 'The Core Commitments of Critical Terrorism Studies', in Breen-Smyth, Marie, Jackson, Richard and Gunning, Jeroen (eds.) *Critical Terrorism Studies*. Abingdon: Routledge.

10. *Ibid*; see also Breen-Smyth, Marie, 2005. 'Insider/outsider issues in researching violence and divided societies', in Porter, Elisabeth, Robinson, Gillian, Breen-Smyth, Marie, Schnabel, Albrecht and Osaghae, Eghosa, eds. *Researching Conflict in Africa: Insights and Experiences*. Tokyo: United Nations University Press, pp. 9–23.

11. Breen-Smyth, Marie, 2004. 'Using Participative Action Research with War Affected Populations: Lessons from research in Northern Ireland and South Africa', in Breen-Smyth, M. and Williamson, E. eds., *Researchers and their 'Subjects': Ethics, power knowledge and consent*. Bristol: Policy Press. pp 137–156.

12. Gillespie, M., 2006. 'Transnational Television Audiences after September 11', *Journal of Ethnic and Migration Studies*, 32, (6) 903–921.

13. *Ibid.*, p. 913.

14. *Ibid.*, p. 913.

15. *Ibid.*, p. 913.

16. Flick, Uwe, 2006. *op. cit.*

17. *Ibid.*

18. Balloch, S. and Taylor, M. eds, 2001. *op. cit*; Garland, J., Spalek, B. & Chakraborti, N., 2006. 'Hearing Lost Voices: Issues in Researching Hidden Minority Ethnic Communities', *British Journal of Criminology*. 46, pp. 423–437.

19. *Ibid.*

20. Punch, Maurice, 1993. 'Observation and the Police: The Research Experience', in Hammersley M, ed, *Social Research: Philosophy, Politics and Practice*. London: Sage, p. 184.

21. *Ibid.*, p. 184; see also Waddington, P.A.J., 1999. 'Police (Canteen) Sub-Culture: An Appreciation', *British Journal of Criminology*. 39(2), pp. 287–309; Tupman, W, and Tupman, A, 1999. *Policing in Europe: Uniform in Diversity*. Exeter: Intellect; Graef, Roger, 1990. *Talking Blues:The Police in their own words*. London: Fontana.

22. Baker, Abdul Haqq, 2010, forthcoming. 'Countering Terrorism in the UK: A Convert Community Perspective', PhD, University of Exeter.
23. Robson, Colin, 2004. *op. cit*, p. 109.
24. *Ibib.*
25. *Ibid.*
26. *Ibid.*
27. Godson, Dean. 2006a. *op. cit.*
28. Garland, Jon., Spalek, Basia & Chakraborti, Neil, 2006. *op. cit*; Alvesson, Mats and Sköldberg, Kaj, 2000. *Reflexive Methodology. New Vistas For Qualitative Research.* London: Sage.
29. Spalek, B and Imtoual, 2007. *op. cit.*
30. *Ibid.*
31. *Ibid.*
32. *Ibid.*
33. Alvesson, Mats and Sköldberg, Kaj, 2000. *op. cit.*
34. *Ibid.*
35. Spalek, Basia and Lambert, Robert, 2008. 'Muslim Communities, Counter-terrorism and Counter-radicalisation: a critically reflective approach to engagement', *International Journal of Law, Crime and Justice.* 36 (4), pp. 257–270.
36. Poynting, S. and Mason, V, 2006. 'Tolerance, freedom, justice and peace? Britain, Australia and anti-Muslim racism since 11th September 2001', *Journal of Intercultural Studies.* 27 (4), pp. 365–392.
37. Spalek, Basia and Lambert, Robert, 2008. *op. cit.*
38. *Ibid.*
39. Gerring, John, 2006. *Case Study Research: Principles and Practices.* New York: Cambridge University Press, p. 17.
40. *Ibid.*
41. Yin, Robert, 2003. *Case Study Research Design and Methods.* Thousand Oaks: CA: Sage, p. 13.
42. Whyte, W.F., 1993. *Street Corner Society: The Social Structure of an Italian Slum.* London: University of Chicago Press.
43. Pryce, K, 1979. *Endless Pressure.* Harmondsworth: Penguin.
44. Wacquant, Loic, 2004. *Body and Soul: notebooks of an apprentice boxer.* Oxford: Oxford University Press.
45. *Ibid.*, p. x.
46. *Ibid.*, p. x.
47. Burnham, Peter *et al*, 2004, p. 53.
48. Abercrombie, Nicholas, Hill, Stephen and Turner, Bryan, 1984. *Dictionary of Sociology.* London: Penguin, p. 34.
49. Flyvbjerg, Bent, 2006. *op. cit.*
50. *Ibid.*, p. 221.
51. *Ibid.*, p. 221.
52. *Ibid.*, p. 221.
53. Kenney, Michael, 2007 and 2008. *op. cit.*

54. Kenney, 2008. *op. cit*, p. 25.
55. Hamm, Mark S., 2005. 'After September 11: Terrorism research and the crisis in criminology', *Theoretical Criminology*. 9 (2), p. 243; see also Hamm, Mark S., 2002. *In Bad Company: America's Terrorist Underground*. Boston: Northeastern University Press; Hamm, Mark S., 2005. *Terrorism as Crime: From Oklahoma City to Al-Qaeda and Beyond* New York: New York University Press.
56. *Ibid.*, p. 242.
57. See footnote 1, Chapter 1.
58. Kenney, Michael, 2008. *op. cit*, p. 143.
59. *Ibid.*, p. 143.
60. *Ibid.*, p. 144.
61. Burnham, Peter, Gilland, Karin, Grant, Wyn and Layton-Henry, Zig, 2004. *Research Methods in Politics*. Basingstoke: Palgrave Macmillan, p. 188.
62. *Ibid.*, p. 187.
63. Scott, J, 1990. *A Matter of Record*. Cambridge: Polity.
64. *Ibid.*
65. *Ibid.*, p. 144; see also Bernard, H. Russell, 2005. *Research Methods in Anthropology*. Lanham, MD: AltaMira Press.
66. *Ibid.*
67. *Ibid.*, p. 145; see also Tashakkori, Abbas, and Teddlie, Charles, 2007. *Handbook of Mixed Methods in Social & Behavioral Research*. London: Sage.
68. *Ibid.*, p. 145.
69. *Ibid.*, p. 145.
70. *Ibid.*, p. 145.

BIBLIOGRAPHY

ABBAS, Tahir, 2004. 'After 9/11: British South Asian Muslims, Islamophobia, Multiculturalism, and the State', *American Journal of Social Sciences*. 21 (3), pp. 26–38.

ABBAS, Tahir, 2005. 'Recent Developments to British Multicultural Theory, Policy and Practice: the Case of British Muslims', *Citizenship Studies*. 9 (2), pp. 153–166.

ABDULLAH, Daud, 2002. 'September 11 as Cover for Mayhem', in *The Quest for Sanity: Reflections on September 11 and the Aftermath*. London: Muslim Council of Britain, pp. 131–136.

ACKROYD, Peter, 2001. *London: The Biography*. London: Vintage.

ALDERSON, John, 1979. *Policing Freedom*. Plymouth: Macdonald & Evans.

ALDERSON, John, 1998. *Principled Policing: Protecting the Public with Integrity*. Winchester: Waterside Press.

Al FARUQI, Ismail, 1983. 'Islam and Zionism', in John L. Esposito, ed., *Voices of Resurgent Islam*. Oxford: Oxford University Press, pp. 261–267.

ALI, Ayaan Hirsi, 2004. *The Caged Virgin*. London: The Free Press.

ALLEN, Chris, 2004. 'Justifying Islamophobia: A Post-9/11 Consideration of the European Union and British Contexts', *American Journal of Islamic Social Sciences*. 21 (3), pp. 1–25.

ALLEN, Chris, 2005. 'From Race to Religion: the New Face of Discrimination', in T. Abbas, ed. *Muslim Britain: Communities Under Pressure*. London: Zed Books, pp. 49–65.

Al-QARADAWI, Yusuf, 1991. *Islamic Awakening Between Rejection & Extremism*. London: Zain International.

Al-QARADAWI, Yusuf, 2003. *The Lawful and the Prohibited in Islam*. Trans. Kamal El-Helbawy et al. London: Al-Birr Foundation.

ALTIKRITI, Anas, 2007. 'The New Fundamentalism', *Guardian Unlimited—Comment is Free*, 2 July.

Al-TURABI, Hassan, 1983. 'The Islamic State', in John L. Esposito, ed., *Voices of Resurgent Islam*. Oxford: Oxford University Press, pp. 241–251.

AMELI, Saied R., Elahi, Manzur and Merali, Arzu, 2004. *British Muslims' Expectations of Government: Social Discrimination: Across The Muslim Divide*. London: Islamic Human Rights Commission (IHRC).

AMELI, Saied R. and Merali, Arzu, 2004. *British Muslims' Expectations of Government: Dual Citizenship: British, Islamic or Both? Obligation, Recognition, Respect and Belonging*. London: Islamic Human Rights Commission (IHRC).

ANDERSON, Benedict, 1983. *Imagined Communities: Reflections on the Origin and Spread of Nationalism*. London: Verso.

ANSARI, Farhad, 2006. *British Anti-Terrorism: A Modern Day Witch-Hunt: Updated Version*. London: Islamic Human Rights Commission (IHRC).

ANSARI, Humayan, 2004. *'The Infidel Within': Muslims In Britain since 1800*. London: Hurst.

ANSARI, Humayan, 2005. 'Attitudes to Jihad, Martyrdom and Terrorism among British Muslims', in T. Abbas, ed. *Muslim Britain: Communities Under Pressure*. London: Zed Books, pp. 144–163.

ARCHIK, Kristin, Rollins, John and Woehrel, Steven, 2005. 'Islamist Extremism in Europe', *Congressional Research Service (CRS): Report for Congress*. Library of Congress, 29 July.

AHMED, Nafeez Mosaddeq, 2006. *The London Bombings: An Independent Inquiry*. London: Duckworth.

AHMED, Zaheer, 2008. 'Million miles from reality', *Jane's Police Review*. 21 March.

ARBLASTER, Anthony, 1977. 'Terrorism, Myths, Meanings and Morals', *Political Studies*. 25(3), pp. 413–424.

Aaronovitch, David, 2011. 'You don't set a thief to catch a terrorist', *The Times*. 10 February.

BAMFORD, Bradley W. C., 2004. 'The United Kingdom's "War Against Terrorism"', *Terrorism and Political Violence*. 16 (4), pp. 737–756.

BAKER, Abdul Haqq, 2009. *Countering Terrorism in the UK: A Convert Community Perspective*. PhD. University of Exeter.

BALLOCH, S., and Taylor, M. eds., 2001. *Partnership Working: Policy and Practice* Bristol: The Policy Press.

BARAK, Gregg, 2004. 'A Reciprocal Approach to Terrorism and Terrorist Like Behaviour', in Mathieu Deflem, ed. *Terrorism and Counter-Terrorism: Criminological Perspectives*. Oxford: Elsevier, pp. 33–52.

BARAN, Zeyno, 2005. 'Fighting the War of Ideas', *Foreign Affairs*. 84 (6), pp. 68–78.

BBC News, 2001. 'Richard Reid case', 28 December. http://news.bbc.co.uk/1/hi/uk/1731568.stm accessed 12 January, 2010.

BBC News, 2001. 'Shoe bomb suspect one of many', 26 December. http://news.bbc.co.uk/1/hi/uk/1729614.stm accessed 12 August, 2008.

BBC News, 2005. 'Peter Clarke', 28 February. http://news.bbc.co.uk/1/hi/england/gloucestershire/4304223.stm accessed 12 January, 2009.

BIBLIOGRAPHY

BBC News, 2005. 'London bomber video aired on TV', 2 September. http://news.bbc.co.uk/1/hi/uk/4206708.stm accessed 23 July, 2010.

BBC News 2005. '"Muslim" gangs target vulnerable', 12 August. http://news.bbc.co.uk/1/hi/england/london/4145198.stm accessed 12 August, 2009.

BBC News, 2005. 'Blair vows hard line on fanatics', 5 August. http://news.bbc.co.uk/1/hi/uk_politics/4747573.stm accessed 29 December, 2010.

BBC News online, 2005. 'Full text of Tony Blair speech on terror', 5 August. http://news.bbc.co.uk/1/hi/uk/4689363.stm accessed 2 February, 2010.

BBC News, 2006. 'Bomber influenced by preacher', 11 May. http://news.bbc.co.uk/1/hi/uk/4762123.stm accessed 20 February, 2009.

BBC News, 2006. 'Kidnap Envoy meeting Iraqi Sunnis', http://news.bbc.co.uk/1/hi/uk/4494456.stm accessed 12 November, 2008.

BBC News, 2006. 'Terrorists bid to infiltrate MI5', 3 July. http://news.bbc.co.uk/1/hi/uk/5142908.stm accessed 10 October, 2008.

BBC News, 2006. 'Profile: Shehzad Tanweer'. 6 July', http://news.bbc.co.uk/1/hi/uk/4762313.stm accessed 29 December, 2010.

BBC News, 2006. 'Call to Muslims over police help', 7 June. http://news.bbc.co.uk/1/hi/uk/5054600.stm accessed 13 November, 2008.

BBC News, 2006. 'Reid heckled during Muslim speech', 20 September. http://news.bbc.co.uk/1/hi/5362052.stm accessed 6 January, 2011.

BBC News, 2007. 'Profile: Mohammad Sidique Khan', 30 April. http://news.bbc.co.uk/1/hi/uk/4762209.stm accessed 29 December, 2010.

BBC News, 2008. 'Top Extremist Recruiter Is Jailed', 26 February. http://news.bbc.co.uk/1/hi/uk/7256859.stm accessed 3 January, 2009.

BBC News, 2008. 'Fatal wartime crush marked', 2 March. http://news.bbc.co.uk/1/hi/england/london/7273488.stm accessed 29 December, 2010.

BBC News, 2009. 'Reaction to Bob Quick Resignation', 9 April. http://news.bbc.co.uk/1/hi/uk/7991590.stm accessed 6 August, 2009.

BBC News 2009. 'Tories condemn 'terror' comment', 16 August. http://news.bbc.co.uk/1/hi/uk/8204159.stm accessed 3 September, 2010.

BBC Radio, 2006. 'Today Programme, interview of Abdul Haqq Baker', 20 April 2006 Radio 4 (7.40am). http://www.bbc.co.uk/radio4/today/listenagain/listenagain_20060420.shtml accessed 22 February, 2008.

BBC TV Newsnight, 2007. 'Jeremy Paxman Interview with Dean Godson', 12 December. http://news.bbc.co.uk/player/nol/newsid_7140000/newsid_7142300/7142300.stm accessed 4 October, 2008.

BBC WW2 peoples archive, 2004. 'Interview with Alf Roberts, survivor of Bethnal Green underground station crush'. http://www.bbc.co.uk/ww2peopleswar/stories/11/a2964611.shtml accessed 29 December, 2010.

BECKETT, Andy, 2008. 'What can they be thinking?', *Guardian online*. 26 September. http://www.guardian.co.uk/politics/2008/sep/26/thinktanks.conservatives accessed 12 December, 2010.

BEGG, Moazzam, 2006. *Enemy Combatant: A British Muslim's Journey to Guantanamo and Back*. London: Free Press.

BEN-DOR, Gabriel and Pedahzur, Ami, 2004. 'The Uniqueness of Islamic Fundamentalism and the Fourth Wave of International Terrorism', in L. Weinberg and A. Pedahzur, eds. *Religious Fundamentalism and Political Extremism*. London: Frank Cass, 2004, pp. 71–90.

BENARD, Cheryl, 2003. *Civil Democratic Islam: Partners, Resources and Strategies*. Santa Monica: Rand.

BENARD, Cheryl, 2005. 'Democracy and Islam: The Struggle in the Islamic World—A Strategy for the United States', in David Aaron, ed., *Three Years After: Next Steps in the War on Terror*. Santa Monica: Rand pp. 15–20.

BENTHALL, Jonathan and Bellion-Jourdan, Jérôme, 2009. *The Charitable Crescent: Politics of Aid in the Muslim World*. 2nd ed. London: I.B.Taurus.

BERGEN, Peter, 2006. *The Osama bin Laden I Know*. London: Free Press

BERMAN, Paul, 2003. *Terror and Liberalism*. London: Norton.

BIRT, Yahya, 2005. 'Lobbying and Marching: British Muslims and the State', in T. Abbas, ed. *Muslim Britain: Communities Under Pressure*. London: Zed Books, 2005, pp. 92–106.

BIRT, Yahya, 2006. 'Islamic Citizenship in Britain after 7/7: Tackling Extremism and Preserving Freedoms', in Aftab Ahmad Malik, ed., *The State We Are In: Identity, Terror and the Law of Jihad*. Bristol: Amal Press, pp. 3–13.

BJORGO, Tore and Horgan, John, eds. 2008. *Leaving Terrorism Behind* London: Routledge.

BLACK, Donald, 2004. 'Terrorism as Social Control', in Mathieu Deflem, ed. *Terrorism and Counter-Terrorism: Criminological Perspectives*. Oxford: Elsevier, pp. 9–18.

BLAIR, Ian, 2005. The Dimbleby Lecture, London—transcript. http://cms.met. police.uk/news/policy_organisational_news_and_general_information/commissioner/the_richard_dimbleby_lecture_2005_by_sir_ian_blair_qpm accessed 11 September, 2010.

BLAIR, Ian, 2009. *Policing Controversy*. London: Profile.

BLAIR, Tony, UK Prime Minister, 2003. 'Statement to Parliament after visit to President Bush', 3 February. http://www.number10.gov.uk/output/Page1770. asp accessed 9 August, 2010.

BLAIR, Tony, UK Prime Minister, 2006. 'Transcript of speech on Middle East to Los Angeles World Affairs Council', 1 August.

BLAIR, Tony, 2010. *A Journey*. London: Random House.

BLEARS, Hazel, 2008. 'DCLG Secretary. Speech at Policy Exchange', 17 July. http://www.policyexchange.org.uk/Events.aspx?id=688 accessed 12 October, 2008.

BLICK, Andrew, Chouhury, Tufyal and Weir, Stuart, 2006. *The Rules of the Game: Terrorism, Community and Human Rights*. York: Joseph Rowntree Reform Trust.

BLOOM, Clive, 2010. *Violent London: 2000 years of riots, rebels and revolts*. Palgrave Macmillan.

BLOOM, Mia, 2005. *Dying to Kill: The Allure of Suicide Terror*. New York: Columbia University Press.

BOYCOTT, Owen, 2008. 'Mohammed Hamid and his followers', *Guardian*, 26 February. http://www.guardian.co.uk/uk/2008/feb/26/uksecurity.july7 accessed 20 January, 2010.

BREEN-SMYTH, Marie, 2007. *A Critical Research Agenda for the Study of Terrorism*. European Consortium for Political Research Symposium paper, p. 1.

BREEN-SMYTH, Marie and Jeroen Gunning, 2007. 'The abuse of research', *Guardian comment*, 13 February. http://www.guardian.co.uk/politics/2007/feb/13/thinktanks.uksecurity accessed 3 June, 2009.

BREEN-SMYTH, Marie, Jackson, Richard and Gunning, Jeroen, 2009. 'The Core Commitments of Critical Terrorism Studies', in Breen-Smyth, Marie, Jackson, Richard and Gunning, Jeroen (eds.) *Critical Terrorism Studies*. Abingdon: Routledge.

BRIGGS, Rachel, 2002. 'Introduction: The Unlikely Counter-Terrorists', in Rachel Briggs, ed., *The Unlikely Counter-Terrorists*. London: Foreign Policy Centre. pp. 1–8.

BRIGGS, Rachel, Feschi, Catherine and Lownsbrough, Hannah, 2006. *Bringing it Home: Community-based approaches to counter-terrorism*. London: Demos.

BRIGHT, Martin, 2006. *When Progressives Treat With Reactionaries*. London: Policy Exchange. http://www.policyexchange.org.uk/images/libimages/176.pdf accessed 3 November, 2010.

BRIGHT, Martin, 2009. 'We must lead fight against extremists', *Jewish Chronicle*. 19 November.

BRIGHT, Martin, 2010. 'Amnesty International, Moazzam Begg and the Bravery of Gita Sahgal', *Spectator*. 7 February. http://www.spectator.co.uk/martinbright/5757557/amnesty-international-moazzam-begg-and-the-bravery-of-gita-sahgal.thtml accessed 29 August, 2010.

BRODEUR, Jean-Paul, 1983. 'High Policing and Low Policing: Remarks about the Policing of Political Activities', *Social Problems*. 30 (5), pp. 507–520.

BRODEUR, Jean-Paul, 2007. 'High policing and Low Policing in post 9/11 times', *Policing: a Journal of Policy and Practice*. 1(1), pp. 25–37.

BRODEUR, Jean-Paul and Dupont, Benoit, 2006. 'Knowledge Workers or "Knowledge" Workers?', *Policing & Society*. 16 (1), pp. 7–26.

BROWN, Eric, 2005. 'After the Ramadan Affair; New Trends in Islamism in the West', *Current Trends in Islamist Ideology*, vol 2, Hudson Institute, pp. 7–29.

BUENO de MESQUITA, Ethan, 2005. 'Conciliation, Counterterrorism, and Patterns of Terrorist Violence', *International Organisation*. 59 (1), pp. 145–76.

BUENO de MESQUITA, Ethan, and Dickson, E. S., 2007. 'The Propaganda of the Deed: Terrorism, Counterterrorism, and Mobilization', *American Journal of Political Science*, 51 (2), 364–81.

BUILDING BRIDGES FOR PEACE, 2010. 'Founder's story'. http://www.buildingbridgesforpeace.org/founders_story.html accessed 29 December, 2010.

BUNYAN, Tony, 1977. *The History and Practice of the Political Police in Britain*. London: Quartet Books.

BURGAT, Francois, 2003. *Face to Face with Political Islam*. London: I.B. Taurus.

BURNETT, Jonathan, 2004. 'Community, cohesion and the state', *Race and Class*. 45(3). pp. 1–18.

BURNETT, Jonny and Whyte, Dave, 2005. 'Embedded Expertise and the New Terrorism', *Journal for Crime, Conflict and the Media*. 1 (4) pp. 1–18.

BURR, J. Millard and Collins, Robert O., 2006. *Alms for Jihad: Charity and Terrorism in the Islamic World*. Cambridge: Cambridge University Press.

BUSH, George, 2006. 'Remembering 9/11', 9 September 2006. http://www.whitehouse.gov/news/releases/2006/09/20060909.html accessed 12 August, 2010.

BUTT, Hassan, 2007. 'My Plea to Fellow Muslims: You Must Renounce Terror', *Guardian*. 1 July. http://www.guardian.co.uk/commentisfree/2007/jul/01/comment.religion1 accessed 12 January, 2011.

CAMPBELL, Alistair and Stott, Richard, 2008. *The Blair Years: extracts from the Alistair Campbell Diaries*. London: Arrow Books.

CAMPBELL, Duncan, 2010. 'The lessons of Blair Peach', *Guardian*. 27 April. http://www.guardian.co.uk/commentisfree/2010/apr/27/blair-peach-policing-lessons?INTCMP=SRCH accessed 14 January, 2011.

CARRELL, Severin and Raymond Whitaker, 2005. 'Ricin: the plot that never was', *Independent on Sunday*, 17 April.

CASCIANO, Dominic, 2005. 'Top Jewish group "terror" apology', *BBC News Online*, 29 December. http://news.bbc.co.uk/1/hi/uk/4564784.stm accessed 3 August, 2009.

CESARI, J., 2008. 'Muslims in Europe and the Risk of Radicalism', in R. Coolsaet, ed., *Jihadi Terrorism and the Radicalisation Challenge in Europe*. Aldershot: Ashgate, pp. 97–107.

CHAKRABORTI, Neil & Garland, Jon, 2004. 'Justifying the Study of Racism in the Rural', in Neil Chakraborti and Jon Garland, eds, *Rural Racism*. pp. 1–13. Collumpton: Willan.

CHARITY COMMISSION, 2009. 'Charity Commission publishes Interpal inquiry report', Press release, 27 February. http://www.charity-commission.gov.uk/news/printerpal.asp accessed 7 August, 2010.

CHUCKMAN, John, 2005. 'Of War, Islam & Israel', in Aftab Ahmad Malik, ed., *With God On Our Side: Politics & Theology of the War on Terrorism*. Bristol: Amal Press, pp. 125–132.

CLARKE, Peter, 2007. *Learning from Experience*. Colin Cramphorn Memorial Lecture. London: Policy Exchange.

CLEGG, Nick, 2008. 'Clegg attacks think-tank's "underhand" briefing on "Unity" festival', http://www.politicshome.com/Landing.aspx?Blog=4060&perma=link# accessed 4 August, 2009.

CLUTTERBUCK, Lindsay, 2006. 'Countering Irish Republican Terrorism in Britain: Its Origin as a Police Function', *Terrorism and Political Violence*. 18, pp. 95–118.

CLUTTERBUCK, Richard, 1977. *Guerrillas & Terrorists*. London: Faber & Faber.

COADY, C.A.J., 2004. 'Defining Terrorism', in Igor Primoratz ed. *Terrorism: The Philosophical Issues*. Basingstoke: Palgrave, pp. 3–14.

COHEN, David, 2009. Andy Hayman: 'I deeply regret not challenging Ian Blair on de Menezes', *Evening Standard*, 26 June. http://www.thisislondon. co.uk/standard/article-23711377-details/Andy+Hayman:I+deeply+regret+ not+challenging+Ian+Blair+on+de+Menezes/article.do accessed 27 July, 2009.

COHEN, Nick, 2008. 'Scandal of the persecuted peacemakers', *Observer*, 23 March. http://www.guardian.co.uk/commentisfree/2008/mar/23/islam.uksecurity accessed 6 August, 2009.

COLL, Steve, 2004. *Ghost Wars: The Secret History of the CIA, Afghanistan, and Bin Laden, from the Soviet Invasion to September 10, 2001*. London: Penguin.

COMMISSION ON BRITISH MUSLIMS AND ISLAMOPHOBIA, 1997. ed. Robin Richardson. *Islamophobia: a challenge for us all*. London: Runnymede Trust.

COMMISSION ON BRITISH MUSLIMS AND ISLAMOPHOBIA, 2001. ed. Robin Richardson and Kaushika Amin. *Addressing the Challenge of Islamophobia: progress report, 1999–2001*. London: Commission on British Muslims and Islamophobia.

COMMISSION ON BRITISH MUSLIMS AND ISLAMOPHOBIA, 2004. ed. Robin Richardson. *Islamophobia: issues, challenges and action*. Stoke on Trent: Trentham Books.

CORBYN, Jeremy, 2005. 'Jeremy Corbyn report, February', http://www. epolitix.com/Resources/epolitix/MPWebsites/Images/i-l/Jeremy%20 Corbyn%20FEBReport.pdf accessed 4 August, 2009.

COX, Caroline and Marks, John, 2006. *The West, Islam and Islamism: Is Ideological Islam Compatible with Liberal Democracy?* London: Civitas.

CRAGIN, Kim, and Gerwehr, Scott, 2005. *Dissuading Terror: Strategic Influence and the Struggle Against Terrorism*. Santa Monica: Rand.

CRELINSTEN, Ronald, 1987. 'Terrorism as Political Communication: The Relationship between the Controller and the Controlled', in Paul Wilkinson and A. M. Stewart eds., *Contemporary Research on Terrorism*. Aberdeen: Aberdeen University Press, pp. 3–23.

CRELINSTEN, Ronald D., 2002. 'Analysing Terrorism and Counter-terrorism: A Communication Model', *Terrorism and Political Violence*. 14 (2), pp. 77–122.

CRENSHAW, Martha, 1983a. 'Introduction: Reflections on the Effects of Terrorism', in Martha Crenshaw, ed., *Terrorism, Legitimacy, and Power: The Consequences of Political Violence*. Connecticut: Wesleyan University Press, pp. 1–37.

CRENSHAW, Martha, 1983b. 'Conclusions', in Martha Crenshaw, ed., *Terrorism, Legitimacy, and Power: The Consequences of Political Violence*. Connecticut: Wesleyan University Press, pp. 143–150.

CRENSHAW, Martha, 1985. 'An Organisational Approach to the Analysis of Political Terrorism', *Orbis*. 29 (3) pp. 473–487.

CRENSHAW, Martha, 1998. 'The Logic of Terrorism: Terrorist Behaviour as a Product of Strategic Choice', in Walter Reich, ed., *Origins of terrorism: Psychologies, Ideologies, Theologies, States of Mind*. Washington, DC: Woodrow Wilson Center Press, pp. 7–24.

CRENSHAW, Martha, 2001. 'Why America? The Globalisation of Civil War', *Current History*. December, pp. 425–432.

CRENSHAW, Martha, 2003. 'The Causes of Terrorism', in Charles W. Kegley, Jr, ed. *The New Global Terrorism: Characteristics, Causes, Controls*. New Jersey: Prentice Hall, pp. 92–105.

CRENSHAW, Martha, 2006. 'Terrorism, Strategies, and Grand Strategies', in Audrey Kurth Cronin and James M. Ludes, eds., *Attacking Terrorism: Elements of a Grand Strategy*. Washington: Georgetown University Press.

CROFT, Stuart, 2006. *Culture, Crisis and America's War on Terror*. Cambridge: Cambridge University Press.

CROFT, Stuart, 2007. 'British Jihadis and the British War on Terror', *Defence Studies*. 7 (3), pp. 317–337.

CRONIN, Audrey Kurth, 2002. 'Behind the Curve: Globalism and International Terrorism', *International Security*. 27.3. pp. 30–58.

CROWN PROSECUTION SERVICE, 2006. 'Racist & Religious Incident Monitoring Report'. http://www.cps.gov.uk/publications/docs/rms05–06.pdf accessed 27 May, 2008.

CRUICKSHANK, Paul and Ali, Mohammad Hage, 2007. 'Abu Musab Al Suri: Architect of the New Al Qaeda', *Studies in Conflict & Terrorism*, 30 (1) pp. 1–14.

CRUIKSHANK, Paul and Bergen, Peter, 2008. 'The Unraveling: the jihadist revolt against bin Laden', *The New Republic*. 11 June.

DANNER, Mark, 2005. *Torture and Truth: America, Abu Ghraib, and the War on Terror*. London: Granta Books.

DARWISH, Nonie, 2006. *Now They Call Me Infidel: Why I Renounced Jihad for America, Israel and the War on Terror*. London: Sentinel.

DAVIES, Nick, 1998. 'Freemasons in the police', *Guardian*. January. http://www.nickdavies.net/1997/01/01/freemasons-in-the-police/ accessed 6 January, 2011.

DEFLEM, Mathieu, 2002. *Policing World Society: Historical Foundations of International Police Cooperation*. Oxford: Oxford University Press.

DEFLEM, Mathieu, 2004. 'Introduction: Towards a Criminological Sociology of Terrorism and Counter-Terrorism', in Mathieu Deflem, ed. *Terrorism and Counter-Terrorism: Criminological Perspectives*. Oxford: Elsevier, 2004, pp. 1–8.

de GUZMAN, M.C., 2002. 'The changing roles and strategies of the police in time of terror', *ACJS Today*, pp. 8–13.

de LINT, Willem, 2000. 'Autonomy, Regulation and the Police Beat', *Social & Legal Studies*. 9 (1), pp. 55–83.

de LINT, Willem, 2004. 'Neo-conservatism and American Counter-Terrorism: Endarkened Policy?', in Mathieu Deflem, ed. *Terrorism and Counter-Terrorism: Criminological Perspectives*. Oxford: Elsevier, pp. 131–153.

de LINT, Willem, 2006. 'Intelligence in Policing and Security: Reflections on Scholarship (editorial)', *Policing & Society*. 16 (1), pp. 1–6.

DELLA PORTA, Donatella, 1992. 'Institutional Responses to Terrorism: The Italian Case', in Conor Gearty, ed. (1996) *Terrorism*. Aldershot: Dartmouth, pp. 499–518.

DELLA PORTA, Donatella, 2009. 'Leaving underground organisations: a sociological analysis of the Italian Case', in Tore Bjorgo and John Horgan eds. (2009) *Leaving Terrorism Behind: Individual and collective disengagement*. London: Routledge, pp. 66–87.

DELONG-BAS, Natana, J., 2004. *Wahhabi Islam: From Revival and Reform to Global Jihad*. London: I.B. Tauris.

DENECE, Eric, 2005. 'The Development of Islamic Fundamentalism in France: Security, Economic and Social Aspects', *Cf2R: French Centre for Intelligence Research*, Research Report no. 1.

DENOEUX, Guilain, 2002. 'The Forgotten Swamp: Navigating Political Islam', *Middle East Policy*. 9 (2), pp. 56–81.

DESAI, Meghnad, 2007. *Rethinking Islamism: The Ideology of the New Terror*. London: I. B. Taurus.

DISPATCHES, 2007. *Undercover Mosque* Channel 4, UK, first broadcast 15 January. http://www.hardcashproductions.com/recent29.html accessed 27 January, 2009.

DODD, Vikram, 2005. 'Special Branch to track Muslims across UK', *The Guardian*, 26 July. http://www.guardian.co.uk/uk/2005/jul/20/religion.july7 accessed 26 April, 2010.

DODD, Vikram, 2006. 'Eleven charged over alleged airline terror plot', *The Guardian*, 22 August. http://www.guardian.co.uk/terrorism/story/0,,18555 21,00.html accessed 28 December, 2010.

DODD, Vikram, 2006. 'Interview with Peter Herbert', *Guardian online*, 26 August. http://www.guardian.co.uk/world/2006/aug/24/alqaeda.terrorism accessed 4 May, 2010.

DODD, Vikram, 2009. 'Al-Qaeda fantasist tells court: I'm a professional liar. Manchester man admits to tricking media into believing he was a jihadi', *The Guardian*, 9 February.

DONOHUE, Laura, K., 2008. *The Cost of Counterterrorism: Power, Politics and Liberty*. Cambridge: Cambridge University Press.

DUNN, Tim and Booth, Ken, Tim, 2002. 'Worlds In Collision', in Ken Booth and Tim Dunne eds. *Worlds In Collision: Terror and the Future of Global Order*. Basingstoke: Palgrave, 2002, pp. 1–26.

DUTTON, Yasin, 1999. *The Origins of Islamic Law: The Qur'an, the Muwatta' and Madinan' Amal*. London: Routledge Curzon.

DUYVESTEYN, Isabelle, 2004. 'How New Is the New Terrorism?', *Studies in Conflict & Terrorism*, 27 pp. 439–454.

EATON, Gai, 1994. *Islam and the Destiny of Man*. Cambridge: Islamic Texts Society.

EICKELMAN, Dale F., and Piscatori, James, 2004. *Muslim Politics*. Princeton: Princeton University Press.

El-AFFENDI, Abdelwahab, 2005. 'The Conquest of Muslim Hearts and Minds? Perspectives on U.S. Reform and Public Diplomacy Strategies', *The Brooking Project on U.S. Policy Towards the Islamic World*. Washington DC: Saban Center for Middle East Policy.

El-FADL, Khaled Abou, 2005. *Islam and the Challenge of Democracy*. Princeton: Princeton University Press.

El-FADL, Khaled Abou, 2005. 'Islam & the Theology of Power', in Aftab Ahmad Malik, ed., *With God On Our Side: Politics & Theology of the War on Terrorism*. Bristol: Amal Press, pp. 299–311.

ELWORTHY, Scillia and Rifkind, Gabrielle, 2005. *Hearts and Minds: Human security approaches to political violence*. London: Demos.

ENDERS, Walter and Sandler, Todd, 2005. 'After 9/11: Is it all Different Now?', *Journal of Conflict Resolution*. 49 (2) pp. 259–277.

ESPOSITO, John L., 1983. 'Introduction: Islam and Muslim Politics', in John L. Esposito, ed., *Voices of Resurgent Islam*. Oxford: Oxford University Press, pp. 67–98.

ESPOSITO, John L., 1999. *The Islamic Threat: Myth or Reality?* 3rd ed., Oxford: Oxford University Press.

ESPOSITO, John L., 2003. 'Islam and the West after September 11: Civilizational Dialogue or Conflict?', in Aftab Ahmad Malik, ed., *The Empire and the Crescent: Global Implications for a New American Century*. Bristol: Amal Press, pp. 112–129.

ESPOSITO, John, L., 2003. 'Islam and Civil Society', in John L. Esposito, and François Burgat, eds, *Modernizing Islam: Religion in the Public Sphere in Europe and the Middle East*. New Brunswick: Rutgers University Press, p. 95.

ESPOSITO, John L., ed., 2003 *The Oxford Dictionary of Islam*, Oxford: Oxford University Press.

FANON, Franz, 2001 (fifth ed.). *The Wretched of the Earth*. London: Penguin.

FATTIHI, Kambiz, 2007. 'US Army enlists anthropologists', *BBC News Online*, 16 October. http://news.bbc.co.uk/1/hi/world/americas/7042090.stm accessed 2 April, 2010.

FEKETE, Liz, 2004. 'Anti-Muslim racism and the European security state', *Race & Class*. 46 (1), pp. 3–29.

FIELDING, Nick and Abul TAHIR, 2005. 'Hamas link to London Mosque', *Times Online*, 13 February. http://www.timesonline.co.uk/tol/news/uk/article513868.ece accessed 21 October, 2010.

FIELDING, Nigel G., 2005. 'Concepts and Theory in Community Policing', *The Howard Journal*. 44 (5), pp. 460–472.

FIELDING, Nigel G., 2005. *The Police and Social Conflict*. 2nd ed. London: Glass House Press.

FITZGERALD, Marion and Hale, Chris, 2006. 'Ethnic minorities and community safety', in Peter Squires ed., *Community Safety: Critical perspectives on policy and practice*. Bristol: Policy Press, pp. 71–92.

FLANAGAN, Shawn Teresa, 2006. 'Charity as Resistance: Connections between Charity, Contentious Politics, and Terror', *Studies in Conflict & Terrorism*. 29 pp. 641–655.

FLYVBJERG, Bent, 2006. 'Five Misunderstandings About Case-Study Research', *Qualitative Inquiry*. 12 (2) pp. 219–245.

FORTIER, Anne-Marie, 2005. 'Pride politics and multiculturalist citizenship', *Ethnic and Racial Studies*. 28 (3) pp. 559–578.

FOUREST, Caroline, 2008. *Brother Tariq: The Doublespeak of Tariq Ramadan*. New York: Encounter.

FREEMAN, Hadley, 2010. 'Tony Blair interviewed by Katie Couric', *Guardian*. 15 September. http://www.guardian.co.uk/news/blog/2010/sep/15/tony-blair-katie-couric accessed 15 September, 2010.

FREY, R.G and Morris, Christopher M., 1991. 'Violence, Terrorism and Justice', in R.G. Frey and Christopher M. Morris, eds., *Violence, Terrorism and Justice*. Cambridge: Cambridge University Press.

GAMBETTA, Diego, 2005. 'Can We Make Sense of Suicide Missions?', in Diego Gambetta, ed., *Making Sense of Suicide Missions*. Oxford: Oxford University Press. pp. 259–299.

GARGINI, Richard, 2008. 'ACPO reply', *Jane's Police Review*, 21 March.

GARLAND, Jon, Spalek, Basia and Chakraborti, Neil, 2006. 'Hearing Lost Voices: Issues in Researching Hidden Minority Ethnic Communities', *British Journal of Criminology*. 46, pp. 423–437.

GARTON ASH, Timothy, 2008. 'Standing Together Against Extremism. Speech at Quilliam Foundation Launch: "Reviving Western Islam & Uniting Against Extremism"', British Museum, London, 22 April. http://www.quilliamfoundation.org/index.php/component/content/article/142 accessed 9. February, 2009.

GATES, Stephen, 2011. 'Sidney Street siege resonates even 100 years on', *The Guardian*, 2 Jan 2011. http://www.guardian.co.uk/uk/2011/jan/02/sidney-street-siege-100-years?INTCMP=SRCH accessed 4 January, 11.

GEARTY, Conor, 2005. 11 September 2001, 'Counter-terrorism, and the Human Rights Act', *Journal of Law and Society*. 32 (1), pp. 18–33.

GEERTZ, Clifford, 1973. *The Interpretation of Cultures*. New York: Basic Books.

GERGES, Fawaz A., 2005. *The Far Enemy: Why Jihad Went Global*. Cambridge: Cambridge University Press.

GERMAN, Mike, 2007. *Thinking Like a Terrorist: Insights of a Former FBI Undercover Agent*. Washington DC: Potomac Books. p. 121.

GHANOUSHI, Soumayya, 2005. 'The Origins of Extremism: Theory or Reality?', in Aftab Ahmad Malik, ed., *With God On Our Side: Politics & Theology of the War on Terrorism*. Bristol: Amal Press, pp. 291–298.

GHAZALI, Abdus Sattar, 2005. 'Rand reports attempt to change Islam', *Islamic Awakening.Com*, p. 14. http://www.islamicawakening.com/viewarticle.php?articleID=1214 accessed 12 May, 2010.

GITHENS-MAZER, Jonathan, 2006. *Myths and Memories of the Easter Rising: Cultural and Political Nationalism in Ireland*. Dublin: Irish Academic Press.

GITHENS-MAZER, Jonathan, 2007. 'Myths of Massacre and Nationalist Mobilisation: Ireland and Algeria in Comparative Perspective', in *Ireland and the Middle East*. In: R. Miller, ed. Dublin: Irish Academic Press.

GITHENS-MAZER, Jonathan, 2008a. 'Locating Agency in Collective Political Behaviour: Nationalism, Social Movements, and Individual Mobilisation', *Politics*. 28 (1), pp. 41–49.

GITHENS-MAZER, Jonathan, 2008b. 'Variations on a Theme: Radical Violent Islamism and European North African Radicalisation', *PS: Political Science and Politics*. 41 (1).

GITHENS-MAZER, Jonathan, 2009a. 'Mobilisation, Recruitment and Violence: Radical violent *takfiri* Islamism in early 21st Century Britain', in Roger Eatwell and Matthew Goodwin, eds. *Extremism in 21ˢᵗ Century Britain*. London: Routledge.

GITHENS-MAZER, Jonathan and Robert Lambert, 2009b. 'The demonisation of British Islamism', *Guardian cif*. 1 April. http://www.guardian.co.uk/commentisfree/belief/2009/mar/31/religion-islam accessed 17 January, 2010.

GITHENS-MAZER, Jonathan and Robert Lambert, 2009c. 'Quilliam on Prevent: the wrong diagnosis', *Guardian cif*. 19 October. http://www.guardian.co.uk/commentisfree/belief/2009/oct/19/prevent-quilliam-foundation-extremism accessed 17 January, 2010.

GITHENS-MAZER, Jonathan and Robert Lambert, 2009d. 'Re-shaping Prevent', *Guardian cif*. 31 October. http://www.guardian.co.uk/commentisfree/belief/2009/oct/31/counter-terrorism-prevent-muslims accessed 17 Janurary, 2010.

GITHENS-MAZER, Jonathan and Robert Lambert, 2009e. 'Let's be honest about Prevent', *Guardian cif*. 9 December. http://www.guardian.co.uk/commentisfree/belief/2009/dec/09/prevent-denham-violent-extremism accessed 3 August, 2010.

GITHENS-MAZER, Jonathan and Robert Lambert, 2010a. 'Why conventional wisdom on radicalization fails: the persistence of a failed discourse', *International Affairs* 86: 4, 2010.

GITHENS-MAZER, Jonathan and Robert Lambert, 2010b. *Islamophobia and Anti-Muslim Hate Crime: a London case study*. Exeter: European Muslim Research Centre, University of Exeter. http://centres.exeter.ac.uk/emrc/publications/Islamophobia_and_Anti-Muslim_Hate_Crime.pdf accessed 26 January, 2010.

GLEES, Anthony, and Pope, Chris, 2005. *When Students Turn to Terror: Terrorist and Extremist Activity on British Campuses*. London: Social Affairs Unit.

GODDARD, Hugh, 2000. *A History of Christian-Muslim Relations*. Edinburgh: Edinburgh University Press.

GODSON, Dean, 2005. 'You'll never guess who's to blame for 7/7', *The Times*, 13 December. http://www.timeonline.co.uk/article/0,,1922518,00.html accessed 2 August, 2008.

GODSON, Dean, 2006a. 'Already Hooked on Poison', *The Times*, 8 February. http://www.timesonline.co.uk/article/0,,1072–2029734,00.html accessed 2 August, 2008.

GODSON, Dean, 2006b. 'The feeble helping the unspeakable', *Times online*, 5 April. http://www.timesonline.co.uk/tol/comment/columnists/guest_contributors/article702053.ece http://www.timesonline.co.uk/tol/comment/.../guest .../article2310437.ece accessed 8 July, 2009.

GODSON, Dean, 2007a. 'The Old Bill Should Choose its Friends Carefully: What on Earth are West Midlands Police up to?', *The Times*, 23 August.

GODSON, Dean, 2007b. 'Introduction to Peter Clarke's Colin Cramphorn Lecture', *Policy Exchange*. http://www.policyexchange.org.uk/images/libimages/260.pdf accessed 14 August, 2010.

GOVE, Michael, 2006. *Celsius 7/7*. London: Weidenfield & Nicholson.

GOVE, Michael, 2006. 'We must engage with moderate Muslims', *The Guardian*, 23 August.

GRAEF, Roger, 1990. *Talking Blues: the Police in their Own Words*. London: Collins.

GREAT BRITAIN. Foreign and Commonwealth Office (F&CO), 2005. *Counter-Terrorism Legislation and Practice: A Survey of Selected Countries*. London: F&CO.

GREAT BRITAIN. Home Office, 2006. *Countering International Terrorism: the United Kingdom's Strategy*. July, London: HMSO.

GREAT BRITAIN. Home Office. 2006. *Covert Human Intelligence Sources: Code of Practice*. London: HMSO.

GREAT BRITAIN. Home Office. 2008. 'The Prevent Strategy: A Guide for Local Partners in England', June. http://www.dcsf.gov.uk/violentextremism/downloads/Prevent%20Strategy%20A%20Guide%20for%20Local%20Partners%203%20June%202008.pdf accessed 8 September, 2010.

GREGORY, Frank and Wilkinson, Paul, 2005. 'Riding Pillion for Tackling Terrorism is a High-Risk Policy', in Christopher Browning, ed., *Security, Terrorism and the UK*. London: Chatham House. pp. 2–3.

GRIEVE, John G.D & Julie French, 2000. 'Does Institutional Racism Exist In the Metropolitan Police Service?', in David G. Green, ed. *Institutional Racism and the Police: Fact or Fiction?* London: Institute for the Study of Civil Society (Civitas).

GRIFFIN, Tom, 2008. 'Conrad Black's favourite Commissar', *Spinwatch*, 15 May. http://www.spinwatch.org.uk/-articles-by-category-mainmenu-8/49-propaganda/4908-dean-godson-conrad-blacks-favourite-commissar accessed 6 May, 2010.

GRIFFITH-DICKSON, Gwen, 2005. *The Philosophy of Religion*. London: SCM Press.

GRIFFITH-DICKSON, Gwen, 2008. 'Countering Extremism and the Politics of "Engagement"', *Gresham College lecture*, Allen & Overy, London Docklands. 29 April. http://www.gresham.ac.uk/event.asp?PageId=108&EventId=658 accessed 2 November, 2010.

GUNARATNA, Rohan, 2002. *Inside Al Qaeda: Global Network of Terror*. London: Hurst.

GUNNING, Jeroen, 2004. 'Peace with Hamas? The transforming potential of political participation', *International Affairs*. 80 (2), pp. 233–255.

HADDAD, Yvonne Y., 1983. 'Sayyid Qutb: Ideologue of Islamic Revival', in John L. Esposito, ed., *Voices of Resurgent Islam*. Oxford: Oxford University Press, pp. 67–98.

HAGGERTY, Kevin D. and Kauger, Erin, 2006. 'Review Essay: Intelligence Exchange in Policing and Security', *Policing & Society*. 16 (1), pp. 86–91.

HAIN, Peter (ed.), 1979. *Policing the Police*. Vols. 1 & 2. London: John Calder.

HALLIDAY, Fred, 2002. *Two Hours That Shook The World—September 11, 2001: Causes & Consequences*. London: Saki Books.

HALLIDAY, Fred, 2004. 'Review article: 9/11 and Middle Eastern Studies past and future: revisiting Ivory towers on sand', *International Affairs*. 80 (5), pp. 953–962.

HALEEM, M.A.S. Abdel, trans., 2004. *The Qur'an*. Oxford: Oxford University Press.

HAMM, Mark S., 2002. *In Bad Company: America's Terrorist Underground*. Boston: Northeastern University Press.

HAMM, Mark S., 2005. *Terrorism as Crime: From Oklahoma City to Al-Qaeda and Beyond* New York: New York University Press.

HAMM, Mark S., 2005. 'After September 11: Terrorism research and the crisis in criminology', *Theoretical Criminology*. 9 (2), pp. 237–251.

HAYMAN, Andy (with Margaret Gilmore), 2009. *The Terrorist Hunters*. London.

HEGGHAMMER, Thomas, 2004. 'Indonesia Backgrounder: Why Salafism and Terrorism Mostly Don't Mix', *IAG Asia Report No. 83*, International Crisis Group.

HILLYARD, Paddy, 1993. *Suspect Community: People's Experience of the Prevention of Terrorism Acts in Britain*. London: Pluto Press.

HILLYARD, Paddy, 2005. *The 'War on Terror': lessons from Ireland*. Essays for civil liberties and democracy in Europe. http://www.ecln.org/essays/essay-1.pdf accessed 7 February, 2010.

HIZB ut TAHRIR website, 2009. 'British Foreign Secretary "Glorifies Terrorism" In Radio Interview', 16 August. http://www.hizb.org.uk/hizb/press-centre/press-release/british-foreign-secretary-glorifies-terrorism-in-radio-interview.html accessed 23 August, 2010.

HOFFMAN, Bruce,1998. *Inside Terrorism*. London: Victor Gollancz.

HOFFMAN, Bruce, 2004. 'Foreword'. In: A.Silke, ed. *Research on Terrorism: Trends, Achievements and Failures*. London: Frank Cass.

HONDERICH, Ted, 2003. *After the Terror*. Expanded, Revised Edition. Edinburgh: Edinburgh University Press.

HONDERICH, Ted, 2006. *Humanity, Terrorism, Terrorist War: Palestine, 9/11, Iraq, 7/7*. London: Continuum.

HOPKINS, Nick and Kahahni-Hopkins, Verad, 2004. 'The antecedents of identification: A rhetorical analysis of British Muslim activists' constructions of community and identity', *British Journal of Social Psychology*. 43, pp. 41–57.

HORGAN, John, 2005. *The Psychology of Terrorism*. London: Routledge.

HOSKEN, Andrew, 2008. *Ken: The Ups and Downs of Ken Livingstone*. London: Arcadia.

HOURANI, Albert, 1991. *Islam in European Thought*. Cambridge: Cambridge University Press.

HOUSE OF COMMONS HOME AFFAIRS COMMITTEE, 2005. *Terrorism and Community Relations*. Sixth Report of Session 2004–5, HC 1656–1. London: The Stationery Office.

HOWE, Darcus, 2000. 'Why Brixton is a place of pilgrimage for "black diamonds"', *Independent Online*, 20 January. http://www.independent.co.uk/news/uk/this-britain/why-brixton-is-a-place-of-pilgrimage-for-black-diamonds-727745.html accessed 7 July, 2009.

HUNTINGTON, Samuel P., 1996. *The Clash of Civilisations and the Remaking of World Order*. London: Touchstone Books.

HURRELL, Andrew, 2002. '"There are no Rules" (George W. Bush): International Order after September 11', *International Relations*. 16 (2), pp. 185–204.

HUSAIN, Ed, 2007. *The Islamist*. London: Penguin.

IGNATIEFF, Michael, 2001. 'Its war', *The Guardian*. 1 October. http://www.guardian.co.uk/Archive/Article/0,4273,4267406,00.html accessed 3 February, 2010.

IGNATIEFF, Michael, 2004. *The Lesser Evil: Political Ethics in an Age of Terror*. Princeton: Princeton University Press.

INNES, Martin, 2006. 'Policing Uncertainty: Countering Terror Through Community Intelligence and Democratic Policing', *Annals of the American Academy*. 605, May, pp. 1–20.

INNES, Martin, Abbot L, Lowe, T, and Roberts, C. 2007. *Hearts and Minds and Eyes and Ears: Reducing Radicalisation Risks Through Reassurance-Oriented Policing*. London: ACPO.

INNES, Martin and Thiel, Daniel, 2008. 'Policing Terror', in Newburn, Tim, ed. *The Handbook of Policing* 2nd ed. Cullompton: Willan. pp. 553–579.

INTERNATIONAL CRISIS GROUP (ICG), 2004. *Saudi Arabia Backgrounder: Who are the Islamists?* ICG Middle East Report No. 31. Amman/Riyaadh/Brussels, 21 September.

ISLAM, Yusuf, et al, 2005. *'Preventing Extremism Together' Working Groups: August—October 2005*. London: Home Office.

BIBLIOGRAPHY

ISMAIL, Salwa, 2006. *Rethinking Islamist Politics: Culture, the State and Islamism*. London: I.B. Taurus.

ISRAELI, Raphael, 2002. 'A Manual of Islamic Fundamentalist Terrorism', *Terrorism and Political Violence*. 14 (4), pp. 23–40.

JACKSON, Richard, 2005. *Writing the War on Terrorism: Language, Politics and Counter-Terrorism*. Manchester: Manchester University Press.

JACKSON, Richard, 2007. 'Constructing enemies: "Islamic terrorism" in political and academic discourse', *Government and Opposition*. 42 (3), pp. 394–426.

JACKSON, Richard, 2008a. 'Counter-terrorism and communities: an interview with Robert Lambert', *Critical Studies on Terrorism*. August, pp. 293–308.

JACKSON, Richard, 2008b. 'The ghosts of state terror: knowledge, politics and terrorism studies', *Critical Studies on Terrorism*. December, 1 (3), pp. 377–392, p. 372.

JONES, David Martin, and Smith, M.L.R. 2009. 'We're All Terrorists Now: Critical—or Hypocritical—Studies "on" Terrorism?', *Studies in Conflict & Terrorism*. 32, pp. 292–302.

JORDAN, Javier, 2004. 'Al-Qaeda and Western Islam', *Terrorism and Political Violence*. 16 (1), pp. 1–17.

JUERGENSMEYER, Mark, 2001. *Terror in the Mind of God: The Global Rise of Religious Violence*. London: University of California Press.

JUERGENSMEYER, Mark, 2006. 'Religion and the New Terrorism', in Andrew T. H. Tan, ed., The *Politics of Terrorism: a survey*. London: Routledge, pp. 73–79.

KALYAS, S., and Sanchez-Cuenca, I., 2005. 'Killing Without Dying: the Absence of Suicide Missions', in Diego Gambetta, ed., *Making Sense of Suicide Missions*. Oxford: Oxford University Press.

KAMALI, M. Hashim, 2003. 'Fanaticism and its Manifestations in Muslim Societies', in Aftab Ahmad Malik, ed., *The Empire and the Crescent: Global Implications for a New American Century*. Bristol: Amal Press, pp. 175–207.

KAPITAN, Tomis, 2004. 'Terrorism in the Aba-Israeli Conflict', in Igor Primoratz, ed. *Terrorism: The Philosophical Issues*, Basingstoke: Palgrave. pp. 175–192.

KARAGIANNIS, Emmanuel and McCauley, Clark, 2006. 'Hizb ut-Tahrir al-Islami: Evaluating the Threat Posed by a Radical Islamic Group That Remains Nonviolent', *Terrorism and Political Violence*. 18, pp. 315–334.

KATZ, Ian, 2008. 'Sir Ian's Siege: a footnote', *The Guardian*, 1 December. http://www.guardian.co.uk/uk/2008/dec/01/ian-blair-police-met-balcombe accessed 3 August, 2010.

KEEBLE, Harry (with Kris Hollington), 2010. *Terror Cops*. London: Simon and Schuster.

KELLY, Ruth, 2006a. 'DCLG Secretary. Our values, our responsibilities—speech to Muslim community groups', 11 October. http://www.communi-

BIBLIOGRAPHY

ties.gov.uk/archived/speeches/corporate/values-responsibilities accessed 27 December 2010.

KELLY, Ruth, 2006b. 'DCLG Secretary. Speech at launch of Commission on Integration and Cohesion', 24 August. http://www.communities.gov.uk/speeches/corporate/commission-integration-cohesion accessed 29 March, 2010.

KELLY, Ruth, 2006c. 'DCLG Secretary. Speech at launch of Sufi Muslim Council', 19 July http://www.communities.gov.uk/speeches/corporate/sufi-muslim-council accessed 27 April, 2010.

KENNEY, Michael, 2007. *From Pablo to Osama*. Philadelphia: Penn State University Press.

KENNEY, Michael, 2008. *Organizational Learning and Islamic Militancy*. Final Report. School of Public Affairs, Capital College, Pennsylvania State University.

KEPEL, Gilles, 2002. *Jihad: The Trail of Political Islam*. Trans. Anthony F. Roberts. London: I.B. Taurus.

KEPEL, Gilles, 2004. *The War for Muslim Minds: Islam and the West*. London: Harvard University Press.

KEPEL, Gilles, 2005. Radical secularism. *The Independent opinion page*, 22 August, p. 12.

KEPEL, Gilles, 2005. *The Roots of Radical Islam*. London: Saki.

KERBAJ, Richard and Kennedy, Dominic, 2008. 'Terrorism adviser to Met is on wanted list: Interpol notice urges arrest of Islam TV chief', *Times online*. http://www.timesonline.co.uk/tol/news/uk/crime/article5342730.ece accessed 7 August, 2010.

KINGSTON, Peter, 2007. 'Confronting risk', *Guardian*, 3 July. http://www.guardian.co.uk/education/2007/jul/03/academicexperts.highereducation accessed 30 December, 2010.

KIRBY, Terry, 1993. 'Protesting police put on an overflowing show of force against Sheehy report at Wembley', *The Independent*. 21 July. http://www.independent.co.uk/news/uk/protesting-police-put-on-an-overflowing-show-of-force-against-sheehy-report-at-wembley-1486099.html accessed 3 May, 2009.

KHALIL, As'ad Abu, 2005. 'Shattering Illusions', in Aftab Ahmad Malik, ed., *With God On Our Side: Politics & Theology of the War on Terrorism*. Bristol: Amal Press, pp. 265–272.

KHAN, Amjad, 2010. 22 October. 'A Dummy's Guide to Lambertism'. http://hurryupharry.org/2010/10/22/a-dummy%E2%80%99s-guide-to-lambertism/ accessed 29 December, 2010.

KHOSROKOVA, Farhad, 2005. *Suicide Bombers: Allah's New Bombers*. trans. David Macey. London: Pluto Press.

KILCULLEN, David, J., 2006. 'Counter-Insurgency Redux', *Survival*. 48(4), pp. 111–130.

KILCULLEN, David, J., 2007. 'Subversion and Counter-Subversion in the Campaign against Terrorism in Europe', *Studies In Conflict and Terrorism*, 30 (8).

373

KILCULLEN, David, 2009. *The Accidental Guerrilla: Fighting Small Wars in the Midst of a Big One*. Oxford: Oxford University Press.

KINGSTON, Peter, 2007. 'Confronting risk', *Guardian*, 3 July. http://www.guardian.co.uk/education/2007/jul/03/academicexperts.highereducation accessed 30 December, 2010.

KIRBY, A., 2007. 'The London Bombers as "Self-Starters": A Case Study in Indigenous Radicalization and the Emergence of Autonomous Cliques', *Studies in Conflict and Terrorism*. 30 (5), pp. 415–28.

KITSON, Frank, 1971. *Low-Intensity Operations: Subversion Insurgency and Peacekeeping*. London: Faber & Faber.

KLEINIG, John, 1996. *The Ethics of Policing*. Cambridge: Cambridge University Press.

KLAUSEN, Jytte, 2005. *The Islamic Challenge: Politics and Religion in Western Europe* Oxford: Oxford University Press.

KOHLMANN, Evan F., 2004. *Al-Qaeda's Jihad in Europe: The Afghan-Bosnian Network*. Oxford: Berg.

KUNDNANI, Arun, 2007. *The End of Tolerance: Racism in 21st Century*. London: Pluto.

KUNDNANI, Arun, 2008. 'Islamism and the Roots of Liberal Rage', *Race & Class*. 50 (2) pp. 40–68.

KURZMANN, Charles, 2004. 'Social Movement Theory and Islamic Studies', in Quintan Wiktorowicz, ed. *Islamic Activism: a Social Movement Theory Approach*. Indiana: Indiana University Press, pp. 289–304.

LA FREE, Gary and Dugan, Laura, 2004. 'How Does Studying Terrorism Compare to Studying Crime?', in Mathieu Deflem, ed. *Terrorism and Counter-Terrorism: Criminological Perspectives*. Oxford: Elsevier, pp. 53–74.

LAMBERT, Robert, 2008a. 'Empowering Salafis and Islamists Against Al-Qaeda: A London Counter-terrorism Case Study', *Political Science and Politics* 41 (1).

LAMBERT, Robert, 2008b. 'Salafi and Islamist Londoners: Stigmatised minority faith communities countering al-Qaeda', *Crime, Law & Social Change*. 50, pp. 73–89.

LAMBERT, Robert, 2010. *The London Partnerships: an insider's analysis of legitimacy and effectivenss*. Unpublished PhD. University of Exeter.

LAMBERT, Robert, 2011. 'Community Intervention as an Engagement Strategy—al-Qaeda in London', in W. Zartman and G.O. Faure, eds., *Engaging Extremists: States and Terrorists Negotiating Ends and Means* Washington DC: United States Institute of Peace (USIP).

LAMBERT, Robert, and Jonathan Githens-Mazer, 2010. 'Suicide terrorism; Grievance & the final act: The 7/7 bombers & suicide terrorism in the 21st Century', in Leo Sher and Alexander Vilens, eds., *Terror and Suicide* New York: Nova Science Publishers.

LAMBERT, Robert and Jonathan Githens-Mazer, 2010. *Islamophobia and Anti-Muslim Hate Crime: UK case studies*. Exeter: EMRC, University of Exeter.

BIBLIOGRAPHY

BIBLIOGRAPHY

LAMBETH COUNCIL website. 2005. 'Brixton Mosque', 25 July. http://www.lambeth.gov.uk/News/NewsArchive/2005/250705CommunityLeaders.htm accessed 3 August, 2010.

LAQUEUR, Walter, 1999. *The New Terrorism: Fanaticism and the Arms of Mass Destruction*. New York: Continuum.

LAQUEUR, Walter, 2004. *No End To War: Terrorism in the Twenty-First Century*. New York: Continuum.

LAWRENCE, Bruce, ed. 2005. *Messages to the World: The Statements of Osama bin Laden*. London: Verso.

LEHENY, David. 2005. 'Terrorism, Social Movements, and International Security: How Al Qaeda Affects Southeast Asia', *Japanese Journal of Political Science*. 6 (1), pp. 87–109.

LEIKEN, Robert S., 2005. 'Europe's Angry Muslims', *Foreign Affairs*. July, pp. 1–8.

LEIKEN, Robert S. and Brooke, Steven. 'The Moderate Muslim Brotherhood', *Foreign Affairs*. 86 (2) March/April 2007.

LEISER, Burton M., 2004. 'The Catastrophe of September 11 and its Aftermath', in Igor Primoratz, ed. *Terrorism: The Philosophical Issues*, Basingstoke: Palgrave, pp. 192–208.

LEWIS, Philip, 2002. *Islamic Britain: Religion, Politics and Identity among British Muslims*. London: I.B. Taurus.

LEWIS, Philip, 2007. *Young, British and Muslim*, London, Continuum.

LEVITT, Matthew 2004. 'Hamas from Cradle to Grave', *Middle East Quarterly*. 11(1), pp. 1–12.

LIA, Brynjar, 2007. *Architect of Global Jihad: The Life of al-Qaeda Strategist Abu Mus'ab al-Suri*. London: Hurst.

LINCOLN, Bruce, 2003. *Holy Terrors: Thinking about Religion after September 11*. Chicago: Chicago University Press.

LINGS, Martin, 1983. *Muhammad: his life based on the earliest sources*. Cambridge: Islamic Texts Society.

LIPS, Lucy, 2010. 'A depressing little story in the Sunday Times', 1 August. http://hurryupharry.org/2010/08/01/a-depressing-little-story-in-the-sunday-times/ accessed 29 December, 2010.

LOADER, Ian and Mulcahy, Aogan., 2003. *Policing and the Condition of England: Memory, Politics and Culture*. Oxford: Oxford University Press.

LUSTICK, Ian S. 2006. *Trapped in the War on Terror*. Philadelphia: University of Pennsylvania Press.

LUSTICK, Ian S, 2007. 'Fractured Fairy Tale: The War on Terror and the Emperor's New Clothes', *Homeland Security Affairs*. 3 (1). http://www.hsaj.org/?fullarticle=3.1.2 accessed 7 September, 2010.

LYONS, William, 2002. 'Partnerships, information and public safety: community policing in a time of terror', *Policing: an International Journal of Police Strategies & Management*. 25 (3) pp. 530–542.

MacEOIN, Dennis, 2007. *The Hijacking of British Islam*. London: Policy Exchange. http://www.policyexchange.org.uk/images/libimages/307.pdf accessed 23 September, 2010.

BIBLIOGRAPHY

MACPHERSON, Lord, 1999. *The Stephen Lawrence Inquiry: Report*, Cm. 4262-1.

MAGUIRE, Mike and John, Tim, 2006. 'Intelligence Led Policing, Managerialism and Community Engagement: Competing Priorities and the Role of the National Intelligence Model in the UK', *Policing & Society*. 16 (1) pp. 67–85.

MAHER, Shiraz and Martin FRAMPTON, 2009. *Choosing our friends wisely: Criteria for engagement with Muslim groups*. London: Policy Exchange. http://www.policyexchange.org.uk/publications/publication.cgi?id=108 accessed 20 March, 2009.

MALCOLM X, 1968. *The Autobiography of Malcolm X*. London: Penguin.

MALIK, Aftab Ahmad, 2005. 'The Betrayal of Tradition', in Aftab Ahmad Malik, ed., *With God On Our Side: Politics & Theology of the War on Terrorism*. Bristol: Amal Press, pp. 133–163.

MALIK, Aftab Ahmad, 2006. 'The State We Are In', in Aftab Ahmad Malik, ed., *The State We Are In: Identity, Terror and the Law of Jihad*. Bristol: Amal Press, pp. 14–31.

MALIK, Kenan, 2005. 'Multiculturalism has fanned the flames of Islamic Extremism', *The Times*, 16 July. http://www.timesonline.co.uk/article/0,,1072-1695604,00.html accessed 27 January, 2008.

MALIK, Kenan, 2009. *From Fatwa to Jihad: The Rushdie Affair and its Legacy*. London Atlantic Books.

MALIK, Maleiha, 2006. 'Muslims are now getting the same treatment Jews had a century ago', *Comment is Free: Guardian Online*, 2 February. http://www.guardian.co.uk/commentisfree/story/0,,2004258,00.html accessed 25 January, 2008.

MALIK, Shiv, 2007. 'My brother the bomber', *Prospect*. 30 June. http://www.prospectmagazine.co.uk/2007/06/mybrotherthebomber/ accessed 2 May, 2009.

MANJI, Irshad, 2004. *The Trouble With Islam: A Wake-Up call for Honesty and Change*. Edinburgh: Mainstream Publishing.

MANNINGHAM-BULLER, Eliza, 2006. *The International Terrorist Threat to the UK*. Speech by the Director General of the Security Service at Queen Mary College, London, 9 November. http://www.mi5.gov.uk/output/Page568.html accessed 12 December, 2006.

MARXISM TODAY, 1982. 'Policing in the Eighties. Interview with Chief Constable John Alderson', April, pp. 8–14. http://www.amielandmelburn.org.uk/collections/mt/index_frame.htm accessed 3 July, 2010.

MAYOR OF LONDON, 2005. *Why the Mayor of London will maintain dialogues with all of London's faiths and communities: a reply to the dossier against the Mayor's meeting with Dr. Yusuf al-Qaradawi*. London: Greater London Authority.

MAYOR OF LONDON, 2006. *Muslims in London*. London: Greater London Authority.

MAYOR OF LONDON, 2006. 'Ken Livingstone's plenary address', State of London Debate, 13 May, 2006, QE II Conference Centre, Westminster. http://www.london.gov.uk/stateoflondon/transcript.jsp accessed 6 August, 2010.

MAYOR OF LONDON, 2007. 'The search for common ground: Muslims, non-Muslims and the UK media', London: Greater London Authority. http://www.london.gov.uk/mayor/equalities/docs/commonground_report.pdf accessed 6 August, 2010.

McAULEY, Dennis, 2005. 'The Ideology of Osama Bin Laden: Nation, tribe and world economy', *Journal of Political Ideologies*. 10 (3), pp. 269–287.

McCANTS, William, ed., 2006. *Militant Ideology Atlas: Research Compendium*. West Point: Combating Terrorism Center.

McCULLOCH, Jude, 2003. '"Counter-terrorism", human security and globalisation—from welfare to warfare state?', *Current issues in Criminal Justice*. March, 14 (3) pp. 283–298.

McCULLOCH, Jude and Pickering, Sharon, 2005. 'Suppressing the Financing of Terrorism', *British Journal of Criminology*. 45, pp. 470–486.

McFATE, Montgomery, 2007. 'The Cultural Knowledge Gap and Its Consequences for National Security. Project report summary', *Institute for Peace*. 10 May. http://www.usip.org/fellows/reports/2007/0510_mcfate.htm accessed 16 January, 2010.

McGHEE, Derek, 2005. *Intolerant Britain? Hate, citizenship and difference*. Maidenhead: Open University Press.

McGHEE, Derek, 2008. *The End of Multiculturalism: Terrorism, Integration and Human Rights*. Maidenhead: Open University Press.

McROY, Anthony, 2006. *From Rushdie to 7/7: The Radicalisation of Islam in Britain*. London: Social Affairs Unit.

McTERNAN, Oliver, 2003. *Violence in God's Name: Religion in an Age of Conflict*. London: Darton, Longman & Todd.

MEER, Nasar, 2006. '"Get off your knees!" Print media public intellectuals and Muslims in Britain', *Journalism Studies*. 7 (1) pp. 35–59.

MEER, Nasar and Noorani, Tehseen, 2008. 'A sociological comparison of anti-Semitism and anti-Muslim sentiment in Britain', *The Sociological Review*. 56 (2) pp. 195–219.

MEIJER, Roel, 2009. 'Towards a Political Islam', *Clingendael Diplomacy Papers No. 22*. Netherlands Institute of International Relations, The Hague.

METROPOLITAN POLICE, 1977. *Instruction Book*. London: MPS.

METROPOLITAN POLICE AUTHORITY, 2005. 'Ascent 2000 citizenship centre-request for funding'. http://www.mpa.gov.uk/access/committees/cop/2003/030519/05.htm accessed 2 July, 2010.

METROPOLITAN POLICE AUTHORITY, 2007. *Counter-Terrorism: The London Debate*. London: MPA.

MICHOT, Yahya, 2006. *Muslims Under Non-Muslim Rule: Ibn Taymiyya*. Oxford: Interface.

MILES, Alice, 2005. 'After all the sneering, at least someone is sticking up for the middle classes', *The Times opinion page*, 23 Nov. http://www.timesonline.co.uk/article/O,,1058–1884407,00.htm accessed 12 December, 2010.

MILNE, Seumas, 1994. *The Enemy Within: The Secret War Against the Miners*. London: Verso.

MIRZA, Munira, 2007. *Living Apart Together: British Muslims and the paradox of multiculturalism*. Policy Exchange, London.

MODOOD, Tariq, 2005. *Multicultural Politics: Racism, Ethnicity and Muslims in Britain*. Edinburgh: Edinburgh University Press.

MODOOD, Tariq, 2006. 'British Muslims and the politics of multiculturalism', in Tariq Modood, Anna Triandafyyllidou, and Richard Zapata-Barrero, eds., *Multiculturalism, Muslims and Citizenship: A European Approach*. London: Routledge, pp. 37–56.

MOORE, Charles, 2008. 'How To Beat the Scargills of Islam', *The 2008 Keith Joseph Memorial Lecture*. Centre for Policy Studies, 10 March. http://www.policyexchange.org.uk/images/libimages/362.pdf accessed 23 July, 2010.

MOUSSAOUI, Abd Samad (with Florence Bouquillat), trans. Simon Pleasance & Fronza Woods, 2003. *Zacarias Moussaoui: The Making of a Terrorist*. London: Serpent's Tail.

MURAD, Abdul-Hakim, 2001. *Recapturing Islam from the Terrorists*. http://www.masud.co.uk/ISLAM/ahm/recapturing.htm accessed 5 September, 2010.

MURRAY, Andrew and German, Lindsey, 2005. *Stop the War*. London: Bookmarks.

MUSLIM COUNCIL of BRITAIN, 2003. 'Response to Islamophobia—Identity, Inclusion, Cohesion, and equality in Modern Britain', a report by the Runnymede Commission on British Muslims and Islamophobia, 20 November. http://www.mcb.org.uk/library/Islamophobia.pdf accessed 3 February, 2010.

MUSLIM COUNCIL of BRITAIN, 2004. 'Counter-Terrorism Powers: Reconciling Security and Liberty in an Open Society', August. http://www.mcb.org.uk/library/ATCSA.pdf accessed 3 February, 2010.

MUSLIM COUNCIL of BRITAIN, 2005. 'Interview with Fadi Itani, 24 January', http://www.mcb.org.uk/features/features.php?ann_id=727 accessed 3 May, 2009.

MYHILL, Andy, 2006. 'Community engagement in policing: Lessons from the literature', London: Stationery Office http:/www.crimereduction.gov.uk/policing18.htm accessed 3 May, 2010.

NADWI, Sayyed Abdul Hasan 'Ali, 2005. Trans. *Muhyiddin Ahmad. Sheikh ul Islam—Ibn Taimiyah: Life and Achievements*. Leicester: UK Islamic Academy.

NAFI, Bashir, 2004. 'The Rise of Islamic Reformist Thought and its Challenge to Traditional Islam', in Nafi, Bashir M., and Taji-Farouki, Suha, eds., *Islamic Thought in the Twentieth Century*. London: I. B. Taurus.

NAFI, Bashir M., 2004. 'Fatwa and War: On the Allegiance of the American Muslim Soldiers in the Aftermath of September 11', *Islamic Law and Society*. 11(1) pp. 78–116.

NAHDI, Fuad, 2003. 'Young, British, and Ready to Fight: New laws and the war have pushed our Islamic radicals underground', *The Guardian*, 1 April. http://www.guardian.co.uk/world/2003/apr/01/religion.uk accessed 4 August, 2009.

NAGL, John A., 2005, new ed. *Learning to Eat Soup with a Knife: Counterinsurgency Lessons from Malaya and Vietnam*. Chicago: Chicago University Press.

NAQSHBANDI, Mehmood, 2006. *Islam and Muslims in Britain: a Guide for Non-Muslims*. London: City of London Police.

NAQSHBANDI, Mehmood, 2006. 'Problems and Practical Solutions to Tackle Extremism; and Muslim Youth and Community Issues', *The Shrivenham Papers*, No. 1, August, Defence Academy of the United Kingdom.

NASR, Seyyed Hossein, 2005. 'Islam & the Question of Violence', in Aftab Ahmad Malik, ed., *With God On Our Side: Politics & Theology of the War on Terrorism*. Bristol: Amal Press, pp. 291–298.

NATIONAL ARCHIVES, Kew. 'History of Special Branch', http://www.nationalarchives.gov.uk/securityhistory/branch.htm accessed 23 September, 2010.

NATIONAL COMMISSION ON TERRORISM ATTACKS UPON THE UNITED STATES, 2004. *The 9/11 Commission Report: Authorised Edition*. London: W.W. Norton & Company.

NEUMANN, Peter R., 2006. 'Europe's Jihadist Dilemma', *Survival*. 48 (2) pp. 71–84.

NEUMAN, Peter, R, 2006. 'What precisely constitutes a moderate Muslim?'. http://www.madrid11.net/node/114 accessed 2 January, 2008.

NEUMANN, Peter R., 2008. 'Joining al-Qaeda: Jihadist Recruitment in Europe', *Adelphi Paper 399*. International Institute for Strategic Studies. pp. 31–34.

NFO NEWSFILM, 2006. 'Transcript of ITV early evening news', 6 July, 06. http://www.nfo.ac.uk/collections/records/0014–0005–4741–0000-0-0000-0000-0.html accessed 29 December, 2010.

OBORNE, Peter, 2006. *The Use and Abuse of Terror: The Construction of a False Narrative on the Domestic Terror Threat*. London: Centre for Policy Studies.

O'CALLAGHAN, Sean, 1999. *The Informer*. London: Corgi Books.

OFCOM, 2008. Broadcast Bulletin, 97. 19 November. Ofcom: London http://www.ofcom.org.uk/tv/obb/prog_cb/obb97/ accessed 2 November, 2010.

OLIVETI, Vincenzo, 2002. *Terror's Source: The Ideology of Wahhabi-Salafism and its Consequences*. Birmingham: Amadeus Books.

O'NEILL, Sean and McGrory, Daniel, 2006. *The Suicide Factory: Abu Hamza and the Finsbury Park Mosque*. London: Harper Perennial.

OWEN, David, 2007. *The Hubris Syndrome: Bush, Blair and the intoxication of power*. London: Politicos.

BIBLIOGRAPHY

PANTUCCI, Raffaello, 2009. 'British Government Debates Engagement with Radical Islam in New Counterterrorism Strategy', *Terrorism Monitor*. 7 (10) 24 April. Category: Terrorism Monitor, Global Terrorism Analysis, Home Page, Military/Security, Europe

PAPE, Robert A., 2006. *Dying to Win: Why Suicide Terrorists Do It*. London: Gibson Square.

PAZ, Reuven, 2005. 'Global Jihad and WMD: Between Martyrdom and Mass Destruction', *Current Trends in Islamist Ideology*, vol. 2, Hudson Institute, pp. 74–86.

PEDAHZUR, Ami, 2005. *Suicide Terrorism*. Cambridge: Polity.

PELFREY, William V., 2005. 'Parallels between Community Oriented Policing and the War on Terrorism: Lessons Learned', *Criminal Justice Studies*. 18 (4) pp. 335–346.

POYNTING, S. and Mason, V, 2006. 'Tolerance, freedom, justice and peace?: Britain, Australia and anti-Muslim racism since 11th September 2001', *Journal of Intercultural Studies* 27 (4) pp. 365–392.

PHILLIPS, Melanie, 2006. *Londonistan: How Britain Is Creating a Terror State Within*. London: Gibson Square.

PHILLIPS, Melanie, 2008a. 'Lunacy at the Yard', *The Spectator*, 15 December. http://www.spectator.co.uk/melaniephillips/3088576/lunacy-at-the-yard.thtml accessed 4 August, 2010.

PHILLIPS, Melanie, 2008b. *Master of Islamist doublespeak. The Australian*, 3 March. http://www.melaniephillips.com/articles-new/?p=570 accessed 23 April, 2010.

PHILLIPS, Richard, 2008. 'Standing together: the Muslim Association of Britain and the anti-war movement', *Race & Class*. 50 (2) pp. 101–113.

PIPES, Daniel, 2003. *Militant Islam Reaches America*. London: W.W. Norton & Company.

PIPES, Daniel, 2005. 'Does a "Covenant of Security" Protect the United Kingdom?', *Daniel Pipes.org*. http://www.danielpipes.org/blog/2004/08/does-a-covenant-of-security-protect-the accessed 19 April, 2010.

PIPES, Daniel, 2007. 'My debate with London mayor', *www.danielpipes.org*. http://www.danielpipes.org/blog/2007/01/my-debate-with-london-mayor-ken-livingstone.html accessed 19 February, 2009.

POOLE, Elizabeth, 2006. 'The Effects of September 11 and the War in Iraq on British Newspaper Coverage', in Poole, Elizabeth and John E. Richardson, eds., *Muslims and the News Media*. London: I.B. Taurus, pp. 96–97.

PRESS COMPLAINTS COMMISSION, 2005. 'Brixton Mosque'. http://www.pcc.org.uk/news/index.html?article=NDc1Mg accessed 2 October, 2010.

PUNCH, Maurice, 1993. 'Observation and the Police: The Research Experience', in Hammersley M, ed, *Social Research: Philosophy, Politics and Practice*. London: Sage.

PUNCH, Maurice and Colin Cramphorn, 2006. 'The Murder of Theo van Gogh, and the Islamic Jihad Division in the Netherlands', *Police Research & Management*. 6 (3) pp. 11–31.

PYSZCZNSKI, T., Solomon, S. and Greenberg, J., 2002. *In the Wake of 9/11: The Psychology of Terror*. Washington, DC: American Psychological Association.

QUILLIAM FOUNDATION, 2008. 'Pulling Together to Defeat Terror. Policy document', April. http://www.quilliamfoundation.org/images/stories/pdfs/pulling-together-to-defeat-terror.pdf accessed 2 January, 2010.

QUTB, Sayyid, 2000. *In the Shade of The Qur'an. Volume II. Al 'Imran*. Trans. and ed. Adil Salahi, and Ashur Shamis. Leicester: The Islamic Foundation.

QUTB, Sayyid, 1990. *Milestones*. Indianapolis: American Trust Publications.

RABASA, Angel, 2005. 'Radical and Moderate Islam', *Testimony presented to the House Armed Services Committee, Subcommittee on Terrorism, Unconventional Threats and Capabilities on February 16, 2006*. Santa Monica: Rand. http://www.rand.org/pubs/testimonies/CT250–1/ accessed 2 February, 2009.

RAI, Milan, 2006. *7/7: The London Bombings, Islam & The Iraq War*. London: Pluto Press.

RAMADAN, Tariq, 1999. *To Be A European Muslim*. Leicester: The Islamic Foundation.

RAMADAN, Tariq, 2004. *Western Muslims and the Future of Islam*. Oxford: Oxford University Press.

REES, Wyn and Aldrich, Richard J., 2005. 'Contending cultures of counterterrorism: transatlantic divergence or convergence', *International Affairs*. 81 (5) pp. 905–923.

REINER, Robert, 1985. *The Politics of the Police*. Brighton: Wheatsheaf.

REINER, Robert, 2000. *The Politics of the Police*. 2nd ed. Oxford: Oxford University Press.

RENNIE, David, 2005. 'I'd do it all again, say's film-makers killer', *Daily Telegraph*, 13 July. http://www.telegraph.co.uk/news/main.jhtml?xml=/news/2005/07/13/wbouy13.xm accessed 4 August, 2010.

REUT INSTITUTE, 2010. 'Building a Political Firewall against the Assault on Israel's Legitimacy: London as a Case Study', November, pp. 40–41, http://www.reut-institute.org/Publication.aspx?PublicationId=3949 accessed 29 August.

RICHARDSON, Louise, 2006. *What Terrorists Want: Understanding the Terrorist Threat*. London: John Murray.

ROBERT, Na'ima, R., 2005. *From My Sister's Lips*. London: Bantam.

ROBSON, Colin, 2004. *Real World Research*. 2nd ed. Massachusetts: Blackwell.

ROSENFELD, Richard, 2004. 'Terrorism and Criminology', in Mathieu Deflem, ed. Terrorism and *Counter-Terrorism: Criminological Perspectives*. Oxford: Elsevier, pp. 9–18.

ROY, Olivier, 2004. *Globalised Islam: The Search for a New Ummah*. London: Hurst.

RUBIN, H.J., and Rubin, I.S., 1995. *Qualitative Interviewing: The Art of Hearing Data*. London: Sage.

RUTHVEN, Malise, 2002. *A Fury For God*. London: Granta.

SADIKI, Larbi, 2004. *The Search For Arab Democracy: Discourses and Counter-Discourses*. London: Hurst.

SAGEMAN, Marc, 2004. *Understanding Terror Networks*. Philadelphia: University of Pennsylvania Press.

SAGEMAN, Marc, 2007. *Leaderless Jihad: Terror Networks in the Twenty-First Century*. Philadelphia: University of Pennsylvania Press.

SAGGAR, Shamit, 2009. *Pariah Politics: Understanding Western Radical Islamism and What Should be Done*. Oxford: Oxford University Press.

SAID, Edward W., 1997. *Covering Islam*. London: Vintage.

SALAFIMANHAJ.COM, 2006. 'The Devil's Deception of 'Abdullaah Faysal'. http://www.salafimanhaj.com/ebook.php?ebook=45 accessed 26 May, 2010.

SALAFIMANHAJ.COM, 2007. 'Is the Salafi Manhaj an Indicator of Terrorism, Political Violence and Radicalisation? A Critical Study of the NYPD Document "Radicalisation in the West—the Home Grown Threat" by Mitchell D, Silber and Arvin Bhatt', http://www.salafimanhaj.com/ebook.php?ebook=45 accessed 26 May, 2010.

SARDAR, Ziauddin, 2004. *Desperately Seeking Paradise*. London:Granta.

SCARMAN, Lord, 1982. *The Scarman Report: The Brixton Disorders 10–12 April, 1981*. London: Pelican.

SCRATON, Phil, 2002. 'In the Name of a Just War', in Phil Scraton, ed., 'Beyond September 11: an Anthology of Dissent'. London: Pluto Press, pp. 216–233.

SCHEUER, Michael ('Anonymous'), 2003. *Through Our Enemies' Eyes: Osama bin Laden, Radical Islam, and the Future of America*. Washington, D.C: Brassey's.

SCHBLEY, Ayla, 2003. 'Defining Religious Terrorism: A Causal and Anthological Profile', *Studies in Conflict & Terrorism*. 26, pp. 105–134.

SCHMID, Alex P., and Jomgman, A, 1988. *Political Terrorism: A Guide to Actors, Authors, Concepts, Data Bases, Theories and Literature*. Oxford: North Holland.

SCHMID, Alex P., 2004. 'Frameworks for Conceptualising Terrorism', *Terrorism and Political Violence*. 16 (2) pp. 197–221.

SCHWEITZER, Yoram, 2006. 'Al-Qaeda and the Global Epidemic of Suicide Attacks', in Ami Pedahzur, ed., *Root Causes of Suicide Terrorism: The globalisation of martyrdom*. Oxford: Routledge, pp. 122–131.

SEATON, Matt, 1995. 'Charge of the New Red Brigade', *Independent on Sunday*, January. Reproduced at http://libcom.org/library/red-action-ira-london-bombs-independent accessed 2 July, 2009.

SHARP, Douglas, 2002. 'Policing after Macpherson: some experiences of Muslim police officers', in Basia Spalek, ed., *Islam, Crime and Criminal Justice*. Cullompton: Devon. pp. 76–93.

SHIBLI, Murtaza, 2010. *7/7: Muslim Perspectives*. London: Rabita.

SILBER, Mitchell D and Arvin Bhatt, 2007. 'Senior Intelligence Analysts—NYPD Intelligence Division Radicalisation in the West—The Homegrown Threat'. http://www.nyc.gov/html/nypd/pdf/dcpi/NYPD_Report-Radicalization_in_the_West.pdf accessed 3 January, 2010.

SILKE, Andrew, 2003. 'Becoming a Terrorist', in Andrew Silke, ed. *Terrorists, Victims and Society: Psychological Perspectives on Terrorism and its Consequences*. Chichester: Wiley, pp. 29–54.

SILKE, Andrew, 2003. 'The Psychology of Suicidal Terrorism', in Andrew Silke, ed. *Terrorists, Victims and Society: Psychological Perspectives on Terrorism and its Consequences*. Chichester: Wiley, pp. 93–108.

SILKE, Andrew, 2003. 'Retaliating Against Terrorism', in Andrew Silke, ed. *Terrorists, Victims and Society: Psychological Perspectives on Terrorism and its Consequences*. Chichester: Wiley, pp. 231–256.

SILKE, Andrew, 2004. 'An introduction to Terrorism Research', in Andrew Silke, ed. *Research on Terrorism: Trends, Achievements and Failures*. London: Frank Cass, pp. 1–29.

SILKE, Andrew, 2004. 'The Devil You Know: Continuing Problems with Research on Terrorism', in Andrew Silke, ed. *Research on Terrorism: Trends, Achievements and Failures*. London: Frank Cass, pp. 57–71.

SILKE, Andrew, 2004. 'The Road Less Travelled: Recent Trends in Terrorism Research', in Andrew Silke, ed. *Research on Terrorism: Trends, Achievements and Failures*. London: Frank Cass, pp. 186–213.

SIVANANDAN, A., ed., 1987. *Policing Against Black People*. London: Institute of Race Relations.

SLUKA, J. ed. 2000. *Death Squad: an Anthropology of State Terror*. Philadelphia: University of Pennsylvania Press.

SOOKHDEO, Patrick, 2004. *Understanding Islamic Terrorism*. Pewsey: Isaac Publishing.

SOOKHDEO, Patrick, 2006. 'The Schools That Divide the Nation'. *London Evening Standard*, 14 September, p. 15.

SOUHAMI, A., 2007. 'Understanding Institutional Racism: the Stephen Lawrence Inquiry and the police service reaction', in *Policing beyond Macpherson: Issues in policing, race and society*. Devon: Willan, pp 66–87.

SPALEK, Basia, 2002. 'Religious diversity, British Muslims, crime and victimisation', in Basia Spalek, ed., *Islam, Crime and Criminal Justice*. Cullompton: Devon. pp. 50–71.

SPALEK, Basia, 2005. 'Muslims and the Criminal Justice System', in T. Choudhury, ed., *Muslims in the UK: policies for engaged citizens*. Budapest: Open Society Institute, pp. 253–340.

SPALEK, Basia, 2005. 'British Muslims and Community Safety post-September 11th', *Community Safety Journal*. 4(2), pp. 12–20.

SPALEK, Basia, 2006. 'Disconnection and Exclusion: pathways to radicalisation?', in T. Abbas, ed., *Islamic Political Radicalism* Edinburgh: Edinburgh University Press.

BIBLIOGRAPHY

SPALEK, Basia, and El-Hassan, Salah, 2007. 'Muslim Converts in Prison', *The Howard Journal of Criminal Justice*. 46 (2), pp. 99–114

SPALEK, Basia and Lambert, Robert, 2007. 'Terrorism, Counter-Terrorism and Muslim Community Engagement post 9/11', *Social Justice and Criminal Justice conference papers*, Centre for Crime & Justice Studies, Kings College, London. July, pp. 202–215.

SPALEK, Basia and Lambert, Robert, 2008. 'Muslim Communities, Counterterrorism and Counter-radicalisation: a critically reflective approach to engagement', *International Journal of Law, Crime and Justice*. 36 (4), pp. 257–270.

SPALEK, Basia, El-Awa, Salwa, and McDonald, Liza Z., 2008. *Police-Muslim Engagement and Partnerships for the Purposes of Counter-terrorism*. Summary report. 18 November. University of Birmingham. http://muslimsafetyforum.org/docs/summary%20report%20ct%20police%20community%20partnership%20bham accessed 2 February, 2010.

SPALEK, Basia and Robert Lambert, 2009. 'The Importance of Partnership, Dialogue and Support when Engaging with Muslim Communities', in Matthew Goodwin and Roger Eatwell, eds., *The New Extremism in 21st Century Britain*. London: Routledge.

SPENCER, Alexander, 2006. 'Questioning the Concept of "New Terrorism"', *Peace, Conflict & Development*. 8, January, pp. 1–33.

STAIRWAY TO HEAVEN memorial, 2010. http://www.stairwaytoheavenmemorial.org/gpage5.html accessed 29 December, 2010.

STEPANOVA, Ekatarina, 2008. *Terrorism in Asymmetrical Conflict: Ideological and Structural Aspects*. Stockholm International Peace Research Institute (SIPRI) Research Report No. 23. Oxford: Oxford University Press.

STERN, Jessica, 2003. *Terror in the Name of God: Why Religious Militants Kill*. New York: Harper Collins.

SUN newspaper, 2008. *Osama bin London*. 27 February. http://www.thesun.co.uk/sol/homepage/news/article851255.ece accessed 23 August, 2010.

SYLVESTER, R & Thompson, A. 2007. 'Dr. Bari—Government Stoking Muslim Tension', *Daily Telegraph*, 12 November. http://www.telegraph.co.uk/news/main.jhtml?xml=/news/2007/11/10/nbari110.xml accessed 28 November, 2010.

TAARNBY, Michael, 2005. *Recruitment of Islamist Terrorists in Europe: Trends and Perspectives*. Aarhus, Denmark: University of Aarhus.

TAMIMI, Azzam, 2001. *Rachid Ghannouchi: a Democrat within Islam*. Oxford: Oxford University Press.

TAMIMI, Azzam, 2002. 'Human Rights—Islamic & Secular Perspectives', in *The Quest for Sanity: Reflections on September 11 and the Aftermath*. London: Muslim Council of Britain, pp. 229–236.

TARROW, Sidney, 1998. *Power in Movement*. New York: Cambridge University Press.

TASEER, Aatish, 2005. 'A British Jihadist: An interview with Hassan Butt', *Prospect*. August, pp. 18–24.

384

TAYLOR, Matthew, 2010. 'Inside the violent world of the new far right', 28 May. http://www.guardian.co.uk/uk/2010/may/28/english-defence-league-guardian-investigation accessed 30 December, 2010.

TAYLOR, Maxwell, 1988. *The Terrorist*. London: Brassey's.

TAYLOR, Maxwell and Quayle, Ethel, 1994. *Terrorist Lives*. London: Brassey's.

TAYLOR, Nick, 2006. 'Covert Policing and Proportionality', *Covert Policing Review*. March, pp. 22–33.

THIEL, Darren, 2009. *Policing Terrorism: A Review of the Evidence*. London: The Police Foundation.

THOMAS, David and Inkson, Kerr, 2003. *Cultural Intelligence* San Francisco: Berrett-Koehler.

TIBAWI, A. L., 2000. 'English-Speaking Orientalists', in A. L. Macfie, ed., *Orientalism: A Reader*. Edinburgh: Edinburgh University Press, pp. 57–78.

TIBI, Bassam, 2005. *Islam Between Culture and Politics*. Basingstoke: Palgrave.

TILLY, Charles, 2003. *The Politics of Collective Violence*. Cambridge: Cambridge University Press.

TILLY, Charles, 2004. 'Trust and Rule', *Theory and Society*. 33 (1) pp. 1–30.

TIMES online, 2007. 'BBC took terrorists paintballing', 5 December. http://www.timesonline.co.uk/tol/news/uk/crime/article3001102.ece accessed 12 August, 2008

TIMES online, 2007. 'Policy Exchange apology to Dr. Mohammad Abdul Bari', 17 December. http://www.timesonline.co.uk/tol/news/uk/article3059836.ece accessed 23 August, 2009.

TRAVIS, Alan, 2008. 'The Making of an Extremist', *Guardian*. 20 August.

TRAVIS, Alan, Clare Dyer, and Michael White, 2005. 'Britain "sliding into police state"', *Guardian*, 28 January.

TREVERTON, Gregory, et al., 2005. 'Exploring Religious Conflict', *RAND National Security Research Division Conference Proceedings*. Santa Monica: Rand.

TULLOCH, John, 2006. *One Day in July: Experiencing 7/7*. London: Little, Brown.

TUPMAN, W.A., 1989. *Beyond Terrorism: towards a theory of scenarios of political violence*. Brookfield Papers No. 1. Exeter: Centre for Police & Criminal Justice Studies.

TUPMAN, W.A., 2000. 'Multiculturalism, minorities and policing', *Europa*. 4 (1) http://www.intellect-net.com/europa/index.html accessed 3 January, 2010.

TUPMAN, W.A., 2002. 'The Business of Terrorism Part 1', *Intersec. The Journal of International Security*. 12 (1), pp. 6–8.

TUPMAN, W.A., 2002. 'The Business of Terrorism Part 2', *Intersec. The Journal of International Security*. 12 (6) pp. 186–8.

TUPMAN, W.A. and O'Reilly, C., 2004. 'Terrorism, Hegemony and Legitimacy: Evaluating success and failure in the War on Terror', in *Political Stud-*

ies Association conference, Lincoln, August. http://www.psa.ac.uk/cps/2004/tupman.pdf accessed 14 July, 2010.

TUPMAN, W, and TUPMAN, A, 1999. *Policing in Europe: Uniform in Diversity*. Exeter: Intellect.

TURK, Austin, 2002. 'Policing International Terrorism: Options', *Police Practice and Research*. 3 (4), pp. 279–286.

TURK, Austin, 2002. 'Confronting enemies foreign and domestic: An American dilemma?', *Criminology and Public Policy*. 1, pp. 345–350.

TURK, Austin, 2004. 'Sociology of Terrorism', *Annual Review of Sociology*. 30, pp. 271–286.

US v. Omar Abdul Rahman et al; 'S5 93 Cr. 181. Court transcript'. http:/intelfiles.egoplex.com/61HKRAHS-sentencing.htm accessed 7 July, 2010.

VENESS, David, 2001. 'Terrorism and Counterterrorism: An International Perspective', *Studies in Conflict & Terrorism*. 24, pp. 407–416.

VENESS, David, 2002. 'The Role of the Police', in Rachel Briggs, ed., *The Unlikely Counter-Terrorists*. London: The Foreign Policy Centre, 2002, pp. 52–58.

VERSI, Ahmed J., 2006. 'Interview with Sir Ian Blair, Commissioner, Metropolitan Police', *Muslim News*. 29 September, pp. 4–5.

VICTOROFF, J., 2005. 'The Mind of the Terrorist: A Review and Critique of Psychological Approaches', *Journal of Conflict Resolution*. 49 (1), pp. 3–42.

VIDINO, Lorenzo, 2005. 'The Muslim Brotherhood's Conquest of Europe', *Middle East Quarterly*, Winter, 12 (1). http://www.meforum.org/687/the-muslim-brotherhoods-conquest-of-europe accessed 3 April, 2010.

VIDINO, Lorenzo, 2006. *Al Qaeda In Europe: the New Battlefield of International Jihad*. London: Prometheus Books.

VIDINO, Lorenzo, 2009. 'Europe's New Security Dilemma', *Washington Quarterly*, Centre for Strategic and Internal Studies. October 32 (4), pp. 61–75.

WACQUANT, Loic, 2004. *Body and Soul: Notebooks of an apprentice boxer*. Oxford: Oxford University Press.

WADDINGTON, P. A. J., 1999. 'Police (Canteen) Sub-Culture: An Appreciation', *British Journal of Criminology*. 39 (2), pp. 287–309.

WADDINGTON, P. A. J., 2005. 'Slippery Slopes and Civil Libertarian Pessimism', *Policing & Society*. 15 (3), pp. 353–375.

WALT, Stephen M., 2002. 'Beyond bin Laden: Reshaping U.S. Foreign Policy', *International Security*. 26 (3), pp. 56–78.

WARD, Tony, 2005. 'State Crime in the Heart of Darkness', *British Journal of Criminology*. 45(4), pp. 434–445.

WARDLAW, Grant, 1982. *Political Terrorism: Theory, tactics and countermeasures*. Cambridge: Cambridge University Press.

WARE, John, 2009. 'Panorama's Faith, Hate and Charity: standing by the allegations', *Guardian Organ Grinder blog*. http://www.guardian.co.uk/media/organgrinder/2009/mar/03/panorama-stands-by-charity-allegations accessed 26 June, 2010.

WARRAQ, Ibn, 1995. *Why I Am Not a Muslim*. London: Prometheus.

WEIR, Stuart, 2006. *Unequal Britain: Human Rights as a Route to Social Justice*. London: Politicos.

WERBNER, Pnina, 2000. 'Divided Loyalties, Empowered Citizenship? Muslims in Britain', *Citizenship Studies*. 4 (3), pp. 307–324.

WHINE, Michael, 2005a. The Penetration of Islamist Ideology in Britain. *Current Trends in Islamist Ideology*. 1, Hudson Institute.

WHINE, Michael, 2005b. 'The Advance of the Muslim Brotherhood in the UK', *Current Trends in Islamist Ideology*. 2, Hudson Institute, pp. 30–40.

WHYTE, Dave, 2002. 'Business as Usual? Corporate Moralism and the "War Against Terrorism"', in Phil Scraton, ed., *Beyond September 11: An Anthology of Dissent*. London: Pluto Press, pp. 150–157.

WHYTE, W.F., 1993. *Street Corner Society: The Social Structure of an Italian Slum*. London: University of Chicago Press.

WIKTOROWICZ, Quintan, 2004. 'Islamic Activism and Social Movement Theory', in Quintan Wiktorowicz, ed., *Islamic Activism: a Social Movement Theory Approach*. Indiana: Indiana University Press, pp. 1–36.

WIKTOROWICZ, Quintan, 2005. 'A Genealogy of Radical Islam', *Studies in Conflict & Terrorism*. 28 (2), pp. 75–97.

WIKTOROWICZ, Quintan, 2005. *Radical Islam Rising: Muslim Extremism in the West*. Oxford: Rowman & Littlefield. p. 787

WIKTOROWICZ, Quintan, 2006. 'Anatomy of the Salafi Movement', *Studies in Conflict & Terrorism*. 29 (4), pp. 207–239.

WILKINSON, Paul, 2000. *Terrorism Versus Democracy: The Liberal State Response*. London: Frank Cass.

WILSON, Richard Ashby, 2005. 'Human Rights in the "War on Terror"', in Wilson, Richard Ashby, ed., *Human Rights in the 'War on Terror*. Cambridge: Cambridge University Press. pp. 1–37.

WINNETT, Robert and Leppard, David, 2004. 'Britain's secret plans to win Muslim hearts and minds', *Times Online*. 30 May. http://www.timesonline.co.uk/tol/news/uk/article436135.ece accessed 21 August, 2010.

WINNETT, Robert and Leppard, David, 2005. 'Young Muslims and Extremism', *Times Online*. 10 July. http://www.timesonline.co.uk/tol/news/uk/article542420.ece accessed 3 July, 2009.

WOLFENDALE, Jessica, 2006. 'Terrorism, Security, and the Threat of Counterterrorism', *Studies in Conflict & Terrorism*. 29, pp. 753–770.

YACOOB, Salma, 2007. 'British Islamic Political Radicalism', in Abbas, Tahir, ed., *Islamic Political Radicalism: A European Perspective*. Edinburgh: Edinburgh University Press. pp. 279–294.

YOUNG, Robert, 2004. 'Political Terrorism as a Weapon of the Politically Powerless, in Igor Primoratz, ed., *Terrorism: The Philosophical Issues*, Basingstoke: Palgrave, pp. 3–14.

ZULAIKA, Joseba and Douglass, William A., 1996. *Terror and Taboo*. London: Routledge.

ABOUT THE AUTHOR

For the bulk of his police service (1977–2007) Robert Lambert worked for Metropolitan Police Special Branch (MPSB) countering all forms of terrorism and political violence in the UK, from Irish republican to the many strands of international terrorism including the al-Qaeda movement. One common denominator in all the many and varied terrorist recruitment strategies he witnessed over the years was the exploitation of a sense of political injustice. Remedying injustice, he came to understand, was a crucial if neglected part of counter-terrorism that should not be perceived as appeasing terrorists. In parallel, throughout his police career Lambert placed value on street or grassroots perspectives over more rigid top-down security approaches to counter-terrorism.

In the final phase of his police career, together with a police colleague, Lambert set up the Muslim Contact Unit (MCU), with the purpose of establishing partnerships with Muslim community leaders both equipped and located to help assess and tackle the spread of al-Qaeda's influence in London. This role enabled him to participate in some pioneering and successful counter-terrorism community engagement projects. It also provided Lambert with opportunities to support Muslim community groups when they faced Islamophobic attacks. In recognition of his work he was presented with the first 'Friends of Islam' award by Dr Mohammad Abdul Bari, Secretary General of the Muslim Council of Britain, at the annual Global, Peace and Unity event in November 2007 and the first 'Dialogue and Building Bridges' award by Anas Altikriti, Chief Executive of The Cordoba Foundation, at Islam Expo in July 2008. In addition, on his retirement from the Metropolitan Police he was presented with awards from the Finsbury Park Mosque, Brixton Masjid, Islamic Human Rights Commission, Interpal, and many other mosques and Muslim charities and organisations. In June 2008 he was awarded an MBE by Her Majesty the Queen for his MPSB service.

Lambert was awarded a PhD for his research dissertation 'The London Partnerships: an Insider's Analysis of Legitimacy and Effectiveness' at the University of Exeter in 2010 which provides the basis for this book. As a mature part-time student Robert was awarded a distinction for his MA dissertation on early modern English encounters with Islam at Birkbeck College, University of London in 2004; and in 2002, first class honours for an inter-disciplinary European cultural history BA at the Open University.

Since September 2009 Lambert has been co-director of the European Muslim Research Centre (EMRC) at the University of Exeter and a part-time lecturer at the Centre for the Study of Terrorism and Political Violence (CSTPV) at the University of St. Andrews. In 2010 EMRC published two reports on *Islamophobia and Anti-Muslim Hate Crime* co-authored by Lambert, the first two reports in a ten-year programme of Europe-wide research. Lambert's twin research interests are community-based approaches to counter-terrorism and Islamophobia. Since January 2008 Lambert has conducted research and written reports and articles in partnership with Dr Jonathan Githens-Mazer, co-director, EMRC. He has also worked in partnership researching community-based approaches to counter-terrorism with Dr Basia Spalek, Dr Salwa el Awa and Dr Laura McDonald at the University of Birmingham.

INDEX

ism in, 169; Ritzy Cinema, 169; Salafi population of, 61–2, 71–2, 84, 105, 125, 155, 157–8, 161, 163, 165–6, 169, 174, 178, 181–2, 184–5, 192, 196, 200–1, 205–6, 210, 229, 261, 274, 277, 282, 284, 292

Brixton Mosque: 57, 183, 202–3, 210; counter-terrorism operations in, 49; location of, xv; Salafis in, 125

Brixton Riots (1981/ 1985/1995): 127; example of, 9

Broadwater Farm Riot (1985): 127

Brooke, Stephen: writings of, 32

Brown, Gordon: administration of, 120; foreign policy of, 27

Brown, Mousa: BBC interview, 163; trial of, 162

Bullman, Joe: documentaries of, 4

Bunyan, Tony: 7

Bush, George W.: 39, 67, 226, 271; administration of, 19, 37; expansion of War on Terror, 55; foreign policy of, 28, 45, 59, 129, 138, 208

Butt, Hassan: *Leaving al-Qaeda*, 259; questioning of legitimacy of claims made by, 259–60

Cameron, David: British Prime Minister, 289; foreign policy of, 27

Campaign against Criminalising Communities (CAM-PACC): participants in, 225

Campbell, Alistair: 41

Catholicism: 207; Irish, 62–3, 239; Nationalist, 63; Republican, 63

Charity Commission: 100, 131, 133, 140; officials of, 81, 84–5, 104, 132; role in Finsbury Park Mosque raid (2003), 146

Chilcot Inquiry: Tony Blair's testimony to, 38

Choudhury, Anjem: 260, 288; leader of Islam For The UK, 287; Shari'ah Roadshow (2009), 287

Chouet, Alain: former head of Direction Générale de la Sécruité Extérieure, 281

Christianity: 74, 149, 168; evangelical, 166, 168

Churchill, Winston: 26; British Home Secretary, 18; intervention at Sidney Street Siege (1911), 5

Clarke, Kenneth: British Home Secretary, 277–8

Clarke, Peter: 139; former head of London Metropolitan Police CTC, 11, 138; *Learning from Experience*, 11

Clegg, Nick: support for connection between Muslim community and counter-terrorism police forces, 27–8

Coalition government: members of, 284, 288

Conservative Party: 283; partner in coalition government, 284, 288

Corbyn, Jeremy: 95, 100, 103–4, 122, 139, 147, 249–50, 286; elected to parliament (1987), 119; political activism of, 121; support for reintegration of disaffected young Muslims, 97

Counter Terrorism Command (CTC): officials of, 11, 138; structure of, 60, 265

Cragan, Kim: Rand report by, 55

Cramphorn, Colin: 11

Croft, Stuart: study of domestic cultural context of War on Terror, 244

Daily Mail: 8; readers of, 275

Daily Telegraph: journalists of, 253

Deobandi: 87, 197, 207; Barelvism, 167

Mustafa, Taji: spokesman for HT, 120

Myers, General Richard: US commander-in-chief, 137

Nahdi, Fuad: 123

Naqshbandi, Mehmood: 165; influence of, 69

National Assocation of Muslim Police (NAMP): complaint registered with ACPO (2008), 266

National Council for Civil Liberties (NCCL): 'Your Rights' cards, 8

Nation of Islam: ideology of, 171; members of, 168

National Front: protest outside Finsbury Park Mosque (2002), 94

Nawaz, Majid: 249; co-director of Quilliam Foundation, 250

Neville-Jones, Dame Pauline: opposition to connection between Muslim community and counter-terrorism police forces, 27–8

New Scotland Yard (NSY): 139, 238, 280; MCU officers at, 57, 141; offices of, xvi, 40, 264; international image of, 268; personnel of, 5; public order control room, 43

New Statesman: editorial staff of, 31

New York: 38, 42; newspapers of, 75; Police Department (NYPD), 214; subway system of, xiii; World Trade Center (WTC), 39, 41–2, 45, 75, 80, 124, 156

Norman, Barry: 95, 100, 103–4, 145; deputies of, 142; Islington police commander, 97, 209, 285; retirement of, 285; support for reintegration of disaffected young Muslims, 97

North Atlantic Treaty Organization (NATO): airbases of, 203

North London Central Mosque Working Party: campaign activity against trustees of Finsbury Park Mosque (2004), 99

Northern Ireland: 'Bloody Sunday' (1969), 21; Royal Ulster Constabulary (RUC), 279

Oborne, Peter: 36–7; analysis of use of counter-terrorism operations for justification of Operation Iraqi Freedom (2003), 136–7

O'Neill, Sean: analysis of Finsbury Park Mosque raid (2003), 136

Operation Kratos (2005): 'shoot to kill' policy, xiv

Osman, Hussain: role in attempted 21/7 bombings, 210

Owen, David: 36–7

Paisley, Reverend Ian: influence of, 66

Pakistan: 85, 260

Palestine: 25, 37, 125, 129, 148; Gaza, 122; Israeli policies regarding, 33, 149, 178; West Bank, 122, 131

Palestine Solidarity Campaign (PSC): founding of (1982), 119

Paris: metro system of, xiii

Pasquill, Derek: 32; former civil servant, 31

Petraeus, General David: 280; Commander of Centcom, 279; invitation to deliver fourth Colin Cramphorn memorial lecture, 279

Phillips, Melanie: 284–5; *Londonistan*, 116, 227

Pipes, Daniel: views regarding *zakat*, 132; writings of, 32

Police Federation: members of, 278; opposition to Shelhy Report (1993), 277–8